CW00607320

POLITICAL SOCIOLOGY FOR THE 21st CENTURY

RESEARCH IN POLITICAL SOCIOLOGY

Series Editor: Betty A. Dobratz

Associate Series Editors: Timothy Buzzell and
Lisa K. Waldner

RESEARCH IN POLITICAL SOCIOLOGY   VOLUME 12

POLITICAL SOCIOLOGY FOR THE 21st CENTURY

EDITED BY

BETTY A. DOBRATZ

Iowa State University, Ames, USA

LISA K. WALDNER

University of St. Thomas, St. Paul, USA

TIMOTHY BUZZELL

Baker University, Baldwin City, USA

2003

JAI
An imprint of Elsevier Science

Amsterdam – Boston – London – New York – Oxford – Paris
San Diego – San Francisco – Singapore – Sydney – Tokyo

ELSEVIER SCIENCE Ltd
The Boulevard, Langford Lane
Kidlington, Oxford OX5 1GB, UK

First edition 2003

Library of Congress Cataloging in Publication Data
A catalogue record from the British Library has been applied for.

ISBN: 0-7623-0895-8
ISSN: 0895-9935 (Series)

⊗ The paper used in this publication meets the requirements of ANSI/NISO Z39.48-1992 (Permanence of Paper).
Printed in The Netherlands.

CONTENTS

v

Mark S. Mizruchi
University of Michigan

Claus Mueller
Hunter College CUNY

John Myles
Florida State University

Anthony M. Orum
University of Illinois at Chicago

Fred Pampel
University of Colorado – Boulder

Alejandro Portes
Princeton University

William G. Roy
University of California at Los Angeles

Alan Rudy
Michigan State University

Barbara Ryan
Widener University

Mildred A. Schwartz
New York University
University of Illinois – Chicago

Sarah A. Soule
University of Arizona

John Walton
University of California at Davis

Frederick D. Weil
Louisiana State University

John F. Zipp
University of Akron

SPECIAL REVIEWERS

We would like to thank the following special reviewers who assisted the editorial board in the preparation of Volume 12 of *Research in Political Sociology*.

Mabel Berezin
Cornell University

David Brady
Duke University

Craig Calhoun
New York University

Terry N. Clark
University of Chicago

Marc Dixon
Ohio State University

Jennifer Earl
University of California, Santa Barbara

John E. Farley
Southern Illinois University

John Galliher
University of Missouri, Columbia

Drew Halfmann
University of Michigan

David Jacobs
Ohio State University

James Jasper

Gloria Jones Johnson
Iowa State University

Rob Kleidman
Cleveland State University

Paul Lichterman
University of Wisconsin

John McCarthy
Pennsylvania State University

Karyn D. McKinney
Pennsylvania State University, Altoona

Gwyneth Mellinger
Baker University

David S. Meyer
University of California, Irvine

Beth Mintz
University of Vermont

Pedro Payne
University of California, Riverside

Eric Plutzer
Pennsylvania State University

Theodore Sasson
Middlebury College

Michael D. Schulman
North Carolina State University

Mack Shelley
Iowa State University

David A. Snow
University of California, Irvine

Sarah A. Soule
University of Arizona

Suzanne Staggenborg
McGill University

Charles Tilly
Columbia University

Donald Tomaskovic-Devey
North Carolina State University

Jonathan Turner
University of California, Riverside

David Weakliem
University of Connecticut

PREFACE

Since *Research in Political Sociology* (*RPS*) started, its primary objective has been to publish high quality, original scholarly manuscripts in order to increase our understanding and knowledge of political sociology. *RPS* and the Section on Political Sociology of the American Sociological Association share this similar goal, and the publication cooperates with the section to achieve sociological understanding of political phenomena.

RPS should help political sociologists strengthen and develop the unique perspectives and skills they bring to the profession. The articles in *RPS* are directed toward identifying, understanding and explaining the various interrelations that exist within and between social and political phenomena. This includes exploring the underlying social roots or origins of politics and power; the organization, management, and process of political power structure; and the effects of political decision making and power structures on the surrounding society and culture. The intent of *RPS* is to share with fellow political sociologists the full array of theoretical, methodological, and substantive interests that exist in the field. *RPS* is open to all theoretical, methodological, and scholarly points of view, irrespective of their political content, so long as they add to our understanding and knowledge of political sociological problems and behavior.

For four volumes *RPS* was superbly edited by Richard G. Braungart and Margaret M. Braungart. This was followed by four more excellent volumes very capably edited by Philo Wasburn. Currently Betty A. Dobratz is the series editor with Timothy Buzzell and Lisa K. Waldner as associate editors. Their first volume (No. 9) was entitled *The Politics of Social Inequality* followed by *Sociological Views on Political Participation in the 21st Century* (No. 10) and then *Theoretical Directions in Political Sociology for the 21st Century* (No. 11). Our current Volume 12 focuses on *Political Sociology for the 21st Century*. Volumes 10–12 provide a trilogy on the state of the field of political sociology.

INTRODUCTION: POLITICAL SOCIOLOGY FOR THE 21st CENTURY

Betty A. Dobratz, Timothy Buzzell and Lisa K. Waldner

After publishing our initial volume of *Research in Political Sociology* (*RPS*) on "The Politics of Social Inequality" (Dobratz, Waldner & Buzzell, 2001), we decided to direct our attention toward assessing the state of the field of political sociology at the start of the twenty-first century. What was originally conceived as a one volume work has turned into three volumes, with "Political Sociology for the 21st Century" concluding our discussion. Volume 10 of the *RPS* series and our first on the state of the field is entitled "Sociological Views on Political Participation in the 21st Century" (Dobratz, Buzzell & Waldner, 2002a). That volume contains several articles on social movements and the state and a symposium on the U.S. Presidential Election of 2000. In the realm of electoral politics, this election is one of the most, if not *the* most, controversial in American history and certainly was an interesting way to usher in the 21st century. Our current volume examines electoral politics more broadly by including articles on voting behavior and a rather unique case study of North Carolina politics authored by a political sociologist who is also a state legislator. It also contains two chapters on social movements and another two on historical comparative studies of the state.

Although our Volume 10 certainly embraces articles relevant to theory, especially social movement theory, Volume 11 focuses more directly on "Theoretical Directions in Political Sociology for the 21st Century" (Dobratz, Buzzell & Waldner, 2002b). In it we publish three chapters that provide a new look at the class, elite, and pluralist debate, two articles on world systems and nation states, and two more on what is commonly referred to as "post-modern" political

Political Sociology for the 21st Century
Research in Political Sociology, Volume 12, 1–16
Copyright © 2003 by Elsevier Science Ltd.
All rights of reproduction in any form reserved
ISSN: 0895-9935/PII: S0895993503120013

sociology. Our current volume again offers a discussion of divergent theoretical paths in political sociology through an examination of conceptualizations that address political divisions, political change, and political processes.

As we were compiling Volumes 10 and 11, we realized, as previously mentioned, other assessments of electoral politics should be included. We also wanted to extend our collection's coverage of social movements and states by adding further discussion of theoretical, methodological and empirical issues. This volume includes considerations of quantitative and qualitative methods and discussions of topics like civil society, public opinion, and historical comparative studies that will increasingly occupy the field's research agenda in the years ahead.

PUBLIC OPINION AND CIVIL SOCIETY

Political Sociology at century's end has brought greater attention to the study of "civil society." This construct is typically used to describe the social space where politics are considered, usually through dialogue, the construction of political conflict, and the emergence of political narratives over time. Themes related to political participation are explored in Volume 10 of this series (Dobratz, Buzzell & Waldner, 2002a). In this collection we expand the analysis to consider more specifically the concept of the public sphere, the nature of public opinion and politics, and issue emergence. The collection of articles in this first section of Volume 12 in fact offers the reader glimpses into the state of current research on civil society, which now occupies a significant place in current political sociology. This volume includes studies which demonstrate continued interest in the ways in which political ideology and public opinion are shaped by social forces, the structure of societal discussions related to political issues, and the politicization of race relations in America.

Ronald N. Jacobs opens this volume with an analysis of the concept of civil society for the field of political sociology. With the emergence of "pro-democracy movements throughout the world," Jacobs argues that civil society as an analytical lens has advanced a number of areas of inquiry in political sociology. This discussion contributes to contemporary political sociology in several ways. First, Jacobs argues for refinements in political sociology's empirical understanding of the ways in which citizens are engaged in a variety of associational contexts specifically related to politics. For example, Jacobs discusses findings related to voluntary associations in society and explores the recently popular thesis reporting the softening of "social capital" in America. Jacobs finds in this review more questions suitable for the work of political sociology. Is the change in voluntary civic association cyclical? Are there shifts in the kinds of associations found in

American politics? What factors contribute to participation in "political spaces"? Second, the chapter summarizes advances in current research on the "contours" of the public sphere. Noting advances that emerge from criticisms of Habermas' model of the public sphere, Jacobs again points to significant opportunities for political sociology in refining empirically informed understandings of the "practice of open discussion about matters of common public concern." Is this societal discussion guided by rationality or, as Habermas suggested, are there distortions in these discussions interjected by participants such as the media? Jacobs also argues that work be done on understanding what constitutes a "public" in societal discussions about the common good (politics). This chapter suggests that political sociology at the end of the 20th century made important advances in describing the truly sociological nature of the democratic political culture, and thus, offers possibilities for additional research in the years ahead.

A parallel development to the rise of the use of the concepts of civil society and the public sphere is what Weakliem notes is a "revival of interest in some aspects of public opinion." This chapter traces the decline in political sociology's work in the study of public opinion, attributing its near demise to the strength of social psychological explanations of voting, the emergence of Marxist sociology in the 1960s, and the focus on social movements studies. But according to Weakliem, political sociologists began to show some interest in public opinion as a researchable concept in the 1980s. Here again he traces the factors influencing this renewed interest. As political sociologists became interested in the state and policy, so too was their interest in the role of public opinion in shaping policy processes and outcomes. Moreover, interest in "national character" in long-term patterns in public opinion spawned interest in the ways social forces play a role in shaping public attitudes about family and economics as well as race, gender, and sexual politics. Weakliem also points out that given the advances in research on social and political movements, political sociology has missed an opportunity to connect public opinion with movement dynamics, including movement effects on public attitudes towards political issues. He points to work on "framing" as ripe for creating linkages between what are otherwise disparate literatures.

In prior volumes, we offered examples of research that suggests political move- ments play a significant role in pushing political issues in the public sphere (see Adam, 2002; Menéndez-Alarcón, 2001; Reger & Taylor, 2002; Schroer, 2001; Waldner, 2001). These studies suggest that the ways in which political issues are understood or framed is important to social-political dynamics in general. Moreover, these prior works gave attention to continuing tensions in civil society especially tensions related to race (Berlet, 2001; Blee, 2001; Turner & Payne, 2002). Given the focus of this section's analysis on civil society, political discus- sion, and public attitudes about issues creating political division, we include two examples of recent work related to public policy and social/political relations. The first work offers a conceptualization of "the contentious politics of crime" by using theoretical constructs from social movements theory. The second work develops an analysis of racism in the context of ideological frames and social structural shifts.

Haines outlines an analysis of crime as a political issue at century's end, placing current discussions about crime policy in the context of what he calls "domain structures" which he conceptualizes in this chapter as not only the "complexity" of political issues, but also "how many facets it has – and in turn, how many different audiences it touches upon." The significance of issue domains is found in mobilization of movement participants, including participants who may pay attention to movement activity just enough to be activated by the issue in some manner of political expression. By further delineating this idea, Haines offers political sociology a rich theoretical field of work in suggesting that the breadth of an issue domain can in turn affect the energies needed to challenge current policy coalitions and structures. For example, he describes the "entrenchment" of policy makers supporting the use of the death penalty as a punishment option for selected crimes. Haines identifies several directions for research. How can the anti-death penalty movement mobilize effectively given the apparent steadfastness of the policy establishment? Do movements that construct an issue domain that is overly broad in its appeal fractionalize? The chapter offers yet another example of political sociology's contribution to understanding public political discussions about common public concerns.

Race and race relations in society continue to hold significance for current discussions in civil society. The chapter presented in this section of Volume 12 outlines first an analysis of current racist ideologies in America, and then presents an intriguing prediction about the nature of racism in the 21st century. Tackling the concept of "new racism" Bonilla-Silva, Forman, Lewis and Embrick map out what they argue are four ideologies that reinforce racist attitudes and behaviors in society. "Abstract liberalism" describes beliefs that "decontextualize" racist patterns; belief in racial equality is supported, but programs designed to assist racial minorities are not. "Naturalization" refers to an understanding of race relations as "that's the way it is" in our society, which results in a diminution for community responsibility for addressing racism. The third ideology identified in the chapter is "cultural racism." As pointed out by the authors, this ideology is much like the "culture of poverty" argument of the 1960s, where believed inferiority of certain racial groups is constructed to be a function of "difference." Finally, the authors identify the ideology of "minimization of race" to describe a complex of beliefs that acknowledge the existence of racism in society but fail to see societal patterns of discrimination resulting in "blacks' collective standing." The impact of these ideologies according to the authors is significant to the politics of race at the end of the 20th century. Moreover, they suggest these patterns will become more acute as society is changed by "the Latin Americanization of race relations." The authors argue that an interplay between racist ideology and racial stratification will create a social context in which race relations shift from an "us versus them racial dynamic" to an "honorary whites" system where up to three racial distinctions are constructed. The result will be a new "white supremacy" suggesting race will continue to be significant in contentious politics. Here again, political sociology has an opportunity to study evolving belief systems and consequent patterns of inequality in American civil society.

ELECTORAL POLITICS

While political participation in the 21st century was the theme for Volume 10 of *RPS*, most of these articles dealt with specific social movements and not electoral politics per se with the exception of the election 2000 symposium and an article including a discussion of the disenfranchisement of African-Americans (Turner & Payne, 2002). The controversy surrounding the 2000 election highlighted the importance of voting and barriers faced by African-Americans attempting to exercise their voting rights. The election 2000 symposium discussed methodological forecasting issues (Lewis-Beck & Tien, 2002), ballot irregularities (Adams & Fastnow, 2002), the declining significance of the labor vote (Eimer, 2002), the role of the courts in selecting the next president (Brigman, 2002), and how the Internet contributed to the 2000 election controversy (Jackson, 2002). This volume strengthens our coverage of elections and voting by including three articles that examine different facets of electoral politics.

Brooks, Manza and Bolzendahl discuss the revitalization of sociological voting behavior research, the usefulness of a variety of theoretical approaches, methodological issues, contemporary debates, and productive avenues of future research. In reviewing the theoretical orientations that have been used to frame questions about voting behavior, the authors discuss several current debates in the literature. For example, the social psychological approach to voting behavior has raised questions concerning the malleability of partisan identity over the life course. Does partisan identity predict voting behavior or is party identity influenced by economic performance, the context of elections, or more long-term changes such as shifts in voter preferences? The authors review interesting theoretical questions raised by social psychological, social structural, economic, and political cultural approaches. Rational Choice is advocated as a useful meta-theoretical orientation that can be used to unify theories of voting behavior if scholars discover what preferences motivate voters and the historical and cultural context informing those preferences. Brooks, Manza and Bolzendahl also examine methodological considerations in the study of voting behavior, pointing out that although there are a variety of research methods used, survey research has played the central role and there is "widespread consensus regarding the utility of quantitative techniques."

Besides differences in theoretical orientations and methodological approaches, other debates highlighted by the authors include class, religious, and ideological cleavages, the complexity of economic voting, and explanations of political change. While Brooks, Manza and Bolzendahl suggest that there is a lack of consistent support for the declining relevance of class in voting and note methodological problems with class research, they argue that other cleavages including religion and ideology deserve more attention by political sociologists including potential divisions around issues relating to race and individual rights. In Volume 10 of *RPS*, Turner and Payne (2002) discuss the racial cleavage by conceptualizing it as the "New Dilemma" in American politics forcing us to ask how a society that values equality can continue to discriminate against African Americans. Using National Elections Study Data they demonstrated that while Americans no longer oppose equal opportunities for blacks in the public sphere, they continue to oppose government programs for assuring equal access such as affirmative action. They also suggest that the growing Latino population, while sharing similar civil rights agendas, may have divergent interests in terms of actual social policy. Turner and Payne make a case for the existence of a racial cleavage and combined with Brooks and associates' call for more empirical research looking at non-class cleavages, political sociologists would be well advised to heed the call for more empirical investigation of race, religion, and ideology.

A final debate considered by Brooks and colleagues concerns aggregate-level political change or the changes in public policy fueled by election outcomes. Causal factors for changes over time include economics and demographic composition of political party support that fosters election outcomes and articulates voter policy preference. The authors argue that more research is needed to resolve the question regarding the causal weight of these factors.

Brooks, Manza and Bolzendahl end their discussion of the current state of electoral politics research by suggesting avenues of potentially fruitful research around non-class cleavages such as gender and religion, and also economic and ideological factors such as welfare state attitudes and racism or anti-immigrant sentiments. Specifically, political sociologists are encouraged to empirically investigate potential connections between voting behavior and pressures encouraging or discouraging policy retrenchment.

Class cleavages in voting behavior is the focus of the article by Kerbo and Gonzalez. Unlike Brooks, Manza and Bolzendahl who argue that while investigating class cleavages is important, other non-class factors may be more important, Kerbo and Gonzalez argue that class continues to be an important variable for political sociologists because of its causal role in non-voting. The higher rates of non-voting by blacks was also discussed by Turner and Payne (2002) who assert that the gap between white and black voting is due to a higher representation of blacks among the poor. These authors argue that while other sociologists have found a decline in class voting it is only because the lower class has stopped participating, rendering active voters more similar in their class backgrounds. Kerbo and Gonzalez make their case by using a comparative perspective focusing on the United States and western European democracies. While the authors cannot make a definite causal argument, they note that there is strong evidence that higher levels of income inequality are related to lower levels of voter turnout when contrasting the United States with other European countries that have lower levels of income inequality, more concessions to workers, and higher voter turnouts. Kerbo and Gonzalez consider non-voting in the context of the class cleavage question as opposed to Brooks and associates' advocacy of non-class based divisions based on religion and ideology including race-based attitudes and beliefs. Ideally, political sociologists will heed Kerbo and Gonzalez's call to pursue greater clarity in class cleavage questions while also paying close attention to religious and ideological explanations for voting preferences.

Luebke's article is written from the unique perspective of a political sociologist who is also a member of the North Carolina state legislature. He details some of his experiences working with both "inside and outside progressive activists" and other progressive legislators in trying to win legislative battles in a state well known for its conservative culture. While Brooks, Manza and Bolzendahl argue that aggregate political change should be studied as election outcomes that communicate voter preferences influencing policy, Luebke's observations provide some anecdotal evidence on how higher levels of political participation influence legislators after elections and suggest new avenues of research for political sociologists wishing to examine this process which has traditionally been the domain for political scientists. Activists wishing to be more effective in their dealings with legislators will also benefit from this discussion.

SOCIAL MOVEMENTS

This section includes two articles focusing on social movements that potentially can influence our field's discussion of electoral politics and shape social-political dynamics in the public sphere. In their chapter Gongaware and Benford draw on Tarrow to suggest social movements have the potential to become an institutionalized part of at least some democratic societies. Also in this collection, Oliver,

Cadena-Roa, and Strawn point out that social movement scholars at times have viewed protest as "politics by other means." However, what has often been referred to as extra-institutional politics is intertwined and interdependent with institutional politics. Nowhere can this be seen better than in Amenta et al.'s (2002) article on "Challengers and States: Toward a Political Sociology of Social Movements." The authors criticize the conceptualization of states in "political opportunity" frameworks, urging researchers to move beyond political opportunity and examine the reciprocal relationship between the state and social movements. States are pictured as political contexts with the key question being "How are political contexts likely to influence challengers?" The structure of authority in the polity, democratization, the rules on how representatives are selected (e.g. winner take all, proportional representation, the use of 'direct democracy' techniques), state bureaucracies and repressive capacities, and state policies are key concerns that could influence social movements. Social movements also target the state. They may influence the structure of the polity and the degree of centralization of authority and also challenge the state's policies, democratic procedures, and electoral rules.

In this volume Oliver et al. identify and discuss four major trends in the subfield of social movements that together should ultimately result in broader theory that is better equipped to consider the diversity of social movements. The first trend illustrates the importance of grounding theory in empirical cases. While mainstream social movement theory grew and developed using cases in the U.S. and Western Europe, the case base is now expanding to include Eastern Europe, Latin America, Africa and Asia. Substantively this leads to more attention being directed toward topics like ethnic conflict, democratization movements, and revolutions and toward regimes typically viewed as less democratic and less stable. The second trend involves the increasing attempts "to theorize the dynamic interplay and interconnections between movements, parties, regimes and other actors as social change unfolds." Part of this shift has resulted in reframing movement issues from movement outcomes to broader discussions about consequences including considering change in culture, opinions, and lifestyles.

The two other trends involve work in event-based and social constructionist studies which play crucial roles in improving theory about social movement processes. Typically, event researchers favor quantitative methods and constructionists use qualitative ones. The use of event-history analysis by a number of social scientists has resulted in the growth of quantitative analyses of protest and more specific testing of hypotheses. Event-centered analysis can incorporate time dynamics and mutual causality and consider how certain events influence other events. In addition to analyzing the rise of a movement, it can deal with mobilization failure and decline. Some believe that event-centered research could result in a unification of collective action-theory and research.

In addition to the increase in quantitative event studies, Oliver et al. identify a rise in social constructionist theories of social movements. They explore framing, identity, culture, and emotions as key concepts in social-constructionist orientations and call for an integration of structuralist and constructionist theories to facilitate our understanding of "how structures constrain social construction and how social construction gives meaning to structures."

Gongaware and Benford complement the Oliver et al. piece by describing for political sociologists the significance of qualitative methods in the study of social movements. They argue qualitative methods have a unique capacity "for capturing the naturalistic context, the interactional dynamic and the meanings of subjective experiences in a setting and/or phenomena under study." Qualitative methods are seen as especially effective in advancing our understanding of movement processes and the situated actions of participants. The authors argue that especially in the last 20 years or so, we have seen "a resurgent interest in ideational and other cultural foci" and a growing need to answer complex questions about "the contexts in which meanings are constructed and transformed . . . about the processes by which actors are defined, resist hegemonic labels and redefine themselves, and about the language that aids in all of these."

Gongaware and Benford review a wide variety of qualitative techniques including secondary source analysis, document analysis, participatory action research, ethnographic fieldwork, and individual and group interviews. The authors address the future direction of qualitative research regarding the issues of globalization, framing processes, collective identities, narratives, and emotions. For example, qualitative methods should be extremely useful in looking at the relationships between emotions, social movements, and contentious politics. Even though Buechler (2002), in our Volume 10 of *RPS*, called for a structural approach to social movements and criticized the ahistorical approach of past movement theory and the overemphasis on micro-meso levels of analysis, Gongaware and Benford argue that qualitative research can be helpful to the work of people like Buechler because qualitative research findings can potentially be generalized and provide researchers with rich in-depth accountings of historical context.

HISTORICAL COMPARATIVE ANALYSIS OF THE STATE

Gongaware and Benford in their discussion of social movements describe historical analysis as "examinations of events or combinations of events via primary and secondary sources in order to uncover and describe accounts of what happened." As they point out, most sociologists "do history" (Tuchman, 1994, p. 307). The value of historical analysis in the study of politics cannot be denied, although Pfaff and Kiser in this volume criticize most political sociologists for a "presentist" bias. Previous *RPS* volumes also had articles where historical analysis was very important. For example, in Volume 11 of *RPS*, Hall (2002) discusses world-systems analysis and the state in the core and periphery. He argues that globalization processes have deep historical roots and are a logical continuation of long-standing trends although there have been major changes in the world economy in recent decades. Buechler (2002) too points out that world systems theory is extremely important in analyzing global structures of inequality in the core and the periphery. In Volume 11 Vujacić (2002) critiques contemporary state-centered theories of European nationalism and advocates a Weberian comparative-historical political sociology to explain the rise of nationalism as a political, ideological and cultural phenomenon.

In this section, Pfaff and Kiser call for increased attention to comparative-historical work in political sociology. They suggest that comparative-historical research is at a crossroads where one direction favors history, emphasizing the complexity and uniqueness of certain events, places and times, and stressing contingency and chance in shaping outcome. The other is oriented more toward social science and the testing of theoretical propositions by using general causal models and attempting to resolve anomalies to advance theoretical contributions. The authors argue developing transportable propositions and arguments with abstractly defined scope conditions is essential for theoretical progress. They point out that the use of transportable causal mechanisms promotes cumulative knowledge by bringing together research from different times and places.

In their chapter Pfaff and Kiser present evidence showing a recent increase in studies following what they consider to be the more social scientific path. They maintain this trend is encouraging with comparative-historical research in political sociology advancing to a more productive middle ground. The authors focus their analysis on the making, unmaking and remaking of states. In examining state formation, Pfaff and Kiser argue that the neo-Weberian, state-centered perspective that supports the idea that war made states has superceded the Marxist framework examining class power and economic structure. Regarding the making of modern states or bureaucratization, they believe sociologists have not devoted much time to the implementation of state policy, in part because of the previously mentioned presentist bias. Two of the interesting debates though have concerned whether either war or revolution promote or detract from bureaucratization.

Although revolutions may be important forces in state formation, revolutions are particularly significant in the unmaking of states. Pfaff and Kiser seem more favorable to the state centered approach rather than the class conflict perspective because all successful revolutions deal with the incapacitation and capitulation of states. A number of causal factors leading to revolution have been identified, such as states encountering internal and external challenges, intra-elite conflict, and large-scale changes in loyalty to the government. The authors maintain that many of the causal mechanisms predicting revolution are transportable to non-European contexts.

Democratization of formerly authoritarian states has been a frequent topic in work on remaking states. Transition theory has identified key stages (liberalization, democratization, and consolidation), but Pfaff and Kiser argue its contribution to political sociology has been more descriptive than analytical. The contention model based on political process theory has tried to bridge micro and macro discussions of political change by introducing a synthetic model of social movements that considers structural, organizational, and cultural explanations. However, the social mechanisms identified may need further work, Pfaff and Kiser contend, as they seem too broad or include multiple mechanisms and may not be transportable beyond Western European type democracies.

The authors point out that a particularly encouraging development for political sociology in the 21st century is the refinement of certain formal methods of historical analysis. Narrative analysis, process-tracing, and the comparison of historical sequences are beginning to make important methodological contributions to historical and comparative political sociology as is the work emphasizing the path dependence of social and political processes. Such contributions may well advance the discussions between social science and history.

Although also advocating historical comparative research of the state, Prechel's work goes down a different path emphasizing contingency theory and a structural neo-Marxist approach rather than a state-centered one. Prechel, in his study of U.S. business political behavior and corporate malfeasance, argues that an explicitly historical theory is needed to understand the policy formation process. In a sense, his work is an attempt to correct what Pfaff and Kiser noted as a failure of much of political sociology to study the implementation of state policy. Prechel uses the social structure of accumulation framework that maintains that corporate profitability depends on institutional arrangements that are external to the firm. Exploration, consolidation, and decay are the three distinct stages in accumulation that are repeated over time. Specifically, Prechel examines three decay-exploration transitions in the U.S. where breakdowns in the institutional arrangements have negatively affected capital accumulation and markets have weakened during times of economic instability and decline.

Prechel draws on the historical contingency theory of class power and state power in structural neo-Marxism identifying class unity and state autonomy as key factors that vary historically. The time-dependent variation in the interdependencies of capital-state relations is considered to facilitate understanding the process of policy formation. Prechel argues one must recognize that class interests are embedded in state structures and that when there is capital dependence, capitalists mobilize politically. State autonomy is influenced by variation in capitalist class consciousness, and the degree of class consciousness influences the ability of the capitalist class to unify and thus affect public policy. Prechel suggests that political sociologists need to theorize key concepts like state structure, state autonomy, and class unity as variables that change over time and also recognize that state structures may be means for classes and class fractions to dominate the state.

The three decay-exploration transitions that Prechel identifies are the 1870–1890s, the 1920s–1930s, and the 1970s–1990s; each involves a key policy paradigm shift. For example, during the 1870–1890s the balance between capitalist-class power and state power shifted by giving property rights that were previously reserved for individuals to industrial corporations. Financial and industrial capitalists used the holding-company subsidiary form to assemble great private wealth. In the 1920s–1930s era, legislation was passed providing for a tax on capital transfers from subsidiary corporations. This law was key in the public policy shift deinstitutionalizing the holding company subsidiary form. Corporations then started to restructure as the multidivisional form where capital transfers among divisions were not subject to tax. Finally in the late 20th century capital dependent corporations changed to the multi-layered subsidiary form (MLSF), representing another transformation in corporate property rights. The MLSF resulted in business having more financial flexibility. In addition, the new arrangements provided incentives for corporate managers to participate in business activities that undermined capitalist stability and started a very volatile period in the stock market.

Prechel identifies three characteristics that the major historical transformations at the end of the 19th and 20th centuries had in common: capital dependence, the formation of a capitalist class power block, and the transformation of state structures. Studies looking at historical contingencies encourage researchers to focus on multiple causes that influence formulations of public policy and allow us to examine whether causes vary historically.

Finally, Prechel questions the pluralist state autonomy framework that states are power holders in their own right and state managers are autonomous when they engage in the policy formation process. Prechel further suggests that "studies that examine the extent to which state managers' professional and class backgrounds cause policy paradigm shifts can aid in resolving the long-term debate between pluralist and neo-Marxist theories." Other articles in previous volumes have also considered this debate. In Volume 11, Mintz (2002) criticized pluralist theory but believed the pluralist-elite debate would need to be revisited after political sociologists better understand how corporate elites and the capitalist class unify, what the relationship is between class and organization in the wielding of elite power, and what the consequences of elite and capitalist class unity are for state policy. Misra (2002) showed how welfare state theorizing has changed over time and examined theorizing welfare states from a class perspective, a race-centered approach, and feminist perspectives. She proposed an integrated model of race/class/gender theorizing as well. Drawing on research from various disciplines and traditions, Lo (2002) examined the "politics of the state in advanced capitalist societies" as he identified and analyzed four "currents of thought" in contemporary Marxist political sociology.

The two studies presented in this section suggest how historical comparative studies about the state can be used in different ways and support different theoretical approaches. Also one focuses on the United States comparing different key periods of historical transition while the other stresses the portability of testable propositions to non-Western societies and different time periods.

CONCLUSION

In this collection we consider differing theoretical approaches to age-old questions in political sociology, and we highlight the continuing importance of variety in research methods in the framing of questions and the analysis of the relationship between politics and society. We examine the concepts of civil society, public opinion, and historical comparative research and have extended our analyses of political participation and the state. Our authors review electoral politics including non-voting and examine theories, methods, and empirical studies in social movements and the state.

In our three volumes on the state of political sociology, we find chapters that are indeed diverse and advance our understanding of the interrelations between society and politics and within politics. Almost all of our articles suggest the growing maturity in political theorizing and offer further suggestions for continued development in this area. As Braungart (1976, p. 39) points out in his book on society and politics, "Political sociology has a past, present, and future." Our authors discuss the historical foundations of their topics, detail present contributions, and suggest future directions for theory and research. The chapters in this volume as well as the previous two volumes of *RPS* highlight areas of political sociology that need further work. In closing our three-volume discussion of political sociology at the beginning of the 21st century, we identify a specific weakness in our research that needs attention and poses a related but broader issue of concern for the field.

First, we believe that the events surrounding September 11, 2001 reveal one glaring absence in political sociology's research agenda: terrorism. There has been little work done in the study of terrorism using a genuinely political sociological approach. We briefly surveyed the articles of the last two years in *Studies in Conflict and Terrorism* and looked at affiliations of authors. As we anticipated, several authors were from political science departments. Others were from Departments of Government, Centers or Schools of Public Affairs or Government (e.g. the John F. Kennedy School of Government at Harvard), History, Political Psychology or Communications Departments, government agencies (e.g. Office of Intelligence and Threat Analysis, Department of State), and organizations like Rand Corporation. We argue the study of terrorism could benefit from the insights of political sociology, and political sociologists can contribute to our empirical understanding of terrorism and its social-political roots as they build interdisciplinary linkages.

Second, we suggest that the field should endeavor to build linkages among the subfields of sociology as well as interdisciplinary ones as ways to advance our knowledge of social-political connections. As Kourvetaris and Dobratz (1982, p. 313) suggested more than twenty years ago, "Political sociology should draw on the developments in related areas of sociology as they impinge on politics." Doing this, of course, has already resulted in examinations of diverse topics and more thorough appreciation and understanding of the breadth of political sociology. A cursory look at articles in the last decade (1992–2002) in the *Annual Review of Sociology* supports this idea. Routinely the *Annual Review of Sociology* lists articles under the heading of Political and Economic Sociology. We found eighteen papers on political sociology under that heading. In addition, we felt at least another 27 articles were about as equally relevant to political sociology as those under that particular heading. Most of the work on social movements was listed under the topic of "Social Processes." Many of the other chapters we identified had politics, political or the state in their titles. For example, an article on "Ideas, Politics and Public Policy" (2002) was listed under social policy, an article on "Prejudice, Politics, and Public Opinion" (2000) was classified under Individual and Society, work on "Politics and Institutionalism" (1999) under formal organizations, and "Class Voting in Capitalist Democracies since World War II" (1995) under Differentiation and Stratification.

It is not our intent to critique any classification system but rather to illustrate the complex intertwinings of political sociology with other subfields and topics in political sociology and to advocate building even greater linkages between political sociology and other subfields of sociology. Many of our articles touch on this in our volumes. For example, Buechler's (2002) piece on social movements especially called for a more structural and historically specific approach that would draw on the broader discipline of sociology. Oliver et al. in this volume argue that "the study of social movements has long stood at the intersection of political sociology and social psychology," noting the false dichotomy of politics versus social psychology.

Prechel reflects on how political sociology can benefit from organizational studies, historical sociology, and formal theory. The task of integrating different theoretical approaches in political sociology may well benefit from political sociologists developing greater linkages with other subfields in sociology and other disciplines. Political sociologists must continue to use the work in other subfields and other disciplines as well their own to further develop political sociology. Our three volumes should also advance the discussions of those linkages, facilitate the growth of current knowledge in the field, and stimulate further research.

REFERENCES

Adam, B. (2002). Theorizing the globalization of gay and lesbian movements. In: B. Dobratz, T. Buzzell & L. Waldner (Eds), *Research in Political Sociology: Sociological Views on Political Participation in the 21st Century* (Vol. 10, pp. 123–138). Oxford: Elsevier Science.

Adams, G., & Fastnow, C. (2002). A note on the voting irregularities in Palm Beach county. In: B. Dobratz, T. Buzzell & L. Waldner (Eds), *Research in Political Sociology: Sociological Views on Political Participation in the 21st Century* (Vol. 10, pp. 189–199). Oxford: Elsevier Science.

Amenta, E., Caren, N., Fetner, T., & Young, M. (2002). Challengers and States: Toward a political sociology of social movements. In: B. Dobratz, T. Buzzell & L. Waldner (Eds), *Research in Political Sociology: Sociological Views on Political Participation in the 21st Century* (Vol. 10, pp. 47–83). Oxford: Elsevier Science.

Berlet, C. (2001). Hate groups, racial tension and ethnoviolence in an integrating Chicago neighborhood. In: B. Dobratz, L. Waldner & T. Buzzell (Eds), *Research in Political Sociology: The Politics of Social Inequality* (Vol. 9, pp. 117–166). Oxford: Elsevier Science.

Blee, K. (2001). What else we need to know: An agenda for studying the racist movement. In: B. Dobratz, L. Waldner & T. Buzzell (Eds), *Research in Political Sociology: The Politics of Social Inequality* (Vol. 9, pp. 172–180). Oxford: Elsevier Science.

Braungart, R. (Ed.) (1976). *Society and politics*. Englewood Cliffs, NJ: Prentice Hall.

Brigman, W. (2002). The Chad legal wars: The role of the courts in the 2000 presidential election. In: B. Dobratz, T. Buzzell & L. Waldner (Eds), *Research in Political Sociology: Sociological Views on Political Participation in the 21st Century* (Vol. 10, pp. 223–260). Oxford: Elsevier Science.

Buechler, S. (2002). Toward a structural approach to social movements. In: B. Dobratz, T. Buzzell & L. Waldner (Eds), *Research in Political Sociology: Sociological Views on Political Participation in the 21st Century* (Vol. 10, pp. 1–45). Oxford: Elsevier Science.

Dobratz, B., Waldner, L., & Buzzell, T. (Eds) (2001). *Research in political sociology: The politics of social inequality*. Oxford: Elsevier Science.

Dobratz, B., Buzzell, T., & Waldner, L. (Eds) (2002a). *Research in political sociology: Sociological views on political participation in the 21st century*. Oxford: Elsevier Science.

Dobratz, B., Buzzell, T., & Waldner, L. (Eds) (2002b). *Research in political sociology: Theoretical directions in political sociology for the 21st century*. Oxford: Elsevier Science.

Eimer, S. (2002). Labor and the 2000 election: Reinventing union politics. In: B. Dobratz, T. Buzzell & L. Waldner (Eds), *Research in Political Sociology: Sociological Views on Political Participation in the 21st Century* (Vol. 10, pp. 213–222). Oxford: Elsevier Science.

Hall, T. (2002). World-systems analysis and globalization directions for the twenty first century. In: B. Dobratz, T. Buzzell & L. Waldner (Eds), *Research in Political Sociology: Theoretical Directions in Political Sociology for the 21st Century* (Vol. 11, pp. 81–122). Oxford: Elsevier Science.

Jackson, R. (2002). Now the ballot boxes are transparent: How Internet-based research made election controversy. In: B. Dobratz, T. Buzzell & L. Waldner (Eds), *Research in Political Sociology: Sociological Views on Political Participation in the 21st Century* (Vol. 10, pp. 201–212). Oxford: Elsevier Science.

Kourvetaris, G., & Dobratz, B. (1982). Political power and conventional political participation. *Annual Review of Sociology, 8,* 289–317.

Lewis-Beck, M., & Tien, C. (2002). Presidential election forecasting: The Bush-Gore draw. In: B. Dobratz, T. Buzzell & L. Waldner (Eds), *Research in Political Sociology: Sociological Views on Political Participation in the 21st Century* (Vol. 10, pp. 173–187). Oxford: Elsevier Science.

Lo, C. (2002). Marxist models of the capitalist state and politics. In: B. Dobratz, T. Buzzell & L. Waldner (Eds), *Research in Political Sociology: Theoretical Directions in Political Sociology for the 21st Century* (Vol. 11, pp. 197–231). Oxford: Elsevier Science.

Mintz, B. (2002). Elites and politics: The corporate elite and the capitalist class in the United States. In: B. Dobratz, T. Buzzell & L. Waldner (Eds), *Research in Political Sociology: Theoretical Directions in Political Sociology for the 21st Century* (Vol. 11, pp. 53–80). Oxford: Elsevier Science.

Misra, J. (2002). Class, race, and gender and theorizing welfare States. In: B. Dobratz, T. Buzzell & L. Waldner (Eds), *Research in Political Sociology: Theoretical Directions in Political Sociology for the 21st Century* (Vol. 11, pp. 19–52). Oxford: Elsevier Science.

Menéndez-Alarcón, A. (2001). National identity in France and the process of European integration. In: B. Dobratz, L. Waldner & T. Buzzell (Eds), *Research in Political Sociology: The Politics of Social Inequality* (Vol. 9, pp. 307–334). Oxford: Elsevier Science.

Reger, J., & Taylor, V. (2002). Women's movement research and social movement theory: A symbiotic relationship. In: B. Dobratz, T. Buzzell & L. Waldner (Eds), *Research in Political Sociology: Sociological Views on Political Participation in the 21st Century* (Vol. 10, pp. 85–121). Oxford: Elsevier Science.

Schroer, T. (2001). Issue and identity framing within the white racialist movement: Internet dynamics. In: B. Dobratz, L. Waldner & T. Buzzell (Eds), *Research in Political Sociology: The Politics of Social Inequality* (Vol. 9, pp. 207–232). Oxford: Elsevier Science.

Tuchman, G. (1994). Historical social science: Methodologies, methods, and meanings. In: N. Denzin & Y. Lincoln (Eds), *Handbook of Qualitative Research* (pp. 306–323). Thousand Oaks, CA: Sage Publications.

Turner, J., & Payne, P. (2002). Power, politics and African Americans. In: B. Dobratz, T. Buzzell & L. Waldner (Eds), *Research in Political Sociology: Sociological Views on Political Participation in the 21st Century* (Vol. 10, pp. 139–169). Oxford: Elsevier Science.

Vujacić, V. (2002). States, Nations, and European nationalism: A challenge for political sociology. In: B. Dobratz, T. Buzzell & L. Waldner (Eds), *Research in Political Sociology: Theoretical Directions in Political Sociology for the 21st Century* (Vol. 11, pp. 123–156). Oxford: Elsevier Science.

Waldner, L. (2001). Lesbian and gay political activism: An analysis of variables predicting political participation. In: B. Dobratz, L. Waldner & T. Buzzell (Eds), *Research in Political Sociology: The Politics of Social Inequality* (Vol. 9, pp. 59–81). Oxford: Elsevier Science.

PART I:
PUBLIC OPINION AND
CIVIL SOCIETY

TOWARD A POLITICAL SOCIOLOGY
OF CIVIL SOCIETY

Ronald N. Jacobs

ABSTRACT

This article reviews sociological research on civil society, by focusing on two areas of debate: (1) the question of civic engagement; and (2) the public sphere. Research on civic engagement has identified new types of associations and new forms of organization that have transformed the voluntary sector. While some of these changes suppress engagement, others encourage participation. Research on the public sphere has helped to map out a discourse of civil society, which identifies utopian images of civic purity as well as anti-utopian images of civic pollution. This discourse circulates in multiple publics, and, increasingly, in mass-mediated forums. In both areas, sociologists have contributed a level of analytical precision and empirical detail that had previously been missing from the more theoretical and normative debates about democracy and civil society.

INTRODUCTION

The idea of civil society has become increasingly popular for those who are interested in political culture, public opinion, civic engagement, social movements, and other aspects of democratic life that extend beyond formal procedures of decision-making. The concept's appeal derives from three sources. First, civil society has been invoked explicitly by pro-democracy movements throughout the

Political Sociology for the 21st Century
Research in Political Sociology, Volume 12, 19–47
Copyright © 2003 by Elsevier Science Ltd.
ISSN: 0895-9935/PII: S0895993503120025

world (Alexander, 1998; Cohen & Arato, 1992; Seligman, 1992). Second, it is one of the only concepts in the social sciences that require a normative engagement with issues of solidarity and democracy (Bryant, 1995; Perez-Diaz, 1995). And third, the concept of civil society has for a long time maintained a relatively ambiguous and multivalent status, allowing it to mean different things to different people, and allowing its users to claim an intellectual heritage that includes Tocqueville, Montesquieu, Rousseau, Hegel, Kant, Marx, Adam Smith, and even Aristotle (Cohen & Arato, 1992; Seligman, 1992). For social scientists, the challenge has been to preserve what is useful in the concept of civil society, but to refine it in more analytically rigorous and empirical ways (Alexander, 1998; Hall, 1995). Sociologists have taken up this challenge in earnest, focusing their attention on two areas in particular: (1) the public sphere; and (2) the question of civic engagement. The result is a growing field of civil society studies, which is beginning to make a significant impact on our understanding of politics and public life.

In its broadest sense, civil society refers to the entire web of associations and public spaces in which citizens can have conversations with one another, discover common interests, act in concert, assert new rights, and try to influence public opinion and public policy (Cohen & Arato, 1992, p. 23). This is a useful definition, because it identifies the two institutional arrangements that are distinctive to civil society: (1) a set of voluntary associations; and (2) a public sphere of communication and debate. On their own, neither voluntary associations nor public spheres can (or should) be thought of as equivalent to civil society (Calhoun, 1993). Taken together, however, they show why the study of civil society is so important for political sociology: namely, because civil society provides the social spaces for activating democratic identities and encouraging practices of effective citizenship (Berezin, 1997a, pp. 365–367).

In order to understand the important relationship between voluntary associations and public spheres, it is helpful to distinguish between weak and strong versions of civil society. As Charles Taylor (1991) has argued, the weak version of civil society refers to the simple existence of free and voluntary associations that are independent of the state. These associations are valuable for the simple fact that they organize a variety of contexts where civic participation can occur – by bringing people together, allowing them to discover common interests, providing them opportunities to volunteer their time in the service of the public good, helping them to develop civic skills, and encouraging them to be involved in public life. In other words, voluntary associations create the conditions for individuals to become more active citizens. The possibility of more *effective* citizens, however, requires that the individuals involved in these associations have the ability to *influence* the state. This stronger version of civil society requires that, in addition to associations, there are also free public spaces of communication – public spheres – where people introduce new issues onto the political agenda, where they attempt to influence public opinion, where they debate their adversaries and try to resolve disputes, and where they force political elites to pay attention to them.[1] Without these kinds of communicative spaces, it would be impossible for engaged citizens and their associations to be politically effective.

Surprisingly, while voluntary associations and public spheres are both such important parts of civil society, they tend to be kept separate in the scholarly literature. In part, this is because specialized theoretical and empirical literatures have developed around each area. Indeed, most debates about the public sphere and modern politics are in dialogue, to a large degree, with Jurgen Habermas's (1989, 1962) *The Structural Transformation of the Public Sphere*. Along similar lines, current debates about voluntary associations and civic engagement tend to begin from Robert Putnam's (1995a, b, 2000) arguments about declining social capital in the United States. My goal in this article is to bring the two literatures into closer contact. After reviewing the theoretical frameworks established by Habermas and Putnam, I show how sociological interventions have helped to bring a level of analytical precision and empirical detail that had previously been missing from the more theoretical and normative debates. I also point to interesting similarities in the kinds of contributions that sociologists are making to the literature on voluntary associations and public spheres. Finally, I outline several areas for future research, in which political sociologists are particularly well-suited to make a significant contribution to the civil society debates.

HABERMAS AND THE PUBLIC SPHERE

The concept of the public sphere refers to a particular type of practice that takes place in civil society: the practice of open discussion about matters of common public concern. The concept owes much of its academic popularity to Habermas, and the publication of his now-classic *The Structural Transformation of the Public Sphere*. Habermas wanted to explain why the normative model of politics changed, during the seventeenth and eighteenth centuries (particularly in the Anglo-American world), so that the principle of open public discussion came to replace that of parliamentary secrecy.[2] He explained this change in politics as being caused by the development of a bourgeois public sphere, which he defined as the sphere of private people[3] come together as a public, who claimed the space of public discourse from state regulation, and demanded that the state engage them in debate about matters of political legitimacy and common concern. "The medium of this political confrontation," Habermas (1989, p. 27) wrote, "was peculiar and without historical precedent: people's public use of their reason."

The Structural Transformation of the Public Sphere continues to stand as one of the most authoritative historical studies of the public sphere; nevertheless, as Calhoun (1992, p. 41) has argued, the primary significance of Habermas's book is its ability to generate new research, theory and analysis. For his own part, Habermas has elaborated on many of the assumptions that informed his historical argument, developing a normative theory of communicative ethics that continues to influence scholarly debates about civil society and democracy (e.g. Habermas, 1987, 1990). There are three principles that inform his historical and theoretical writing, which I summarize below:

(1) *The main value of the public sphere is its potential for promoting rational-critical debate and reasoned forms of consensus.* When Habermas extolled the "people's public use of their reason," what he had in mind was a form of *critical rationality*, in which private persons discussed political issues in a setting where the *best argument* carried the day. Public opinion was only "real" if it was subjected to "critical publicity," in which private individuals had the ability to discuss the issue openly, without penetration from authoritative institutions (Habermas, 1989, pp. 248–249). Ultimately, Habermas developed this idea of critical publicity into a formal, procedural model of communicative ethics, in which public discussions would center on the norms of symmetry, reciprocity, and reflexivity. This is the "ideal speech situation," referring to "the rules participants would have to follow if they were to strive for an agreement motivated by the force of the better argument alone" (Cohen & Arato, 1992, p. 348). If symmetry or reciprocity were absent from a speech situation, or if the discussants were not committed to the possibility of being persuaded to change their mind by a better argument, than any consensus that might have been achieved was "merely empirical," and lacked the criteria necessary for critical rationality.

(2) *While there are many spaces of discussion within civil society, it is necessary that they be integrated through a single public sphere.* Because he emphasized symmetrical and reciprocal debate motivated by the goal of rational-critical consensus, Habermas insisted on actual dialogue organized through a single, integrated public space (Cohen & Arato, 1992, p. 349). This did not necessarily mean that there had to be one immense town hall that could fit all of a society's citizens, but it did mean that actual discussions had to be connected together in a way that made possible "a rationally founded agreement on the part of all those who might be affected" (Habermas, 1992, p. 447). In practice, this meant that everybody had to be reading the same newspapers, using those newspapers to set the agenda for their own discussions, and organizing their discussions according to common norms of communicative practice (i.e.

symmetry, reciprocity, reflexivity). Importantly, it also meant that there had to be a feedback loop, whereby the discussions taking place among individuals found their way back into the media.[4] In the absence of these conditions, Habermas believed that it would be impossible to maintain the public sphere as an important political force, because speakers would become disconnected from the effects of their speech (Garnham, 1992, pp. 367–375).

(3) *The democratic and progressive potential of the public sphere has been continually eroded throughout the twentieth century.* Ultimately, Habermas's account of the public sphere turned into a tragic tale of degeneration and lost potential, in which the progressive features of the public sphere have been continually eroded throughout the twentieth century. Habermas pointed to several historical trends that he thought were responsible for this erosion. First, there was a growing split between the public world of work and the private realm of intimacy, transforming the intimate sphere into a space dominated by consumption and leisure (Habermas, 1989, p. 159). Second, the technologies of radio, film, and television – because of their putatively greater "natural" intimacy – reduced the capacity for rational-critical orientation (Habermas, 1989, p. 172). Finally, the political public sphere became dominated by an advertising logic, interested more in the choices of consumers than in the process by which they arrived at these choices. "Public opinion" became an "object to be molded in connection with a staged display of . . . publicity in the service of persons and institutions, consumer goods, and programs" (Habermas, 1989, p. 236).

SOCIOLOGICAL RESEARCH ON THE PUBLIC SPHERE

While Habermas is without question the dominant theoretical figure in contemporary debates about democracy and the public sphere, he is not without critics. Feminists have criticized his commitment to rational consensus, arguing that it privileges bourgeois and masculinist communicative practices that reproduce hegemony (e.g. Benhabib, 1992; Fraser, 1992).[5] Eley (1992) has argued that Habermas wrongly dismissed the plebeian public sphere, failing to recognize how it helped to institutionalize resistance through more carnivalesque forms of publicity. Zaret (2000, p. 35) has argued that Habermas's criticism of the contemporary, commercialized public sphere is based on a description of English history that "is very nearly the opposite of the reality of early-modern printing and print culture." Postmodern theorists have argued that Habermas's critical theory completely misunderstood the television age, wrongly subjecting it to normative modes of evaluation derived from speech-act theory (Lee, 1992; Warner, 1992).

And hermeneutically-inclined theorists have argued that Habermas's procedural model of communication failed to grasp the aesthetic, cultural, and communitarian bases of political discussion (e.g. Jacobs & Smith, 1997; Rorty, 1989; Walzer, 1983, 1995). In each area of debate, sociological research has helped considerably to clarify the issues and adjudicate between the competing positions. Three distinct streams of research have emerged.

Rational-Critical Debate or the Discourse of Civil Society?

One important area of research has investigated the extent to which the communicative norm of rational-critical debate actually operates in empirical publics, either past or present. In his historical study of political participation and civic life in the United States, for example, Schudson (1998) argues that there has *not* been a strong correlation between rational-critical debate and political participation. The Lincoln-Douglas debates provide a case in point. Typically characterized as the high point of American political discourse and civic participation, these debates were as much about entertainment as deliberation, with both participants incorporating a mixture of careful argument, polemical rhetoric, ad hominem attack, and ethnic/racial/religious fear-mongering. It was not until the Progressive movement of the early twentieth century that a model of informed, educated, and dispassionate citizens came to predominate. The irony of this movement is that, in the process of putting forth a vision of rational-critical debate, it killed political participation:

> The outcome was a world in many respects more democratic, inclusive, and dedicated to public, collective goals, and, for all that, less politically engaging. By the close of the Progressive Era, the cultural contradictions of democracy would reach a point of mournful clarity (Schudson, 1998, p. 147).

Schudson argues that the Progressive movement's image of an informed, educated, dispassionate, debating citizenry has operated primarily as an idealized image of a utopian civic climate, which can be held up against the present as a way to urge people to become better citizens.

Many cultural sociologists argue that it is in this way, as a sacred signifier in a broader *discourse of civil society*, that images of rational-critical debate have found most of their political power in the public sphere. In a series of studies, Alexander and his colleagues have begun to map the empirical contours of this discourse, showing that debates in the public sphere are structured by a central tension between utopian and dystopian visions of solidarity (Alexander, 1992, 1997; Alexander & Smith, 1993; Jacobs, 2000; Kane, 1997; Ku, 1999, 2001; Smith, 1998). On the utopian or "sacred" side of the discourse, the descriptive terms bear a striking resemblance to the normative vision outlined by Habermas. Pure motives are active, autonomous, rational, reasonable, self-controlled, and realistic. Pure relationships are open, trusting, critical, truthful, straightforward, and deliberative. Pure institutions are formal, rule-regulated, inclusive, and impersonal. But these terms only get their meaning through a semiotic principle of binary opposition, which outlines the qualities of equally *impure* motives, relationships, and institutions: passive, dependent, irrational, unreasonable, out of control, emotional, unrealistic, secretive, deferential, deceitful, calculating, conspiratorial, arbitrary, exclusive, and personal.

Research on the discourse of civil society suggests that the public sphere is only rarely an arena of reason or consensus; more typically, it operates as an agonistic arena for aesthetic politics and symbolic contestation. In empirical publics, actors make use of the binary structure of civil discourse to "purify" themselves and their allies, and to "pollute" their enemies. In order to narrate themselves as powerful and heroic, public actors must describe others as dangerous, foolish, weak, or antiheroic in some other way. They describe their enemies as irrational, out of control, secretive, or deceitful; by contrast, they describe themselves and their allies as rational, reasoned, and straightforward. They describe the projects and policies of their enemies as perverse, futile, and jeopardizing, while those of their friends are synergistic, mutually supportive, and progressive (Hirschman, 1991). People know when they are being "symbolically polluted," and must spend a great deal of their time trying to repair the symbolic damage. Groups and associations who find themselves continually polluted in the public sphere must continually operate from a defensive and reactive position.

As my research on race and the media demonstrated (Jacobs, 2000), the binary discourse operates as an effective tool used by those wishing to shut down discussion. The 1965 Watts uprising provides a good example. In "mainstream" newspapers such as the *Los Angeles Times* and *Chicago Tribune*, politicians, journalists, and other public figures described the rioters as "youthful," "boastful," "irrational," and "insane," and described the riot zone as "terrifying" and "hysterical." Placed on the front page of the paper to signal that evaluation was the appropriate frame for talking about the crisis, editorials contrasted the "shameful, senseless, bloody rioting" with the tremendous debt the community owed to its "heroic law enforcement personnel." Linking criticism of the police to "Communist press agencies worldwide," they used the Watts crisis to criticize all forms of civil disobedience, including the leaders of the Civil Rights, student, and anti-war movements. In such an environment, where the polluting discourse of civil society had been so vigorously mobilized, reasoned deliberation about causes and appropriate policy responses was nearly impossible, and the primary effect of public debate was to *shut down* any discussion.

Thus, at the same time that the discourse of civil society promotes an idealized image of a rational, debating public committed to fairness and inclusion, it also provides the symbolic resources for truncating debate and excluding people from public debate. This is the "paradox of civil society": namely, that the discourse of repression is inherent in the discourse of liberty (Alexander, 1997). Indeed, even the most "obvious" democratic principles are part of an aesthetic politics, in which political actors make strategic decisions about whom to include in reasoned deliberation, and whom to exclude. Those who are to be included are assumed to be rational, critical, and autonomous; those who are to be excluded must "prove" that they possess these skills and characteristics. There is no procedural fix to guarantee that people operate according to principles of justice or morality, since those very principles are part of a discursive system that contains their opposites. What matters, then, is the specific way that people mobilize the discourse in particular situations.

Other research on the discursive structure of the public sphere has been more critical of Alexander's approach, arguing that he fails to appreciate the way that the "official" discourse of civil society is a normalizing agent that marginalizes alternative cultural forms of representation. For these critics, empirical publics are even *further* from the Habermasian vision of critical rationality and communicative coherence than Alexander suggests. For example, in a study of nineteenth-century American women's movements, Rabinovitch (2001) argues that women were able to get their issues onto the public agenda not only by mobilizing the dominant discourse of civil society, but also – and, perhaps, more importantly – by mobilizing an alternative discourse of compassion and affection. By trying to relate empirical public debates to a single underlying cultural logic, Rabinovitch (2001) argues, Alexander's approach ignores the possibility that a civil society may contain two or more universal moral discourses that may be irreconcilably at odds with each other. Along similar lines, Meeks (2001) argues that the discourse of civil society forces marginalized groups to adopt particular kinds of strategies when they participate in the public sphere. In his study of the sexual politics of difference, Meeks reveals how the public sphere acts as a force of normalization, privileging those within the gay community who adopt an "assimilationist" sexual politics, designed to emphasize what homosexuals and heterosexuals share in common.[6] The problem with this is not only that the dominant discourse of civil society forces marginalized groups to present a homogenized and normalized image of themselves. It is also that the dominant discourse exacerbates the antagonisms that exist within these marginalized groups, making it more likely that their identity movements will eventually self-destruct (Gamson, 1996). In other words, the hierarchies and contradictions inherent to the discourse of civil society may have real and negative consequences for the associational life of marginalized groups.

One Public or Many?

In theoretical debates about the public sphere, perhaps the most vigorous criticism of Habermas is that his idealized vision of "the public sphere" has in reality operated as an arena of hegemony, exclusion, and subordination. For critics like Nancy Fraser (1992), dominant groups attempted to create a unified public sphere in order to create "active consent," where they included the subordinate groups, but did so under discursive rules which favored the dominant group. Historically, the establishment of "rational, critical discourse" and "objectivity" as the organizing tropes of the bourgeois public sphere and the "mainstream" news media was accomplished through a binarism intended to delegitimate excluded groups. These exclusions were created through discourse that criticized the "undisciplined" and "mob-like" activity of the working class, the "natural" sexuality and desire of women, and the "natural" passivity and indolence of non-whites (Eley, 1992; Jacobs, 1998). In other words, as I suggested in the previous section, the discourse of civil society has developed through a semiotic binary in which criteria of inclusion were intertwined with criteria of exclusion, and where the ideal of civic virtue required an anti-ideal of civic vice. As a form of social closure, this binary discourse advantages dominant groups and associations by being formally open yet informally closed; while in principle anyone can enter a dominant public sphere, "insiders" and "outsiders" are defined and identified by the tacit, uncodified classificatory schemes of the binary code, the practical mastery of which is unequally distributed among the participants. Thus, while the bourgeois public sphere was organized according to the open and democratic principles of rationality and publicity, it was at the same time "the arena, the training ground, and eventually the power base of a stratum of bourgeois men who were coming to see themselves as a 'universal class' and preparing to assert their fitness to govern" (Fraser, 1992, p. 114).

Historically, subordinated groups have turned to alternative publics as a way to compensate for their exclusion from the dominant public sphere. In these alternative communicative spaces, groups have been able to discover common interests, to develop arguments that could more effectively engage the dominant public, and to provide deliberative spaces that could nurture the development of new public leaders. Motivations to participate in these alternative publics were reinforced by the experiences of exclusion, but also by the hope that new arguments and new rhetoric would be able to capture "mainstream" public attention and shift public opinion.

My own research on the African-American press provides an example of an empirical public sphere that provided an alternative to the dominant public (Jacobs, 2000). African-American newspapers emerged early in the nineteenth century, carved out of the mutual aid societies, independent churches, and educational institutions of the African-American community in the Northern cities. *Freedom's Journal* was first, published in 1827; but at least forty different newspapers were published by African-Americans before the Civil War, and the establishment of a national black press was generally agreed upon as the second most pressing issue among African-American leaders of the time. The historical need for a strong black press was three-fold: (1) to provide a forum for debate and self-improvement; (2) to monitor the mainstream media; and (3) to increase black visibility in white civil society. African-Americans could not count on the "mainstream" press of the time to publicize black voices or to represent black issues in a non-patronizing manner. Most of the Northern papers were against slavery and in favor of eman-cipation, but their positions were crafted through stories that favored the voices of white politicians over black abolitionists. Even in dealings with their white aboli-tionist allies, black leaders often found their voices excluded and marginalized. The white abolitionist press, while receiving most of its early subscription support from African-Americans, eventually decreased its coverage of black news items in favor of reports about the activities of white abolitionists; in fact, William Lloyd Garrison actively discouraged the establishment of early black papers such as *Colored American* and Frederick Douglass's *North Star*. By establishing an independent black press, African-Americans were able to secure a space of self-representation: not only to craft common identities and solidarities, but also to develop arguments that might effectively engage white civil society. As Frederick Douglass argued, the problem was that white society did not have a true knowledge of black affairs; the solution was to develop active, aggressive, and critical black spaces of debate and opinion formation. Thus, the formation of a national black press was seen as the solution to the ills of black society, white society, and the nation as a whole.

The history of the African-American public sphere and the black press is neither an isolated nor an exceptional case; numerous historical studies point to the existence of non-bourgeois, non-male, and otherwise "non-official" publics. As early as the eighteenth century, there were plebian publics, women's publics, and an entire set of public spheres that were organized more around "festive communication" than rational discourse.[7] During the women's suffrage movement of the nineteenth century, there developed national, regional and local women's papers simultaneously articulating the principles of women's rights and the vision of a new kind of media organization (Steiner, 1993). The working class press at the turn of the century consisted of hundreds of newspapers in dozens of languages (Bekken, 1993). What these alternative publics and alternative media point to is the fact that Habermas's account of the rise of the bourgeois public sphere "is an extremely idealized abstraction from the political cultures that actually took shape at the end of the eighteenth and the start of the nineteenth century" (Eley, 1992, p. 307). Empirical civil societies have always contained plural and partial publics.

Another way sociologists have studied multiple publics has been to investigate the different styles of talk that people adopt when moving from subsidiary to dominant publics, in order to see which types of publics do a better job of approximating the ideal of rational deliberation. For example, in an ethnographic study of sexual identity politics, Lichterman (1999) found that people in insular, highly solidaristic forums frequently engaged in open-ended, self-critical, multi-perspectival talk about matters of sexual concern; yet those same individuals, when transported into a multi-group coalition-building arena, adopted narrower forms of identity talk that assumed a single gay interest and a common enemy. In other words, the smaller public encouraged more critical rationality than the larger one. Along similar lines, Eliasoph (1998) argued that open, critical, and forthright discussions about politics can be found much more often in *small private spaces* than they can in large public ones, where most people carefully avoid talking about politics. Eliasoph and Lichterman both argue that rational deliberation gets short-circuited because large publics encourage a culture that privileges doing things over talking about them. The problem is that, in the absence of ordinary voices, the larger, more dominant publics get filled up with experts, power-brokers, and activists, with the result being a more polarized public debate that discourages ordinary citizens even further from participating.[8] In this sense, the issue agendas and the styles of talk that dominate large publics have a dampening effect on the political effectiveness of voluntary associations.

Has the Public Sphere Really Degenerated?

A third area of sociological research has questioned Habermas's mass-culture critique of and his story of tragic decline. For historical sociologists, a key problem with Habermas's tale of degeneration is its inconsistency.

> Habermas tends to judge the eighteenth century by Locke and Kant, the nineteenth century by Marx and Mill, and the twentieth century by the typical suburban television viewer. Thus, Habermas's account of the twentieth century does not include the sort of intellectual history, the attempt to take leading thinkers seriously... that is characteristic of his approach to seventeenth, eighteenth, and nineteenth centuries. Conversely, his treatment of the earlier period doesn't look at 'penny dreadfuls,' lurid crime and scandal sheets, and other less than altogether rational-critical branches of the press or at the demagoguery of traveling orators, and glances only in passing at the relationship of crowds to political discourse... Moreover, the public consequences of mass media are not necessarily as uniformly negative as *Structural Transformation* suggests, and there may be more room than Habermas realized for alternative democratic media strategies (Calhoun, 1992, p. 33).

In his historical study of printing and petitions in early-modern England, Zaret (2000) makes a similar argument about the way Habermas selectively treats historical evidence in order to develop a linear story of past glory and present decline. As Zaret demonstrates, the communicative changes that Habermas glorifies did not develop magically from the salons, pubs, and coffeehouses where bourgeois men gathered to discuss matters of common concern. Rather, they developed out of a dialogic order that was imposed by print technology, in the form of petitions, cross-petitions, broadsides, and newspapers – all of which were shaped in fundamental ways by commerce and textual reproduction, and not by the teleological, functionalist releases of critical rationality that Habermas imagines (Zaret, 2000, p. 278).

By looking more even-handedly at the history of the public sphere, sociologists have provided a useful counterpoint to the overly pessimistic view toward mass culture and the contemporary public sphere that critical theorists tend to put forth. If commercialization and mediated communication have always been a central part of the public sphere, as Calhoun and Zaret both suggest, then there may be important democratic possibilities made possible by the modern media age. Indeed, as sociologists have turned their attention to mass media and the public sphere, they have focused on two types of media forms in particular: (1) televised media events; and (2) the Internet.

In its earliest history, television was primarily an entertainment-based industry, focusing on dramas, music, comedies, and games. News was an afterthought, provided as a public service, but limited to fifteen minutes every evening.[9] Eventually, television executives discovered that they could make money broadcasting the news, provided that they could create new and more dramatic forms of presentation. The first new form they discovered was the media event, or the "live broadcasting of history" (Dayan & Katz, 1992). By televising live coverage of presidential debates and inaugurations, royal weddings and funerals, the Olympics, wars, civic crises and countless other events, television has helped to create a national – and, increasingly, a global – public sphere of a size and scope that had never before been possible.

According to Dayan and Katz (1992, pp. 5–7), media events display the following features: (1) an interruption of routine broadcasting; (2) which is usually monopolistic (that is, all stations switch to coverage of the event); and (3) is typically broadcast live. During media events, people take time out of their daily routines to watch television, often collectively. Media events serve the legitimation needs for societies whose members cannot gather together in a direct way. They provide common rituals and common symbols, which citizens can experience contemporaneously with everyone and interpersonally with those around them. According to Dayan and Katz (1992, p. 25) media events approximate Weber's three ideal-typical forms of authority: "rationality, charisma, and tradition are inscribed respectively in Contest, Conquest, and Coronation." In the "production" of media events, news workers tend to exhibit a much higher level of involvement in the story, and they make extensive use of the more inflated genres of high-mimetic fiction, such as romance, tragedy, and epic (Jacobs, 1996; Smith, 1994). In other words, media events are rituals writ large.[10]

The political power of media events is their capacity to create an integrated global public sphere, by concentrating public attention onto a single event. Indeed, media events tend to draw the largest audience among all types of television broadcasts (Dayan & Katz, 1992). Addressed to a fictional world audience that is believed to be an important source of international public opinion, these events allow individuals and associations to force the state to engage them in debate about matters of common concern, in a situation where refusal results in a loss of international legitimacy. The 1989 events in Tienanmen Square provide a case in point. Chinese protesters carried signs quoting Abraham Lincoln and other American democratic heroes, which were translated into English for the audiences of CNN; so long as international media cameras were there, it was believed, Chinese authorities would not turn violent (Calhoun, 1994; Keane, 1995). By increasing the global reach of television news, and by captivating public attention, media events help to expand the scope of discussions that take in the public sphere. To be sure, these publics are imperfect, as measured against the ideal of critical rationality. Powerful gate-keeping forces regulate who gets media access, and the media coverage tends to present a picture of sporadic events that bear little connection to one another. Nevertheless, the live coverage presents an opportunity for typically excluded groups to "hijack" the event, and to gain a global public forum that could not be duplicated through any other mechanism (Dayan & Katz, 1992, pp. 68–77). Not surprisingly, voluntary associations approach media events as a prime opportunity to get their message out to the public, and they descend on these events with protests, street theater, and other forms of symbolic action (Sobieraj, 2002).

If the power of television is its ability to create incredibly large publics, the power of the Internet is its ability to sustain smaller, more particularistic counter-publics. As Castells (2001, p. 164) has argued, the Internet serves democratization well, "by relatively leveling the ground of symbolic manipulation, and by broadening the sources of communication." Social movements and voluntary associations have used the Internet to establish global networks of discussion, organization, and publicity that bypass the gatekeepers of traditional media, and by so doing have been able to avoid the politics of public visibility. Local communities, which have increasingly found themselves ignored by the dominant media conglomerates, have used the Internet to reproduce local forms of culture, citizenship, and solidarity. Websites, list-serves, and chat rooms have been produced for an almost infinite variety of particularistic groups who have never been able to carve out a successful (i.e. profitable) niche using print or television media. And yet, there is good reason to believe that the result will *not* be undue balkanization, because a majority of these Internet users are also exposed to general-interest, non-partisan portal sites such as yahoo.com, aol.com, and msn.com (Jacobs, 2001). While more research is needed to determine exactly how these new forms of media practice are influencing civil society, one thing is clear. The current media environment offers much more than the simple, tragic erosion of the public sphere.

THE QUESTION OF CIVIC ENGAGEMENT

While the debates about the public sphere revolve around the organization of public debate, they also involve the ability of associations to get their issues onto the public agenda and to influence public policy. Oriented primarily to the strong version of civil society (cf. Taylor, 1991), most research on the public sphere assumes the existence of a set of voluntary associations that are independent from the state. Many of the sociological contributions to the public sphere debates (e.g. Calhoun, 1994; Dayan & Katz, 1992; Eliasoph, 1998; Lichterman, 1999, 2001; Perez-Diaz, 1993; Sobieraj, 2002) are interested in the relationship between public spheres and voluntary associations. Implicitly, though, all debates about the public sphere imply an interest in the relationship between voluntary associations and civic engagement.

Ever since de Tocqueville (1969), scholars have argued that effective democracies needed strong voluntary associations, and that the exceptionalism of American democracy could be attributed to the fact that it had a more vibrant associational life than other nations. Americans seemed to join associations much more than they did in Europe, and they tended to do so for a much wider variety of purposes, both political and non-political. For the most part, empirical studies have continued to find higher levels of association membership in the United States than in other industrialized nations (Almond & Verba, 1963; Ladd, 1999), though a good deal of this is due to the high rates of American participation in religious associations (Curtis, Grabb & Baer, 1992; Wuthnow, 1999).

For de Tocqueville, the importance of voluntary associations was primarily political. When people gathered together in an association, they: (1) discovered shared interests in common; (2) learned to describe these shared interests as a collective *public* interest; and (3) attempted to interject this collective interest into political debates and public policy decisions. In the process, they developed important civic skills, increased their involvement in political life, developed solidaristic forms of attachment to their fellow association members, and felt a sense of general political efficacy (Schlozman, Verba & Brady, 1999). Furthermore, by aggregating the private interests of their members, associations helped to diversify the sources of political influence in civil society, since there was legitimacy in the simple fact of being able to claim a large base of supporters (Knoke, 1990, pp. 54–55; Parsons, 1982, pp. 251–252).

Since the 1980s, however, that has been growing concern about the health of the American voluntary sector. The first major warning call was sounded by Bellah, Madsen, Sullivan, Swidler and Tipton (1985), who criticized the ways that liberal individualism had impoverished American political culture and turned people away from associations. The second warning came from the non-profit sector, where researchers warned of declining total membership, threats of reduced government funding, and demands for greater accountability (Hall, 1987; Kanter & Sumner, 1987; Leat, 1990). But the most important warnings have come from Robert Putnam. Drawing on national survey data, Putnam showed that voluntary association membership had decreased dramatically since the 1950s and 1960s – in all age groups, at all levels of education, and in every type of association (Putnam 1995a, b, 2000). As a result of this decline, Putnam argued, there had been a decrease in civic engagement. Disconnected from voluntary associations, Putnam worried, Americans would experience less trust and less social connection, and political institutions would function less efficiently as a result.

Putnam has received an unusual amount of attention in academia and beyond, sparking a renewed interest in the question of civic engagement. Like Habermas's work on the public sphere, Putnam's arguments about civic engagement have been particularly valuable as a spur for further theory, research, and analysis. As a consequence, "scholars are asking much more precise questions about the full range of individuals' involvement in groups, social activities, and political activities of all kinds" (Skocpol & Fiorinia, 1999, p. 8). Three questions in particular seem to be attracting sociological attention:

(1) Are there really fewer people participating in voluntary associations?
(2) What organizational changes have taken place in the voluntary sector since the 1950s and 1960s, and how have these changes impacted civic engagement?
(3) Under what conditions does participation in voluntary associations produce trust, tolerance, and other forms of social capital?[11]

In attempting to answer these questions, sociologists have frequently challenged Putnam's claims about the state of civil society. They have also raised important new questions about civic engagement, which are at least as important as the question of whether or not there has been a real decline.

Are There Really Fewer People Participating in Voluntary Associations?

Putnam's empirical findings center on the claim that Americans today are less likely to join voluntary associations, less likely to volunteer their time when they do join, and, as a result, less likely to campaign, to vote, or to express confidence in public leaders. Are these findings correct? On the one hand, there is strong evidence that would seem to support Putnam's concerns. Americans today are much more likely to donate their money to an organization than to offer their time or involvement (Verba, Schlozman & Brady, 1995, p. 77). For those who do offer their time, they are more likely than ever to treat their volunteer work as a one-time event rather than an ongoing commitment (Wilson & Musick, 1999; Wuthnow, 1998). There has been a decline in voter turnout (Miller & Shanks, 1996). And many of the largest, most important civic groups of the past have experienced dramatic declines in membership, with some disappearing altogether (Skocpol, 1999a).

On the other hand, there are many who disagree with Putnam's claims about civic decline. Ladd (1996) finds that more people are attending school board meetings. Jenks (1987) finds that people are *more* likely to do volunteer work, and that the mean level of hours volunteered per week has actually increased. Skocpol and Fiorinia (1999) argue that the GSS data Putnam relied on does not account for multiple memberships, and therefore is unable to document a decisive decline in membership. Verba, Schlozman and Brady (1995, pp. 71–73) argue that voter turnout may have declined, but most other measures of civic and political engagement have not. And besides, membership in voluntary associations continues to be higher in the United States than in other industrialized nations (Ladd, 1999; Verba, Schlozman & Brady, 1995, p. 80). Thus, the evidence about decline appears to be mixed, at best.

For others, the question about the correctness of Putnam's empirical findings elides a more significant issue. Is Putnam asking the right questions? What if the real story has less to do with levels of membership, and more with the changing *forms* of civic engagement? Indeed, this is precisely what Wuthnow (1998) found in his study of American civic involvement. The people Wuthnow interviewed were joining very different kinds of associations, which were more porous and informal than the kinds of organizations that Putnam was counting, and they were joining the organizations for very specific purposes and delimited time periods. To be sure, this created real challenges for the organizations. The association representatives that Wuthnow interviewed had to devote significant amounts of energy in order to attract members, volunteers, and public attention. Often, they were forced to rely heavily on public relations specialists, newspapers, television, and the Internet, with the result being virtual communities of interest that were very geographically dispersed. Because these associations were more transient and scattered, they were less central to the quotidian life of the community, and they did little to help bring neighbors together in relations of trust or solidarity. Furthermore, because they relied more on mass mediated forms of communication, these associations were more dependent on the existence of a coherent and inclusive public sphere, making their ability to promote civic engagement more tenuous. Nevertheless, these organizations did provide real and substantial civic connections. "Even though they may be more sporadic or span greater distances than in the past," Wuthnow (1998, p. 204) concluded, "they do link people together in a community of interest." In other words, these new kinds of associations may be *different*, but that does not necessarily translate to a tragic loss of citizenship.

Other scholars have pointed to the fact that civic engagement is a cyclical process, linked to the periodic appearance of rituals and crises. Trust, solidarity, and other forms of social capital do not need to be reproduced at every moment of time, but simply require regular periods of heightened collective attention. This is a good thing, since most people do not have the time to retire at the end of the day to the salon or coffeehouse, in order to discuss matters of common concern. Nor do they have the time to spend three or four evenings at the Rotary Club each week. Indeed, it is quite possible that these idealized images of civic engagement are undesirable and anachronistic, almost always requiring a patriarchal division of household labor as well as a healthy dose of residential segregation. In this sense, there are strong similarities and common limitations shared by Habermas's idealized vision of the public sphere and Putnam's idealized image of voluntary associations. During ritual events, however, people who are otherwise disengaged from public life turn on their television sets, open their newspapers, and talk about important public matters. They seek out civic organizations, they volunteer their time, and they pay attention to important public matters. In short, they increase their levels of civic engagement at the same time as they become more involved in the public sphere.

While more research is needed to document the full range of ritual events that produce an increase in civic engagement, one important type of event that has been studied is the national election. At the individual level, elections allow people to renew their symbolic attachment to national society, leading to an increase in social capital. Indeed, as Rahn, Brehm and Carlson (1999) found in an analysis of the American National Election Studies, levels of social and political trust increased significantly after the 1996 Presidential election, as did perceptions of external efficacy. At the organizational level, elections increase political mobilization, spurring the formation of new associations, social movements, and other civic activities, while contributing to the heightened sense of collective effervescence that helps to define the modern political campaign (Sobieraj,

2002). While cautioning that more research on ritual and civic engagement is needed, Rahn, Brehm and Carlson (1999, p. 140) have raised the intriguing possibility that "the simple ritual of elections . . . may be a crucial component in the development of the high quality of life represented by high levels of social capital."

What Changes have Taken Place in the Voluntary Sector?

One thing that has become increasingly apparent is that the "advocacy explosion" has transformed the nature and organization of the voluntary sector. The traditional picture of American association building was one of grass roots, local membership organizations, linked in a federated structure to other chapter affiliates at both the state and the national level (Skocpol, 1999a). These groups met regularly, providing their members with multiple opportunities for participation, engagement, and leadership. As the earlier discussion of Wuthnow's research suggests, these kinds of organizations are being replaced by more porous institutions and informal networks. But they are also being replaced by another kind of organization: the advocacy group (Berry, 1997; Cigler & Burdett, 1983).

The primary goal of an advocacy group is to *represent* the interests of its members and constituents, through legislative lobbying and media activism. Because of this goal, most advocacy groups rely heavily on paid professionals to do their work, and only secondarily (if at all) on the labor of unpaid volunteers (Berry, 1999). As compared to other types of associations, advocacy groups are generally less interested in providing opportunities for their members to participate in meetings or to interact with other chapter affiliates. Indeed, their preferred techniques of civic influence – patron grants, direct mail, and media publicity – share one thing in common: namely, the desire to minimize or eliminate extended interactions with real groups of members (Skocpol, 1999b, pp. 491–494). This does not necessarily mean that advocacy groups have eliminated members altogether; indeed, some of the most successful advocacy groups have more than a half-million members (Berry, 1999, p. 368). Nevertheless, members of groups such as the National Audubon Society or the Environmental Defense Fund experience the non-profit sector much differently than do members of traditional associations like the Elks or Rotary.

In many ways, the shift toward advocacy and publicity has been good for civil society. One of the reasons that membership-based service and fraternal organizations had begun to fall out of favor, after all, was that an increasing number of people found them to be too narrow in their interests and too segregated in their membership patterns (Skocpol, 1999b, pp. 481–487). In contrast, many of the advocacy groups developed directly out of the 1960s social movements, and seem to be better aligned with the cultural changes taking place in American civil society (Minkoff, 1995). Moreover, advocacy groups seem to "get things done" more efficiently, and on a much larger scale, than local volunteer-based groups. Indeed, advocacy groups have been surprisingly effective at getting their issues on the media agenda, and they have succeeded in many instances in getting legislation passed (Berry, 1999). In a pragmatist political culture that privileges doing things over talking about them, advocacy groups seem much more "realistic" than other kinds of associations (Lichterman, 2001).

Still, many scholars are concerned about the growing emphasis on publicity, advocacy, and politics in the voluntary sector. After all, the historical importance of non-profit associations and civic groups was connected to a large degree to the role they played in generating civic engagement, solidarity, trust, and social capital. In other words, associations provided a valuable civic service when they offered their members opportunities to gather together and talk about matters of common concern. When non-profit associations shift their emphasis too far in the direction of publicity and advocacy, there is a danger that they will become less interested in organizing these kinds of face-to-face participatory activities. From this point of view, the emphasis on advocacy and publicity hurts an association's ability to provide opportunities for generating social capital, at the same time that it increases the association's effectiveness in the public sphere. Further research is needed to explore this tension between civic engagement and political effectiveness among advocacy associations.

Another problem with the advocacy explosion is that it intensifies the preference that associations have for wealthy, highly educated, professionally skilled members. After all, these kinds of members are much more likely to be able to provide the kinds of volunteer resources that advocacy organizations want. If volunteers can offer the same kind of labor power as professional public relations workers, and can do so within a temporal framework that matches the news day, they can act as effective substitutes for a paid professional staff. If the volunteers come from high-status groups, they can serve as attractive sources to journalists, fulfilling another useful function for the organization.[12] It is perhaps not surprising, then, that active recruitment into civic groups tends to be disproportionately biased toward wealthier, more professional, and more educated individuals (Schlozman, Verba & Brady, 1999). Thus, as more associations shift their emphasis toward advocacy and publicity, it is likely to decrease social capital and civic engagement much more rapidly in disadvantaged communities than it is in privileged ones. It remains to be seen whether the rise of porous institutions and informal networks will be enough to offset the rise of advocacy groups, in terms of the opportunities that individuals have for civic engagement.

Does Participation in Voluntary Associations Always Produce Social Capital?

Finally, ethnographic studies of actual associations have revealed that participation in voluntary associations does not always produce an increase in trust or social capital. As the earlier discussion of Lichterman's (1999) work suggested, individuals who are trusting, reflective, and tolerant in small, solidaristic spaces often become uncritical, narrow, and shrill in larger, more "political" spaces. Others, who are open-minded, thoughtful, and compassionate in private spaces become virtually mute in public, trying hard to produce a performance of political apathy that leaves the public sphere open for activists and other professional politicians (Eliasoph, 1998). These studies and others reveal the "dark side of civic engagement": specifically, that "civic engagement may not necessarily be a good thing" (Fiorina, 1999, p. 396). What Lichterman, Eliasoph and Fiorina are suggesting is that civic engagement only produces trust and social capital in specific kinds of contexts.

Fiorina (1999) has sketched the argument about the contextual effects of engagement in its clearest form. Because of the rise of advocacy organizations, the formal inclusion of previously excluded groups, and the decline in political parties, there has been a marked increase in participatory politics since the 1960s. Yet, while this has been a positive and progressive change, it has had an unintended consequence: specifically, the demands of participation are so severe that the people willing to pay the costs tend to have the most intensely held and extreme views (Fiorina, 1999, p. 416). As a result, participants tend to care about different issues than non-participants, and they tend to discuss those issues in more extreme terms than non-participants (Verba, Schlozman & Brady, 1995, pp. 463–508). As public sphere debates become more polarized, the effect is to discourage moderate citizens from participating in voluntary associations.

In order to resolve this dilemma, Fiorina (1999, p. 416) suggests lowering the costs of political participation, by "reconsidering the notion that people must be physically present, or must invest large blocks of their time." This could be accomplished through a number of mechanisms, all of which have been suggested at various points in the present chapter: (1) the use of new communication technologies, such as the Internet; (2) a more effective integration of large and small publics; (3) the empowerment of porous institutions and informal networks; and (4) the focus on (mass-mediated) ritual events such as political campaigns, civil crises, and (inter)national tragedies. The point is to encourage the kinds of civic talk and civic practices that actually produce social capital, while disempowering the ones that tend to produce apathy, cynicism, and distrust.

CONCLUSION

A great deal of empirical research has already contributed to a growing sociology of civil society. Indeed, as I have suggested, a number of distinct streams of research are beginning to emerge in the area. Needless to say, much important work is still left to be done. Indeed, while some of the areas I have described are well established, others have only begun to be explored. For this reason, I want to conclude by outlining four specific areas where more research is needed, and where political sociologists are particularly well suited to contribute to the civil society debates:

(1) *Studies that examine processes of civic activation during ritual events.* As I argued earlier in the chapter, while studies have documented the effects that national elections have on civic engagement and the public sphere, more research is needed to document the full range of ritual practices that increase civic engagement and political effectiveness. Indeed, there is already a large and significant literature on politics and ritual, that identifies the ways that ritual activity provides symbolic representation of political parties, promotes solidarity among political party members, promotes particular understandings of political reality, and provides legitimation and mystification (Kertzer, 1996, p. 125; also see Alexander, 1988; Berezin, 1997b; Kertzer, 1988; Smith, 1991; Wagner-Pacifici, 1986). Civil society scholars can make effective use of this tradition of scholarship, in order to answer the following kinds of questions: What kinds of rituals are most effective at promoting engagement and increasing solidarity? What kinds of rituals are most effective at getting a new issue onto the public agenda, and influencing public sphere debates? Do large publics respond to different kinds of rituals than small publics? Are the rituals that increase civic engagement the same ones that increase political effectiveness? These kinds of questions can help to specify more precisely the relationship between voluntary associations and public spheres.

(2) *Studies that examine the relationship between porous institutions and advocacy organizations.* As research on the advocacy explosion suggests, there may be a growing tension between civic engagement and political effectiveness in contemporary civil society. As voluntary associations get more interested in getting their issues onto the public agenda and influencing public sphere debates, there is the danger that they will decrease their emphasis on providing engagement contexts for their members. More research is needed to determine the extent to which this is actually occurring, and what effect it may be having on civic participation. Do advocacy groups discourage people from being involved in voluntary associations, or do they

lower the costs of participation? Are there specific forms of communication technology that make it easier for today's associations to combine civic engagement with political effectiveness in the public sphere? To what extent are the porous institutions that Wuthnow (1998) describes filling in the gaps left behind by advocacy organizations and an increasingly professionalized world of voluntary associations? How effective are these porous institutions at helping individuals to discover new interests, develop civic skills, and maintain an active involvement in public life? In short, is it possible to have a vibrant world of voluntary associations without frequent meetings and regular opportunities for participation and membership? Is it possible to be actively engaged in civil society from the privacy of one's home, by reading news, watching television, talking on the phone, and using the Internet?

(3) *Studies of the Internet and civil society.* While Habermas and Putnam both privilege face-to-face interactions in their theories of civil society, this preference may not be warranted. Indeed, as Calhoun (1993) and Zaret (2000) persuasively argue, the historical evidence for privileging face-to-face communication in the public sphere is unconvincing. After all, the idea that political actions should be supervised in civil society by the practice of criticism and according to standards of disinterested public virtue implied the existence of an impersonal mass audience, put into place precisely by the *anonymity* of print technology (Lee, 1992, pp. 409–411; Warner, 1993, pp. 34–35). In newspapers, pamphlets, and literary journals, individuals developed the techniques of reasoned argumentation to a mass audience; they also established the expectation that their autonomy and their citizenship was to be pursued primarily through the practices of *reading* and *publishing*.

Today, television and the Internet have replaced print as the dominant form of cultural transmission in the public sphere. I have already suggested how televised media events are influencing the public sphere. But television has a limited ability to directly influence voluntary associations, since it is such a mass medium. The Internet, however, is a much different medium, with capabilities of one-to-one, one-to-many, and many-to-many communication. More research is needed to determine how this new medium is changing the world of voluntary associations and public spheres. In what ways do Internet content providers actually inform public sphere debates? To what extent is the Internet improving the viability and the circulation of smaller, alternative publics? How is the Internet changing the communicative practices of voluntary associations? These questions need to be answered in order to chart the impact that this new form of cultural transmission is having on the public sphere.

(4) *Studies that examine the relationship between voluntary associations and the public sphere.* Finally, as I have suggested throughout this article, there

needs to be more research that examines the relationship *between* voluntary associations and the public sphere. On the one hand, associations constitute a significant portion of the "small publics" that make up civil society. On the other hand, many associations spend a great deal of energy trying to attract publicity and influence the dominant publics. In other words, there is an interaction between civic engagement and the public sphere that merits further attention. Lichterman (1999, 2001) and Eliasoph (1998) have done exemplary work that highlights this interaction. Hopefully, future scholars will continue this work, contributing in important ways to our understanding of politics, public life, and the shape of civil society.

There is one area in particular where research in political sociology could go a long way toward highlighting the relationship between voluntary associations and public spheres: political campaigns. Indeed, recent research by Sobieraj (2002) has revealed how campaigns mobilize the voluntary sector, encouraging associations to increase their activities. Interestingly, Sobieraj also notes that campaigns encourage many associations to shift their priorities toward a "public sphere orientation." Seeing the campaign as a prime opportunity to get their issue(s) into the arena of public discussion and debate, many associations become almost obsessed with media publicity. They believe that if they can get publicity during a campaign, it will force the political candidates to address the matters about which they are the most concerned. Sobieraj finds that most associations fail to get the media publicity they seek, and when they do get publicity they usually still fail to influence the agenda of issues organizing the campaign. Nevertheless, when associations believe that a political campaign is a critical moment of opportunity for them, there is a powerful effect on the kinds of civic activities they pursue. More research is needed to determine what long-term impacts campaigns have on those associations that adopt a public sphere orientation.

Looking at campaigns from the perspective of the candidates, there is an equally interesting relationship between voluntary associations and public spheres. Political candidates often seem compelled to visit as many different locales as possible, in order to show that they are interested in the entire population of their governing territory. In the process, they give speeches and news interviews. They shake hands and kiss babies. They visit schools and civic groups. They have "town-hall meetings," where they answer the questions of "ordinary people." And, of course, they do all of these things under the watchful gaze of news media. But what are the effects of these activities? Do they bring about any changes in the issues and agendas of public discussion? Do they encourage voluntary associations to hold more meetings, or to provide other kinds of opportunities for civic participation? What kinds of opportunities do campaigns present for the porous organizations described by Wuthnow? Is there any relationship between the type of campaign – e.g. local, state, national – and its effects on public spheres and voluntary associations? These questions, as well as others, suggest many exciting areas of future research for a political sociology of civil society.

NOTES

1. As Lichterman's (1999, 2001) research demonstrates, voluntary associations frequently create free spaces of public communication, and as such they operate very much like public spheres. What is required by the "stronger version" of civil society I am describing, however, is the existence of public spheres which have the power to force public authorities and political elites to pay attention to them.

2. This shift in the norms and practice of politics can be seen in two historical changes that occurred in England. The first occurred during the early 1700s, when Bolingbroke developed a new theory and practice of political opposition, whereby the opposition sought to influence policy from outside of government, by mobilizing public opinion through political journalism. The second came to pass during the early 1800s, when journalists were provided an official place in the Houses of Parliament (Cohen & Arato, 1992, p. 658; Habermas, 1989, p. 62).

3. By "private persons," what Habermas had in mind was that the discussions took place between individuals, in a manner where the power of each utterance was determined by the force of the argument rather than the public status of the speaker.

4. Habermas's model for how this might work is revealed in his description of English pubs and coffee houses. By the beginning of the eighteenth century, there were already so many spaces of public discussion that they could only be integrated through print media, which were central to the public life of the English pub and coffee house; their articles were frequently made the object of coffee house discussions, and the discussions often resulted in letters to the editor that were published the following week (Habermas, 1989, p. 42).

5. As I discuss later in the chapter, Fraser (1992) also criticizes Habermas for not appreciating alternative publics, and for over-emphasizing the "official" public sphere of predominantly elite communication.

6. On this point, also see Seidman (1993), Seidman, Meeks and Traschen (1999).

7. For historical accounts of the plebian public sphere, see Eley (1992) and Tucker (1996a). For historical accounts of women's publics, see Ryan (1992), Baker (1992), and Landes (1988). On festive communication and the public sphere, see Keane (1984) and Tucker (1996b).

8. Lichterman (2001) has proposed an interesting solution to this problem: an ethic of translation, in which individuals who are involved in a large set of diverse associations take on the responsibility for facilitating communication between different kinds of publics.

9. CBS increased its network news broadcast to thirty minutes in 1963, with NBS following suit later in the year and ABC waiting until 1967.

10. While Habermas has tended to dismiss rituals as pre-modern and degenerative deformations that are unnecessary in modern society (e.g. Habermas, 1987, pp. 86–92), many sociologists and anthropologists have shown that ritual continues to be a powerful

and important force in the modern public sphere (e.g. Berezin, 1997b; Kertzer, 1996; Wagner-Pacifici, 1986). In this sense, media events provide a mass-mediated forum for a type of political action that has been important throughout modernity.

11. While there are competing definitions of social capital, what is common to all of them is the idea that generalized forms of trust emerge out of social relationships and social networks.

12. In her ethnographic study of the social organization of the news room, Tuchman (1978, pp. 68–81) found that a journalist's status is often parasitic upon the status of his or her sources, such that "important journalists have important sources."

REFERENCES

Alexander, J. C. (1988). Culture and political crisis: 'Watergate' and Durkheimian sociology. In: J. Alexander (Ed.), *Durkheimian Sociology: Cultural Studies* (pp. 187–224). NY: Cambridge University Press.

Alexander, J. C. (1992). Citizen and enemy as symbolic classification: On the polarizing discourse of civil society. In: M. Fournier & M. Lamont (Eds), *Where Culture Talks: Exclusion and the Making of Society* (pp. 289–308). Chicago, IL: University of Chicago Press.

Alexander, J. C. (1997). The paradoxes of civil society. *International Sociology, 12*, 115–133.

Alexander, J. C. (1998). Civil Society I, II, III: Constructing an empirical concept from normative controversies and historical transformations. In: J. Alexander (Ed.), *Real Civil Societies: Dilemmas of Institutionalization* (pp. 1–19). London: Sage Publications.

Alexander, J. C., & Smith, P. (1993). The discourse of American civil society: A new proposal for cultural studies. *Theory and Society, 22*, 151–207.

Almond, G., & Verba, S. (1963). *The civic culture: Political attitudes and democracy in five nations*. Princeton, NJ: Princeton University Press.

Baker, K. (1992). Defining the public sphere in eighteenth-century France: Variations on a theme by Habermas. In: C. Calhoun (Ed.), *Habermas and the Public Sphere* (pp. 181–211). Cambridge, MA: The MIT Press.

Bekken, J. (1993). The working-class press at the turn of the century. In: W. Solomon & R. McChesney (Eds), *Ruthless Criticism: New Perspectives in U.S. Communication History* (pp. 151–175). Minneapolis, MN: University of Minnesota Press.

Bellah, R., Madsen R., Sullivan, W., Swidler, A., & Tipton, S. (1985). *Habits of the heart*. Berkeley, CA: University of California Press.

Benhabib, S. (1992). In the shadow of Aristotle and Hegel: Communicative ethics and current controversies in practical philosophy. In: *Situating the Self: Gender, Community and Postmodernism in Contemporary Ethics* (pp. 23–67). NY: Routledge.

Berezin, M. (1997a). Politics and culture: A less fissured terrain. *Annual Review of Sociology, 23*, 361–383.

Berezin, M. (1997b). *Making the fascist self: The political culture of inter-war Italy*. Ithaca, NY: Cornell University Press.

Berry, J. M. (1997). *The interest group society*. NY: Longman.

Berry, J. M. (1999). The rise of citizen groups. In: T. Skocpol & M. Fiorina (Eds), *Civic Engagement in American Democracy* (pp. 367–394). Washington, DC: Brookings Institution Press.

Bryant, C. G. A. (1995). Civic nation, civil society, civil religion. In: J. Hall (Ed.), *Civil Society: Theory, History, Comparison* (pp. 136–157). Cambridge: Polity Press.

Calhoun, C. (1992). Introduction: Habermas and the public sphere. In: C. Calhoun (Ed.), *Habermas and the Public Sphere* (pp. 1–50). Cambridge, MA: The MIT Press.

Calhoun, C. (1993). Civil society and the public sphere. *Public Culture, 5*, 267–280.

Calhoun, C. (1994). *Neither Gods nor Emperors: Students and the struggle for democracy in China*. Berkeley, CA: University of California Press.

Castells, M. (2001). *The Internet galaxy: Reflections on the Internet, business, and society*. Oxford University Press.

Cigler, A., & Burdett, L. (Eds) (1983). *Interest group politics*. Washington, DC: Congressional Quarterly, Inc.

Cohen, J., & Arato, A. (1992). *Civil society and political theory*. Cambridge, MA: The MIT Press.

Curtis, J., Grabb, E., & Baer, D. (1992). Voluntary association membership in fifteen countries: A comparative analysis. *American Sociological Review, 57*, 139–152.

Dayan, D., & Katz, E. (1992). *Media events*. Cambridge, MA: Harvard University Press.

Eley, G. (1992). Nations, publics, and political cultures: Placing Habermas in the nineteenth century. In: C. Calhoun (Ed.), *Habermas and the Public Sphere* (pp. 289–339). Cambridge, MA: The MIT Press.

Eliasoph, N. (1998). *Avoiding politics: How Americans produce apathy in everyday life*. Cambridge University Press.

Fiorina, M. (1999). Extreme voices: A dark side of civic engagement. In: T. Skocpol & M. Fiorina (Eds), *Civic Engagement in American Democracy* (pp. 395–426). Washington, DC: Brookings Institution Press.

Fraser, N. (1992). Rethinking the public sphere: A contribution to the critique of actually existing democracy. In: C. Calhoun (Ed.), *Habermas and the Public Sphere* (pp. 109–142). Cambridge, MA: The MIT Press.

Gamson, J. (1996). Must identity movements self destruct? In: S. Seidman (Ed.), *Queer Theory/Sociology* (pp. 351–367). Cambridge, MA: Blackwell.

Garnham, N. (1992). The media and the public sphere. In: C. Calhoun (Ed.), *Habermas and the Public Sphere* (pp. 359–376). Cambridge, MA: The MIT Press.

Habermas, J. (1987). *The theory of communicative action* (Vol. 2). T. McCarthy (Trans.). Boston: Beacon Press.

Habermas, J. (1989, 1962). *The structural transformation of the public sphere*. T. Burger (Trans.). Cambridge, MA: The MIT Press.

Habermas, J. (1990). *Moral consciousness and communicative action*. Cambridge, MA: The MIT Press.

Habermas, J. (1992). Further reflections on the public sphere. In: C. Calhoun (Ed.), *Habermas and the Public Sphere* (pp. 421–461). Cambridge, MA: The MIT Press.

Hall, J. A. (1995). In search of civil society. In: J. Hall (Ed.), *Civil Society: Theory, History, Comparison* (pp. 1–31). Cambridge: Polity Press.

Hall, P. D. (1987). A historical overview of the private non-profit sector. In: W. Powell (Ed.), *The Non-profit Sector: A Research Handbook* (pp. 3–26). New Haven and London: Yale University Press.

Hirschman, A. O. (1991). *The rhetoric of reaction*. Cambridge, MA: Harvard University Press.

Jacobs, R. N. (1996). Producing the news, producing the crisis: Narrativity, television, and news work. *Media, Culture and Society, 18*, 373–397.

Jacobs, R. N. (1998). The racial discourse of civil society: The Rodney King affair and the city of Los Angeles. In: J. Alexander (Ed.), *Real Civil Societies: Dilemmas of Institutionalization* (pp. 138–161). London: Sage Publications.

Jacobs, R. N. (2000). *Race, media, and the crisis of civil society: From Watts to Rodney King.* Cambridge University Press.

Jacobs, R. (2001). Different media? *Boston Review, 26,* 13–14.

Jacobs, R., & Smith, P. (1997). Romance, irony, and solidarity. *Sociological Theory, 15,* 60–80.

Jenks, C. (1987). Who gives to what. In: W. Powell (Ed.), *The Non-profit Sector: A Research Handbook* (pp. 321–339). New Haven and London: Yale University Press.

Kane, A. (1997). Theorizing meaning construction in social movements: Symbolic structures and interpretation during the Irish land war, 1879–1882. *Sociological Theory, 15,* 249–276.

Kanter, R. M., & Sumner, D. V. (1987). Doing well while doing good: Dilemmas of performance measurement in non-profit organizations and the need for a multiple-constituency approach. In: W. Powell (Ed.), *The Non-profit Sector: A Research Handbook* (pp. 154–166). New Haven and London: Yale University Press.

Keane, J. (1984). *Public life and late capitalism: Toward a socialist theory of democracy.* Cambridge: Cambridge University Press.

Keane, J. (1995). Structural transformations of the public sphere. *The Communication Review, 1,* 1–22.

Kertzer, D. (1988). *Ritual, politics, and power.* New Haven, CT: Yale University Press.

Kertzer, D. (1996). *Politics and symbols: The Italian communist party and the fall of communism.* New Haven, CT: Yale University Press.

Knoke, D. (1990). *Organizing for collective action: The political economy of associations.* NY: Aldine de Gruyter.

Ku, A. (1999). *Narratives, politics, and the public sphere: Struggles over political reform in the final transitional years in Hong Kong.* Aldershot, UK: Ashgate.

Ku, A. (2001). The public up against the state: Narrative cracks and credibility crisis in post-colonial Hong Kong. *Theory, Culture & Society, 18,* 121–144.

Ladd, E. C. (1996). The data just don't show Erosion of America's social capital. *Public Perspective, 7,* 5–22.

Ladd, E. C. (1999). *The Ladd report.* NY: Free Press.

Landes, J. (1988). *Women and the public sphere in the age of the French revolution.* Ithaca, NY: Cornell University Press.

Leat, D. (1990). Voluntary organizations and accountability: Theory and practice. In: H. Anheier & W. Seibel (Eds), *The Third Sector: Comparative Studies of Non-profit Organizations* (pp. 141–153). NY: Walter de Gruyter.

Lee, B. (1992). Textuality, mediation, and public discourse. In: C. Calhoun (Ed.), *Habermas and the Public Sphere* (pp. 402–420). Cambridge, MA: The MIT Press.

Lichterman, P. (1999). Talking identity in the public sphere: Broad visions and small spaces in sexual identity politics. *Theory and Society, 28,* 101–141.

Lichterman, P. (2001). From tribalism to translation: Bridging diversity for civic renewal. *The Hedgehog Review, 3,* 40–61.

Meeks, C. (2001). Civil society and the sexual politics of difference. *Sociological Theory, 19,* 325–343.

Miller, W. E., & Shanks, J. M. (1996). *The new American voter.* Cambridge, MA: Harvard University Press.

Minkoff, D. (1995). *Organizing for equality: The evolution of women's and racial-ethnic organizations in America, 1955–1985.* New Brunswick, NJ: Rutgers University Press.

Parsons, T. (1982, [1963]). On the concept of influence. In: L. Mayhew (Ed.) *Talcott Parsons: On Institutions and Social Evolution* (pp. 224–252). Chicago, IL: University of Chicago Press.

Perez-Diaz, V. (1993). *The Return of Civil Society.* Cambridge, MA: Harvard University Press.

Perez-Diaz, V. (1995). The possibility of civil society: Traditions, character, and challenges. In: J. Hall
    (Ed.), *Civil Society: Theory, History, Comparison* (pp. 80–109). Cambridge: Polity Press.
Putnam, R. (1995a). Bowling alone: America's declining social capital. *Journal of Democracy, 6,*
    65–78.
Putnam, R. (1995b). Tuning in, tuning out: The strange disappearance of social capital in America.
    Political Science and Politics, 28, 664–683.
Putnam, R. (2000). *Bowling alone: Civic disengagement in America.* NY: Simon and Schuster.
Rabinovitch, E. (2001). Gender and the public sphere: Alternative forms of integration in nineteenth
    century America. *Sociological Theory, 19,* 344–370.
Rahn, W. M., Brehm, J., & Carlson, N. (1999). National elections as institutions for generating
    social capital. In: T. Skocpol & M. Fiorina (Eds), *Civic Engagement in American Democracy*
    (pp. 111–160). Washington, DC: Brookings Institution Press.
Rorty, R. (1989). *Contingency, irony, and solidarity.* Cambridge University Press.
Ryan, M. (1992). Gender and public access: Women's politics in nineteenth-century America. In: C.
    Calhoun (Ed.), *Habermas and the Public Sphere* (pp. 259–288). Cambridge, MA: The MIT
    Press.
Schlozman, K., Verba, S., & Brady, H. (1999). Civic participation and the equality problem. In:
    T. Skocpol & M. Fiorina (Eds), *Civic Engagement in American Democracy* (pp. 427–460).
    Washington, DC: Brookings Institution Press.
Schudson, M. (1998). *The Good Citizen: A History of American Civic Life.* NY: The Free Press.
Seidman, S. (1993). Identity and politics in a postmodern gay culture. In: M. Warner (Ed.), *Fear of a
    Queer Planet* (pp. 105–142). Minneapolis, MN: University of Minnesota Press.
Seidman, S., Meeks, C., & Traschen, F. (1999). Beyond the closet? The changing social meaning of
    homosexuality in the United States. *Sexualities, 2,* 9–34.
Seligman, A. (1992). *The idea of civil society.* NY: Free Press.
Skocpol, T. (1999a). How Americans became civic. In: T. Skocpol & M. Fiorina (Eds), *Civic Engage-
    ment in American Democracy* (pp. 27–80). Washington, DC: Brookings Institution Press.
Skocpol, T. (1999b). Advocates without members: The recent transformation of American civic life.
    In: T. Skocpol & M. Fiorina (Eds), *Civic Engagement in American Democracy* (pp. 461–510).
    Washington, DC: Brookings Institution Press.
Skocpol, T., & Fiorinia, M. (1999). Making sense of the civic engagement debate. In: T. Skocpol &
    M. Fiorina (Eds), *Civic Engagement in American Democracy* (pp. 1–23). Washington, DC:
    Brookings Institution Press.
Smith, P. (1991). Codes and conflict: Toward a theory of war as ritual. *Theory and Society, 20,* 103–138.
Smith, P. (1994). The semiotics of media narratives. *Journal of Narratives and Life Histories, 4,* 89–120.
Smith, P. (1998). Barbarism and civility in the discourses of fascism, communism, and democracy:
    Variations on a set of themes. In: J. Alexander (Ed.), *Real Civil Societies: Dilemmas of Institu-
    tionalization* (pp. 115–137). London: Sage Publications.
Sobieraj, S. (2002). Voluntary associations, the news media, and the political culture of presidential
    campaigns: The promise and limitations of civil society and the public sphere. Unpublished
    doctoral dissertation, University at Albany, State University of New York.
Steiner, L. (1993). Nineteenth-Century suffrage periodicals: Conceptions of womanhood and the Press.
    In: W. Solomon & R. McChesney (Eds), *Ruthless Criticism: New Perspectives in U.S. Com-
    munication History* (pp. 38–65). Minneapolis, MN: University of Minnesota Press.
Taylor, C. (1991). Modes of civil society. *Public Culture, 3,* 95–118.
de Tocqueville, A. (1969). *Democracy in America* (2 vols). NY: Doubleday.
Tuchman, G. (1978). *Making news: A study in the construction of reality.* NY: Free Press.

Tucker, K. H. (1996a). *French revolutionary syndicalism and the public sphere*. Cambridge: Cambridge University Press.

Tucker, K. H. (1996b). Harmony and transgression: Aesthetic imagery and the public sphere in Habermas and post-structuralism. *Current Perspectives in Social Theory, 16*, 101–120.

Verba, S., Schlozman, K. L., & Brady, H. E. (1995). *Voice and equality: Civic voluntarism in American politics*. Cambridge, MA: Harvard University Press.

Wagner-Pacifici, R. (1986). *The Moro morality play: Terrorism as social drama*. Chicago, IL: University of Chicago Press.

Walzer, M. (1983). *Spheres of justice*. NY: Basic Books.

Walzer, M. (1995). The communitarian critique of liberalism. In: A. Etzioni (Ed.), *New Communitarian Thinking: Persons, Virtues, Institutions, and Communities* (pp. 52–70). Charlottesville, VA: University Press of Virginia.

Warner, M. (1992). The mass public and the mass subject. In: C. Calhoun (Ed.), *Habermas and the Public Sphere* (pp. 377–401). Cambridge, MA: The MIT Press.

Warner, M. (1993). The public sphere and the cultural mediation of print. In: W. Solomon & R. McChesney (Eds), *Ruthless Criticism: New Perspectives in U.S. Communication History* (pp. 7–37). Minneapolis, MN: University of Minnesota Press.

Wilson, J., & Musick, M. (1999). Attachment to volunteering. *Sociological Forum, 12*, 243–272.

Wuthnow, R. (1998). *Loose connections: Joining together in America's fragmented communities*. Cambridge, MA: Harvard University Press.

Wuthnow, R. (1999). Mobilizing civic engagement: The changing impact of religious involvement. In: T. Skocpol & M. Fiorina (Eds), *Civic Engagement in American Democracy* (pp. 331–363). Washington, DC: Brookings Institution Press.

Zaret, D. (2000). *Origins of democratic culture: Printing, petitions, and the public sphere in early modern England*. Princeton, NJ: Princeton University Press.

PUBLIC OPINION RESEARCH AND POLITICAL SOCIOLOGY

David L. Weakliem

ABSTRACT

Since the 1960s, political sociologists have not paid much attention to public opinion research. Recent studies, however, find that public opinion has a substantial influence on government policy. Moreover, the accumulation of data over a substantial period of time and a large number of countries facilitates comparative and historical studies of public opinion. Hence, public opinion research and political sociology have much to offer each other. This paper reviews research in four areas: the effect of opinion on policy, influences on public opinion, framing, and modifications to conventional survey design, and suggests that the first two areas offer particularly promising opportunities.

INTRODUCTION

During the 1950s and early 1960s, public opinion was a key area in political sociology. Since that time, its place has declined to the point that recent textbooks such as Kourvetaris (1997) and Orum (2001) do not even have entries for "public opinion" or "opinion" in their indexes. As Orum (1996, p. 141) puts it, "what had once been the meat and potatoes for political sociologists had now become a side order, at best." Public opinion is a vigorous research area in its own right, but it is now often left to specialists, many of them from disciplines other than sociology. Since the 1970s, political sociologists have turned to areas such as social

Political Sociology for the 21st Century
Research in Political Sociology, Volume 12, 49–80
Copyright © 2003 by Elsevier Science Ltd.
All rights of reproduction in any form reserved
ISSN: 0895-9935/PII: S0895993503120037

movements, the theory of the state, and welfare policy. Nevertheless, some recent research in public opinion research is very relevant to the concerns of political sociologists, and some work in political sociology is returning to issues involving public opinion. In order to put the recent work in context, it is necessary to consider the reasons for the decline of the older research tradition.

The Decline of Public Opinion Research in Political Sociology

In the 1940s and 1950s, Columbia University was the center of a vigorous program of research on public opinion. Lazarsfeld, Berelson and Gaudet (1944) conducted a panel study in Erie County, Ohio, during the 1940 presidential campaign, focusing on patterns of communication and influence among individuals. Subsequently, Berelson, Lazarsfeld and McPhee (1954) conducted a study of Elmira, New York, during the 1948 campaign. As in the 1940 study, they paid considerable attention to communication and personal influence. However, they also proposed a theory of the development and maintenance of "cleavages": enduring group differences in attitudes and voting patterns. This theory was based on their work on patterns of communications: they argued that cleavages did not follow directly from differences of interest, but also on transmission and maintenance through personal interaction. Lipset, Lazarsfeld, Barton and Linz (1954) developed some of these ideas to produce a model of variations in working class consciousness, which was further extended in Lipset (1963).

Thus, the Columbia research program had two distinct foci: networks of communication and influence among individuals, and the analysis of social cleavages. These interests demanded different forms of data and methods of analysis, and as time went on they became increasingly separate. In later work, Lipset and his followers developed the analysis of social cleavages, but paid less attention to their grounding in individual interactions. Meanwhile, the work on personal influence helped to spur the development of network analysis, which became an important area of sociology. Few applications of network analysis, however, focused on public opinion.

During the 1950s, an alternative approach, which became known as the "Michigan school," was developing in political science. Representatives of the Michigan school were primarily interested in individual decision-making, rather than group processes. In the first major work from this group, Campbell, Gurin and Miller (1954) suggested that the Columbia studies had exaggerated the strength and stability of social cleavages. In later work, Campbell, Converse, Miller and Stokes (1960) developed a sophisticated theory of the voting decision, but they had relatively little to say about the flows of communication and influence that had interested the Columbia group. The influence of the Michigan group helped to shift the focus of public opinion research toward psychological issues. Hence, many political sociologists, particularly those with a macrosociological orientation, turned away from public opinion research. Moreover, the success of the Michigan group in establishing the American National Election Studies (ANES) had an indirect but important effect on research. The ANES were based on representative national samples, making it difficult to take account of group processes or local context. As Coleman (1986; see also Stimson, 1995) observes, the shift in samples produced a "shift in the unit of analysis . . . from the community to the individual." Although research on public opinion flourished during the 1960s and 1970s, it became increasingly remote from the concerns of most political sociologists.

A second reason that political sociologists turned away from public opinion research after the 1950s was the revival of Marxist theory. Lazarsfeld and Lipset had been influenced by what might be called a social democratic form of Marxism, in which broad economic and social changes promoted or impeded the development of class consciousness. In the 1960s, however, attention shifted to the structuralist Marxism of Althusser (1971) and Poulantzas (1976) and the revolutionary tradition associated with figures such as Rosa Luxemburg (1906).[1] Neither approach had much use for traditional public opinion research.[2] Structuralists downplayed the role of consciousness entirely. Followers of Luxemburg regarded class consciousness as important, but they made a sharp separation between normal and revolutionary consciousness. In their view, class consciousness could develop very rapidly in times of crisis, so efforts to gauge opinion in "normal" times, particularly in the artificial setting of a survey, were of little interest.

Another contributing factor was the rise of resource mobilization theory in the study of social movements. After Olson (1965) demonstrated that shared interests are not a sufficient condition for collective action, social movement researchers began to focus on resources and incentives rather than grievances. Although most sociologists did not pursue a rigorous rational-choice approach, many were influenced by Olson's contention that actions should be explained by interests rather than by values or beliefs. Moreover, some resource mobilization theorists argued that "social movement entrepreneurs" could create the beliefs necessary to sustain collective action (McCarthy & Zald, 1977). Thus, to the extent that opinion influenced collective action, it was as an intervening variable rather than an autonomous cause.

Finally, the appearance of political and labor conflict and "new social movements" in the 1960s contributed to the popularity of the new approaches. Early research had suggested that changes in public opinion were usually gradual, and that "extremism" tended to decline with economic development, leading to a prediction that the political stability of the 1950s would endure. As Lipset (1963, pp. 444–446) put it, ideological conflict had been replaced by the "politics of collective bargaining."[3] The revival of class conflict and the appearance of new social movements suggested that something important was missing from this analysis. Moreover, most of the new activity was not sponsored by political parties or traditional interest groups – in fact, it was often directed at the leaders of established institutions. Hence, scholarly attention shifted from electoral politics to collective action, especially its more novel and disruptive forms.

Those working to construct a theory of politics without public opinion, however, ran into problems of their own. Structuralist Marxists argued that state policy was constrained by the need to promote capital accumulation, so that governments had little room for choice (Block, 1977). However, there is almost invariably disagreement over the effectiveness of different policies. For example, there is no consensus on whether social welfare spending helps or hinders economic growth. Consequently, even if governments are concerned about capital accumulation, their policies are still driven by beliefs rather than objective "requirements."[4]

Within the resource mobilization tradition, some scholars observed that identity and commitment could be regarded as resources. For example, McCarthy and Zald (1977, p. 1222) noted that social movements could draw support from "conscience constituents" – that is, people who would not benefit directly from the success of the movement. Also, evidence suggested that social movement activity was affected by "political opportunity structure," one component of which is a sympathetic government or public (Tarrow, 1988).

Finally, as in the 1960s, political developments influenced sociological thought. The most important development was the revival of the right. Ronald Reagan and Margaret Thatcher were surprisingly successful in carrying out their programs, suggesting that the constraints on state action had been overstated. Moreover, the new right seemed to change the terms of political debate, with supporters of the welfare state and government intervention now on the defensive. It was natural to ask whether the shifts in political climate reflected a change in public opinion. In particular, observers from the left sought to refute the idea that public opinion had moved to the right (Ferguson & Rogers, 1986).

Despite the shift in focus discussed above, some public opinion research has continued to address sociological themes. The increased availability of historical and comparative data has facilitated this kind of research. At the same time, more political sociologists are returning to questions related to public opinion. Hence, there is good deal of recent work on public opinion that is relevant to political sociology, although it is scattered over a number of specific research areas and some of it is not well known among sociologists. The remainder of this paper will review this work and discuss opportunities for future research.

CONTEMPORARY RESEARCH

This section reviews four strands of recent work: the connection between public opinion and policy, influences on public opinion, framing, and modifications of conventional survey design. In addition, it discusses an empirical observation that has not received much attention in research or theory: that average opinions on many, but not all, questions move fairly steadily in one direction over a long period of time. Although any discussion of public opinion must touch on voting and political parties, these areas will not be considered in detail. Recent sociological work on voting and turnout has been reviewed in several places, notably Manza and Brooks (1999) and Evans (1999).

Methodological Issues

Before discussing research, it is necessary to address a fundamental methodological issue. Although most contemporary opinion research employs standardized surveys, a number of observers have argued that surveys are fundamentally unsuited to measuring public opinion. Five decades ago, Blumer (1948, p. 542) asked whether "public opinion polling actually deals with public opinion" and concluded that it did not. Similar criticisms have surfaced repeatedly over the years. Marshall (1983 [1988], p. 121), in a discussion of working class consciousness, argues that "workers' responses to sociologists' questions are not all of one piece; they may perform a variety of cognitive, emotional, and social functions for the subject." He concludes (pp. 122–123) that this complexity can be grasped only by observing people over a period of time, mainly in a natural setting, and that qualitative research "provides a more suitable alternative to the large-scale survey, and . . . generates data that the latter are incapable of uncovering no matter how much care is taken in piloting the survey and in compiling the questions." Gans (1991, p. 160) argues that opinions measured in surveys "are frequently abstracted or disconnected from those in everyday life," although he acknowledges that surveys can "provide hypotheses about people's thoughts . . . which can be tested with more detailed and intensive interviewing or through fieldwork."

Nevertheless, the standardized survey is the only method with which it is generally possible to obtain large and reasonably representative samples. Moreover, the standardized format means that results can be replicated and re-analyzed by other researchers. For this reason, surveys are likely to remain the dominant method in the study of public opinion, and most of the research discussed below is based on surveys. Nevertheless, the critics raise some worthwhile points, which will be discussed in the section on modifications of conventional survey design.

Also, qualitative research can certainly provide information that is difficult or impossible to obtain in surveys. Consequently, efforts to supplement surveys with less structured questions, as in Campbell, Converse, Miller and Stokes (1960), or to supplement qualitative methods with surveys, as in Wolfe (1998) and Lendler (1997), are often illuminating.

Public Opinion and Policy

Whether public opinion influences government policy is a classic question in the study of politics. Many authors have made arguments for or against the influence of public opinion, but until recently there was very little systematic evidence. In the last decade, this question has been the focus of a great deal of attention in political science, and considerable progress has been made in answering it. The key works in this area are Stimson, MacKuen and Erikson (1995), Stimson (1999), and Erikson, MacKuen and Stimson (2002).

Stimson (1999) undertakes a comprehensive analysis of questions on government policy included in national surveys since the 1950s, and finds that most of the change can be summarized by a single variable, which he calls "policy mood." That is, when opinions on one issue become more liberal, opinions on most other opinions do as well.[5] This pattern is quite different than that found in cross-sectional studies of individuals, in which associations among opinions are generally weak, and opinions on economic and social issues are almost independent. Stimson's (1999) estimates suggest that public mood was at its most liberal in the late 1950s, and at its most conservative around 1980. There were also several other striking movements, such as a gradual move to the right during the early 1960s and a shift back to the left in the second half of the decade.

Stimson, MacKuen and Erikson (1995) and Erikson, MacKuen and Stimson (2002) analyze the relationship between policy mood and several indexes of public policy, including congressional votes, the content of laws passed, and Supreme Court decisions. They find a substantial correlation – for example, the liberal mood of the early 1960s was accompanied by the passage of major civil rights laws and an extension of anti-poverty programs, and the conservative mood of the late 1970s and early 1980s was accompanied by deregulation and tax cuts. The connection is only partly accounted for by party control of the Presidency and Congress. For example, policy was relatively conservative in the late 1970s, despite a Democratic president and Democratic majorities in both houses of Congress. Thus, their results suggest that political leaders respond directly to public opinion. However, their work does not systematically address the possibility that changes in both policy and public opinion reflect some other factor, such as the activities of organized groups.

Burstein (1998) fills this gap by reviewing a number of studies that take account of both social movement activity and public opinion. He concludes that opinion has the stronger influence; indeed, he finds no evidence that social movement activity has any consistent effect after controlling for public opinion.

Taken as a whole, this research makes a compelling case that public opinion has influenced public policy in the United States over the past 50 years. In effect, it shows that β has a positive coefficient in the regression equation $y = \alpha + \beta x + e$, where y is a measure of policy and x is a measure of public opinion, with both variables conceptualized in terms of left and right. This is an extremely important result, but there are a number of other questions that arise even in the framework of this simple model.

First, one might ask whether the influence of public opinion varies among nations, times, or types of issues (Manza & Cook, 2002). Several well-known analyses of modern capitalist democracy suggest that public influence is limited to questions of secondary importance. Mills (1956), for example, argued that the most important government decisions, by which he meant primarily issues of war and peace, were made by elites. Marxists such as Miliband (1969) have suggested that public opinion has little influence on policies that directly affect the interests of capital.

Although much of the work on the connection between opinion and policy has relied on general indexes, there have been a number of studies of policy in particular areas. Smith's (2000) study of policies related to business is of particular interest for political sociologists. He examines issues on which business is united in support or opposition and finds that public opinion has a substantial effect. Smith's (2000) explanation of this finding is that issues that unite business tend to be visible and relatively easy to interpret in terms of interests, so that the public is easily mobilized. His account suggests that public opinion will have less effect on issues that are obscure and harder to interpret. In a sense, Smith reverses Miliband's argument – he suggests that public opinion will matter for "big" issues, but may have little influence on many secondary questions such as the regulation and taxation of particular industries.

There have been a number of other studies that examine the effect of opinion on particular policies. Wlezien (1995), for example, examines spending on defense and social programs, and finds that public opinion affects both. Only a few studies, however, have focused on comparisons across areas. Sharp (1999), after case studies of six broad policy areas, argues that there are several distinct patterns – policy responded to public opinion in some areas, but not in others. Manza and Cook (2002) offer several hypotheses about the types of issues for which public opinion will have more or less effect. They suggest, for example, that public opinion will have less effect in areas where there are strongly organized interest groups, such as health care policy. Now that the general point that public opinion makes a difference has been convincingly established, it seems likely that researchers will increasingly turn their attention to comparisons of this type.

The effects of public opinion might also vary among nations. It seems likely that political institutions affect government responsiveness. Most obviously, one would expect opinion to have more influence under democratic governments. Even within democracies, however, the size of the effect may differ depending on the electoral system, the nature of the parties, or the extent of popular participation. Moreover, it is possible that the public can influence policy even under non-democratic governments through informal pressures or the threat of disorder. Social factors might also have an effect even apart from differences in political institutions. For example, many observers have suggested that the United States has what Almond and Verba (1963) call a "participant" culture, in which people are inclined to organize to demand action from the government. A participant culture might either enhance or reduce the connection between public opinion and policy. Under such a culture, governments would have less autonomy, but if they responded to the demands of organized minorities the effect of general public opinion might be diminished rather than increased.

For similar reasons, the influence of public opinion might change over time. For example, in the last several decades, American politics has seen developments such as the increased use of primary elections and a decline of urban political machines. In other nations, observers have pointed to an "Americanization" of politics, with more emphasis on individual leaders and less on parties and their traditions. Some observers also see changes in political culture, particularly a decline of deference and move toward a "participant" orientation (Inglehart, 1997). Hence, if the effects of public opinion depend on political institutions or social factors, one would expect some changes over time. There have been very few studies of change within nations. The most extensive is Monroe's (1998) analysis of the United States, which finds some decline in the influence of public opinion between 1960–1979 and 1980–1993.

Studies of nations other than the United States are also rather uncommon. Soroka and Wlezien (2002) analyze the effect of public opinion on public expenditure in Great Britain. They find that spending generally responds to public opinion, as it does in the United States. In Britain, however, spending in specific areas is less closely tied to opinion about those areas – "it is as though policy makers receive cures for increased (decreased) spending . . . but exercise discretion in deciding where spending increases (decreases) occur" (Soroka & Wlezien, 2002, pp. 23–24). This research, like that of Erikson, MacKuen and Stimson (2002), is based on what Monroe (1998) calls a "congruence" approach, in which opinion change is analyzed in relation to policy change. While this approach is attractive in principle, it requires identical questions repeated over a significant period of time, and many nations lack such data. Hence, most comparative studies have used an alternative that Monroe (1998) calls the "consistency" approach, in which opinion about proposed policies is compared to subsequent change in policy. In effect, this approach asks how often the policy supported by the majority is actually adopted. Since the consistency approach is based on the absolute level of opinion, rather than change in opinion, it makes it possible to use questions that are asked only once. Brooks (1985, 1987, 1990) examines policy and opinion in Canada, France, the United States, and Germany, and finds only small differences among them. His most striking finding is that in all nations the policy favored by the majority was adopted in less than half of the cases. This conclusion depends on the way that policy is coded, and most other studies have obtained somewhat more optimistic estimates (Petry, 1999). Nevertheless, all find that government policy frequently does not match majority preferences, a point that will be discussed at more length below.

An alternative to studies of policy change is cross-sectional analysis based on multi-national surveys. This approach has been applied to comparisons of the American states. Erikson, Wright and McIver (1993) find a strong correlation between average opinion and policy – states in which public opinion is more liberal have more liberal policies. As yet, this approach does not seem to have been applied to national differences, but with comparative data from sources such as the International Social Survey Programme, World Values Study (WVS), and Global Barometer surveys it is clearly possible to do so. Since these surveys include relatively diverse samples of nations, it is also possible to examine variations in the strength of the relationship. For example, one could ask whether any relationship between policy and opinion is stronger in nations with more democratic forms of government.

A second way in which the analysis of the opinion-policy relationship might be extended involves the definition of the independent variable, public opinion. Previous research has simply used the average opinion in the entire sample, which amounts to assuming that all people have equal influence on policy.[6] This assumption, although convenient, is not very plausible, and it was one of the major targets in Blumer's (1948) critique of survey research. In particular, since political participation and resources generally increase with socioeconomic status (Verba, Nie & Kim, 1978), one might expect influence on policy to do so as well. If this is the case, better predictions of policy could be obtained by using a weighted average of opinions. To take an extreme case, suppose that people with below-average incomes had no influence on the government. In that case, "effective" public opinion would not be the average opinion among the whole population, but the average among people in the upper half of the income distribution.[7] Socioeconomic status is probably the most obvious potential source of variation in influence, but it is not the only one. For example, it is possible that political leaders focus on groups that are regarded as potential "swing voters." In this case, the opinions of these groups would have more weight than those of others.

There are two major practical obstacles to research on differential influence. First, surveys may not contain the necessary information on group membership. For example, some surveys do not ask about income, and those that do use a variety of response categories. Second, the opinions of all groups seem to move roughly in parallel over time (Page & Shapiro, 1992), so that measures using alternative definitions of public opinion will be highly correlated. Nevertheless, the question is important enough to deserve attention despite these difficulties.

A third extension is to ask whether there are systematic biases in policy – that is, whether certain policies are consistently more liberal or conservative than the public would like. In terms of the regression equation $y = \alpha + \beta x + e$, this amounts to asking whether the intercept term α is zero. This question is not always meaningful. For example, the General Social Survey asks people to place themselves on a scale ranging from "the government in Washington ought to reduce the income differences between the rich and the poor" to "the government should not concern itself with reducing the income difference." With a general question of this kind, one cannot say whether government policy on redistribution is more or less liberal than what the public wants. Some questions, however, give people a choice between specific courses of action – for example, whether the death penalty should or should not be abolished. In this case, it is meaningful to ask whether the government's policy is the one preferred by the majority.

This is effectively the approach taken by the "consistency" studies discussed previously. As mentioned, these studies find many cases in which policy does not match majority preferences. Moreover, it does not appear that the discrepancy is merely a matter of a lag in government response. There are some issues on which government policy seems to remain out of step with popular opinion over a long period of time (Sharp, 1999). There is no conflict between this observation and the evidence of government responsiveness reported in Erikson, MacKuen and Stimson (2002). That is, the government could respond to shifts in public opinion, while remaining consistently to the left or right of what the public wanted.

One reason that such discrepancies might occur is because of the unequal influence of different groups. For example, Stouffer (1963) found that, compared to the general public, elites were less likely to support the repression of unpopular opinions. Hence, one might expect policy on civil liberties to be more libertarian than the general public desires. For the same reason, policy on some economic issues might be to the right of public opinion. This question presents a promising opportunity for future research. As Davis (1987) points out, elite opinions are usually similar to those of educated people generally. Hence, even when information on elites is lacking, one could compare the match of policy with the preferences of people at different educational levels.

Another possibility is that the difference reflects political leaders' views about the feasibility and effectiveness of policies. To the extent that voters' decisions are based on performance, politicians will have an interest in implementing policies that they think will be successful, rather than policies that are currently popular. Beliefs about effectiveness may be even more relevant for administrators. For example, survey evidence suggests that the American public generally disapproves of affirmative action programs but approves of strong enforcement of laws against discrimination. Sharp (1999, p. 89), drawing on Skrentny (1996) argues that the less popular path was chosen because "the leadership of any bureaucratic agency is driven toward workable strategies and the avoidance of demonstrable agency failure." Prosecuting individual cases was slow, expensive, and difficult, and consequently was not seen as a "workable" strategy of pursuing racial equality.

Studies of differences between policy and opinion must be based on the analysis of specific issues, rather than general indexes of policy. Policies seem to be consistently more conservative than the public wants in some areas, and more liberal in other areas. For example, in every year of the General Social Survey, the public has supported more spending on education, and less spending on welfare. Such differences would be lost when a general index of policy is computed. Some of the consistency studies, particularly Brooks (1985), Monroe (1998), and Petry (1999) have attempted to compare consistency over different policy areas. No consensus, however, has emerged from these studies. For example, Brooks (1985) finds that policy is less likely to match public opinion on redistributive issues, but Petry (1999) finds the opposite. Hence, more work needs to be done in this topic.

Influences on Public Opinion

The preceding section has discussed the influence of public opinion on policy. The natural next step is to ask what factors influence public opinion. Over the years, there have been an enormous number of studies that seek to explain opinions. The great majority of these studies, however, have dealt with differences among individuals. Even researchers with macrosociological interests have often been obliged to focus on the individual level because of limitations of data. This section will emphasize work that is relevant to explaining the overall distribution of opinions. Of course, the population is composed of individuals, so differences in the composition of the population will help to explain differences in the distribution of opinions in the population. Usually, however, a substantial fraction of the differences among nations, times, or other units remains after taking account of differences in composition. Thus, the explanation of differences among populations is not simply a matter of aggregating differences among individuals. Four areas will be considered: general social and demographic conditions, networks and social context, the news media, and social movements.

The greatest emphasis will be on factors that might explain historical change in the distribution of opinions. The explanation of change has long presented a difficult problem for theories of public opinion. Early sociological accounts emphasized stability, and held that there were strong forces promoting return to an equilibrium distribution of opinions (Berelson et al., 1954, pp. 296–303). Hence, they suggested that over the long term, changes in population composition were the major source of change in public opinion. For example, if education reduces ethnic and racial prejudice, then the average level of prejudice in the population will decline as the average educational level rises. Some observers, such as Campbell, Converse, Miller and Stokes (1966) argued that this account of change was inadequate, and empirical studies have supported the critics. For example, Davis (1980) examines long-term change in a variety of opinions and finds that only a fraction can be explained by changes in factors such as educational levels.

General Social and Demographic Conditions

Using the limited comparative information at his disposal, Lipset (1963) argued that factors such as economic development and ethnic heterogeneity had consistent effects on public opinion. His best-known claim was that economic development led to a decline in "extremism" and in the intensity of class conflict. Lipset's conclusions were based largely on cross-sectional correlations between average opinions and economic development. As political sociologists became more historically oriented in the 1960s and 1970s, this method of analysis fell out of favor. There is an ongoing body of research on "national character" (e.g. Inkeles, 1997), but it seems to have had little influence on political sociologists over the last few decades.

In recent years, however, this tradition has experienced some revival as the availability of comparative data has increased. Inglehart (1977, 1997) has made a substantial contribution by proposing and testing a theory of the development of values. His account is based on the idea that virtually all people have the same basic needs, which include physical well-being, freedom, and aesthetic concerns. Physical security and comfort are primary in the sense that they take precedence when resources are scarce, but as they are satisfied, people begin to place more emphasis on other values. In turn, these value priorities influence opinions on many social and political issues. Empirical evidence from the World Values Surveys appears to support his claim – there is a strong correlation between economic development and support for the values he identifies as "postmaterialist."

In recent work, Inglehart and Baker (2000) have considered economic development in connection to a wider range of social and political attitudes. In a modification of Inglehart's previous model, they suggest that there is a second dimension of values, which they label as traditional versus secular/rational (Inglehart & Baker, 2000). They suggest that the earlier stages of economic development produce a shift towards secular/rational values, but that in the later stages the main result is a shift towards the post-material or "self-expression" values. Hence, a key claim of Inglehart's recent work is that the effect of economic development on opinions is non-linear (Inglehart, 1997).

Although critics have raised a number of objections to this model, most of the attention has focused on individual-level influences on values or on technical points of measurement. There has been little effort to evaluate his account of the relationship between economic development and opinion. Moreover, there are several alternative accounts of the relationship, including those of Lipset (1963), Inkeles (1997), and Triandis (1993). Although these accounts agree with Inglehart's on some points, there are some significant differences. Hence, a systematic study of alternative views about the effects of development on opinions would be very valuable. Moreover, factors other than economic development have received little attention, although some theoretical accounts hold that opinions will be influenced by conditions such as ethnic diversity (Blau, 1977) or family systems (Todd, 1985). Thus, the study of national differences presents many opportunities for research.

One objection to this type of research is that the effects of economic development or other general factors are unlikely to be uniform. Rather, they may vary depending on culture or history. Authors such as Inglehart do not deny the possibility of such variation, but they assume that it is small. In contrast, critics such as Blumer (1960) suggest that it is so large that any generalizations about the effects of economic development are unwarranted. In principle, this issue can be subjected to empirical study, but until recently public opinion data have been available only for a small and relatively homogeneous group of nations. With data sets such as the WVS, it is possible to examine variation in the effects of general social conditions. For example, one could ask whether the effects of societal affluence differ between Moslems and Christians, or between traditionally Moslem and Christian nations.

Existing comparative work focuses almost exclusively on averages, although the extent of variation within nations is also of considerable theoretical interest. Thirty years ago, Mann (1970) argued that liberal democracy does not require consensus on values. His evidence was necessarily limited to a few nations, all of them liberal democracies. It would now be possible to conduct a much more thorough comparative analysis, asking whether liberal democracies show more or less consensus than other nations. Similarly, many observers hold that class differences on certain opinions decline with economic development (e.g. Clark & Lipset, 1991). The appearance of cross-national opinion surveys covering a large number of nations greatly increases our ability to investigate such claims empirically.

Some studies of the effect of general social conditions on opinion consider change over time. Page and Shapiro (1992, p. 338) argue that people respond in a broadly rational way to changes in the world. For example, opinions about crime and the death penalty became more conservative as the crime rate increased. In contrast, studies of "moral panics" generally suggest a more skeptical view of public rationality. Typically, these studies have found that popular concern about various social problems rises and falls with little or no connection to actual conditions (Best, 1989). There appear, however, to have been few systematic empirical studies of the effect of "moral conditions" such as crime or divorce rates on public opinion.

Economic conditions have been the subject of more attention than moral conditions. Lipset (1968) argued that economic hardship produces a turn to the left by causing people to focus on class interests. Durr (1993), however, finds that in the 1968–1988 period, public opinion moved to the left when the public was generally optimistic about economic prospects and to the right when it was pessimistic. He argues that economic worries cause people to focus on self-interest, and hence to give less weight to the concerns of the disadvantaged. Erikson, MacKuen and Stimson (2002) suggest a way to reconcile these arguments, finding that unemployment causes policy mood to shift to the left while inflation causes a shift to the right. Their study, like Durr's, is restricted to the United States. It seems possible that the relationship between economic conditions and public opinion varies depending on political or social factors. For example, the response might differ between nations with individualistic traditions and those with class-conscious traditions. Hence, similar studies of other nations would make a valuable contribution.

Networks and Social Context

As mentioned above, the Columbia studies regarded public opinion and voting as the result of a social process. One of Berelson, Lazarsfeld and McPhee's (1954, p. 300) central principles was that "by the very process of talking to one another, the vague dispositions which people have are crystallized into specific attitudes, acts, or votes." This principle implies that social context will influence opinions or votes. For example, when the community contains a large number of manual workers, people of all classes will be more exposed to the views of manual workers. Hence, the opinions of middle-class people living in predominantly working-class communities may be different from those of middle-class people living in middle-class communities.

Ideally, contextual analysis uses data from both the individual and the community levels. In the example above, one would want to measure individual class membership and the class composition of the community. However, since representative surveys of individuals generally contained little or no information on social context, many early studies of contextual effects were based exclusively on aggregate data. As warnings against the "ecological fallacy" became widely known, sociologists became wary of this kind of work. More recently, however, data sets including information on multiple levels have become more widely available, making it possible to carry out more valid contextual analyses (Huckfeldt & Sprague, 1993). Research using contextual analysis has found a number of consistent results. In particular, the Columbia group's hypothesis that "social interaction creates a political bias favorable to political majorities" was confirmed by several later studies (Huckfeldt & Sprague, 1993, p. 291). As Finifter (1974) observed, however, this tendency could be mitigated if people with "deviant" views tended to form friendship groups.

One area where contextual analysis can usefully be applied is the study of national differences discussed above. For example, Weakliem (2002), using WVS data, finds evidence that the effects of education vary depending on economic development. Banaszak and Plutzer (1993) consider contextual influences on feminist attitudes in Europe, and find that both men's and women's attitudes are influenced by women's presence in the paid labor force and in higher education. Moreover, Banaszak and Plutzer (1993) find that women's entry into the labor force has influenced different types of women in different ways: women in paid employment become more feminist while homemakers become more anti-feminist. Their results imply that increased participation of women in the labor force will increase the differences of opinion between the two groups. As this example shows, contextual analysis can help to explain differences in the strength of social cleavages as well as differences in overall opinion.

Contextual analysis can also be used to evaluate the effects of different communities and institutions. As Huckfeldt, Plutzer and Sprague (1993) note, people are simultaneously embedded in a number of contexts – jobs, religious groups, neighborhoods and so on. It is likely that many of these contexts have an influence. Moreover, this is not simply a matter of one context being more important – say, religious denomination counting more than neighborhood. For example, Wald, Owen and Hill (1990) find that conservative Protestant churches promote cohesion on moral issues, while liberal Protestant churches do not. That is, members of conservative congregations tend to share similar views, while members of liberal ones show more diversity. Wald, Owen and Hill (1990) argue that this difference gives conservative churches an advantage in the political arena.

Another value of contextual analysis is in providing a model for the diffusion of new ideas. It cannot easily to explain the origins of new ideas but can help explain their spread, or failure to spread. For example, an idea that meets a hostile reception from the majority might be more likely to endure if its adherents form a cohesive group than if they are widely scattered.

Simple models of diffusion suggest that changes in public opinion will be smooth and gradual. In many cases, actual changes do follow this pattern. At times, however, there is rapid change, as support for a particular opinion rises or falls dramatically within a short period of time. More complex models of contextual analysis can help to account for this type of change. Although he does not offer a formal model, Legro (2000) sketches a theory of collective opinion change that makes use of ideas about social context. He argues that support for a consensus view is based partly on the assumption that everyone else supports the consensus. When expectations are disappointed, people are more likely to reveal their doubts. As people realize that others share their doubts, support for the orthodox position may collapse suddenly. His approach has obvious appeal in explaining events like the collapse of the Soviet Union, but it may also apply to public opinion on more specific issues. There are many cases in which a previously popular view fades quickly – for example, the idea that homosexuality is a mental disorder.

Contextual models also have implications concerning the relative rates of change in different groups. If people have different sorts of networks, as they certainly do, opinion change will not be uniform across groups – different people will encounter new ideas at different times, and will respond more or less favorably to them. Empirical research, however, has not generally found substantial differences of this kind. Page and Shapiro (1992), after examining a large number of issues, concluded that the opinions of different groups largely move in parallel – all groups change at the same time and at about the same rate. Nevertheless, there are a number of exceptions to this generalization. Manza and Brooks (1999) find that over the last forty years or so, women's opinions about social services have moved to the left relative to those of men, while professionals' opinions on a number of social issues have moved to the left relative to other classes. It is also possible that there are smaller or subtler differences between groups that would emerge on closer examination. In any case, Page and Shapiro's (1992) evidence that the opinions of various groups move in parallel presents a significant puzzle given the strong evidence of contextual effects in cross-sectional analyses.

Media Effects

Models of social context assume that people obtain ideas and information from other people. An alternative assumption is that people obtain them from the news media. The two possibilities are not mutually exclusive – most people receive information both from other people and from the media. Moreover, much of the information that people pass on to others is originally obtained from the media. Hence, the study of media effects is a complement to the study of contextual effects.

Many recent studies have examined the effect of news coverage on opinions. Although early studies such as Lazarsfeld, Berelson and Gaudet (1944) suggested that media effects were small, most recent studies have found substantial effects. As Page and Shapiro (1992, p. 340) put it, "public opinion often responds not to events or social trends themselves but to *reported events*" [emphasis in original]. It appears, however, that people make distinctions among different sources of information. Page, Shapiro and Dempsey (1987) examine the influence of television news coverage on changes in a variety of opinions. They find that statements by parties and interest groups have little effect on opinion, but that news commentary and statements by "experts" have a substantial effect. Smith (2000) finds that changes in public opinion are influenced by the relative media coverage of liberal and conservative think tanks. Although his statistical analysis begins only in 1977, he suggests that growing business support for conservative think tanks beginning around 1970 had a lasting effect on the climate of opinion (Smith, 2000, pp. 194–196).

More detailed studies of particular opinions have also found significant media effects. For example, Iyengar (1990) finds that the content of television news affects answers to general questions on poverty – specifically, people are less likely to favor societal action after viewing stories on blacks or single mothers. Gilens (1999) finds that between the 1960s and 1990s blacks became more prominent in news stories on welfare. He suggests that this change in media coverage led to increasingly negative attitudes towards welfare in the general public.

It is possible to extend the work on media effects in several ways. First, it seems likely that the size of media effects will vary depending on the type of question – in particular, media coverage might have more influence on views when people have less information from personal experience. Page and Shapiro (1992) use such reasoning to suggest that media coverage has more influence on foreign policy opinions than on domestic policy opinions. Second, the distinction between independent sources and special interest groups might be investigated further. Existing studies have simply classified sources based on intuitive judgments, and have not asked how people come to define particular sources as independent or biased. Possible influences might include simple cues such as the name of the organization, the way in which it is presented by journalists, and the positions it has taken in the past. For example, if a think tank invariably takes pro-business positions, journalists or the public may eventually come to respond to it as a representative of business interests rather than an independent source. Third, most of the research on the media deals with relatively specific political issues, and usually with short-term changes in opinion. There has been less work on how the media affects more general outlooks and values such as those discussed by Inglehart (1997).

Social Movements

Research on social movements has flourished over the last few decades. There have, however, been surprisingly few studies of their effect on public opinion. As Giugni (1998, pp. 385–386) observes, most studies of the effects of social movements have focused on government policy. While government policy is certainly important, casual observation suggests that the effect of social movements on the general climate of opinion may be even more important. Even movements that do not achieve their stated goals may influence opinion, and hence improve the prospects of future movements devoted to the same general goal. For example, it is often said that Socialist parties in the United States, despite their electoral failure, had an indirect impact by introducing ideas that were later borrowed by the major parties. Hence, observers who restrict their attention to public policy may understate the effects of social movements.

In principle, it seems unlikely that there is any simple conclusion about how social movements affect public opinion – different movements are likely to have different effects. Some movements might not attain enough visibility to have any impact. Others might actually alienate the public at large and retard the acceptance of new ideas. The public response to social movements, even peaceful ones, is often negative or at best mixed. For example, contemporary opinion on Martin Luther King was divided – in 1963 a Gallup poll found that 41% of the public viewed him favorably and 37% viewed him unfavorably. The public tends to react negatively to groups that are associated with conflict and controversy, even when it approves of their goals. On the other hand, even unpopular groups may have a positive effect by changing the limits of what people regard as possible. In effect, the demands of extreme groups would work like the opening positions in a negotiation – by comparison, more moderate proposals for change seem like reasonable compromises. A position that is too extreme, however, may be ignored or provoke a strong negative reaction. Hence, the influence of social movements on public opinion is likely to depend on a combination of factors including the number, size, demands, and tactics of groups devoted to the same general end. Hence, research on this topic would require a combination of statistical analyses of time series and more detailed case studies.

Framing

The concept of framing has a complex history. Goffman (1974) applied it to the study of personal interaction, and it has continued to be used in that area. After an influential article by Snow, Rochford, Worden and Benford (1986) it has been widely adopted in research on social movements. When applied to social movements, however, it has been interpreted in a variety of ways and sometimes used quite loosely (Benford, 1997). Moreover at about the same time, many political scientists have adopted the related concept of the "schema" (Conover & Feldman, 1984). Tannen and Wallat (1987, p. 207) make a careful attempt to distinguish frames from schemas. They state that "frame . . . refers to a sense of what activity is being engaged in, how speakers mean what they say" while a schema involves "participants' expectations about people, objects, events and settings in the world, as distinguished from alignments being negotiated in a particular interaction." However, in the literature on social movements, the term "schema" is rarely used and "frame" is often applied to both aspects.

Hence, the following discussion will not attempt to distinguish between frames and schemas. In keeping with most public opinion research, the focus will be on enduring structures of belief rather than interaction. Nevertheless, the idea of the frame (or schema) is still relevant. It may be contrasted to a traditional perspective in opinion research – the idea of "attitude constraint" (Converse, 1964). Attitude constraint involves the correlation among opinions – for example, whether support for legal abortion tends to go with support for gun control. The key assumption of most research on attitude constraint is that differences are essentially a matter of larger or smaller. For example, Converse (1964) argued that attitude constraint was very weak among the majority of the public. A vigorous debate ensued, with some observers arguing that attitude constraint was stronger than Converse had suggested, or that it had increased since the time of his study. On both sides of the debate, however, the issue was understood as involving high versus low constraint. An alternative view is that people organize their opinions in different ways – beliefs A and B may be highly correlated in one outlook and largely independent in another. This is the implication of the idea of frames or schemas. It should be noted that despite the intuitive appeal of this view, there is little evidence for it. Hence, it is possible that the idea of frames, however useful it may be in the study of personal interaction, is not applicable to public opinion. Nevertheless, it has several important implications that deserve to be tested.

On the population level, the major implication is that the content of the frames offered by supporters and opponents will influence public acceptance of a position. Cress and Snow (2000, p. 1072) suggest that the success of social movements is "partly contingent on the development of coherent and well-articulated accounts of the problems and who or what is to blame . . . and what needs to be done in order to remedy it." At the same time, some frames may have more "resonance" than other equally well-developed frames (Snow et al., 1986, p. 477). A frame that appeals to values that are not widely shared is unlikely to succeed, no matter how sophisticated it is.

There have, however, been few attempts to test these hypotheses. As Benford (1997, p. 412) observes, the "resonance" of a frame is often judged by its success: "we tend to work backward from successful mobilization to the framings activists proffered and then posit a causal linkage between the two." Benford (1997) also notes that much of the research relies on case studies. In order to discover the effects of frame development or "resonance," it is necessary to have some kind of comparison, whether among different movements in the same nation, or among similar movements in different nations or at different times. For example, in the United States, movements for prison reform have faded since the early 1970s, while movements for the legalization of drugs have endured without making substantial gains in support. Evidence that such unsuccessful movements had used weak or unappealing frames would provide a compelling demonstration of the value of the framing perspective. Comparative studies of movements for similar causes in different nations would also be useful. National differences in typical values and beliefs would produce differences in the effectiveness of frames – for example, a frame that worked in an individualistic society like the United States might be ineffective in Japan.

On the individual level, one major implication of the perspective is that tension or conflict among frames will sometimes occur.[8] If people can freely combine elements of different frames, then a "frame" is no more than a summary description of a person's position on a number of issues, much like the terms "liberal," "moderate," and "conservative." On the other hand, if a frame is a real structure of thought, some signs of strain will be visible when people attempt to combine incompatible frames.

Gamson and Modigliani (1989) develop specific arguments of this kind in a study of public attitudes toward nuclear power. They argue that the combination of favorable and unfavorable frames produces "ambivalence." They argued that this ambivalence can explain several forms of instability in opinions such as "the temporary decline in apparent support for nuclear power during moments of peak media coverage, followed by a partial rebound to former levels when the media attention subsides" and the "volatility of response with slight changes in question wordings" (Gamson & Modigliani, 1989, pp. 34–35). They also suggest that ambivalence accounts for the popularity of an apparently inconsistent position – support for nuclear power in general combined with opposition to building plants in one's own vicinity.

Feldman and Zaller (1992) suggest a different way to measure ambivalence. They find that, when asked to give reasons for their position, Americans who support welfare programs appeal mainly to practical reasons, while those who oppose them appeal mainly to principles. In their interpretation, supporters of the welfare state are ambivalent in the sense that they treat their positions on specific is-sues as departures from their basic values. Unfortunately, there have been few sub-sequent efforts to define ambivalence, conflict, or contradiction in testable ways.[9]

A second implication for the individual level is that a switch from one frame to another will produce some kind of reorganization of beliefs. In extreme cases, the change of frames may amount to a conversion experience, or what Snow and Machalek (1983, pp. 265–266) call the "displacement of one universe of discourse by another." Even with less encompassing frames, however, some reorganization should occur – that is, under the new frame certain considerations will become more relevant to a particular opinion while others become less relevant.

Testing this claim is difficult, since it requires not only longitudinal data but also some way of identifying frames. The frame that a person holds is not a directly observable characteristic like age or gender, but must be inferred from the pattern of opinions. There is consequently a good deal of uncertainty in classification, making it difficult to identify changes. Also, changes of frames are presumably rather uncommon, so a general sample of the public might not yield enough cases for analysis. Hence, it would be useful to examine targeted samples of people who are experiencing substantial pressures to change – for example, people who have just entered a particular profession or training program. The idea of framing suggests that the experience would produce not only changes in particular beliefs, but also changes in the relations among beliefs.

The preceding discussion has assumed that the idea of frames, if valid, will apply to all people. An alternative possibility is that certain people organize their thought in terms of frames, while others do not. In particular, frames might be found among people who are more interested in public affairs or active in social movements. Using surveys of the general public, it is easy to establish that people who are more interested in politics show more attitude constraint. The idea of framing goes beyond this, however, since it suggests that people who are active in different causes will not just have more structure, but different structures. For example, Luker (1984) suggests that pro-life activists are not simply more conservative than pro-choice activists, but think about the world in a fundamentally different way. Thus, it is possible that the idea of frames will be useful for understanding the thinking of activists or intellectuals, but less applicable to the general public.

Modifications of Conventional Survey Design

The traditional view of surveys assumes that people have "true" opinions, and that surveys are an attempt to measure them. From this point of view, a good question is one that gets people to reveal their true opinion – for example, one that does not pressure them to answer in a particular way. Recently, some scholars have suggested that people begin, not with an opinion, but with a collection of "considerations" that they apply in answering the question (Zaller, 1992, pp. 40–41). That is, people make up their minds on the spot, but do not begin with a blank slate as in Converse's (1964) model of "non-attitudes." Since there are many potentially relevant considerations, responses will vary depending on which ones are brought to bear on the question. For example, sometimes changes in the wording of a question produce substantial changes in responses. Zaller argues that this does not mean that one form of the question is biased or confusing, but that the wordings bring different considerations to mind. Some observers have criticized Zaller's model (e.g. Sniderman, Tetlock & Elms, 2001). However, there is widespread agreement that researchers should treat responses to survey questions as decisions rather than as mixtures of "true" opinion and measurement error.

To study the decision-making process, survey researchers have started to include elements of experimental design in surveys. As Sniderman and Grob (1996, p. 382) observe, the development of computer-assisted interviewing has facilitated this effort. Surveys were once limited to split-ballot designs offering two or three forms of a question, but now any number of forms can be offered. This development has made it easier to apply the vignette method, in which respondents are asked to make judgments about particular hypothetical cases. For example, a survey may include a question on how much government aid a family should receive, and systematically vary marital status, race, and other potentially relevant factors. Different respondents will receive different forms of the question, so they will not be influenced by their previous answers, as they would if the characteristics were varied in a series of questions. The use of vignettes allows researchers to investigate the possibility that judgments about particular cases may depart from general principles. When combined with a factorial design, vignettes can reveal biases of which even the respondents may be unaware. Hence, the combination of vignettes and factorial designs is particularly useful in studies of topics such as tolerance and racial prejudice. This approach has been employed by a number of political scientists, notably Paul Sniderman and his collaborators (see the references in Sniderman, 1993; Sniderman & Grob, 1996), but has not seen much use by sociologists.

There have been a number of efforts to study the effect of information or arguments on responses. In the simplest form, respondents are randomly selected to receive different information or arguments before answering a question. Kinder and Sanders (1990) compare questions offering different reasons for opposing affirmative action – that it "discriminates against whites" or that it "gives blacks advantages they haven't earned." They find that the overall level of opposition to affirmative action is almost identical in each form, but that its relationship to other opinions is very different. With the reference to unfair advantages, opposition to affirmative action is more closely connected to conservative opinions on a variety of issues, including ones apparently unrelated to race. They suggest that when the issue is framed in terms of unfair advantages, opposition to affirmative action forms part of a general conservative ideology. A more complex approach is to ask for people's opinion, and then present them with counterarguments. Sniderman and Piazza (1993) apply this approach to questions of affirmative action, and find that proponents of government assistance are more easily persuaded to change their minds than are opponents.

The efforts to alter information can be seen as attempts to bring social processes into the survey. One of the classic criticisms of surveys is that they involve little or no social interaction. Hence, the opinions that people express in a survey might be different from the ones that they would express after discussion and debate. This point is of both practical and normative importance. For example, a politician might wonder whether a position that is popular in a pre-election survey would remain popular after an election campaign. From a normative point of view, both Marxist and liberal theory suggest that there is an "ideal" public opinion that would be visible under the right conditions, and that leaders should sometimes be guided by ideal rather than actual opinions. The approaches described above, however, involve small-scale interventions (Sniderman & Grob, 1996, p. 396). Although they can show that differences in information or arguments affect immediate responses, they cannot show whether they lead to more lasting changes. James Fishkin's "deliberative polling" is an ambitious effort to study the effect of a substantial intervention (Fishkin, Luskin & Jowell, 2000). In the deliberative poll, people are first given a standard survey, and then offered a chance to attend a weekend conference in which they hear briefings from experts with a variety of opinions and engage in small group discussions with other participants. After the conference, they are given a survey on the same topics. Views are often fairly stable, but there are some cases of striking change, such as an increase in support for foreign aid (Fishkin, Luskin & Jowell, 2000, p. 664). The deliberative poll is not intended to model actual political processes. Rather, it is intended to represent an ideal form of democratic politics, in which people listen to reasoned arguments from a variety of sources and discuss their views with diverse groups, rather than just with like-minded friends. Of course, Fishkin's ideal political process is a liberal one. It would probably be impossible, and certainly unethical, to design a model for the ideal suggested by some other views, such as classical Marxism. Nevertheless, the general approach of the deliberative poll could be modified to consider other ways of organizing debate.

Trends in Opinions

The preceding sections have considered active research areas. This section will consider the implications of an empirical regularity that is well known but rarely the focus of attention – that change in opinion often takes the form of a slow and relatively steady trend, usually in a liberal direction. For example, support for gender equality and opposition to racial segregation have both grown gradually over the entire period for which survey data are available. As mentioned above, usually only a fraction of the trend cannot be explained by changes in the composition of the population (Davis, 1980). There is a large unexplained residual change composed of a combination of time and cohort effects.

It is plausible to explain a gradual trend in opinion by other gradual social changes such as material affluence or the growth of the mass media. In most cases, however, there are numerous potential independent variables. All variables that show a substantial time trend are highly correlated and all "explain" the trend in opinion about equally well. Hence, it is difficult to conduct a conventional statistical analysis, and in most cases researchers merely remove or control for any trend.

Despite the difficulty of analyzing trends, they should not be disregarded. The presence or absence of a trend is ultimately one of the most important issues involving public opinion. If a trend is continued, a question eventually becomes the subject of consensus. Marxist and other radical theorists have noted that the active political agenda includes a relatively narrow range of issues. On many questions, there is a consensus or "hegemonic" view that goes largely unchallenged. However, these theorists have limited their attention to a few issues – specifically, those related to the organization of production (Lukes, 1974). Yet private ownership of the means of production is only one of many things that are generally taken for granted. In the contemporary United States, for example, virtually everyone assumes that the government should be responsible for funding primary and secondary education, although some argue that funding should take place through vouchers. As Lazarsfeld (1950, p. 622) points out, this was not a matter of consensus in nineteenth century America – many people argued that parents should be responsible for paying for their own children's education, just as they were responsible for paying for their food and clothing. Hence, understanding why questions do or do not become the subjects of consensus is an important task for theories of public opinion.

Berelson, Lazarsfeld and McPhee (1954, pp. 207–212) proposed a model of the "life-history" of issues in which proposals were initially put forward by small minorities, then became subjects of active controversy, and then were implemented and became matters of consensus. Consideration of a variety of issues, however, suggests that there is no single life history. Some questions, such as the Social Security system, become matters of consensus, only to become controversial again. Others, such as the legal rights and responsibilities of labor unions, seem to remain controversial over a long period of time. There are also a few cases like the prohibition of alcohol, which produced a long-lived and powerful movement that attracted considerable public support, but then was rejected and rapidly declined (Gusfield, 1963). Berelson, Lazarsfeld and McPhee (1954) appear to have recognized that a number of life histories were possible and intended their model simply as a framework for further analysis. It is surprising that later researchers have not pursued this point.

For the last fifty years, work on life histories could use the substantial body of repeated survey questions. A researcher could begin by classifying questions as showing a trend or not, and see what the items in each group had in common. As a preliminary generalization, it seems that many questions involving values and moral judgments have a trend, while most questions of policy do not. The "policy preferences" included in Stimson's (1999) index seem to have fluctuated around a constant level since the 1950s. This difference may be partly a result of selection, since surveys usually include questions about policy issues only while they are actively subject to debate. Nevertheless, it seems unlikely that the difference is entirely an artifact.

This generalization is only a first approximation, however, since not all opinions on general values have become more liberal. For example, acceptance of premarital sex and homosexuality has increased since the 1970s, but acceptance of extramarital sex has not. Although survey results would be useful for the study of "life-histories" they would not be essential – even in their absence, it is often possible to tell whether an issue was or was not the subject of substantial controversy. Hence, the question might also be investigated using more traditional comparative and historical studies.

CONCLUSION

This section will consider two questions – whether political sociologists ought to pay more attention to public opinion, and where public opinion research might go in the future. The first question does not require extended discussion, since Burstein (1998) has already provided a compelling argument. Explaining state policy is not the only concern of political sociology, but it is certainly an important one. Hence, if public opinion influences state policy, political sociologists cannot afford to ignore it. Even if a researcher is primarily interested in some other potential influence, such as social movements, any analysis that ignores public opinion is misspecified. As discussed above, there is strong evidence that public opinion does have an influence on government policy.

Turning to the second question, experience shows that the availability of appropriate data has an important effect on the direction of research. As discussed previously, the appearance of academic surveys based on representative national samples shifted public opinion research toward a focus on individual differences. Currently, the volume of cross-national and time series data on public opinion is growing steadily, so that the opportunities for research on the effects and causes of public opinion are expanding. Research involving modifications to conventional survey design has been facilitated by the use of computers in interviewing. It is now relatively easy to carry out experiments involving question wording, framing, and related issues. As discussed above, however, it remains difficult to go beyond small-scale, brief interventions. Projects such as Fishkin's (1996) deliberative poll are difficult to implement, and are likely to remain so. In terms of data, research on framing faces serious difficulties. Direct observation of framing processes requires detailed longitudinal data, which remains difficult to obtain. Hence, most of the studies of framing in social movements and politics have been based on case studies (Benford, 1997). Some authors, such as Cress and Snow (2000), have examined multiple cases. Obtaining data on social movements, however, requires a good deal of archival research, so such studies are usually limited to a small number of cases and often to a single country or time period. The limitations of data mean that only very large effects will be clearly visible. Gamson and Modigliani (1989) propose hypotheses that can be tested with standard survey data, but they involve effects that are generally subtle and difficult to detect, such as differences in stability of opinions. Hence, although the idea of framing is appealing, there is reason to be skeptical about the prospects for research in this area.

Another issue that must be considered is the substantive content of the different areas. Most political sociologists are primarily interested in macrosociology, and are not especially familiar with the techniques and theories that are relevant to research on individual responses to surveys. Hence, social psychologists have a comparative advantage in employing modifications to standard survey design. Since many political sociologists make use of survey data, or at least face a decision about whether to use survey data, they can certainly learn from recent work in this area. However, it seems less likely that they will contribute in an active way, at least in the near future.

Hence, the two areas that appear to offer the best prospects for political sociology are the effects of public opinion on policy and the factors affecting public opinion. Studies of the causes of various policies are common in sociology as well as in political science, and most sociologists already recognize the importance of "political" factors. Hence, it should not be difficult for them to extend their horizons and take account of public opinion in a more systematic way. Sociology also has a strong tradition of research on the sources of public opinion. Moreover, although there is considerable overlap between sociology and political science in this area, there are also some important differences, as sociologists tend to emphasize social cleavages while political scientists emphasize individual choice (Manza & Brooks, 1999, pp. 9–30). Hence, not only can sociologists contribute to research on the sources of public opinion, they can add a distinctive perspective, drawing attention to questions, techniques, or variables that would otherwise be left out.

Perhaps the most interesting questions involve the historical development of opinion and policy. In recent decades, the tendency in sociology has been to emphasize discontinuity and the possibility of rapid change. The idea of social equilibrium is very much out of fashion. In contrast, the most sophisticated recent work on public opinion is based on a model of fluctuation around a stable equilibrium. Wlezien (1995) and Erikson, MacKuen and Stimson (2002) propose a "thermostatic" model in which people compare actual policy with their desired policy. If government policy is to the right of what most people want, public opinion moves to the left; if policy is to the left of what they want, the public moves to the right. Hence, shifts in average public opinion are reactions against governments moving too far in some direction. For example, the conservative public mood in 1980 led to the election of Ronald Reagan, but as the new government moved policy in a conservative direction public opinion moved back to the left. Thus, the model implies that there will be gradual swings around an equilibrium level. While it is possible in principle that the public's "target" will change over time, the data reported in Erikson, MacKuen and Stimson (2002) suggest that it has remained essentially unchanged since the 1950s.

The policy measures used by Erikson, MacKuen and Stimson (2002), however, suggest that policy has followed a definite trend, tending to move to the left over time. They suggest that this tendency reflects "a (more or less) constant public philosophy applied to changing conditions," in which the government is obliged to take on new issues brought about by the increased complexity of society (Erikson et al., 2002, p. 334). Their evidence is at odds with the numerous accounts of contemporary society that see a shift to the right over the past few decades. Such claims may be mistaken, since they are usually based on impressionistic observations. However, the discrepancy suggests that it is necessary to examine general indexes of policy more closely. One possibility is that policy has continued to move to the left in some areas, but has shifted to the right in others. Another is that there have been some changes in the direction of policy that do not fit easily into traditional definitions of left and right. In any case, the striking difference between the trends found in systematic indexes of policy and those perceived by most informed observers must be addressed.

In conclusion, there is no need for public opinion research to focus on differences among individuals. This was simply a temporary limitation imposed by the absence of historical and comparative data. Hence, political sociologists who have not paid much attention to public opinion research may be surprised and interested when they examine recent work. Conversely, public opinion researchers who make use of comparative data can benefit from the work of political sociologists. Thus, after several decades in which it was seen primarily as a branch of social psychology, public opinion may again become a central part of political sociology. If this occurs, both fields will be the richer for it.

NOTES

1. Mann (1973) provides a good review of these developments.
2. Poulantzas gave more attention to class consciousness in his later writings, but the work of his structuralist period seems to have had more influence on American sociologists.
3. Researchers in this tradition did offer a theory of extremist politics in which groups whose social status was threatened would reject the "politics of collective bargaining," often directing their anger against symbolic targets (Bell, 1964). This account, however, did not seem to provide a very compelling explanation of the major social movements of the 1960s.
4. Block acknowledged this point in his later writings, although he focused on the beliefs of state officials rather than general public opinion.
5. There are some exceptions to this generalization. Erikson, MacKuen and Stimson (2002) find evidence of a second dimension involving some issues of crime and poverty. They also report that opinions on a few issues, particularly abortion, move in a distinctive fashion.
6. More precisely, it assumes that influence on policy is proportional to the probability of participating in the survey.
7. In an analysis of the American states, Hill and Leighley (1992) and Hill, Leighley and Hinton-Andersson (1995) find that the rate of lower class turnout is related to more generous welfare spending. Their results provide some indirect evidence for this hypothesis.
8. This is similar to the idea of "cross-pressures" that figured prominently in the work of the Columbia school – a person exposed to pressures in different directions does not simply adopt a middle position, but shows some signs of stress, contradiction, or ambivalence.
9. Smelser (1998) suggests some ways in which ambivalence may be manifested, although he focuses on ambivalence in an emotional rather than an intellectual sense.

ACKNOWLEDGMENTS

I thank the editors and anonymous reviewers for useful comments on a previous draft of this manuscript.

REFERENCES

Almond, G. A., & Verba, S. (1963). *The civic culture.* Princeton, NJ: Princeton University Press.

Althusser, L. (1971). *Lenin and philosophy and other essays.* London: NLB.

Banaszak, L. A., & Plutzer, E. (1993). Contextual determinants of feminist attitudes. *American Political Science Review, 87,* 147–157.

Bell, D. (Ed.) (1964). *The radical right.* Garden City, NY: Anchor.

Benford, R. D. (1997). An insider's critique of the social movement framing perspective. *Sociological Inquiry, 67,* 409–430.

Berelson, B. R., Lazarsfeld, P. F., & McPhee, W. N. (1954). *Voting.* Chicago: University of Chicago Press.

Best, J. (Ed.) (1989). *Images of issues.* New York: Aldine.

Blau, P. (1977). *Inequality and heterogeneity.* New York: Free Press.

Block, F. (1977). The ruling class does not rule: Notes on the Marxist theory of the State. *Socialist Review, 33,* 6–27.

Blumer, H. (1948). Public opinion and public opinion polling. *American Sociological Review, 13,* 542–554.

Blumer, H. (1960). Early industrialization and the laboring class. *The Sociological Quarterly, 1,* 1–14.

Brooks, J. E. (1985). Democratic frustration in the Anglo-American polities. *Western Political Quarterly, 38,* 250–261.

Brooks, J. E. (1987). The opinion-policy Nexus in France. *Journal of Politics, 49,* 465–480.

Brooks, J. E. (1990). The opinion-policy Nexus in Germany. *Public Opinion Quarterly, 54,* 508–529.

Burstein, P. (1998). Bringing the public back in. *Social Forces, 77,* 27–62.

Campbell, A., Converse, P. E., Miller, W. E., & Stokes, D. E. (1960). *The American voter.* New York: Wiley.

Campbell, A., Converse, P. E., Miller, W. E., & Stokes, D. E. (1966). *Elections and the political order.* New York: Wiley.

Campbell, A., Gurin, G., & Miller, W. E. (1954). *The voter decides.* Evanston, IL: Row, Peterson.

Clark, T. N., & Lipset, S. M. (1991). Are social classes dying? *International Sociology, 6,* 397–410.

Coleman, J. S. (1986). Social theory, social research, and a theory of action. *American Journal of Sociology, 91,* 1309–1335.

Conover, P. J., & Feldman, S. (1984). How people organize the political world: A schematic model. *American Journal of Political Science, 8,* 95–126.

Converse, P. E. (1964). The nature of belief systems in mass publics. In: D. A. Apter (Ed.), *Ideology and Discontent* (pp. 75–169). New York: Free Press.

Cress, D. M., & Snow, D. A. (2000). The outcomes of homeless mobilization. *American Journal of Sociology, 105,* 1063–1104.

Davis, J. A. (1980). Conservative weather in a liberalizing climate: Change in selected NORC general social survey items, 1972–1978. *Social Forces, 58,* 1129–1156.

Davis, J. A. (1987). The future study of public opinion. *Public Opinion Quarterly, 51,* S178–S179.

Durr, R. H. (1993). What moves policy sentiment? *American Political Science Review, 87,* 158–170.

Erikson, R. S., MacKuen, M. B., & Stimson, J. A. (2002). *The macro polity.* New York: Cambridge University Press.

Erikson, R. S., Wright, G. C., & McIver, R. P. (1993). *Statehouse democracy: Public opinion and policy in the American States.* Cambridge: Cambridge University Press.

Evans, G. (Ed.) (1999). *The end of class politics?* Oxford: Oxford University Press.

Feldman, S., & Zaller, J. (1992). The political culture of ambivalence: Ideological responses to the welfare state. *American Journal of Political Science, 36*, 268–307.

Ferguson, T., & Rogers, J. (1986). *Right turn: The decline of the democrats and the future of American politics*. New York: Hill and Wang.

Finifter, A. (1974). The friendship group as a protective environment for political deviants. *American Political Science Review, 68*, 607–625.

Fishkin, J. S., Luskin, R. C., & Jowell, R. (2000). Deliberative polling and public consultation. *Parliamentary Affairs, 53*, 657–666.

Gamson, W. A., & Modigliani, A. (1989). Media discourse and public opinion on nuclear power. *American Journal of Sociology, 95*, 1–37.

Gans, H. (1991). *Middle American individualism*. New York: Oxford University Press.

Gilens, M. (1999). *Why Americans hate welfare*. Chicago: University of Chicago Press.

Giugni, M. G. (1998). Was it worth the effort? The outcomes and consequences of social movements. *Annual Review of Sociology, 24*, 371–393.

Goffman, E. (1974). *Frame analysis: An essay on the organization of experience*. Cambridge: Harvard University Press.

Gusfield, J. R. (1963). *Symbolic crusade: Status politics and the American temperance movement*. Urbana: University of Illinois Press.

Hill, K. Q., & Leighley, J. E. (1992). The policy consequences of class bias in state electorates. *American Journal of Political Science, 36*, 351–365.

Hill, K. Q., Leighley, J. E., & Hinton-Andersson, A. (1995). Lower-class mobilization and policy linkage in the U.S. states. *American Journal of Political Science, 39*, 75–86.

Huckfeldt, R., Plutzer, E., & Sprague, J. (1993). Alternative contexts of political behavior: Churches, neighborhoods, and individuals. *Journal of Politics, 55*, 363–381.

Huckfeldt, R., & Sprague, J. (1993). Citizens, contexts, and politics. In: A. Finifter (Ed.), *Political science: The State of the discipline II* (pp. 281–303). Washington, DC: American Political Science Association.

Inglehart, R. (1977). *The silent revolution*. Princeton, NJ: Princeton University Press.

Inglehart, R. (1997). *Modernization and postmodernization: Cultural, economic, and political change in 43 societies*. Princeton, NJ: Princeton University Press.

Inglehart, R., & Baker, W. E. (2000). Modernization, cultural change, and the persistence of traditional values. *American Sociological Review, 65*, 19–51.

Inkeles, A. (1997). *National character: A psycho-social perspective*. New Brunswick, NJ: Transaction.

Iyengar, S. (1990). Framing responsibility for political issues: The case of poverty. *Political Behavior, 12*, 19–40.

Kinder, D. R., & Sanders, L. M. (1990). Mimicking political debate with survey questions: The case of white opinion on affirmative action for blacks. *Social Cognition, 8*, 73–103.

Kourvetaris, G. A. (1997). *Political sociology: Structure and process*. Boston: Allyn and Bacon.

Lazarsfeld, P. F. (1950). The obligations of the 1950 pollster to the 1984 historian. *Public Opinion Quarterly, 14*, 617–638.

Lazarsfeld, P. F., Berelson, B., & Gaudet, H. (1944). *The people's choice*. New York: Duell, Sloan, & Pearce.

Legro, J. W. (2000). The transformation of policy ideas. *American Journal of Political Science, 44*, 419–432.

Lendler, M. (1997). *Crisis and political beliefs: The case of the colt firearms strike*. New Haven: Yale University Press.

Lipset, S. M. (1963). *Political man*. Garden City, NY: Anchor.

Lipset, S. M. (1968). *Revolution and counterrevolution*. New York: Basic.

Lipset, S. M., Lazarsfeld, P. F., Barton, A. H., & Linz, J. (1954). The psychology of voting: An analysis of political behavior. In: G. Lindzey (Ed.), *Handbook of Social Psychology* (pp. 1124–1175). Cambridge, MA: Addison-Wesley.

Luker, K. (1984). *Abortion and the politics of motherhood*. Berkeley: University of California Press.

Lukes, S. (1974). *Power: A radical view*. London: Macmillan.

Luxemburg, R. (1906) [1971]. *The mass strike*. New York: Harper & Row.

Mann, M. (1970). The social cohesion of liberal democracy. *American Sociological Review, 35*, 423–439.

Mann, M. (1973). *Consciousness and action among the western working class*. London: Macmillan.

Manza, J., & Brooks, C. (1999). *Social cleavages and political change*. Oxford: Oxford University Press.

Manza, J., & Cook, F. L. (2002). Policy responsiveness to public opinion: The State of the debate. In: J. Manza, F. L. Cook & B. I. Page (Eds), *Navigating Public Opinion: Polls, Policy, and the Future of American Democracy*. New York: Oxford University Press.

Marshall, G. (1983) [1988]. Some remarks on the study of working-class consciousness. *Politics and Society, 12*, 263–301. Reprinted in: D. Rose (Ed.), *Social Stratification and Economic Change* (pp. 98–126). London: Hutchinson.

McCarthy, J. D., & Zald, M. N. (1977). Resource mobilization and social movements: A partial theory. *American Journal of Sociology, 82*, 1212–1241.

Miliband, R. (1969). *The state in capitalist society*. London: Weidenfeld and Nicolson.

Mills, C. W. (1956). *The power elite*. New York: Oxford University Press.

Monroe, A. D. (1998). Public opinion and public policy, 1980–1993. *Public Opinion Quarterly, 62*, 6–28.

Olson, M. (1965). *The logic of collective action*. Cambridge, MA: Harvard University Press.

Orum, A. M. (1996). Almost a half century of political sociology: Trends in the United States. *Current Sociology, 44*, 132–151.

Orum, A. M. (2001). *Introduction to political sociology* (4th ed.). Upper Saddle River, NJ: Prentice-Hall.

Page, B. I., & Shapiro, R. Y. (1992). *The rational public: Fifty years of trends in Americans' policy preferences*. Chicago: University of Chicago Press.

Page, B. I., Shapiro, R. Y., & Dempsey, G. R. (1987). What moves public opinion? *American Political Science Review, 81*, 23–44.

Petry, F. (1999). The opinion-policy relationship in Canada. *Journal of Politics, 61*, 540–550.

Poulantzas, N. (1976). *Political power and social classes*. Atlantic Highlands, NJ: Humanities.

Sharp, E. B. (1999). *The sometime connection: Public opinion and social policy*. Albany: State University of New York Press.

Skrentny, J. D. (1996). *The ironies of affirmative action*. Chicago: University of Chicago Press.

Smelser, N. J. (1998). The rational and the ambivalent in the social sciences. *American Sociological Review, 63*, 1–15.

Smith, M. A. (2000). *American business and political power*. Chicago: University of Chicago Press.

Sniderman, P. M. (1993). The new look in public opinion research. In: A. Finifter (Ed.), *Political Science: The State of the Discipline II* (pp. 219–245). Washinton, DC: American Political Science Association.

Sniderman, P. M., & Grob, D. B. (1996). Innovations in experimental design in attitude surveys. *Annual Review of Sociology, 22*, 377–399.

Sniderman, P. M., & Piazza, T. (1993). *The scar of race*. Cambridge, MA: Harvard University Press.

Sniderman, P. M., Tetlock, P. E., & Elms, L. (2001). Public opinion and democratic politics: The problem of nonattitudes and social construction of political judgment. In: J. H. Kuklinski (Ed.), *Citizens and Politics* (pp. 254–288). Cambridge: Cambridge University Press.

Snow, D. A., & Machalek, R. (1983). The convert as a social type. *Sociological Theory, 1*, 259–289.

Snow, D. A., Rochford, E. B., Worden, S. K., & Benford, R. D. (1986). Frame alignment processes, micromobilization, and movement participation. *American Sociological Review, 51*, 464–481.

Soroka, S. N., & Wlezien, C. (2002). Opinion-policy dynamics: Public preferences and public expenditure in the United Kingdom. Paper presented at the Elections, Public Opinion and Parties Annual Conference, Salford, England.

Stimson, J. (1995). Opinion and representation. *American Political Science Review, 89*, 179–183.

Stimson, J. A. (1999). *Public opinion in America: Moods, cycles, and swings* (2nd ed.). Boulder, CO: Westview.

Stimson, J. A., MacKuen, M. B., & Erikson, R. S. (1995). Dynamic representation. *American Political Science Review, 89*, 543–565.

Stouffer, S. A. (1963). *Communism, conformity, and civil liberties*. Gloucester, MA: Peter Smith.

Tannen, D., & Wallat, C. (1987). Interactive frames and knowledge schemas in interaction. *Social Psychology Quarterly, 50*, 205–216.

Tarrow, S. (1988). National politics and collective action. *Annual Review of Sociology, 14*, 421–440.

Todd, E. (1985). *The explanation of ideology: Family structures and social systems*. Oxford: Blackwell.

Triandis, H. C. (1993). Collectivism and individualism as cultural syndromes. *Cross-Cultural Research, 27*, 155–180.

Verba, S., Nie, N. H., & Kim, J. (1978). *Participation and political equality*. New York: Cambridge University Press.

Wald, K., Owen, D. E., & Hill, S. S. (1990). Political cohesion in churches. *Journal of Politics, 52*, 197–215.

Weakliem, D. L. (2002). The effects of education on political opinions: An international study. *International Journal of Public Opinion Research, 14*, 141–157.

Wlezien, C. (1995). The public as thermostat: Dynamics of preferences for spending. *American Journal of Political Science, 39*, 981–1000.

Wolfe, A. (1998). *One nation, after all*. New York: Viking.

Zaller, J. R. (1992). *The nature and origins of mass opinion*. Cambridge: Cambridge University Press.

DOMAIN STRUCTURE, OPPORTUNITY, AND THE CONTENTIOUS POLITICS OF CRIME

Herbert H. Haines

ABSTRACT

In struggles over crime control, advocates of punitive measures have attained a distinct advantage over groups favoring less repressive strategies. Nevertheless, social movements that mobilize against the "get tough" trend struggle on, and some fare better than others. What determines their trajectory and fate? I draw upon observations of the anti-death penalty and drug policy reform movements to explore the impact of domain structure, *the configuration of policy issues that movements address. I suggest that multidimensional domains produce favorable structures of political opportunity for assaults upon entrenched policies. In addition, movements operating in such domains display steeper mobilization trajectories than movements operating in narrower domains, but also become more vulnerable to fractionalization as they mature.*

INTRODUCTION

As generations of critical criminologists have observed, crime has always been a political phenomenon, insofar as the legality or illegality of particular forms of conduct always reflects the exercise of power. Since the mid-1960s, however,

Political Sociology for the 21st Century
Research in Political Sociology, Volume 12, 81–110
ISSN: 0895-9935/PII: S0895993503120049

the politicization of crime and criminal justice in the United States has been taken to new and unprecedented levels (Beckett, 1997; Beckett & Sasson, 2000; Chambliss, 2001; Garland, 2001; Savelsberg, 1994). Its elevation into a major public issue was first accomplished by politicians who became aware of the electoral benefits of tough anti-crime rhetoric, by law enforcement groups whose budgets and political influence were wedded to certain perceptions of crime and criminals, and by media decision makers who understood that crime stories attract readers and viewers. The politicization of crime has also been accomplished by social movement organizations devoted to influencing public policy on various crime-related issues; e.g. prison reform, sentencing policy, capital punishment, victims' rights, gun control, and the War on Drugs.

In the political battles over crime and criminal justice in the United States, advocates of punitive anti-crime measures have held a distinct advantage over those who propose rehabilitative and reform-based strategies since the mid-1960s, when conservative Republicans began portraying lawlessness as the fault of a liberal federal judiciary, excesses of the civil rights movement, and generous social welfare programs. Downplaying social and economic root causes, the Right framed the issue in terms of a volitional criminology: lawbreaking was a choice made by bad people in a climate of leniency. By 1970, "penal-welfarism" had been largely displaced by a new paradigm that devalues traditional conceptions of rehabilitation, champions punishment as a form of expressive justice, makes the "victim" its symbolic center of gravity, and defers to populist sentiment rather than criminological expertise (Garland, 2001, pp. 6–20; also see Savelsberg, 1994).

Several explanations for this transformation in the politics of crime and justice have been offered. Some observers have credited it to "democracy in action," in which get-tough, law and order policies are straightforward responses to rising crime rates and changing public opinion (Wilson, 1975). Others have attributed it to an affinity between punitive justice policies and elements of American culture (Scheingold, 1984), to successful manipulation of public sentiment by interest groups (Beckett, 1997; Beckett & Sasson, 2000; Chambliss, 2001; Cullen, Clark & Wozniak, 1985; Greenberg & Humphries, 1980; Jacobs & Carmichael, 2002; Jacobs & Helms, 1996, 1999), to the perceived threat posed by racial minorities (Blalock, 1967; Jackson, 1989; Jacobs & Helms, 1999; Liska, Lawrence & Benson, 1981; Liska, Lawrence & Sanchirico, 1982) or to crises of late modernity (Garland, 2001).

Regardless of the reasons, it is clear that volitional explanations and punitive remedies have attained a marked competitive edge in the politics of American criminal justice, especially among political elites. Nevertheless, the general public is not as uniformly and consistently in favor of get-tough models as is often assumed (Beckett & Sasson, 2000, pp. 119–127; Gaubatz, 1995; Garland, 2001,

p. 203; Lock, Timberlake & Rasinski, 2002; Maguire & Pastore, 2001, p. 131; Scheingold, 1984, p. 46). Activists in the various social movements that seek to mobilize "against the grain" of get-tough policies face daunting but not impossible odds, and some of these movements fare better than others. How can we understand this? What are the factors which determine the trajectory and fate of challenges to the punitive hegemony? This article draws upon observations of two recent crime policy reform efforts, the anti-death penalty (ADPM) and drug policy reform (DPRM) movements, to explore the impact of one such factor, "domain structure." Domain structure refers to the configuration of policy issues that a movement addresses, which is defined by the contentious political interaction of movement actors and government policy makers. I will suggest that, other things being equal: (a) broad, multidimensional domains produce more favorable structures of political opportunity for challengers, thus allowing them to mount more formidable assaults upon relatively entrenched policies; (b) that movements operating in broad, multi-dimensional domains will display steeper mobilization trajectories with more pro-nounced "surge" phases (Lofland, 1993) than movements operating in narrow and unidimensional domains; and (c) that such movements, as they mature, experience greater levels of fractionalization and disunity than those in narrower domains.

MOBILIZING AGAINST THE PUNITIVE GRAIN

In recent decades, several reform movements have sought to exert influence over crime policy in the United States. Some of these have pursued objectives that are consistent with the increasingly punitive trend in criminal justice policy, such as the crime victims' rights movement (Daly, 1994; Elias, 1983, 1986; Henderson, 1985; McShane & Williams, 1992; Viano, 1987; Weed, 1995) and organized opposition to gun control (*Congressional Digest*, 1999; Davidson, 1993; Spitzer, 1998; Weir, 1997). Others, like the anti-death penalty (Haines, 1996; Kirchmeier, 2002; Meltsner, 1973; Palmer, 2000), drug policy reform (Baum, 1996; Bock, 2000; Gray, 1998), sentencing reform, and gun control (Carter, 1997; *Congressional Digest*, 1999; Spitzer, 1998) movements have had to mobilize "against the grain" of get-tough policy models, with varying degrees of success. This article focuses upon two such movements, the collective efforts to abolish capital punishment and to redirect drug control policies.

Data and Methods

The data on which I will base my discussion of domain structure and its impact come from two qualitative studies. The first of these focused on anti-death penalty activists and organizations and was conducted in 1991 and 1992,[1] with supplemental data collection during 1998 and 1999. The investigation produced 59 structured, open-ended interviews with activists, primarily in leadership positions within the movement, and over 5,000 pages of primary documents (e.g. memoranda, minutes from board and committee meetings, and private correspondence) from the files of national organizations (the National Coalition to Abolish the Death Penalty [NCADP], Amnesty International, the American Civil Liberties Union [ACLU], and the NCADP Legal Defense and Educational Fund), various state affiliates, and individual activists. In addition, I was a participant observer at five national conferences over the same time period. The second body of data comes from a study of drug policy reform groups which I began in 1999.[2] To date, I have conducted 39 structured, open-ended interviews with drug policy reformers in national and state organizations, analyzed approximately 2,000 pages of newsletters produced by movement organizations (the Criminal Justice Policy Foundation, Common Sense for Drug Policy, the Drug Policy Foundation, Families Against Mandatory Minimums, the Lindesmith Center, National Organization for the Reform of Marijuana Laws [NORML] and the November Coalition), 429 pages of ACLU documents from the organization's archives at Princeton University, and over two hundred weekly editions of each of two electronic newsletters (The *Week Online with DRCNet* and *DrugSense*). I have also conducted participant observation at two national Drug Policy Foundation conferences and one annual conference of NORML.

The Anti-Death Penalty Movement

The death penalty has been in almost continuous use in this country since the early Colonial period. Organized opposition to capital punishment ("abolitionism") has nearly as long a history as the death penalty itself, with its highest levels of visibility and influence coming during the years preceding the Civil War, the first decade of the twentieth century, the1960s and the years since the late 1970s (Filler, 1952; Galliher, Ray & Cook, 1993; Mackey, 1976). The third of these protest cycles, which began around 1965, brought about a major change of direction. Control of movement shifted from political reformers to attorneys (Haines, 1996, pp. 23–38) who, instead of devoting themselves to convincing legislators and members of the general public that capital punishment is immoral, as abolitionists always had, launched a campaign to have executions declared unconstitutional by the United States Supreme Court. The notion that the Constitution could be interpreted with reference to "evolving standards of decency" rather than the original intent of its 18th century authors suggested that executions might be deemed "cruel and unusual punishments" as prohibited by the Eighth Amendment. Attorneys with the NAACP Legal Defense Fund and the American Civil Liberties Union litigated a series of cases over a seven-year period that culminated in the landmark 1972 *Furman v. Georgia* decision (Meltsner, 1973). All existing capital sentencing laws were rendered null and void, and executions came to an official halt.

The victory was short-lived, however. A backlash of sorts set in (Epstein & Kobylka, 1992, p. 83; Zimring & Hawkins, 1986, pp. 38–45), and lawmakers in most states enacted new death penalty statutes that they hoped would meet the core objection of the *Furman* Justices, i.e. the arbitrary and capricious manner in which death sentences had theretofore been imposed. In 1976, the Supreme Court allowed new death penalty laws to stand, so long as they were non-mandatory, included adequate sentencing guidelines for jurors, and contained various other enhanced due process features. Anti-death penalty lawyers continued to challenge individual death sentences, but by 1982 the federal courts began to move from *refining* capital punishment (Haines, 1996, pp. 55–57) to *deregulating* it (Weisberg, 1983). It became increasingly clear that court action was not going to end executions a second time, and that abolitionists would have to go back to lobbying and public education if they hoped to turn the tide (Haines, 1996, pp. 78–79). Leading ADPM organizations – the National Coalition to Abolish the Death Penalty, Amnesty International U.S.A., and the ACLU – turned toward an incremental approach, hoping to chip away at popular support for the death penalty by focusing on more limited issues – e.g. the execution of juveniles and the mentally retarded, racial disparities in death sentencing, inadequacies in indigent legal defense, and the danger of executing the innocent. The last of these issues has recently begun to make some headway. Illinois declared a moratorium on executions pending an investigation into how eleven innocent people had landed on the state's death row and how to avoid such embarrassments in the future. The state of Maryland declared a similar moratorium two years later, and the moratorium movement may be gaining strength (Kirchmeier, 2002). Other triggering events that may improve the ADPM's prospects include the publicity given to high-profile death row inmates like Mumia Abu Jamal. But for the most part, the battle against the death penalty has been frustrating for those who have waged it. Executions steadily climbed through 1998, states have expanded the scope of their capital sentencing laws, and public approval of the death penalty has exceeded disapproval by wide margins.

The Drug Policy Reform Movement

In a sense, the first "drug policy reformers" in the United States were nineteenth-century prohibitionists who sought to eliminate problems they associated with drunkenness, and anti-narcotic crusaders of the late 19th and early 20th centuries. However, the drug policy reform movement that this paper attends to is comprised of those who have opposed the enactment and enforcement of harsh drug laws in recent decades. During the late 1960s and early 1970s, a substantial portion of the public, as well as many in the media and the government, became critical of the legal prohibition of marijuana, probably as a consequence of the increasing use of the drug by middle-class youth. The first significant U.S. drug reform organization, the National Organization for the Reform of Marijuana Laws, was founded in 1970 (Anderson, 1981). Throughout the 1970s, it sent experts to state legislatures to testify in favor of the drug's decriminalization. The American Civil Liberties Union also began a gradual entrance into the drug policy arena in 1973 when a committee of its board members concluded that the organization's libertarian principles left it no alternative but to endorse the freedom of adults to use drugs without government interference.[3] Reformers won scattered victories on the state level during the 1970s, when Alaska, California, Colorado, Mississippi, Nebraska, North Carolina, New York, Ohio, and Oregon all decriminalized the possession of small amounts of marijuana. However, the movement was stalled by an anti-reform "Parents' Movement" in the late 1970s (Musto, 1999, pp. 270–277). Congress failed to decriminalize marijuana on the federal level, and several of the states that had done so reversed themselves (Inciardi, 1992, pp. 43–45).

In spite of these setbacks, the momentum for a rethinking of drug abuse and drug policy soon resumed, stimulated by the escalation of the Drug War in the 1980s. The apogee of the new War on Drugs came with the passage of the Anti-Drug Abuse Acts of 1986 and 1988, which: (a) imposed heavy mandatory minimum prison sentences for a wide array of drug-related crimes; (b) tied U.S. foreign policy to other nations' cooperation with its drug control mandates; (c) denied public housing and other federal benefits to drug offenders; (d) made government contracts contingent on the provision of "drug-free workplaces"; and (e) broadened the scope of drug conspiracy laws. The new War on Drugs has also expanded the use of drug testing and asset forfeiture as methods for controlling drug use and distribution (Baum, 1996; Musto, 1999, pp. 274–293). Such measures came to be seen by some Americans as more harmful than drugs themselves, and organized opposition to the War on Drugs mounted. Economist Milton Friedman and journalist William F. Buckley, both political conservatives, had already announced their support for sweeping drug legalization in 1984 and 1985, respectively. Soon thereafter, political scientist Ethan Nadelmann organized the "Princeton Group," an informal project that involved many of the people who would soon play leading roles in reform efforts[4] and Arnold Trebach and Kevin Zeese founded The Drug Policy Foundation.[5]

Drug reform activists have attacked the contemporary "War on Drugs" not only as morally flawed (Blum, 1991; Szasz, 1974, 1992), but also as costly, ineffective, and even counterproductive (Bertram, Blachman, Sharpe & Andreas, 1996; Friedman, 1991; Glasser, 1991; Gordon, 1994; Gray, 1998; Morgan, 1991; Nadelmann, 1988a, b; Reuter, 1991). The critics have claimed that harshly punitive drug control policies have a variety of damaging side effects. For example, criminalization has been said to encourage crime by addicts who must obtain their drugs at artificially high black market prices, and by drug dealers who cannot turn to the law to settle disputes with competitors. It has also been charged that the War on Drugs has led Americans to tolerate a diminution of their civil liberties in the form of suspicionless drug tests, racial profiling by police, and other measures (Friedman, 1991, pp. 58–61), and that drug criminalization has played a key role in sustaining such health threats as the AIDS epidemic and fatal drug overdoses, in corrupting law enforcement personnel, in skewing the nation's foreign policy and human rights record (Scott & Marshall, 1991), and in exacerbating racial discrimination in the criminal justice system (Hoelter, 1993; "War on Black People," 1996).

The drug policy reform movement grew rapidly during the 1990s. It is difficult to estimate the number of individual activists that now fill its ranks, but at least forty organizations focusing primarily on drug policy are active at the national level and in larger states alone.[6] These groups advocate across a wide range of issues, including specific drug treatment modalities, the medical utilization of marijuana and/or opiates, asset forfeiture provisions of current drug control laws, mandatory minimum prison terms, and needle exchange programs. While there is scant public support for sweeping drug legalization, reformers have succeeded in undermining faith in the efficacy of the War on Drugs (Lester, 2001; cf. Maguire & Pastore, 2001, p. 131) and in building enthusiasm for less radical reforms (Blendon & Young, 1998). Voters have passed medicinal marijuana initiatives in seven states and have approved treating rather than incarcerating non-violent drug possession offenders in two states thus far. Surveys reveal substantial levels of sympathy not only for these measures, but for needle exchange ("Most U.S. Adults Support Needle Exchange," 1997) as well.

Both the ADPM and the DPRM have aroused opposition from the ranks of ruling elites and, like many other movements, both have stimulated the mobilization of countermovements (Mottl, 1980; Lo, 1982; Zald & Useem, 1987). Their opponents have attempted to undermine these movements by stressing the disreputability of the apparent constituents they seem to represent – convicted murderers and drug users – among other things. The trajectories of these two movements, however, suggest factors that may enhance or impede challenges to punitive orthodoxy. One such factor is found in the configuration of sub-issues they address – i.e. their "domain structures." Before returning to these contrasting cases, however, it is necessary to make a brief foray into social movement theory in order to establish a framework for their analysis.

ISSUE DOMAINS AND POLITICAL OPPORTUNITY

Beginning in the early 1970s, collective action scholars began to reject the assumptions of both pluralist and power-elite models of politics and to offer more nuanced views that allowed for spatial and temporal variation in challengers' political access. Some sought to explain differences in the occurrence of collective action across cities (Eisinger, 1973), states (Amenta & Zylan, 1991) or nations (Della Porta, 1996; Kitschelt, 1986; Kriesi, 1995; Kriesi, Koopmans, Duyvendak & Giugni, 1992; Rucht, 1996) with reference to differences in political opportunity structure. Other movement analysts have employed the political opportunity concept dynamically rather than cross-sectionally, linking the rise and fall of movement activity to changes in the receptivity of polities to claims-making (Jenkins & Perrow, 1977; Piven & Cloward, 1979; Tarrow, 1996). Most of these studies dealt with shifts in the conduciveness of the political environment to "policy-specific" or "group-specific" claims-making (Tarrow, 1996, pp. 42–43; also see Burstein, 1991; Sawyers & Meyer, 1999), the analytic level which is most applicable to my research. Shifts in opportunity may also be limited to particular localities (Einwohner, 1999; Tarrow, 1994, p. 85). But in a larger sense, cyclical variations in the *overall* vulnerability of polities to challenges may be identified. Tarrow (1994, p. 153) uses the phrase *cycle of protest* to refer to "a phase of heightened conflict and contention across the social system that includes: a rapid diffusion of collective action from more mobilized to less mobilized sectors; a quickened pace of innovation in the forms of contention; new or transformed collective action frames; a combination of organized and unorganized participation, and sequences of intensified interaction between challengers and authorities which can end in reform, repression and sometimes revolution."

While it is important to recognize both that larger patterns of collective action exist and that the trajectories of different movements may be related, it is also true that "politics proceeds primarily in numerous relatively self-contained policy domains, each operating more or less autonomously with its own issues, actors, and processes" (Burstein, 1991, p. 329). These domains – which, following McDonagh (1989, p. 121), I will call *issue* domains – are defined by topics and/or policy objectives that interrelate or 'hang together' around some common substantive core; e.g. "women's issues," "the environment," "child welfare," and "drug control" – and constitute the fields on which movement actors, their opponents, and the

State engage each other. Such clustered issues are sometimes viewed as *inherently* connected, but domains are more commonly approached as fluid and socially constructed (Burstein, 1991; Sawyers & Meyer, 1999). A crucial part of issue framing and frame alignment by challengers, in fact, is the task of linking different issues together in such a way as to mobilize participants, allies, and resources behind a common cause.

SOURCES OF POLITICAL OPPORTUNITY

McAdam has written that *"any* event or broad social process that serves to undermine the calculations and assumptions on which the political establishment is structured occasions a shift in political opportunities." He mentioned "wars, industrialization, internal political realignments, prolonged unemployment, and widespread demographic changes" as precursors of such shifts (1982, p. 41). More recently, Brockett (1991), Kriesi et al. (1992), Rucht (1996) and Tarrow (1983, 1994, pp. 85–89) have offered largely overlapping specifications of the most important types or precursors of political opportunity. In the most widely-cited of these, Tarrow (1983) proposed three core dimensions: the *openness or closure of formal political access*, the *degree of stability of political alignment*, and the *presence or absence of influential allies*. He later (1989) added a fourth dimension, *elite divisions*.

Originally, political process theorists tended to speak of opportunities as something external to and independent of movements themselves. It is now generally accepted that challengers also manufacture opportunities for themselves and others. Opportunities can be created when collective action diffuses through social networks, when coalitions are formed, when incentives are created for elites to concede to demands, and when "political space [is opened] for kindred movements and counter-movements" (Tarrow, 1994, p. 82). An important example of the creation of political opportunity is found where the interpretive framework of a particular movement – e.g. "civil rights" – becomes a "master frame" that is adapted by other movements in furtherance of their own agendas (Snow & Benford, 1992).

Moreover, movement researchers have recently begun to look into the *properties of target issues* as potential sources of (or constraints upon) opportunity, asking what qualities make certain issues more conducive to mobilization than others. David Meyer's (1993) analysis of several cycles of American peace activism in the nuclear age concludes that the test ban campaign of 1955–1963 and the nuclear freeze movement of the early 1980s benefitted from addressing problems that were "much larger and more immediate" to the groups the movement sought to mobilize than the more abstract and elite-dominated debates about the Hiroshima/Nagasaki bombings and the anti-ballistic missile treaty. Einwohner (1999) reaches a similar conclusion after examining data from four types of animal rights campaigns. She suggests that opportunities for successful mobilization are minimized when activists challenge practices that target groups define as important and necessary, as has been the case with efforts to restrict hunting and scientific experimentation on animals. But activists' assaults on less cherished, more peripheral activities like circus attendance and the manufacture and use of fur garments have met with greater success.

Ungar's (1998) analysis of mobilization around the issues of global warming and ozone depletion also seeks to return our attention to properties of issues that are partially independent of the framing process. According to Ungar, the marketability of claims are constrained by two interrelated factors: "the accumulated claims, understandings and practices that have recurred sufficiently often and regularly that they come to adhere to the problem as recognizable, attributable and accountable features," and "the various selection principles that prevail in the public, political and policy arenas at a given point in time" (1998, p. 511). Ungar concluded that differences in the outcomes of concurrent environmental claims regarding global warming and depletion of the ozone layer cannot be explained in terms of political opportunities. Rather, global warming was more marketable because, inherently, it evoked a sense of immediate and dreadful consequences.

All of these scholars suggest that properties of issues themselves help shape the political environment that activists confront. This is an important contribution to a more complete understanding of political opportunity and its role in collective action. But a related question has yet to be asked: *are there particular configurations of issues within larger issue domains that are conducive to successful mobilization and challenge?* After all, movements generally address multiple problems, and it is possible that the specific targets that are selected as parts of the movement's domain may have impacts that are not merely additive. That is, certain *domain structures* may bring about opportunities and advantages that are more than the sum of their individual components.

I propose that the complexity and breadth of the issue domain targeted by a movement is among the important determinants of the opportunities available to activists. It is not my intention to add yet another "type" of political opportunity to an already lengthy list (see Almeida & Stearns, 1998, p. 39; Gamson & Meyer, 1996; Schock, 1999, p. 356), but rather to suggest that domain structure contributes to already-recognized elements of political opportunity. Certain constellations of issues, if skillfully framed, will resonate with a larger and more diverse cross-section of society. The size of this cross-section will define the potential scope of mobilization that may be attainable. Its diversity will drive wedges through the opposition, attract allies from unexpected quarters, and counteract opponents' attempts to marginalize the movement.

NARROW AND BROAD ISSUE DOMAINS: CAPITAL PUNISHMENT AND DRUG POLICY

Some social movements operate within issue domains that are complex and multi-faceted, touching upon numerous sub-issues that are interrelated and are of direct concern to multiple constituencies. The objectives of other movements boil down to one or two bedrock controversies that polarize audiences into sharply defined "for" and "against" camps. Until quite recently, the politics of capital punishment have tended to be of the latter sort. Throughout the four historical cycles of protest against capital punishment, the death penalty has been defined and debated in a relatively simple form. The bedrock issue has been the morality or immorality of state-sanctioned killing as a mechanism of retribution or deterrence. Until the early twentieth century, the moral question usually rested upon scriptural interpretation, upon the matter of whether or not it was God's will for certain offenders to die for their crimes, and the two opposing sides scoured the Bible for textual evidence to bolster their views (Masur, 1989, pp. 66–70). The religious character of the debate has diminished considerably over time, but it appears that most people still favor or oppose executions based upon their answer to two interrelated questions: (1) does justice require that murderers pay with their own lives?; and (2) is it morally justifiable for the state to kill? Forty-eight percent of Gallup poll respondents who favor the death penalty cite retributive justice as their main reason, more than twice the number that cite any other justification (Maguire & Pastore, 2001, p. 147). This can be extraordinarily frustrating for abolitionists, who often find that people who concede many of capital punishment's flaws – that it is arbitrary, that it is riddled with racial and class bias, that it fails as a deterrent, and so forth – nevertheless continue to support the death penalty on retributive grounds alone.[7]

Beyond the broad question of its fundamental morality, many other criticisms have been directed at capital punishment over the years. Are particular elements of capital sentencing, such as jury selection and victim impact statements, consistent with the United States Constitution? Do executions of juveniles and the mentally retarded violate international human rights agreements to which the United States is a party? Is capital punishment cost-effective? However, such questions have been subsidiary to the central moral issue until very recently. What is more, positions on all these matters have tended to cleave along conventional ideological lines, with those on the left tending toward one consistent set of answers and those on the right toward another.

While the death penalty debate has taken a narrow, almost one-dimensional form, the battle over drug policy is multidimensional, entailing a wider array of sub-issues that have lives of their own. The moral acceptability of recreational drug use and the question of whether human beings enjoy a fundamental right to use mind-altering substances have not been central in public discussions of drug policy. Rather, the drug policy domain has come to encompass a constellation of issues, none of which fully subsume the rest: should drug control policy be guided by principles of deterrence, prevention, or treatment?; are enforcement practices that were designed for the suppression of addictive narcotics appropriate for cannabis?; should marijuana use be allowed as part of the treatment of certain medical conditions for which it has a demonstrably beneficial effect, but remain prohibited for recreational purposes?; should physicians be authorized to prescribe opiates for the relief of severe chronic pain in terminal cases or for the maintenance of persons who have already become addicted?; are certain drug enforcement tactics (e.g. random drug tests, civil asset forfeiture, no-knock searches, drug courier profiling) justified, or do they do more harm than good?; should injection drug users be provided with clean syringes to prevent the spread of HIV, or with "safe injection rooms" designed to prevent overdoses?; might currently illegal drugs be *regulated* – like alcohol and tobacco – rather than criminalized outright?

Not only is the sheer number of issues that fall within the drug policy domain larger than that in the death penalty domain, but the positions people take on them do not co-vary in as consistent a fashion. Those who favor medical cannabis may or may not favor the decriminalization of recreational marijuana smoking. Those who oppose policies that allow the government to seize the assets of persons marginally and innocently connected to a drug-trafficking operation may also oppose syringe-exchange programs or medical marijuana. New Mexico Governor Gary Johnson became something of a celebrity when he began calling for the legalization of *all* drugs, but he also endorses the right of employers to require random drug tests of their employees and to terminate them for positive results (Johnson, 1999). The drug policy domain is thus broader and more complex than that of capital punishment – and probably broader than *most* issue domains – in that it encompasses a larger number of specific policy issues and produces less predictable clusters of beliefs.

It is important to understand that the property of domain structures that I am referring to as breadth or multi-dimensionality is not merely another way of referring to the "complexity" of *issues* themselves. For instance, we sometimes hear that in today's media-driven political culture, issues must be simplified, "dumbed down" and turned into sound bites because the public lacks the patience to deal with "complexity." This may well be true, and successful claims-making often seems to involve just this sort of strategic distillation. The complexity of an issue *domain*, however, refers not to how complicated or intellectually challenging a policy question is, but rather how many autonomous facets it has – and in turn, how many different audiences it touches upon. Each sub-issue can, and probably must, be distilled and simplified in order to be used successfully in the mobilization of each potential audience.

DOMAIN STRUCTURE, MOBILIZATION POTENTIAL, AND ALLY AVAILABILITY

Klandermans (1989, p. 120) defines mobilization potential as "those members of a society who may possibly be enlisted in some way or other" by a social movement organization. All statements about mobilization potentials are to some extent speculative, since they involve an estimation of a population that is not participating in collective action, but *might* do so if certain things occurred. The concept is useful, nonetheless, because it acknowledges that not all mobilizations have equal potentials in terms of their eventual size and composition.

A rather persistent feature of the ADPM has been its small size and the homogeneity of its mobilization potential. Opinion data indicate that support for capital punishment is relatively great in nearly all demographic and political categories, and abolitionists have been unable to do much to change that. It is true that reported death penalty support has declined during recent years in the face of heightened concerns over potential miscarriages of justice in capital cases. Death penalty support has stood at 64 to 67% in recent years, representing a 20-year low (Death Penalty Information Center, 2002; Taylor, 2000). Whether this trend will continue, and whether or not anti-death penalty activists will be able to capitalize on it, remains to be seen. In any case, opponents of capital punishment have not outnumbered its supporters since the mid-1960s.

In addition to its numerical weakness, the ADPM has drawn active participants from a rather narrow band of American society. Active participants in anti-death penalty organizations and events have come, overwhelmingly, from the ranks of political liberals and members of traditionally progressive religious denominations. Outreach efforts by movement organizations in recent years, especially those aimed at attracting more racial and ethnic minorities to the movement, have met with little success (Haines, 1996; Jones, 2002). As a result, the movement is small, quite poorly funded, and contains few *"wild cards"* (Haines, 1998); i.e. participants who shatter the discrediting stereotypes that adhere to death penalty opponents. The ADPM's enemies have employed what Ibarra and Kitsuse (1993) call "counter-rhetorics of hysteria," attributing to abolitionists an irrational tendency to "take the side of criminals" and to oppose punishment in general.

Further, they have charged that critics of the death penalty would instantly changed their opinion if they were to experience the murder of a loved one (Vandiver, Giacopassi & Gathje, 2002). The most significant wildcards in the death penalty domain are the handful of murder victims' families that speak out publically against capital punishment, especially those who make up the core of Murder Victims' Families for Reconciliation, a group that was founded in the 1970s. But this group's numbers are still too small, and the statewide "Journeys of Hope" it sponsors too low in visibility, to counteract the negative image that still burdens death penalty opponents.

Admittedly, one of the most significant features of the recent crisis of the death penalty's legitimacy is the emergence of *conservative* critics willing to express misgivings in public. The 1998 execution of Karla Tucker, a born-again Christian woman, led a number of such conservative critics to speak out, including Congressman Henry Hyde (R-IL), televangelist Pat Robertson, and columnist George Will (Palmer, 2000). Recent scandals concerning the numbers of innocent people on death row have had the same effect; even the *National Review* ran a piece critical of the death penalty (Cannon, 2000). But these are quite recent developments which may or may not prove durable.

Because of the relative complexity of current drug policy, the DPRM has from its very beginnings drawn sympathizers and participants (albeit at varying levels of intensity) from a wider cross-section of society, crossing traditional political boundaries. The movement has rather broad appeal, is relatively large, and is well-funded in comparison to the ADPM.[8] There are numerous "wild cards" in the DPRM, including political conservatives[9] as well as liberals, law enforcement officials[10] as well as active drug users, federal judges[11] and elected officials[12] as well as academics and social workers, all in highly visible positions. Many of these unexpected sympathizers and participants are drawn to the movement by particular sub-issues that affect them directly. Libertarian conservatives, for example, are attracted by what they see as government intrusion into personal conduct,[13] while other conservatives like Congressman Hyde are upset about the impact of the drug war on property rights (e.g. civil asset forfeiture and proposed regulations that would have required banks to report depositors' financial dealings). Judges often participate in reaction to excessive federalization of drug-related crimes and limitations on their discretion, while some police officials are concerned about the waste of resources in an unwinnable battle against drug use. Opposition to the War on Drugs as a whole or to certain of its parts is less constrained by political and demographic boundaries than are views on many other social issues.

Thus, the breadth of an issue domain affects the composition as well as the size of social movements' mobilization potentials, especially the demographic and ideological heterogeneity of potential supporters. Can a reform effort realistically expect to draw support from African-Americans, Asian-Americans, and other "minority groups," for instance, or is it limited to a largely white membership? Are its supporters and participants from particular religious backgrounds – Catholics, for example, or Evangelicals? Are they primarily political conservatives or primarily political liberals, or does the movement have an appeal that spans the ideological spectrum? The answer to these questions is profoundly important, since the mobilization potential has implications for the movement's opportunity structure and, in turn, its capacity to mount a serious challenge to existing policy.

DOMAIN STRUCTURE AND ELITE DIVISIONS

Policy reform movements that draw upon a narrower social band will usually be weaker in both size and credibility than movements that draw from a wider one. Movements that attract little or no support from powerful elites – and especially movements which *threaten* elites' perceived interests – will be particularly disadvantaged, as many of those elites will devote their considerable influence and resources in opposition to the movement's efforts. On the other hand, we might reasonably expect broad issue domains to be advantageous in that such environments will produce divided and hence weaker elite opposition. The drug policy domain is a case in point. There *are*, without question, entrenched bureaucracies operating at the federal, state, and local levels that are aggressive advocates of the punitive drug war model and which sometimes use repressive tactics against challengers. Nevertheless, political and economic elites are not uniformly supportive of these bureaucracies. As I have noted, opposition to the drug policy status quo extends to current and former government officials, to members of the conservative intelligentsia, and to influential members of the judicial and criminal justice systems. The DPRM has an enormous *potential* advantage in that it does not face the concentrated power of a unified elite. Neither, for that matter, does the anti-death penalty movement at present. Nevertheless, it is apparent that different issue domains vary in the degree to which their appeal extends into elite circles.

DIVERSITY AND PUBLIC IDENTITY MANAGEMENT

Social movement organizations and their leaders attempt to manage their public identities in much the same way individuals attempt to manage the impressions they make (Goffman, 1959). Some SMOs, like the Black Panther Party of the 1960s and more recent groups such as Earth First! and Queer Nation, choose to differentiate themselves from the mainstream by stressing the radical character of their views and by adopting tactics that are widely viewed as extreme. This strategy is unlikely to create widespread public support for movement goals, but it is usually adopted to affirm a collective identity rather than for instrumental purposes. Advocacy groups with focused policy agendas more often seek to establish a consensus regarding issues within their domain. Leaders in this sort of movement tend to be concerned about framing *themselves and their membership* in a manner that enhances their legitimacy in the eyes of potential supporters (Coy & Woehrle, 1996).

In addition to its impact on the mobilization potential, social movement size and diversity may have important consequences for a movement's public image. Most obviously, small movements are taken less seriously than large ones. Knowing this, leaders use techniques such as block recruiting to appear larger than they are, and may avoid tactics like street demonstrations that betray their numerical weakness. Less obvious is the fact that homogeneous movements are more vulnerable than heterogeneous ones to negative caricature and dismissal, especially when they mobilize mostly from discredited groups (like political liberals in recent decades). The ADPM has been severely limited in this regard through much of its history. As one long-time leader put it:

> We're all worried that we are perceived as sort of knee-jerk liberals, sentimentalists, and that we aren't suitably sympathetic with the victim. We don't have enough police officers that are visible in [our organizations]. We don't have enough district attorneys that are visible . . ., we don't have enough husbands and wives, brothers and sisters whose sons, daughters, sisters and brothers have been murdered and who are nonetheless on our side.[14]

Conversely, the DPRM is able to trot out police, judges, conservatives and other stereotype-shattering wildcards to undermine the "counterrhetoric on insincerity" (Ibarra & Kitsuse, 1993) wielded by countermovement activists – e.g. that drug reformers are merely "pot-smoking hippies" or "wine-and-cheese liberals" with hidden agendas[15] – and to position themselves as responsible and well-informed citizens from most every walk of life and political persuasion. Drug policy activists have been deeply involved in "outreach" activities designed to bring in new groups of supporters, such as African-Americans, police chiefs, church officials, and the like.[16] A great deal of the content of drug reformers' public education activity involves "mainstreaming" their cause by trumpeting their own diversity, as in the opening words of an online editorial: "Six or seven years ago, the idea of legalization might have been dismissed by most people as a 'hippie' or 'druggie' idea. Today, most Americans might not yet be on our side, but at least realize there are 'respectable' citizens who agree with us" (Borden, 2001). Mainstreaming is much more widespread and easier to accomplish with "harm-reduction" proposals – e.g. drug courts, higher treatment budgets, and limits on mandatory minimum prison sentences for non-violent drug possession convictions – than with calls for drug legalization.[17]

The opportunity to draw in a diverse array of participants through *frame amplification* and *extension* processes (Snow, Rocheford, Worden & Benford, 1986) would not exist were it not for the broad reach of drug control policy as it has evolved since the 1980s. The arsenal of drug control policy has become so broad that the War on Drugs contains something to offend almost everyone. The breadth of drug policy issues, in turn, maximizes the supply of potential allies for drug reform and divides those groups (government and corporate elites, and conservatives generally) that once supplied much of the support for a punitive drug control regime.

DOMAIN STRUCTURE, MOVEMENT TRAJECTORY, AND FRACTIONALIZATION

If broad issue domains appear likely to open up larger and more diverse mobilization potentials as well as make opponents' discrediting efforts more difficult, as suggested by the contrasting cases of the ADPM and the DPRM, it follows that domain structure may produce different movement trajectories across time. First, it seems likely that *social movements operating in broad issue domains will "surge"* (Lofland, 1993, pp. 5–6, 187–189, 1996, pp. 191–192) *more rapidly than movements targeting narrow issues*. After the United States Supreme Court ended a ten-year moratorium on executions in 1976, there was an initial round of small, scattered protests. But the development of organized opposition to capital punishment was slow. It was not until the mid-1980s, when Amnesty International U.S.A. elevated the priority of its death penalty work and the National Coalition to Abolish Capital Punishment was able to hire more than one or two staffers at a time, that the movement began to develop an organizational infrastructure at the national level. Funding for abolitionist organizations remained pitifully inadequate throughout the period. And most importantly, the ADPM has suffered from a serious organizational deficit at the state level, which is the primary arena for death penalty politics (Haines, 1996, pp. 151–153). Even now, most states have only "paper" anti-death penalty coalitions at best. In other words, movement growth has been slow and sporadic for nearly a quarter-century after the critical event in the recent history of capital punishment.

The critical years in drug policy came in the mid-1980s when the "zero-tolerance" rhetoric exploded in Washington and Congress enacted several new pieces of punitive anti-drug legislation; e.g. the Omnibus Crime Bill of 1984, the Comprehensive Asset Forfeiture Act of 1984, and the Anti-Drug Abuse Acts of

1986 and 1988. In contrast to what happened in the death penalty arena, drug policy reform groups began appearing almost immediately, including the Drug Policy Foundation in 1986, the Criminal Justice Policy Foundation in 1988, The Lindesmith Center in 1994, and Common Sense for Drug Policy in 1995. NORML regained its former stature during the same time span, after having nearly disappeared in the early Reagan years. The human and monetary resources available to these groups rose significantly, and a network of state and local drug policy affiliates began to appear in almost every part of the country. In addition, organizations focused on specific sub-issues proliferated during the same period: marijuana (the Marijuana Policy Project), needle exchange (Harm Reduction Coalition), drug treatment (the National Alliance of Methadone Advocates, Physician Leadership on National Drug Policy, the Trebach Institute) mandatory minimum sentencing (Families Against Mandatory Minimums, the November Coalition), pharmaceutical pain management (American Pain Foundation, American Society for Action on Pain), fact-based drug education (Partnership for Responsible Drug Education, Mothers Against Misuse and Abuse), civil asset forfeiture (Forfeiture Endangers America's Rights), and the denial of federal aid to college students convicted of drug offenses (Students for a Sensible Drug Policy). Most of these specialized organizations coordinate their activities with one or more of the national multi-issue groups. The DPRM, in short, surged rapidly and dramatically as the drug war escalated.

The same domain properties that seem to facilitate rapid mobilization and a capacity to withstand many of the common counterattacks used by opponents also have their downside. The intra-movement diversity that complex domains facilitate brings with it the danger of fractionalization (Zald & Ash, 1966, pp. 336–337). During the surge phase of mobilization within a broad issue domain, when the focus is still on relatively abstract matters, the divisive potential of these disagreements may be suppressed. Participants may be so energized that they will live by the dictum "the enemy of my enemy is my friend." But when the point is reached that movement spokespersons and organizations have to put forth concrete proposals for reform, unity will seem less important and major disagreements about details may start to emerge. Equally important, the polarization of organizations around divergent proposals will exacerbate competition for scarce resources. This suggests another hypothesis: *as they mature, social movements operating in broad issue domains will experience greater levels of fractionalization and disunity than movements targeting narrow domains.*

Diverse movements are at greater risk of several types of divisive "frame disputes" (Benford, 1993). For instance, one faction within the drug policy reform movement prefers to attack the drug war as an intrusion on personal liberty, and it thus advocates the legalization of all currently prohibited drugs (Blum,

1991; Friedman, 1992). A larger faction approaches drug use as a public health matter. It argues that different drugs represent greater or lesser threats to health, and should accordingly be subject to greater or lesser degrees of state regulation, but public policy should emphasize prevention and treatment across the board.[18] Another frame dispute concerns the substances that should be the main foci of claims-making. Since marijuana accounts for the vast majority of illicit drug use in America, some feel that the reform of policies concerning cannabis should be the central objective. Moreover, this group claims that for the foreseeable future the only significant policy changes that are likely to be attainable will concern marijuana, and that efforts aimed at hard drug policy are probably a waste of time.[19] The other side in this debate, "harm reductionists," advocate a far greater focus on the hard, "white powder" drugs. Some harm reductionists view marijuana reformers as concerned only with the largely middle-class users of a mild intoxicant, and insensitive to the devastation that drug policy wreaks on the lives of the often poorer hard drug users.[20]

The ADPM, on the other hand, experienced little internecine warfare over issue framing until quite recently. Differences of opinion over such issues as the primacy of moral arguments and racial issues in abolition efforts do exist (Haines, 1996; Jones, 2002). But open disputes have rarely broken out. This relative unity seems attributable to the similar origins of most participants and the resulting homogeneity of viewpoints within the movement, as well as to an understanding that the movement is already frail enough without further weakening itself through pointless infighting.[21] The disputes that *have* come to the surface often seem to divide white activists from the small contingent of people of color. The latter, for example, often prefer to stress racial disparities in capital sentencing in their organizing and to put the death penalty in a broader, multi-issue context.

Diverse movements may also be more vulnerable to internal disagreements about strategy and tactics. The DPRM has experienced several such strategic disagreements, some of which have already been mentioned. The most basic, however, is what reformers themselves refer to as the "respectability issue." Some, particularly those in leadership positions of the major SMOs, believe that the key to ending the War on Drugs is overcoming the widespread association of drug policy reform with hedonistic drug use, and their efforts to "mainstream" their movement involve distancing it from the drug culture. These individuals tend to dress somewhat conservatively (hence the derogatory label of "suits" used by the grassroots, "tie-dye" faction), to avoid speaking at pot rallies and "smoke-ins," and to carefully tailor their rhetoric so as to appear responsible and reasonable.

In the past, the messenger and the message have been counter-productive, when you have – and I used to have long hair, so I'm allowed to say this – when you have a long-haired person wearing a heavy metal T-shirt at a rally screaming about legalizing marijuana. That's the wrong messenger and the wrong message. Now the movement – this, this drug policy reform movement is getting smarter about having more respectable messengers. But it's easier to convince someone to wear a suit and a tie, than to get them to change what they've been saying for thirty years.[22]

The opposing faction of reformers is less concerned about its counter-cultural image. Many, in fact, revel in it. This symbolic divide overlaps with a tactical one, in that the "suits" often advocate a more incremental approach to policy reform based on opinion polling and focus groups, and avoid "getting too far out in front of public opinion" at any given point in time. The "suits," for example, represented by organizations like The Lindesmith Center (recently renamed the Drug Policy Alliance) and Americans for Medical Rights, have focused considerable resources on carefully-worded state ballot initiatives on the medical cannabis issue. More radical activists see medical marijuana as a phony wedge issue, and prefer a frontal assault exemplified by an initiative on Alaska's November 2000 ballot. The unsuccessful Alaska measure sought to legalize marijuana for recreational as well as medical use, subject it to regulations similar to those for alcoholic beverages, establish an unlimited right to cultivate the plant, clear criminal records of marijuana convictions, and initiate a process for possible reparations to persons who have been punished for marijuana possession or cultivation.

Finally, broad and diverse movements are chronically susceptible to internal mistrust and/or conflict over issues unrelated to primary movement goals. Death penalty opponents have been greatly concerned about this in their coalitions,[23] which often include both traditional liberals with pro-choice attitudes on abortion, and Catholic officials with strong pro-life leanings. It is not difficult to imagine how the topic of abortion might arise in the midst of a discussion of capital punishment, and how disruptive it might be. Differences of opinion over other matters, such as the gay rights, gun control, gender and racial issues in movement organizations, and the like, also exist within the ranks. Through the 1990s at least, abolitionists were able to enforce a single-issue focus that has kept other issues off the table. The price of maintaining abolitionist unity has been a failure to develop more salient frames that put the death penalty in broader contexts (Haines, 1996, pp. 167–193; Jones, 2002).

On the other hand, the DPRM is so diverse that internal conflict over secondary issues is a constant threat. For instance, the emergence of New Mexico Governor Gary Johnson as a reform spokesman was not welcomed by many reformers who recognized his value as a conservative wildcard but abhorred his rightist stance on matters like welfare reform and school vouchers.[24] Similarly, cooperating on asset forfeiture reform with certain conservative Congressmen is more than some of these same activists are able to do in good conscience.

I certainly have had differences with people in their approach . . . you know, people with DPF, Lindesmith, Common Sense for Drug Policy will WORK with a Henry Hyde! Uh, which if you work with a Henry Hyde, who are you NOT gonna work with?! . . . They will work with the Libertarians from the Cato Institute and stuff, which, you know – 'yeah, you can use drugs, personal use! You can also carry *guns* for personal use, those kind of [things]. I'm *not* a Libertarian! I'm sure we have libertarians on the staff, but that's, that's not the way we go in general.[25]

Conversely, libertarians in the DPRM can find it difficult to sit at the same conference table with drug policy allies who are also proponents of national health insurance, gun control or restrictions on free trade. And unlike the death penalty, where "success" can be measured in only one way – a decline in executions – "success" in the expansive domain of drug policy can mean many things. It can mean the legal curtailment of drug testing, the expansion of government-funded drug treatment, the spread of drug courts or the decriminalization of a particular drug. Each of these "successes" would delight some drug reformers and infuriate others.

CONCLUSION: DIRECTIONS FOR FUTURE RESEARCH

I have hypothesized that broad, multidimensional issue domains produce favorable structures of political opportunity for challengers. Multidimensional domain structures increase the number of potential supporters by enabling reformers to address a broader range of sub-issues. Divisions within the ranks of policy making elites are more likely, and reformers are better positioned to counteract negative stereotypes and negotiate appealing public identities.

I also proposed that reform movements operating within these favorable domains tend to mobilize more rapidly, but that such movements are more vulnerable to fractionalization than those in narrower domains. The experiences of the anti-death penalty and drug policy reform movements in the United States are generally supportive of these hypotheses. For most of the period since the return of capital punishment to the American criminal justice system, the issue has been framed largely in narrow moral terms. Throughout that phase, anti-death penalty activists experienced difficulty in mobilizing resources for their efforts, changing public opinion, and reversing the upward trend in executions. The ADPM grew quite slowly, especially at the state and local levels, but remained relatively free of internal conflict. In the last few years, as the attack on capital punishment has become more multifaceted, each of these patterns has shown signs of possible change: mobilization appears to be accelerating, public approval of capital punishment has declined, two states have imposed moratoria on executions, and infighting among activists has risen slightly. In contrast to that of the death penalty, the drug policy domain has been quite complex since the reform groups began to proliferate in response to the Reagan-Bush intensification of the drug war. Drug control raises numerous sub-issues, and in consequence, drug reform efforts have attracted a larger and broader range of activists and supporters, have mobilized more rapidly, and have won several highly visible battles. But the DPRM has also been more internally fractious than anti-death penalty groups.

This paper, of course, is based on qualitative analyses of only two reform campaigns. As a next step, it would be helpful to quantify the concepts it has employed. How, for example, might we *measure* the complexity of a domain structure so as to test in a systematic manner the hypotheses I have introduced? Such measures must gauge more than the sheer number of sub-issues that fall within a given issue domain. They need to capture the degree to which sub-issues represent separate dimensions of the larger domain, and are capable of resonating across conventional cultural, ideological, and demographic boundaries. Similarly, how might the hetero/homogeneity of movements' mobilization potentials and participant bases best be measured? Armed with research designs that adequately address these matters, comparative investigations of the impact of domain structure on other criminal justice (e.g. victims' rights, gun control, sentencing policy) and non-criminal justice issues (e.g. environmental policy, animal rights, economic globalization) can be undertaken.

A related topic about which little research has been carried out concerns the specific ways that activists construct their own public identities (exceptions include Coy & Woehrle, 1996; Hunt, Benford & Snow, 1994). I have observed, for instance, how the active participation of stereotype-shattering "wildcards" can contribute to this process, and have suggested that certain domain structures are likely to make wildcards more available. But to what extent do reformers *consciously* employ wildcard groups in their strategies? How much attention do they give to broadening the ideological, demographic, or occupational range of participants? Since outreach entails crafting appeals to groups that may not be generally like-minded, what recruitment strategies are employed? How are contradictory elements in the recruitment of divergent targets managed? And once recruited, how is the presence of wildcards employed as a part of larger movement strategy? It seems very likely that investigations of these matters will suggest links between identity-framing and domain properties. We also need ways of determining with greater precision how wildcards affect the course and outcome of crime politics on a number of specific levels, including: (a) the perceptions of reform claims by various target publics; (b) the quantity and characteristics of media coverage of reformers; (c) the mobilization of funds and other material resources and, of course; (d) the receptivity of policy makers to movement demands.

Yet another topic deserving of exploration is the extent to which domain structure is dependent on framing and claims-making. As I noted earlier, domains have been approached thus far as social constructs with boundaries that emerge and are transformed in the cauldron of political contention. However, domains cannot be defined by activists with a completely free hand. Characteristics of the problem's environment, as well as the actions of policy makers or counter-movements, both provide the grist for the claims-makers' mill and constrain their framing activities. For instance, I have noted in passing that the drug policy domain's complexity and breadth derives largely from the actions of a drug control bureaucracy that chooses to combat drugs with racial profiles, asset forfeiture, mandatory minimum sentences and the like. A "kinder, gentler" drug war with a narrower enforcement arsenal would not provide as many opportunities for DPRM mobilization, as drug policy reformers themselves recognize.[26] It may be useful to think of broad, multi-dimensional domains as potentially congruent with a greater range of 'individual' frames – i.e. values and interests of specific social groups – than more unidimensional domains, thereby presenting more channels for frame bridging, amplification, and extension (Snow et al., 1986).

Finally, taking full advantage of a favorable domain structure requires activists to be aware of the mobilizing opportunities that their target issues present. When challengers fail to recognize which frames are most likely to resonate with important constituencies, as death penalty opponents have often done in their failure to supplement moralistic frames with pragmatic ones (Haines, 1996, pp. 167–195), or when they fail to recognize which constituencies actually lie within their mobilization potential, they sacrifice the chance to cultivate alliances and divide the opposition. And in order to capitalize fully on the opportunities that their domain offers, movement strategists must also find ways to convince those allies who are mobilized around a particular sub-issue (such as needle exchange or the execution of mentally retarded offenders) to link their special interest with those of other movement segments. Failing this, the "special interest groups" will not coordinate fully with the larger movement, compromising its effectiveness. One reformer recently claimed, optimistically, that "nearly everyone who comes to the issue of drug policy – whether through the issue of AIDS or incarceration or asset forfeiture or marijuana – soon discovers that the problem is the drug war, and the very paradigm within which our nation has chosen to deal with substances . . ." (Smith, 1999). The manner by which reform leaders attempt to get diverse constituencies to "connect the dots"[27] deserves the close scrutiny of students of crime policy change.

NOTES

1. The ADPM project was supported by grants from the National Science Foundation (SES 9109494), the National Endowment for the Humanities, and the Research Foundation of the State University of New York.

2. The DPRM project was supported by National Science Foundation grant No. SES9904984.

3. Minutes: ACLU Due Process Committee, January 23, 1973; ACLU Due Process Committee, June 26, 1973.

4. Interviews: Ethan Nadelmann, The Lindesmith Center, November 17, 1999; Loren Siegel, American Civil Liberties Union, November 19, 1999; Marsha Rosenbaum, The Lindesmith Center-West, July 24, 2001.

5. Interviews: Arnold Trebach, formerly of the Drug Policy Foundation, October 18, 1999, September 5, 2001; Kevin Zeese, Common Sense for Drug Policy, October 20, 1999.

6. Many of these organizations are one- or two-person operations, but a few are rather large. The Drug Policy Foundation and The Lindesmith Center, which recently merged as the Drug Policy Alliance, claim over 24,000 supporting members. The Drug Reform Coordination Network, a cyber-network run out of a Washington, DC headquarters, had 15,000 subscribers as of early 2000, and the National Organization for the Reform of Marijuana Laws has functioning chapters in every state.

7. Interviews: Joe Ingle, Southern Coalition on Jails and Prisons, March 28, 1992; Charles Fulwood, former Death Penalty Coordinator of Amnesty International U.S.A., May 29, 1992; William Bowers, Northeastern University, April 27, 1992; Claudia King, Death Penalty Focus of California, July 1, 1992; Bruce Ledewitz, Western Pennsylvania Coalition Against the Death Penalty, August 20, 1992.

8. In 1992, a veteran leader of the ADPM told the author that he doubted that its component organizations raised a combined total of $1 million a year (Interview: Hugo Bedau, April 27, 1992). Only two years later a single contributor, financier George Soros, committed $3 million over three years to the Drug Policy Foundation, and financed the founding of The Lindesmith Center. TLC's total budget in 1999 was around $1.7 million (Baker, 1999). Other wealthy benefactors have provided relatively generous funding for Common Sense for Drug Policy, Americans for Medical Rights, and other drug policy groups. NORML raised and spent about $900,000 in 1998 (correspondence with Keith Stroup, Executive Director, April 2000).

9. These include economist Milton Friedman, columnist and publisher William F. Buckley, former Reagan administration officials Lyn Nofziger and George Schultz.

10. Most prominent among these are Joseph MacNamara, a veteran of the NYPD who went on to head the Kansas City and San Jose departments; the late Gil Puder of Vancouver, British Columbia; and former police chiefs Nicholas Pastore and Patrick Murphy.

11. U.S. District Judges Robert Sweet, Bruce Jenkins, Scott Wright, and John L. Kane, U.S. Court of Appeals Judge Juan Torruella, U.S. District Court Judge John Curtin.

12. The most prominent elected officials to speak out for reform to date are New Mexico Governor Gary Johnson and former Baltimore Mayor Kurt Schmoke.

13. Interviews: Steve Dasbach and Ron Crickenberger, Libertarian Party National Office, October 25 and 26, 1999.

14. Interview: Hugo A. Bedau, National Coalition to Abolish the Death Penalty, April 27, 1992.

15. Interview: Eric Sterling, Criminal Justice Policy Foundation, October 18, 1999.

16. Interviews: Eric Sterling, October 18, 1999; Carol Bergman, Research and Policy Reform Center, August 15, 2000; Joseph MacNamara, July 26, 2001; Arnold Trebach, October 19, 1999; and September 5, 2001.

17. Interviews: Bill Zimmerman, Campaign for New Drug Policies, August 20, 2001; Dave Fratello, Campaign for New Drug Policies, August 20, 2001; Marsha Rosenbaum, July 24, 2001.

18. Interviews: Ethan Nadelmann, November 17, 1999; Deborah Small, The Lindesmith Center, June 26, 2000; Steve Bunch, New Mexico Drug Policy Forum, July 27, 2000; Eric Sterling, October 18, 1999.

19. Interview: Keith Stroup, National Organization for the Reform of Marijuana Laws, October 21, 1999.

20. Interview: Alan Clear, Harm Reduction Coalition, November 17, 1999.

21. Interview: Henry Schwarzschild, American Civil Liberties Union and National Coalition to Abolish the Death Penalty, March 10, 1992.

22. Interview: Robert Kampia, Marijuana Policy Project, October 20, 1999.

23. Interviews: Leigh Dingerson, National Coalition to Abolish the Death Penalty, February 11, 1992; Bill Lucero, Kansas Coalition Against the Death Penalty, April 2, 1992. Letter, Eugene Wanger to NCADP officers and Executive Committee members, May 3, 1988.

24. Comments by Steven Bunch, President and Executive Director of the New Mexico Drug Policy Forum, at the 13th International Conference on Drug Policy Reform, May 18, 2000, Washington, DC; telephone interview with Steven Bunch, July 25, 2000.

25. Interview: Alan Clear, November 17, 1999.

26. Interview: Adam Smith and Karyn Fish, Drug Reform Coordination Network, October 22, 1999.

27. Interview: Ethan Nadelmann, November 17, 1999.

REFERENCES

Almeida, P., & Stearns, L. B. (1998). Political opportunities and local grassroots environmental movements: The case of Minamata. *Social Problems, 45*(1), 37–60.

Amenta, E., & Zylan, Y. (1991). It happened here: Political opportunity, the new institutionalism, and the Townsend movement. *American Sociological Review, 56,* 250–265.

Anderson, P. (1981). *High in America: The true story behind NORML and the politics of Marijuana.* New York: Viking Press.

Baker, R. (1999). George Soros's long strange trip. *The Nation* (September 20), 32–34, 39–42.

Baum, D. (1996). *Smoke and mirrors: The war on drugs and the politics of failure.* Boston: Little, Brown.

Beckett, K. (1997). *Making crime pay: Law and order in contemporary American politics.* New York: Oxford University Press.

Beckett, K., & Sasson, T. (2000). *The politics of injustice: Crime and punishment in America.* Thousand Oaks, California: Pine Forge Press.

Benford, R. D. (1993). Frame disputes within the nuclear disarmament movement. *Social Forces, 71*(3), 677–701.

Bertram, E., Blachman, M., Sharpe, K., & Andreas, P. (1996). *Drug war politics: The price of denial.* Berkeley: University of California Press.

Blalock, H. M. (1967). *Toward a theory of minority group relations*. New York: John Wiley & Sons.

Blendon, R. J., & Young, J. T. (1998). The public and the war on illicit drugs. *JAMA, 279*, 827–832.

Blum, J. (1991). The right to control one's consciousness. In: A. S. Trebach & K. B. Zeese (Eds), *New Frontiers in Drug Policy* (pp. 16–23). Washington, DC: The Drug Policy Foundation.

Bock, A. (2000). *Waiting to inhale: The politics of medical marijuana*. Santa Ana, CA: Seven Locks Press.

Borden, D. (2001). Editorial: Winning the hearts and minds of the public. *The Week Online with DRC-Net*. [Online]. Available: http://www.drcnet.org/wol/193.html#publicopinion (February 2002).

Brockett, C. D. (1991). The structure of political opportunities and peasant mobilization in central America. *Comparative Politics, 23*(3), 253–274.

Burstein, P. (1991). Policy domains: Organizations, culture, and policy outcomes. *Annual Review of Sociology, 17*, 327–350.

Cannon, C. M. (2000). The problem with the chair: A conservative case against capital punishment. *National Review, 51*, 28–32.

Carter, G. L. (1997). *The gun control movement*. New York: Twayne Publishers.

Chambliss, W. J. (2001). *Power, politics, and crime*. Boulder, CO: Westview Press.

Congressional Digest (1999). Gun control overview: Major laws and controversies (November, 258–259, 288).

Coy, P. G., & Woehrle, L. M. (1996). Constructing identity and oppositional knowledge: The framing practices of peace movement organizations during the Persian Gulf War. *Sociological Spectrum, 16*, 287–327.

Cullen, F. T., Clark, G. A., & Wozniak, J. F. (1985). Explaining the get tough movement: Can the public be blamed? *Federal Probation, 49*(2), 16–23.

Daly, K. (1994). Men's violence, victim advocacy, and feminist redress. *Law and Society Review, 28*, 777–786.

Davidson, O. G. (1993). *Under fire: The NRA and the battle for gun control*. New York: Henry Holt and Co.

Death Penalty Information Center (2002). Summaries of recent poll findings. [Online]. Available: http://www.deathpenaltyinfo.org/Polls.html#Gallup1001 (March 2002).

Della Porta, D. (1996). Social movements and the state: Thoughts on the policing of protest. In: D. McAdam, J. D. McCarthy & M. N. Zald (Eds), *Comparative Perspectives on Social Movements: Political Opportunities, Mobilizing Structures, and Cultural Framings* (pp. 62–92). New York: Cambridge University Press.

Einwohner, R. L. (1999). Practices, opportunities and protest effectiveness: Illustrations from four animal rights campaigns. *Social Problems, 46*(2), 169–186.

Eisinger, P. (1973). The conditions of protest behavior in American cities. *American Political Science Review, 67*, 11–28.

Elias, R. (1983). *Victims of the system: Crime victims and compensation in American politics and criminal justice*. New Brunswick, NJ: Transaction Books.

Elias, R. (1986). *The politics of victimization: Victims, victimology, and human rights*. New York: Oxford.

Epstein, L., & Kobylka, J. F. (1992). *The supreme court and legal change: Abortion and the death penalty*. Chapel Hill: University of North Carolina Press.

Filler, L. (1952). Movements to abolish the death penalty in the United States. *Annals of the American Academy of Political and Social Science, 284*, 124–136.

Friedman, M. (1991). The war we are losing. In: M. B. Krauss & E. P. Lazear (Eds), *Searching for Alternatives: Drug-Control Policy in the United States* (pp. 53–67). Stanford, CA: Hoover Press.

Friedman, M. (1992). Crime. In: A. Trebach & K. Zeese (Eds), *Friedman & Szasz On Liberty and Drugs: Essays on the Free Market and Prohibition* (pp. 33–43). Washington, DC: The Drug Policy Foundation.

Galliher, J. F., Ray, G., & Cook, B. (1993). Abolition and reinstatement of capital punishment during the progressive era and early 20th century. *Journal of Criminal Law and Criminology, 83*(3), 538–576.

Gamson, W. A., & Meyer, D. S. (1996). Framing political opportunity. In: D. McAdam, J. D. McCarthy & M. N. Zald (Eds), *Comparative Perspectives on Social Movements: Political Opportunities, Mobilizing Structures, and Cultural Framings* (pp. 275–290). New York: Cambridge University Press.

Garland, D. (2001). *The culture of control: Crime and social order in contemporary society.* Chicago: The University of Chicago Press.

Gaubatz, K. T. (1995). *Crime in the public mind.* Ann Arbor, MI: University of Michigan Press.

Glasser, I. (1991). Drug prohibition: An engine for crime. In: M. B. Krauss & E. P. Lazear (Eds), *Searching for Alternatives: Drug-Control Policy in the United States* (pp. 271–282). Stanford, CA: Hoover Press.

Goffman, E. (1959). *The presentation of self in everyday life.* New York: Anchor.

Gordon, D. R. (1994). *The return of the dangerous classes: Drug prohibition and policy politics.* New York: W. W. Norton and Company.

Gray, M. (1998). *Drug crazy: How we got into this mess and how we can get out.* New York: Random House.

Greenberg, D. F., & Humphries, D. (1980). The dynamics of oscillatory punishment processes. *Journal of Criminal Law and Criminology, 68,* 643–651.

Haines, H. H. (1996). *Against capital punishment: The anti-death penalty movement in America, 1972–1994.* New York: Oxford University Press.

Haines, H. H. (1998). Wildcard units in activists coalitions. Paper presented at the Annual Meetings of the Midwest Sociological Society, Kansas City, Missouri (April 3).

Henderson, L. (1985). The wrongs of victims's rights. *Stanford Law Review, 37,* 936–1021.

Hoelter, H. (1993). Drug war's racist outcomes cannot be ignored. *The Drug Policy Letter, 17,* 7–9.

Hunt, S., Benford, R. D., & Snow, R. A. (1994). Identity fields: Framing processes and the social construction of movement identities. In: E. Laraña, H. Johnston & J. R. Gusfield (Eds), *New Social Movements: From Ideology to Identity* (pp. 185–208). Philadelphia: Temple.

Ibarra, P. R., & Kitsuse, J. I. (1993). Vernacular constituents of moral discourse: An interactionist proposal for the study of social problems. In: J. A. Holstein & G. Miller (Eds), *Reconsidering Social Constructionism: Debates in Social Problems Theory* (pp. 21–53). Hawthorne, NY: Aldine de Gruyter.

Inciardi, J. A. (1992). *The war on drugs II: The continuing epic of heroin, cocaine, crack, crime, AIDS, and public policy.* Palo Alto, CA: Mayfield.

Jackson, P. I. (1989). *Minority group threat, crime, and policing: Social context and social control.* New York: Praeger.

Jacobs, D., & Carmichael, J. T. (2002). The political sociology of the death penalty: A pooled time-series analysis. *American Sociological Review, 67,* 109–131.

Jacobs, D., & Helms, R. E. (1996). Toward a political model of incarceration: A time-series examination of multiple explanations for prison rates. *American Journal of Sociology, 102*(2), 323–357.

Jacobs, D., & Helms, R. E. (1999). Collective outbursts, politics, and punitive resources: Toward a political sociology of spending on social control. *Social Forces, 77,* 1497–1524.

Jenkins, J. C., & Perrow, C. (1977). Insurgency of the powerless. *American Sociological Review, 42,* 249–268.

Johnson, G. E. (1999). The case for drug legalization. *The Drug Policy Letter, 43*, 6–9.

Jones, S. (2002). Struggling to become racially diverse in the anti-death penalty movement: A political process approach. Unpublished dissertation, Temple University.

Kirchmeier, J. L. (2002). Another place beyond here: The death penalty moratorium movement in the United States. *University of Colorado Law Review, 73*(1), 1–116.

Kitschelt, H. P. (1986). Political opportunity structures and political protest: Anti-nuclear movements in four democracies. *British Journal of Political Science, 16*, 57–95.

Klandermans, B. (1989). Introduction to Part II: Management of social movement organizations. In: B. Klandermans, H. Kriesi & S. Tarrow (Eds), *From Structure to Action: Comparing Social Movement Research Across Cultures. International Social Movement Research* (Vol. 2, pp. 117–128). Greenwich, Conn.: JAI Press.

Kriesi, H. (1995). The political opportunity structure of new social movements: Its impact on their mobilization. In: J. C. Jenkins & B. Klandermans (Eds), *The Politics of Social Protest: Comparative Perspectives on States and Social Movements. Social Movements, Protest, and Contention* (Vol. 3, pp. 167–198). Minneapolis: University of Minnesota Press.

Kriesi, H., Koopmans, R., Duyvendak, J. W., & Giugni, M. G. (1992). New social movements and political opportunities in Western Europe. *European Journal of Political Research, 22*, 219–244.

Lester, W. (2001). Poll: U.S. losing war on drugs. *Los Angeles Times* (March 22) [Online]. Available: http://www.mapinc.org/drugnews/v01/n505/a10.html. July 22, 2002.

Liska, A. E., Lawrence, J. J., & Benson, M. (1981). Perspectives on the legal order: The capacity for social control. *American Journal of Sociology, 87*(2), 413–426.

Liska, A. E., Lawrence, J. J., & Sanchirico, A. (1982). Fear of crime as a social fact. *Social Forces, 60*(3), 760–770.

Lo, C. Y. (1982).Countermovements and conservative movements in the contemporary U.S. *Annual Review of Sociology, 8*, 107–134.

Lock, E. D., Timberlake, J. M., & Rasinski, K. A. (2002). Battle fatigue: Is public support waning for "war"-centered drug control strategies? *Crime and Delinquency, 48*(3), 380–398.

Lofland, J. (1993). *Polite protesters: The American peace movement of the 1980s.* Syracuse, NY: Syracuse University Press.

Lofland, J. (1996). *Social movement organizations: Guide to research on insurgent realities.* New York: Aldine de Gruyter.

Mackey, P. E. (1976). *Voices against death: American opposition to capital punishment, 1787–1975.* New York: Burt Franklin.

Maguire, K., & Pastore, A. L. (Eds) (2001). *Sourcebook of criminal justice statistics* [Online]. Available: http://www.albany.edu/sourcebook/ (February, 2002).

Masur, L. (1989). *Rites of execution: Capital punishment and the transformation of American culture, 1776–1865.* New York: Oxford University Press.

McAdam, D. (1982). *Political process and the development of black insurgency, 1930–1970.* Chicago: University of Chicago Press.

McDonagh, E. L. (1989). Issues and constituencies in the progressive era: House roll call voting on the nineteenth amendment, 1913–1919. *Journal of Politics, 51*, 119–136.

McShane, M. D., & Williams, F. P., III (1992). Radical victimology: A critique of the concept of victim in traditional victimology. *Crime and Delinquency, 38*, 258–271.

Meltsner, M. (1973). *Cruel and unusual: The Supreme Court and capital punishment.* New York: Random House.

Meyer, D. S. (1993). Peace protest and policy: Explaining the rise and decline of antinuclear movements in postwar America. *Policy Studies Journal, 21*, 35–51.

Morgan, J. P. (1991). Prohibition is perverse policy: What was true in 1933 is true now. In: M. B. Krauss & E. P. Lazear (Eds), *Searching for Alternatives: Drug-Control Policy in the United States* (pp. 405–423). Stanford, CA: Hoover Press.

Most U.S. adults support needle exchange (1997). Reuters wire report [Online]. Available: http://www.mapinc.org/drugnews/v97/n561/a04.html?1362 (July 22, 2002).

Mottl, T. L. (1980). The analysis of countermovements. *Social Problems, 27*, 620–633.

Musto, D. F. (1999). *The American disease: Origins of narcotic control* (3rd ed.). New York: Oxford University Press.

Nadelmann, E. A. (1988a). U.S. drug policy: A bad export. *Foreign Policy* (Spring), 83–108.

Nadelmann, E. A. (1988b). The case for legalization. *The Public Interest, 92*, 3–31.

Palmer, E. A. (2000). The death penalty: Shifting perspectives. *Congressional Quarterly Weekly* (June 3), 1324–1329.

Piven, F. F., & Cloward, R. (1979). *Poor people's movements: How they succeed, why they fail.* New York: Vintage.

Reuter, P. (1991). On the consequences of toughness. In: M. B. Krauss & E. P. Lazear (Eds), *Searching for Alternatives: Drug-Control Policy in the United States* (pp. 138–164). Stanford, CA: Hoover Institution Press.

Rucht, D. (1996). The impact of national contexts on social movement structure: A cross-movement and cross-national comparison. In: D. McAdam, J. D. McCarthy & M. N. Zald (Eds), *Comparative Perspectives on Social Movements: Political Opportunities, Mobilizing Structures, and Cultural Framings* (pp. 185–204). New York: Cambridge University Press.

Savelsberg, J. J. (1994). Knowledge, domination, and criminal punishment. *American Journal of Sociology, 99*(4), 911–943.

Sawyers, T. D., & Meyer, D. S. (1999). Missed opportunities: Social movement abeyance and public policy. *Social Problems, 46*(2), 187–206.

Scheingold, S. (1984). *The politics of law and order: Street crime and public policy.* New York: Longman.

Scott, P. D., & Marshall, J. (1991). *Cocaine politics: Drugs, armies, and the CIA in central America.* Berkeley and Los Angeles, CA: University of California Press.

Schock, K. (1999). People power and political opportunities: Social movement mobilization and outcomes in the Philippines and Burma. *Social Problems, 46*(3), 355–375.

Smith, A. J. (1999). Editorial: Growing pains. *The Week Online with DRCNet*, Issue No. 91 [Online]. Available: http://www.drcnet.org/wol/091.html#editorial (March, 2002).

Snow, D. A., & Benford, R. D. (1992). Master frames and cycles of protest. In: A. D. Morris & C. M. Mueller (Eds), *Frontiers in Social Movement Theory* (pp. 133–155). New Haven: Yale University Press.

Snow, D. A., Rocheford, E. B., Jr., Worden, S. K., & Benford, R. D. (1986). Frame alignment process, micromobilization, and movement participation. *American Sociological Review, 51*, 464–481.

Spitzer, R. J. (1998). *The politics of gun control* (2nd ed.). Chatham, NJ: Chatham House Publishers, Inc.

Szasz, T. (1974). *Ceremonial chemistry: The ritual persecution of drugs, addicts, and pushers.* Garden City, NY: Anchor Press.

Szasz, T. (1992). *Our right to drugs: The case for a free market.* Westport, CT: Praeger.

Tarrow, S. (1983). Struggling to reform: Social movements and policy change during cycles of protest. Western Societies Program Occasional Paper No. 15. New York Center for International Studies, Cornell University, Ithaca, N.Y.

Tarrow, S. (1989). Struggle, politics, and reform: Collective action, social movements, and cycles of protest. Western Societies Program, Occasional paper no. 21. Ithaca, NY: Cornell University.

Tarrow, S. (1994). *Power in movement: Social movements, collective action and politics*. New York: Cambridge University Press.

Tarrow, S. (1996). States and opportunities: The political structuring of social movements. In: D. McAdam, J. D. McCarthy & M. N. Zald (Eds), *Comparative Perspectives on Social Movements: Political Opportunities, Mobilizing Structures, and Cultural Framings* (pp. 41–61). New York: Cambridge University Press.

Taylor, H. (2000). Support for death penalty down sharply since last year, but still 64% to 25% in favor [Online]. Available: http://www.harrisinteractive.com/harris_poll/index.asp?PID=101 (March 2002).

Ungar, S. (1998). Bringing the issue back in: Comparing the marketability of the ozone hole and global warming. *Social Problems, 45*(4), 510–527.

Vandiver, M., Giacopassi, D. J., & Gathje, P. R. (2002). I hope someone murders your mother!: An exploration of extreme support for the death penalty. *Deviant Behavior, 23*, 385–415.

Viano, E. (1987). Victim's rights and the constitution: Reflections on a bicentennial. *Crime and Delinquency, 33*, 438–451.

War on Black People (1996). DRCNet *Activist Guide, 8* (January 20) [Online]. Available:http://drcnet. org/guide1–96/waron.html (January, 1999).

Weed, F. (1995). *Certainty of justice: Reform in the crime victim movement*. Hawthorne, NY: Aldine de Gruyter.

Weir, W. (1997). *A well regulated militia: The battle over gun control*. North Haven, CT: Archon Books.

Weisberg, R. (1983). Deregulating death. In: P. B. Kurland, G. Casper & D. J. Hutchinson (Eds), *The Supreme Court Review, 1983* (pp. 305–395). Chicago: The University of Chicago Press.

Wilson, J. Q. (1975). *Thinking about crime*. New York: Basic Books.

Zald, M. N., & Ash, R. (1966). Social movement organizations: Growth, decay and change. *Social Forces, 44*(3), 327–341.

Zald, M. N., & Useem, B. (1987). Movement and countermovement interaction: Mobilization, tactics and state involvement. In: M. N. Zald & J. D. McCarthy (Eds), *Social Movements in an Organizational Society* (pp. 247–272). New Brunswick, NJ: Transaction.

Zimring, F. E., & Hawkins, G. (1986). *Capital punishment and the American agenda*. New York: Cambridge University Press.

"IT WASN'T ME!": HOW WILL RACE AND RACISM WORK IN 21st CENTURY AMERICA

Eduardo Bonilla-Silva, Tyrone A. Forman,
Amanda E. Lewis and David G. Embrick

ABSTRACT

In post-civil rights America, most whites believe the nation is "beyond race." If confronted with the reality of racial inequality, they proclaim they have nothing to do with it ("It wasn't me"). Our goals in this paper are twofold. First, we suggest whites' new common sense reflects a new, more subtle racial ideology: the ideology of color blind racism. We use data from the 1997 Survey of Social Attitudes of College Students and the 1998 Detroit Area Study to document the central frames of this ideology and examine how most whites use them to explain a variety of racial matters. Second, we argue that racial stratification in the United States is becoming Latin America-like. Specifically, we contend racial stratification is becoming tri-racial with a pigmentocratic component to it and that the ideology of color blind racism will bolster this trend. We use a variety of data to test on a preliminary basis our thesis. We conclude examining the implications of this new ideology and racial stratification system for the future of race relations in this country.

Political Sociology for the 21st Century
Research in Political Sociology, Volume 12, 111–134
Copyright © 2003 by Elsevier Science Ltd.
All rights of reproduction in any form reserved
ISSN: 0895-9935/PII: S0895993503120050

INTRODUCTION

In the popular song by Jamaican reggae singer Shaggy,[1] the main character has just been caught by his girlfriend having sex with another woman in his house. His friend advises him to lie and tell his girlfriend, "It wasn't me." Much like the male character in the song, white America responds with a collective "It wasn't me" when it comes to issues of racial inequality. However, unlike the male character in the song, whites are not being duplicitous when they say "It wasn't me" as they truly believe they have nothing to do with racial minorities' standing in society. For instance, in a recent nationwide survey in which whites were asked to explain the disadvantaged status of blacks vis-à-vis whites, 66% thought it was because blacks rely too much on welfare and another 62% thought that blacks lacked the motivation to improve their socioeconomic status (Smith, 1998). In the 2000 General Social Survey, 51% of whites stated that blacks' low social position was due to lack of motivation and willpower and only 33% thought it was because of discrimination. A 1996 survey revealed that if pressed to choose between a structural explanation (e.g. "racial discrimination is the main reason why many black people can't get ahead these days") and an individual explanation (e.g. "blacks who can't get ahead in this country are mostly responsible for their own condition"), whites are more likely to cite personal responsibility over racial discrimination by a 2-to-1 margin (58% said personal responsibility and 28% said discrimination) (Smith, 1998). In fact, a quarter century of trend data indicates that individual explanations have surpassed structural explanations for understanding the condition of blacks. For instance, in 1972, approximately three-quarters of whites (72%) attributed black disadvantage to "generations of slavery and discrimination." By 2000, less than half of whites were willing to make such an attribution (47%) (2000 General Social Survey).

Another example of this mainstream[2] viewpoint is expressed in interviews where whites often go so far as to deny minority claims of discrimination suggesting that such "attitudes" are unhelpful, un-American, or even racist. For instance, in one interview with a suburban mother (Lewis, forthcoming), she stated the following:

> Mrs. Miller: I do get annoyed, when I see all of these Black family TV shows on TV. I have to say that. There's one of these stations that has a lot of those. And I do get annoyed, I don't like to watch them. It just – it just bothers me the, the portrayal I guess, of it.
>
> Amanda: Which part of it?
>
> Mrs. Miller: Maybe that, maybe the hints they might make against the white people. Or … I don't like the corny attitude. I just – that kind of stuff. I'm very strongly into we're in America, now be an American.

Another respondent suggested the real problem for blacks is their "chip on the shoulder" attitude:

> There is a certain amount of that racism that I feel like is, brought on by the groups themselves, and not by the outside group. Because, there's a certain amount of kind of "chip on their shoulder" attitude, that they kinda carry around with them, whomever they meet. And it, it is apparent to whomever they meet, and it turns you off. And that doesn't help the Black image – (laughs). It doesn't help – it doesn't help their case, if they're try – if, if you know, we're all trying to work together – for them to always [be] using that as an excuse constantly.

Thus, whites can use the "it wasn't me" stance not only to deny responsibility, but to suggest that alternative perspectives are the "real" problem (see also Blauner, 1989; Rubin, 1994). Our goals in this paper are to explain whites' "It wasn't me" post-civil rights viewpoint and predict how "race relations" (more properly, racial stratification) will operate in the 21st century. To accomplish our goals, we first explore "color blind racism" or the ideology that has emerged to justify contemporary racial inequality and which produces the "it wasn't me" stance. Secondly, we look to the future and argue that race relations in the United States will become Latin America-like and provide some evidence to support our claim.

COLOR BLIND RACISM: HOW WHITES JUSTIFY CONTEMPORARY RACIAL INEQUALITY

Whites' post-civil rights "common sense" on racial matters is that racists are few and far between, that discrimination has all but disappeared since the 1960s, and that most whites are color blind (see Lewis, 2001; Lewis, Chesler & Forman, 2000). Although whites' common sense is not totally without foundation (e.g. traditional forms of racial discrimination and exclusion as well as Jim Crow-based racist beliefs have decreased in significance), we argue that it is ultimately false. In this section we contend that a new powerful racial ideology[3] has emerged to justify the contemporary racial order: the ideology of color blind racism. This ideology, unlike Jim Crow racism, is anchored on the abstract extension of egalitarian values to racial minorities and the notion that racial minorities are culturally deficient (see also Bobo et al., 1997; Essed, 1996). Furthermore, this ideology fits the subtle, institutional, and apparently non-racial character of the "new racism" (Bonilla-Silva & Lewis, 1999) or America's post-civil rights racial structure[4] (see also Brooks, 1990; Smith, 1995).

Yet, color blind racism is a curious racial ideology. Although it engages, as all ideologies do, in "blaming the victim," it does so in a very indirect, "now you see it, now you don't" style. In this section we examine its central frames[5] and explain how whites use them in ways that justify racial inequality. The quotes in this section come from two similarly structured projects: the *1997 Survey of Social Attitudes of College Students* and *1998 Detroit Area Study* (DAS henceforth). The former is a convenience sample of 627 college students (451 white students) surveyed at a large Midwestern University (MU), a large Southern University (SU), and a medium-sized West Coast University (WU). A 10% random sample of the white students who provided information in the survey on how to contact them (about 90%) were interviewed (41 students, 17 men and 24 women, 31 from middle and upper middle class backgrounds and 10 from the working class) (for more information see Bonilla-Silva & Forman, 2000). The 1998 DAS is a probability survey of 400 black and white Detroit metropolitan area residents (323 whites and 67 blacks). The response rate was an acceptable 67.5%. As part of this study, 84 respondents (a 21% sub-sample) were randomly selected for in-depth interviews (67 whites and 17 blacks).

The interviews were conducted by research assistants who followed a structured interview protocol, were race-matched, and lasted between one and two hours. Research assistants transcribed the material verbatim and the principal investigator for both projects did a content analysis of the interviews to determine broad themes and recurrent discursive rhetorical elements. In this paper, we perform ideological analysis, and hence, we assess if respondents used similar themes and arguments rather than trying to characterize individual respondents' views (against or for integration, interracial marriage, or affirmative action). This strategy limits the likelihood of biased interpretations of respondents' positions on issues or false attributions of intentions to respondents.

Our analysis revealed that color blind racism has four central frames. The four frames are *abstract liberalism*, *naturalization*, *cultural racism*, and *minimization of racism*. We provide examples of how these frames are used by whites to defend, explain, and ultimately justify contemporary racial inequality.

Abstract Liberalism: Unmasking Reasonable Racism

When minorities were slaves, contract laborers, or "braceros"[6] the principles of liberalism and humanism were not extended to them. In the apt words of philosopher Charles W. Mills (1997, p. 27), *"European humanism usually meant that only Europeans were human"* (emphasis in original). Today most whites believe minorities are part of the body politic but extend the ideas associated with liberalism in an *abstract* and *decontextualized* manner that ends up rationalizing racially unfair situations. For example, most whites claim to be for equal opportunity in principle, but oppose any race-based program (affirmative action, busing, etc.) to help minorities. In their protestations, as we will show, they exhibit little concern for the fact that discrimination is alive and well and imposes limitations on minorities' life chances.

Because of the curious way in which liberalism's principles are used in the post-civil rights era, other analysts label modern racial ideology "laissez fare racism" (Bobo, Kluegel & Smith, 1997) or "competitive racism" (Essed, 1996) or argue that modern racism is essentially a combination of the "American Creed" with antiblack prejudice (Sears, 1988). The importance of the abstract liberalism frame is evident in that whites use it on a host of issues ranging from affirmative action and interracial friendship and marriage to residential and school segregation. Because of the pivotal role played by this frame in organizing whites' racial views, we provide three examples of how whites use it. An archetype of how whites use the notion of equal opportunity in an abstract manner to oppose racial fairness is Sue, a student at SU. When asked if minority students should be provided unique opportunities to be admitted into universities, Sue stated:

> I don't think that they should be provided with unique opportunities. I think that they should have the same opportunities as everyone else. You know, it's up to them to meet the standards and whatever that's required for entrance into universities or whatever. I don't think that just because they're a minority that they should, you know, not meet the requirements, you know.

Sue, like most whites, ignores the effects of past and contemporary discrimination on the social, economic, and educational status of minorities. Therefore, by supporting equal opportunity for everyone without a concern for the existing savage racial inequalities between whites and blacks, Sue's stance safeguards white privilege.

College students are not the only ones who use this abstract notion of equal opportunity to justify their racial views. For example, Eric, a corporate auditor in his forties and a very affable man who seemed more tolerant than most members of his generation (e.g. he had dated a black woman for three years, acknowledged that discrimination happens "a lot" and identified multiple examples, and even said that "the system is . . . is white"), erupted in anger when asked if reparations were due to blacks for the injuries caused by slavery and Jim Crow.

> [In a loud and angry tone] Oh tell them to shut up, ok! I had nothing to do with the whole situation. The opportunity is there, there is no reparation involved and let's not dwell on it. I'm very opinionated about that!

Was Eric just a white with a "principled opposition" to government intervention? This does not seem to be the case since Eric, like most whites, made a distinction between government spending on behalf of victims of child abuse, the homeless, and battered women (whom most whites deem as legitimate candidates for assistance) and government spending on blacks (whom most whites deem as unworthy candidates for assistance).

This finding was consistent with DAS survey results. For instance, whereas 64% of whites agreed that "we should expand the services that benefit the poor," only 40% (84% of blacks) agreed with the proposition "the government should make every effort to improve the social and economic position of blacks living in the United States." But was their opposition "racial" or just based on their opposition to government intervention in general? It seems to be racial as the proportion of whites supporting government programs that were not perceived as "racial" was quite large. For example, 75% approved of increasing federal spending for the environment and 60% for social security, however only 32% approved of such increases for programs to assist blacks.

This frame appeared occasionally in discussions on affirmative action, but most often in discussions about the limited level of school and residential integration in America. College students and older adults were adamant in arguing that it is not the government's business to remedy racial problems. For example, Ian, a manager of information security at an automotive company in his forties, used the abstract liberalism frame in response to the question on the limited level of school integration. Although Ian's first reaction was to question the premise of the question ("I guess I don't believe that"), he later addressed the issue of who is to blame by saying the following:

> I don't think I can't put the blame on anybody, not the government. We can't force blacks to move out to Nebraska or Utah or whatever to live. Same thing, you can't make 'em move to the upper peninsula and move to just because you want to have blacks in school. Um, some of it may be partially due to blacks themselves. They don't want to move to certain areas, they are happy with where they're at.

When asked directly if the government should do anything to ameliorate school segregation, Ian reiterated,

> I don't think the government should really play any part in it. If blacks want to stay in Detroit or any other area and continue that pattern, that's fine. If they want to move out to the suburbs and enroll their kid, more power to 'em, go for it! But I don't think there should be any forced integration.

Naturalization: Decoding the Meaning of "That's the way it is"

A frame that has not yet been brought to the fore by social scientists is whites' naturalization of race-related matters. Approximately half of DAS respondents and college students used this frame, particularly when discussing school or neighborhood matters or to explain the limited contact between whites and minorities or even whites' preference for whites as significant others. The word "natural" or the phrase "that's the way it is" is often interjected to normalize events or actions that could otherwise be interpreted as racially motivated (residential segregation) or racist (preference for whites as friends and partners). But, as social scientists know quite well, few things that happen in the social world are "natural," particularly those pertaining to racial matters. Segregation as well as racial preferences is produced through social processes.

One example of how whites insert this frame is Bill, a manager in a manufacturing firm. He explained the limited level of school integration as follows:

> I don't think it's anybody's fault. Because people tend to group with their own people. Whether it's white or black or upper-middle class or lower class or, you know, upper class, you know, Asians. People tend to group with their own. Doesn't mean if a black person moves into your neighborhood, they shouldn't go to your school. They should and you should mix and welcome them and everything else, but you can't force people together. If people want to be together, they should intermix more. [Interviewer: OK. So the lack of mixing is really just kind of an individual lack of desire?] Well, individuals, it's just the way it is. You know, people group together for lots of different reasons: social, religious. Just as animals in the wild, you know. Elephants group together, cheetahs group together. You bus a cheetah into an elephant herd because they should mix? You can't force that [laughs].

Bill's metaphor comparing racial segregation to the separation of species, however, was not the only way of using the naturalization frame. For example, Jim, a 30-year old computer software salesperson for a large company, naturalized school segregation as follows:

> Ah, you know, it's more of the human nature's fault. It's not the government's fault, right? The government doesn't tell people where to live. So as people decide where to live or where to move into or where they wanna feel comfortable, [they] move to where they feel comfortable. We all kinda hang out with people that are like us. I mean, you look at Detroit, we have a Mexican village, why do we have a Mexican village? Why aren't Mexican people spread out all over on metro Detroit? Well, they like being near other Mexican people that way they could have a store that suited them close by the, you know, those sort of things probably together. So, it's more human nature that I would blame for it.

These narratives are noteworthy not only for the way they explain racial patterns but also for the implicit solutions they suggest. That is, nothing needs to be done, thus justifying the status quo and clearly implying that no intervention is necessary.

"They Don't Have It Altogether": Cultural Racism

Pierre Andrè Taguieff (1990) has argued that modern European racism does not rely on an essentialist interpretation of minorities' endowments. Instead, it has *biologized* (presented them as if they were fixed) their presumed cultural practices and used that as the rationale for justifying racial inequality. Thus, Europeans are less likely today to claim that minorities are biologically inferior (i.e. less intelligent, capable, or moral) but Europeans are quick to argue that their culture is "different" (inferior) and the reason for their secondary status in society (Taguieff, 2001). By treating culture as immutable, Europeans deflect any possible accusation of racism ("It is not our fault that they live and behave like that") and can blame minorities for their social status ("If you guys work hard and complain less, you would be able to achieve parity with us").

This cultural racism is very well established in America (Feagin, 2000). Originally labeled as the "culture of poverty" in the 1960s, this tradition has resurfaced many times since in new flesh resurrected by conservative scholars such as Charles Murray (1984) and Lawrence Mead (1986). Even liberals, such as William Julius Wilson (1987), and radicals, such as Cornel West (1993), devote too much attention to blacks' cultural practices and come close to make them independent of the structure that promotes them.[7] The essence of the American version of this frame is "blaming the victim," arguing that minorities' standing is a product of their lack of effort, loose family organization, and inappropriate or deficient values.

Since there is very little disagreement among social scientists about the centrality of this frame in the post-civil rights era, we provide only one example of how whites use this frame. Kim, a student at MU, agreed with the premise of the following question, "Many whites explain the status of blacks in this country as a result of blacks lacking motivation, not having the proper work ethic, or being lazy. What do you think?"

> Yeah, I totally agree with that. I don't think, you know, they're all like that, but, I mean, it's just that if it wasn't that way, why would there be so many blacks living in the projects? You know, why would there be so many poor blacks? If they worked hard, they could make it just as high as anyone else could. You know, I just think that's just, you know, they're raised that way and they see that parents are so they assume that's the way it should be. And they just follow the roles their parents had for them and don't go anywhere.

Minimization of Racism: Whites' Declining Significance of Race Thesis

When whites are asked about discrimination in the abstract, they acknowledge its existence. For example, when DAS respondents were asked the question, "Discrimination against blacks is no longer a problem in the United States," a high proportion of *both* blacks and whites (83% of whites and 90% of blacks) "disagreed" with that statement. Nevertheless, whites and blacks disagree about the centrality of discrimination in explaining blacks' collective standing. Hence in response to the more specific question, "Blacks are in the position that they are today as a group because of present day discrimination," only 33% of whites "agreed" with that statement (compared to 61% of blacks).

College students were more likely than DAS respondents to give at least surface support to the idea of the continuing existence of discrimination. Because students interviewed for this study were enrolled in social science courses at the time of the interviews, they may have become sensitized to the significance of discrimination as well as to the new character of contemporary discrimination. However, despite this exposure, few believed discrimination and institutionalized racism are the reason why blacks lag behind whites in this society. In general, all respondents articulated their declining significance of race thesis in one of two ways. Whereas some used an indirect strategy of denial or minimization of discrimination set by one of the following two phrases "I am not black" or "I don't see discrimination" (strategy favored by college students), others denied outright that discrimination happens.

First is Mary, a student at SU who used the indirect strategy of denial. She answered a direct question on whether or not blacks face lots of discrimination as follows:

> Well, from my point of view, I don't see it necessarily. But then, of course, I am *white*. And so I'm not going to see it. It's something I'm not looking for. Second, it doesn't happen to me so it's very hard for me to look at a minority person and say "Well, they're facing racism right now" because it is something that is not happening to me, and I'm not looking for it. But I'm *sure* it happens.

This answer sounds reasonable because Mary is not black and thus cannot speak about blacks' experiences. However, Mary seriously doubts discrimination is very prominent in blacks' lives. Moreover, she believes that when it happens, it does to few individuals and in an overt manner. This is illustrated in her response to the statement, "Many blacks and other minorities claim that they do not get access to good jobs because of discrimination and that when they get the jobs they are not promoted at the same speed as their white peers,"

> I think before you really start talking about hiring practices and promotion practices, you have to look at credentials. I mean, you know, I've only really had one job. I worked for a general contractor so it was basically me in the office all day with him, my boss. But I, in fact, you have to look at credentials. I mean, I don't know if, you know, a white person gets a job over a minority [and] I can't sit here and say "Well, that's discrimination because I don't know what the factors were. This person got a master's degree versus a bachelor's degree, or more in-depth training than this person, you know? I mean, I definitely do not doubt that [discrimination] happens, that minorities get passed over for promotions and that they are not hired based on their race. I have absolutely no doubt that it happens. I think that before you can sit there and start calling a lot of things discrimination, you need to look into the background, the credentials behind it.

The second example is of respondents who deny discrimination outright. Many of these respondents believe blacks read racism into situations that do not have a racial basis. Sandra, a retail salesperson in her early forties, is one such case as evident by the way she explained her view on discrimination:

> I think if you are looking for discrimination, I think it's there to be *found*. But if you make the best of any situation, and if *you don't use it as an excuse*. I think sometimes it's an excuse because people felt they deserved a job, whatever! I think if things didn't go their way I know a lot of people have tendency to use prejudice or racism or whatever as an *excuse*. I think in some ways, *yes* there is (sic) people who are prejudiced. It's not only blacks, it's about Spanish, or women. In a lot of ways there [is] a lot of *reverse* discrimination. It's just what you wanna make of it.

These frames together form a formidable arsenal of ideas that help *most* whites[8] justify the racial status quo. For example, when whites are asked about affirmative action, they can resort to the frame of abstract liberalism to oppose it: "Why should we use discrimination to combat discrimination?" or "We should judge people by their merits and let the best person get the job, promotion, or be admitted into a good college." When whites are confronted with the tremendous residential and school segregation in the United States, they argue that race has nothing to do with these matters: "This is a natural thing" or "People prefer to be with people who are like them" or "This has nothing to do with race." When whites are faced with evidence of discrimination, they acknowledge its occurrence but classify the episodes as "isolated incidents" (e.g. the reaction to the lynching of James Byrd in Jasper, Texas). If blacks suggest discrimination is systemic, whites usually blame blacks for playing the "race card." For example, in an interview with a white mother, when asked whether she ever talked to her kids about race-related current events, the mother replied, "I mean maybe Rodney King, because he was kind of playing the Black card, you know, 'It's because I'm Black.' " Even in this rather extreme case, the severe beating of a Black man at the hands of white police officers, this person doubted claims of harm (see Lewis, forthcoming).

If color blind racism is the ideology typical of the "new racism" era (Bonilla-Silva & Lewis, 1999), how will it play out in the future given that the demography of the country is changing so dramatically? More significantly, how will racial stratification be organized in a country where most actors believe that "race does not matter" and where minorities are slowly becoming the majority? We examine these matters in the next section.

"WE ARE ALL AMERICANS": THE LATIN AMERICANIZATION OF RACE RELATIONS IN THE USA

So far, we have discussed the nature of post-civil rights racial ideology. Now we want to outline how we think race relations will operate in the 21st century. The basic thread of our argument is that race relations will become Latin America-like. Yet, Latin America-like does not mean exactly like Latin America. The 400-year history of the American "racial formation" (Omi & Winant, 1994) has stained the racial stratification order forever. Thus, we expect some important differences in this new American racial stratification system compared to that typical of Latin American societies. First, "shade discrimination" (Kinsbrunner, 1996) will not work perfectly. Hence, for example, although Asian Indians are dark-skinned, they will still be higher in the stratification order than, for example, Mexican American *mestizos*. Second, Middle Easterners, Asian Indians, and other non-Christian groups will not be allowed complete upward mobility. Third, because of the 300 years of dramatic racialization and group formation, most members of the non-white groups will maintain "ethnic" (Puerto Ricans) or racial claims (e.g. blacks) and demand group-based rights.

In becoming Latin America-like, we contend the United States will begin to exhibit the ostrich approach to racial matters of countries such as Cuba, Mexico, or Brazil that stick their head deep into the social ground and say, "We don't have races here. We don't have racism here. We are all Mexicans, Cubans, Brazilians, or Puerto Ricans!" Nevertheless, researchers have documented that racial minorities in these so-called "racial democracies," tend to be worse off than even racial minorities in Western nations. In Brazil, for example, blacks and *pardos* (tan or brown) earn about 40 to 45% as much as whites; are half as likely as whites to be employed in professional jobs, and have virtually no representation in colleges (Hasenbalg & do Ville Silva, 1999; Lovell & Wood, 1998; Nascimento & Nascimento, 2001; Telles, 1999).

Moreover, we argue that the United States will become Latin America-like not just in reference to racial thinking but also with regard to the structure of racial stratification. We suggest that the bi-racial system typical of the United States (white versus nonwhite) – which was the exception in the world-racial system[9] – will evolve into a more complex racial stratification system. Like in many Latin America countries, we posit the United States will develop a tri-racial system[10] with "whites" at the top, an intermediary group of "honorary whites" – similar to the coloreds in South Africa during formal apartheid – and a non-white group or the "collective black"[11] at the bottom. Furthermore, we contend this system will be further complicated by a pigmentocratic component – the ranking of individuals based on skin tone, facial characteristics, and hair texture, that is, individual members of racial and ethnic groups will also rank themselves *within* groups based on phenotype broadly construed.

As we suggest in Fig. 1, which is a heuristic rather than an analytical device,[12] the "white" group will include groups such as "traditional" whites, new "white"

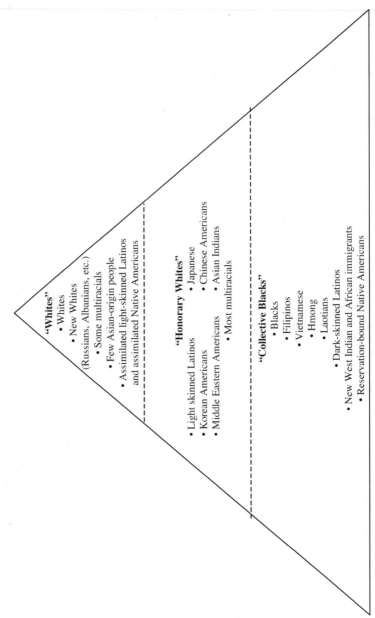

Fig. 1. Preliminary Map of Tri-Racial System in the USA.

immigrants and, in the near future, assimilated light-skinned Latinos. We predict the intermediate racial group or "honorary whites" will include groups such as most light-skinned Latinos (e.g. most Cubans and segments of the Mexican and Puerto Rican communities),[13] Japanese Americans, Korean Americans, Asian Indians, Chinese Americans, and maybe Middle Eastern Americans. Finally, the "collective black" will include groups such as blacks, dark-skinned Latinos, Vietnamese, Cambodians, Laotians, and possibly Filipinos.

Why Latin Americanization Now?

Why do we contend race relations in the United States will become Latin America-like? The reasons are multiple. First, the demography of the nation is changing. Racial minorities are approximately 30% of the population today and, as population projections suggest, may become a numeric majority in the year 2050. These projections may even underestimate the proportion of minorities in the future, as early releases from the 2000 Census suggest that the Latino population was almost one percentage point higher than the highest prior projection (see Grieco & Cassidy, 2001). Thus, the racial demography of the United States may approximate that of many Latin American countries in the future.

Although whitening the population through immigration or by classifying many newcomers as white (Gans, 1999; Warren & Twine, 1997) are possible solutions to the new American demography, for reasons we discuss below, we do not think this is likely. Hence, a more plausible accommodation to the new racial reality is to: (1) create an intermediate racial group to buffer racial conflict; (2) allow some newcomers into the white racial strata; and (3) incorporate most immigrants of color into the collective black strata.

Second, the "new racism" and its accompanying ideology point in the direction of Latin Americanization. The mechanisms and practices to reproduce racial advantage in America have become as subtle and sophisticated as those typical of Latin America. For example, many whites and commentators explain the exclusion of blacks in certain neighborhoods as a matter of class[14] rather than race in the United States as well as in Brazil (Nascimento & Nascimento, 2001; Twine, 1998). And, in both contexts, the specific mechanisms used to accomplish racial segregation are, for the most part, covert (Guimarães, 2001).

Third, the globalization of race relations will reinforce the transformations that are already taking place in the United States' racial structure (Lusane, 1997). The once almost all-white Western nations have now "interiorized the other" (that is, included racial minorities in their midst) (Miles, 1993). The new world-systemic need for capital accumulation has led to the incorporation of "dark" foreigners as "guest workers" and even as permanent workers (Schoenbaum & Pond, 1996). Thus, today, European nations have racial minorities in their midst who are progressively becoming an underclass (Castles & Miller, 1993; Cohen, 1997). European countries now have an internal "racial structure" (Bonilla-Silva, 1997) to maintain white power and have developed a curious racial ideology that combines ethnonationalism with a race-blind ideology similar to the American color blind racism (for more on this, see Bonilla-Silva, 2000). This new global racial reality, therefore, will reinforce the Latin Americanization trend in the United States.

Fourth, the convergence of the political and ideological actions of the Republican Party, conservative commentators and activists, and the so-called "multiracial" movement (Rockquemore & Brunsma, 2001), has created the possibility for the radical transformation of the way we gather racial data in America. One possible outcome of the Census Bureau categorical back-and-forth is either the dilution of racial data or the elimination of race as an official category. At this very moment, Ward Connerly and his colleagues are gathering signatures to place the California Racial Privacy Initiative on the ballot in November 2002 to forbid California from classifying individuals by race.

Connerly himself, and the politics he represents, are emblematic of color blind racism and the Latin Americanization of race relations thesis we are advancing. Connerly is an anti-black black who, through marriage and claims of a racial mix background, has elevated his status to that of almost non-black. He led the political initiative that eliminated affirmative action in college admissions in California and now is involved in this campaign to stop gathering racial data altogether – the data needed to make the case about the significance of race.

Latin Americanization Trends

Although we do not expect Latin Americanization to fully materialize until the middle of the century at the earliest, there are many trends that indicate we are headed in that direction. Here we consider just a few objective and subjective indicators that point in the direction of our thesis.

Objective Indicators

If Latin Americanization is happening, the standing of the various racial strata should match their predicted position in the stratification order. Thus, one would expect whites to have a better social and economic standing than "honorary whites" who in turn should have a better social and economic standing than the "collective black." This ought to be true regarding a range of social indicators. In terms of income, as Table 1 shows, light-skinned Latinos (Argentines, Chileans,

Table 1.   Mean Income ($) of Different Ethnic Groups, 1990.

Latino	Mean Income	Asian Americans	Mean Income
Mexican Americans	6,470.05	Chinese	12,695.05
Puerto Ricans	7,250.20	Japanese	15,801.93
Cubans	11,727.21	Koreans	10,177.38
Guatemalans	7,103.94	Asian Indians	15,857.61
Salvadorans	6,745.21	Filipinos	12,313.99
Costa Ricans	10,615.79	Taiwanese	13,310.58
Panamanians	10,701.25	Hmong	1,191.89
Argentines	15,506.40	Vietnamese	7,930.65
Chileans	12,727.60	Cambodians	3,759.82
Bolivians	10,661.95	Laotians	4,520.04
Whites	12,159.18	Whites	12,159.18
Blacks	7,210.56	Blacks	7,210.56

Costa Ricans, and Cubans) are doing much better than dark-skinned Latinos (Mexicans, Puerto Ricans, etc.). The exceptions in Table 1 (Bolivians and Panamanians) are examples of self-selected immigrants. For example, four of the largest ten concentrations of Bolivians in the U.S. are in the state of Virginia, a state with just 7.2% Latinos (Census Bureau, 2000). Table 1 also shows that Asians have a pattern similar to the Latinos. Hence, a severe income gap is emerging among honorary white Asians (Japanese, Asian Indians, Koreans, Filipinos, and Chinese) and those who we posit belong to the collective black (Vietnamese, Cambodian, Hmong, and Laotians) (see also Murguia & Telles, 1996).

Poverty, educational, and occupational data also reveal that a more complex racial configuration is solidifying in the United States and falls within our expectation (data not shown in paper).

Subjective Indicators

As in the case of objective indicators, if Latin Americanization is becoming a reality, one would expect the various racial strata to exhibit a consciousness that reflects their position in the racial stratification order. Thus, "honorary whites" should be developing the idea that they are different (white-like and, thus, "better") than poor Asians, dark-skinned Latinos, and blacks. Conversely, whites must be beginning to make distinctions among the various strata (e.g. accepting honorary whites more than poor Asians and dark-skinned Latinos). Data on racial self-classification shows this pattern clearly. Light-skinned Latinos (e.g. Cubans, Argentineans, etc.) are anywhere between 25 to 100% more likely than

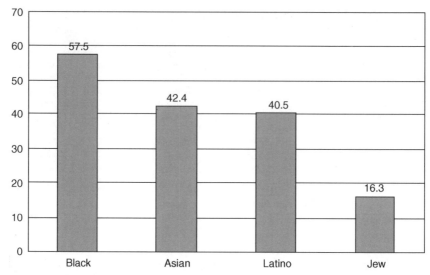

Fig. 2. Whites' Opposition to Intermarraige by Race of Prospective Mate. *Source:* 1990
General Social Survey.

dark-skinned Latinos (e.g. most Puerto Ricans, Dominicans, etc.) to self-classify
as white. Thus, whereas 80% or more of Cubans and Argentineans claim to be
white, fewer than 40% of Central Americans and Dominicans make such a claim
(see Bonilla-Silva & Glover, forthcoming).

In terms of whites' racial attitudes, the available data also seems to support our
argument. Figure 2 shows that whites possess a clear rank order preference for a
close relative marrying a Black, Asian, or Latino. For instance, approximately six
in ten whites object to a close relative marrying a Black compared to only four in
ten objecting to a close relative marrying an Asian or Latino or a little more than
one in ten objecting to a close relative marrying a Jew.

Although it would be ideal to have more recent data on whites' objection to
intermarriage with the various racial and ethnic groups, unfortunately such data
does not exist. The 1990 General Social Survey was the last time that white
respondents were asked this question for each of the four groups. The questions
on intermarriage that have been asked more recently, however, are mostly about
whether or not whites support laws against black-white marriages. Given the core
arguments of this paper, these items have limited analytical use for us. However,
data on attitudes is ultimately less important than behavioral data. If racial actors
are developing attitudes toward other groups based on their location in the racial
structure, their attitudes should correlate to their behavior. That is, the racial

ranking of the groups and concerns over color should correlate with the way the groups make choices about neighborhoods, friends, and significant others. In terms of marital choices, the findings of a recent study on interracial marriage seem to fit this expectation (Quian & Lichter, 2001). These researchers found that although less than 5% of all marriages in this country are interracial, those who choose to marry outside their race, tend to marry people of lighter color. Thus, Asians are more likely to marry whites, followed by Latinos, and lastly blacks. Latinos are more likely to marry whites, followed by Asians, and lastly blacks. Blacks are more likely to marry Latinos than whites or Asians. Furthermore, in a press release about his findings, Quian commented that, "Skin color is still very important. African-Americans are the least likely to be interracially married; light-skinned Latinos are more likely to be interracially married than dark-skinned ones" (Phipps, 2001. See also Moran, 2001).

A similar pattern of preference for light skin also emerged in interviews with white parents in Northern California (Lewis, forthcoming). For instance, Mrs. Karpinsky, a mother of two, when asked whether she thought it would be a problem for her or her husband if one of their children married someone from a different race stated the following:

> Mrs. Karpinsky: It depends what race "I do, to me, Asians aren't – to me it is, I hate to say this, it sounds so prejudiced, but to me it's more like Blacks are, African Americans would be the only . . . to me Asians are just like – white. And I guess I just am realizing I am saying that (laughs), but I wouldn't feel um, uncomfortable at all if my daughter, you know, married a, an Asian person or I wouldn't have felt strange dating an Asian person in college, but I would have felt a little bit – I would have felt uncomfortable dating a Black man.

Another way to assess if Latin Americanization is affecting the racial consciousness of various actors is examining their degree of affect toward other groups. According to Fig. 3, Mexicans and Puerto Ricans have more positive feelings toward Blacks than Asians, whereas Cubans have more positive feelings toward Asians than blacks (see also Murguia & Forman, forthcoming).

In another study, based on the 1990 Latino National Political Survey (de la Garza et al., 1992), the researchers found that this trend was even stronger when "Latinos" were disaggregated by racial self-classification (Forman, Martínez & Bonilla–Silva, 2000). That is, Latinos who self-identified as "black" or as "Latino" expressed warmer feelings toward blacks than those who self-identified as "white." These researchers also reported that 92% of Cubans compared with 58% of Puerto Ricans and 51% of Mexicans self-identified as "white." In all, these results help clarify why Cubans have less positive feelings toward Blacks than Puerto Ricans or Mexicans have toward Blacks.

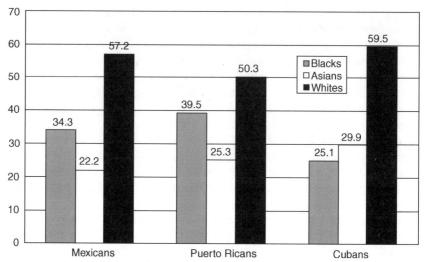

Fig. 3. Latino's Attitudes Toward Blacks, Asians, and Whites. *Source:* 1990 National Social Survey.

CONCLUSIONS

In this paper we have argued two fundamental points about the nature of race relations in the post-civil rights era. First, we suggested that a new racial ideology has emerged to justify the racial status quo fitting of the practices typical of the "new racism" (Bonilla-Silva & Lewis, 1999). This ideology, which we label color-blind racism, includes a series of frames that allow whites to support the mythology of non-racialism. Secondly, we argued that because of national and international changes in race relations, the racial stratification order of the United States will become Latin America-like. Specifically, we suggested – and provided preliminary data to support our claim – that a tri-racial stratification order is developing that will make race relations in the United States as complex as they are all over Latin America.

The consequences of our findings for racial politics in the 21st century are enormous. First, racial politics will change dramatically. We predict that the "us" versus "them" racial dynamic will lessen as "honorary whites" grow in size and social importance. This variegated "group" is likely to buffer racial conflict – or derail it – as intermediate groups do in many Latin American countries (Degler, 1986) as well as provide a path for upward, albeit limited, racial mobility (Nobles, 2000).

Second, the ideology of color blind racism will become even more salient among whites and honorary whites and will also influence members of the collective black.

Color blind racism, which is an ideology similar to that prevalent in Latin American societies, will help glue the new social system and further buffer racial conflict. As we all become more color blind, racial matters will be seen out of (racial) focus and explanations based on class may become more prominent (Harris, 1999; Wilson, 1978).

Third, if the Census Bureau decides to stop gathering racial statistics, documenting the impact of race in a variety of social venues will become extremely hard if not next to impossible. More significantly, because state actions always impact civil society, if the state decides to erase race from above, the *social* recognition of "races" in the polity may become harder. We may develop a Latin American-like "disgust" for even mentioning anything that is race-related.

Fourth, the deep history of black-white divisions in the United States has been such that the centrality of the black identity will not dissipate. For instance, research on even the "black elite" indicates that they exhibit racial attitudes that are similar to lower class blacks (Dawson, 1994). However, even among blacks, we predict some important shifts. Their racial consciousness will become more diffused (see Chap. 6 in Bonilla-Silva, 2001). Furthermore, the external pressure of "multiracials" in predominantly white contexts (Rockquemore & Brunsma, 2001) and the internal pressure of "ethnic" blacks[15] (Vickerman, 1999; Waters, 1999) may change the notion of "blackness" and even the position of some "blacks" in the racial stratification system. Pigmentocracy may become an even more important factor as a way of making social distinctions among "blacks" (Allen, Telles & Hunter, 2000).

Fifth, the new racial stratification system will be more effective in maintaining "white supremacy" (Mills, 1997). Whites will still be at the top of the social structure, but will face fewer race-based challenges. The expanded "collective black" will remain firmly at the bottom with a reduced space for racial contestation and honorary whites will remain *honorary*, that is, they will still face discrimination and will not receive equal treatment in society (for example, although based on their overall status we classify Middle-Eastern Americans as "honorary whites," their treatment in the post-September 11 era indicates their status as "white" and "American" is very tenuous indeed).

We realize that many analysts and commentators regard the disappearance of Jim Crow racism as a sign of tremendous progress (Thernstrom & Thernstrom, 1997). We believe, however, that those at the bottom of the racial hierarchy will soon discover that behind the statement "We are all Americans" and whites' protestation that "It wasn't me" about contemporary racial inequality hides a deeper, hegemonic way of maintaining white supremacy. As a color blind Latin America-*like* society, racial inequality will be part of our landscape but with a much reduced political space for racial contestation.

If color blindness is the new dominant racial ideology in America and racial stratification is becoming tri-racial, what are the best strategies to fight this new, two-headed monster? Unlike researchers in the prejudice paradigm, who advocate education or the internalization of new norms as the cure for "racism," those of us in the racial ideology paradigm focus on the struggle for resource redistribution and the elimination (or mitigation) of racial caste. Therefore, given the well-documented racial inequalities between blacks and whites in terms of wealth, income, neighborhood quality, and education as well as the continuing significance of discrimination, we believe that a Marshall-type race-targeted program and intensive policing against old and new-fashion discrimination will be necessary to eliminate racial inequality and guarantee that blacks and other racial minorities become full citizens of the United States.

But we are not naïve. Given the racial demography of the country and the fact that most whites believe the "it wasn't me" mythology, this kind of political program is unlikely unless a significant segment of the white community joins in the struggle for racial justice. But from where will these white racial progressives come from? Elsewhere one of the authors investigated the identity of "racial progressives" and found they are more likely to be young, white women from a working class background (Bonilla-Silva, forthcoming. See also Feagin & Vera, 1995). In fact, women and racial minorities have already become the *majority* in the working class as well as among those belonging in unions (Kelley, 1997; Roediger, 2002). This is the crack in the system: the possibility that the "(*new*) workers of the world (*might*) unite."

However, if our Latin Americanization prediction is right, the political issue of the future will no longer be restricted to convincing progressive whites to join in the struggle for racial justice. Instead, members of the "collective black" and their allies will have to devise strategies and practices to convince "honorary whites" that their interests are closer to the "collective black" than to whites. The political objective is to show them that their status is *honorary* (awarded by the dominant race) and that, therefore, they always face the possibility of discrimination and debasement (e.g. Middle Eastern Americans in the post-September 11 era). Otherwise "honorary whites" will ally with "whites" and proclaim like them that "It wasn't me" and that "We are all Americans."

NOTES

1. Shaggy (2000). It wasn't me. *Hotshot*. MCA Records.
2. The mainstream view on racism assumes the phenomenon is a matter of prejudiced individuals. For a critique and an alternative interpretation, see Eduardo Bonilla-Silva, "Rethinking Racism: Toward a Structural Interpretation," *American Sociological Review*, *62*, 465–480.

3. By racial ideology we mean the racially-based frameworks used by actors to explain and justify (dominant racial ideology) or challenge (oppositional ideology) the racial status quo. Although all the races in a racialized social system have the *capacity* of developing these frameworks, the frameworks of the dominant race tend to become the master frameworks upon which all racial actors ground (for or against) their ideological positions.

4. A society's *racial structure* includes the totality of social relations and practices that reinforce systemic white privilege. For more on this, see Bonilla-Silva (2001).

5. For a thorough examination of this ideology, see Eduardo Bonilla-Silva (forthcoming). *Color Blind Racism or How Whites Justify Contemporary Racial Inequality*. Boulder: Rowman and Littlefield.

6. "Braceros" refers to Mexican workers brought to the country through the Bracero Program in the post-World War II era.

7. Although West (1993) and Wilson (1987) address the structural factors shaping black life chances, they also insist on the centrality of cultural factors seen as independent from the structural conditions faced by blacks. For a more elaborate analysis of this matter, see Chap. 1 in Bonilla-Silva (2001).

8. Elsewhere Bonilla-Silva and Forman (2000) have argued that there is a segment of the white community that does not subscribe to the new dominant racial ideology. This group, which they label as "white progressives" is mostly comprised of women from working class backgrounds with some college level education.

9. For discussions on the racialization of the word-system, see Balibar and Wallerstein (1991), Goldberg (1993) and Mills (1997).

10. Two central components of Latin American racial stratification are a tri-racial order and "shade discrimination"(Kinsbrunner, 1996) or "colorism" (ranking people according to skin tone). For an excellent review on racial matters in Latin America, see Peter Wade (1997). *Race and Ethnicity in Latin America*. Chicago: Pluto Press.

11. Here we are adapting Tony Negri's idea of the "collective worker" to the situation of all those at the bottom of the racial stratification system (see Negri, 1984).

12. This map is a tentative rather than definitive placement of groups. Hence, the position of some groups may change (e.g. Chinese Americans, Asian Indians, and Arab Americans) and, at this early stage in our analysis, the map is not inclusive of all the groups in the United States (for instance, Samoans, Micronesians, etc., are not in the map). More significantly, if our Latin Americanization thesis is accurate, there will be categorical porosity as well as "pigmentocracy." The former refers to individual members of a racial strata moving up (or down) the stratification system (e.g. a light-skin middle class black person marrying a white woman and moving to the "honorary white" strata) and the latter refers to the rank ordering of groups and members of groups based on the way they look (the more "white" one looks, the higher esteem one receives).

13. For an example of Puerto Ricans becoming "white," see the case of middle class Puerto Ricans in California in Rodriguez (1999).

14. For a recent article claiming that residential segregation is mostly the product of class, see David R. Harris, " 'Property Values Drop When Blacks Move in, Because...': Racism and SESE Determinants of Neighborhood Desirability." *American Sociological Review*, *64*(3), 461–479. For en excellent critique of the class-based explanation of residential segregation, see Camille Charles Zubrinksy and Lawrence Bobo (1996). "Prismatic Metropolis: Race and Residential Segregation in the City of the Angels." *Social Science Research*, *25*, 335–375.

15. By ethnic blacks we refer to first-generation West Indians, Haitians, and most Africans who struggle to distance themselves from African Americans. For more discussion on this matter, see Chapters 1 and 4 in Alex-Assensoh and Hanks (2000).

REFERENCES

Alex-Assensoh, Y. M., & Hanks, L. J. (2000). *Black and multiracial politics in America*. New York: New York University Press.

Allen, W., Telles, E., & Hunter, M. (2000). Skin color, income, and education: A comparison of African Americans and Mexican Americans. *National Journal of Sociology, 12*(1), 129–180.

Balibar, E., & Wallerstein, I. (1991). *Race, nation, and class: Ambiguous identities*. London: Verso.

Blauner, R. (1989). *Black lives, white lives: Three decades of race relations in America*. Berkeley: University of California Press.

Bobo, L., Kluegel, J., & Smith, R. (1997). Laissez faire racism: The crystallization of a kinder, gentler, antiblack ideology. In: S. Turner et al. (Eds), *Racial Attitudes in the 1990s: Continuity and Change* (pp. 15–42). Westport: Praeger.

Bonilla-Silva, E. (1997). Rethinking racism: Toward a structural analysis. *American Sociological Review, 62*, 465–480.

Bonilla-Silva, E. (2000). This is a white country: The racial ideology of the western nations of the world-system. *Sociological Inquiry, 70*(2), 188–214.

Bonilla-Silva, E. (2001). *White supremacy and racism in the post-civil rights era*. Boulder: Lynne Rienner Publishers.

Bonilla-Silva, E. (forthcoming). *Color blind racism or how whites justify contemporary racial inequality*. Boulder: Rowman and Littlefield.

Bonilla-Silva, E., & Forman, T. (2000). I'm not a racist, but . . .: Mapping white college students' racial ideology in the USA. *Discourse & Society, 11*(1), 50–85.

Bonilla-Silva, E., & Glover, K. (forthcoming). We are all Americans: The Latin Americanization of race relations in the USA. In: M. Krysan & A. Lewis (Eds), *Changing Terrain of Race and Ethnicity*. New York: Russell Sage.

Bonilla-Silva, E., & Lewis, A. (1999). The new racism: Toward an analysis of the U.S. racial structure, 1960s–1990. In: P. Wong (Ed.), *Race, Nation, and Citizenship*. Boulder: Westview Press.

Brooks, R. (1990). *Rethinking the American race problem*. Berkeley, Los Angeles, and Oxford: University of California Press.

Castles, S., & Miller, M. (1993). *The age of migration: International population movements in the modern world*. Hong Kong: MacMillan.

Cohen, R. (1997). *Global diasporas*. Seattle: University of Washington Press.

Dawson, M. (1994). *Beyond the mule*. Princeton: Princeton University Press.

de la Garza, R. O., DeSipio, L., Garcia, C. F., Garcia, J., & Falcon, A. (1992). *Latino voices: Mexican, Puerto Rican, and Cuban perspectives on American politics*. Boulder: Westview Press.

Degler, C. N. (1986). *Neither black nor white: Slavery and race relations in Brazil and the United States*. Madison: University of Wisconsin Press.

Essed, P. (1996). *Diversity: Gender, color, and culture*. Amherst: University of Massachusetts Press.

Feagin, J. R. (2000). *Racist America*. New York and London: Routledge.

Feagin, J. R., & Vera, H. (1995). *White racism: The basics*. New York and London: Routledge.

Forman, T., Martínez, G., & Bonilla-Silva, E. (2000). Latinos' perceptions of blacks and Asians: Testing the immigrant hypothesis. Unpublished manuscript.

Gans, H. J. (1999). *The possibility of a new racial hierarchy in the twenty-first century United States* (pp. 371–390). M. Lamont (Ed.). Chicago: University of Chicago Press.

Goldberg, D. T. (1993). *Racist culture: Philosophy and the politics of meaning.* Cambridge: Blackwell Publishers, Inc.

Grieco, E., & Cassidy, R. (2001). *Overview of race and Hispanic origin 2000.* Washington, DC: U.S. Government Printing Office.

Guimarães, A. S. A. (2001). Brazil: The misadventures of nonracialism in Brazil. In: C. Hamilton (Ed.), *Beyond Racism: Race and Inequality in Brazil, South Africa, and the United States.* Boulder: Lynne Rienner.

Harris, D. R. (1999). Property values drop when blacks move in, because . . .: Racial and socioeconomic determinants of neighborhood desirability. *American Sociological Review, 64*(3), 461–479.

Hasenbalg, C., & do Valle Silva, N. (1999). Notes on racial and political inequality in Brazil. In: M. Hanchard (Ed.), *Racial Politics in Contemporary Brazil* (pp. 154–178). Durham: Duke University Press.

Kelley, R. D. G. (1997). *Yo' Mama's Disfunktional.* Boston: Beacon Press.

Kinsbrunner, J. (1996). *Not of pure blood: The free people of color and racial prejudice in nineteenth-century Puerto Rico.* Durham: Duke University Press.

Lewis, A. (2001). There is no race in the schoolyard: Colorblind ideology in an (almost) all white school. *American Educational Research Journal, 38*(4), 781–811.

Lewis, A. (forthcoming). *Race in the schoolyard: Negotiating race in classrooms and communities.* New Brunswick: Rutgers University Press.

Lewis, A., Chesler, M., & Forman, T. (2000). The impact of color-blind ideologies on students of color: Intergroup relations at a predominantly white university. *Journal of Negro Education, 69*(1/2), 74–91.

Lovell, P. A., & Wood, C. H. (1998). Skin color, racial identity, and life chances in Brazil. *Latin American Perspectives, 25*(3), 90–109.

Lusane, C. (1997). *Race in the global era: African Americans at the millennium.* Boston: South End Press.

Mead, L. M. (1986). *Beyond entitlement: The social obligations of citizenship.* New York: Free Press.

Miles, R. (1993). *Racism after race relations.* London: Routledge.

Mills, C. W. (1997). *The racial contract.* Ithaca and London: Cornell University Press.

Moran, R. F. (2001). *Interracial intimacy: The regulation of race and romance.* Chicago and London: University of Chicago Press.

Murguia, E., & Forman, T. (forthcoming). Shades of whiteness and the Mexican origin population: Views from the inside and outside. In: E. Bonilla-Silva & A. Doane (Eds), *Deconstructing Whiteness, Deconstructing White Supremacy.* New York: Routledge.

Murguia, E., & Telles, E. E. (1996). Phenotype and schooling among Mexican Americans. *Sociology of Education, 69*(4), 267–289.

Murray, C. A. (1984). *Losing ground: American social policy, 1950–1980.* New York: Basic Books.

Nascimento, A., & Nascimento, E. L. (2001). Dance of deception: A reading of race relations in Brazil. In: C. Hamilton et al. (Eds), *Beyond Racism* (pp. 105–156). Boulder: Lynne Rienner Publishers.

Negri, A. (1984). *Marx beyond Marx: Lessons on the Grundrisse.* J. Fleming (Ed.). South Hadley: Bergin & Garvey.

Nobles, M. (2000). *Shades of citizenship: Race and the census in modern politics.* Palo Alto: Stanford University Press.

Omi, M., & Winant, H. (1994). *Racial formation in the United States from the 1960s to the 1990s.* New York and London: Routledge.

Phipps, J. (2001). Color solidifies in melting pot. *Health Scout News* (September 21).

Quian, Z., & Lichter, D. T. (2001). Measuring marital assimilation: Intermarriage among natives and immigrants. *Social Science Research, 30,* 289–312.

Rockquemore, K., & Brunsma, D. L. (2001). *Beyond black: Biracial identity in America.* Thousand Oaks: Sage Publications.

Rodriguez, V. M. (1999). Boricuas, African Americans, and Chicanos in the "far west" notes on the Puerto Rican pro-independence movement in California, 1960s–1980s. In: R. Torres & G. Katsiaficas (Eds), *Latino Social Movements: Historical and Theoretical Perspectives* (pp. 79–109). New York: Routledge.

Roediger, D. (2002). *White colored: Transcending the racial past.* Berkeley, Los Angeles, and London: Berkeley University Press.

Rubin, L. (1994). *Families on the fault line.* New York: Harper Collins.

Schoenbaum, D., & Pond, E. (1996). *The German question and other German questions.* New York: St. Martin's Press.

Sears, D. (1988). Symbolic racism. In: P. Katz & D. Taylor (Eds), *Eliminating Racism: Profiles in Controversy* (pp. 53–84). New York: Plenum.

Shaggy (2000). It wasn't me. *Hotshot.* MCA Records.

Smith, R. C. (1995). *Racism in the post-civil rights era.* New York: State University of New York Press.

Smith, T. (1998). Intergroup relations in contemporary America. In: W. Winborne & R. Cohen (Eds), *Intergroup Relations in the United States: Research Perspectives* (pp. 69–106). New York: National Conference for Community and Justice.

Taguieff, P. A. (1990). The new cultural racism of France. *Telos, 83,* 109–122.

Taguieff, P. A. (2001). *The force of prejudice: On racism and its doubles.* Minneapolis and London: University of Minnesota Press.

Telles, E. E. (1999). Ethnic boundaries and political mobilization among African Brazilians: Comparisons with the U.S. Case. In: M. Hanchard (Ed.), *Racial Politics in Contemporary Brazil* (pp. 82–97). Durham: Duke University Press.

Thernstrom, S., & Thernstrom, A. (1997). *America in black and white.* New York: Simon and Schuster.

Twine, F. W. (1998). *Racism in a racial democracy: The maintenance of white supremacy in Brazil.* New Brunswick: Rutgers University Press.

Vickerman, M. (1999). *Crosscurrents: West Indian immigrants and race.* New York: Oxford University Press.

Wade, P. (1997). *Race and ethnicity in Latin America.* Chicago: Pluto Press.

Warren, J. W., & Twine, F. W. (1997). White Americans, the new minority? Non-blacks and the ever-expanding boundaries of whiteness. *Journal of Black Studies, 28*(2), 200–218.

Waters, M. (1999). *Black identities: West Indian immigrant dreams and American realities.* Cambridge: Harvard University Press.

West, C. (1993). *Race matters.* Boston: Beacon Press.

Wilson, W. J. (1978). *The declining significance of race.* Chicago: University of Chicago Press.

Wilson, W. J. (1987). *The truly disadvantaged: The inner city, the underclass, and public policy.* Chicago: The University of Chicago Press.

Zubrinksy, C. C., & Bobo, L. (1996). Prismatic metropolis: Race and residential segregation in the city of the angels. *Social Science Research* (25), 335–375.

PART II:
ELECTORAL POLITICS

VOTING BEHAVIOR AND POLITICAL SOCIOLOGY: THEORIES, DEBATES, AND FUTURE DIRECTIONS

Clem Brooks, Jeff Manza and Catherine Bolzendahl

ABSTRACT

Once a core concern of postwar political sociology, research on voting behavior was largely displaced after the 1960s by new and important controversies concerning state formation, social movements, and globalization. Sociological research on voting enjoyed an intellectual renaissance during the 1990s, however, with emerging connections to research on changing patterns of stratification, ideological conflicts over racism, religion, and individual, rights and variation across national context. This paper evaluates recent developments in the study of voting behavior. We discuss social psychological, social structural, economic, and political cultural approaches to understanding voting behavior, identifying their underlying differences as well as relevant considerations regarding the benefits and limits of rational choice as a meta-theory. We review debates over class, religion, economic voting, new cleavages, and aggregate political change, concluding with a discussion of some productive lines of further research.

INTRODUCTION

Voting in national elections is usually the most consequential form of political behavior in democratic polities. Elections provide not only the most regular

Political Sociology for the 21st Century
Research in Political Sociology, Volume 12, 137–173
ISSN: 0895-9935/PII: S0895993503120062

opportunity for political participation and influence by individual citizens, but also an institutional context in which social conflicts and inequalities involving groups are routinely expressed and often transformed into enduring patterns of political party conflict. Elections are themselves an important causal factor behind national policy-making (e.g. Powell, 2000). For example, the capacity of social democratic parties to control government has been critical to the development of Scandinavian-style welfare states, while the historical popularity of Christian Democratic or liberal parties in other countries has led to the development of corporatist or liberal regimes (Esping-Andersen, 1990; Hicks, 1999; Huber & Stephens, 2001).

Since the proximate source of citizens' control over government rests with the aggregated choices of individual voters in elections, the study of voting behavior has causal relevance to virtually all aspects of political institutions and stratification studied by sociologists. But this broad relevance has not always led to scholarly interest: a core concern of postwar U.S. political sociology in the 1950s and 1960s, voting behavior subsequently experienced a relatively long period of inattention between the mid-1960s to the late 1980s, as political sociologists turned their attention to new and important controversies over state formation, social movements, and globalization.[1]

In the past decade, however, the study of voting by political sociologists has enjoyed something of an intellectual renaissance. This development provides an opportunity to review the state of sociological theorizing and research on voting behavior. Due to the remarkable range of literatures on mass political behavior, our review is deliberately selective, directing attention to the theoretical approaches, scholarly controversies, and research questions of greatest likely relevance to political sociologists. While our focus is primarily on contemporary work, we begin with a discussion of the legacies left by several mid-20th century classics that shaped subsequent innovations. While much of our focus is on the U.S., we consider where relevant studies of voting behavior in other countries and with comparative research.

The paper is in four sections. In the first, we discuss social psychological, social structural, economic, and political cultural approaches to understanding voting behavior, concluding the section with a discussion of the benefits and limits of rational choice as a meta-theory of voting. We next consider a number of methodological issues that have been central to the study of voting behavior. The third section reviews five major contemporary debates concerning voting behavior, discussing key findings that have advanced these debates. We then identify a pair of instructive dead-ends suggested by our review, concluding with a discussion of more productive lines of research that extend the theories and debates we review.

THEORIES OF VOTING BEHAVIOR

A fundamental theorem of political behavior research, and one buttressed by a half-century's worth of survey research, is that the aggregate outcome of elections is shaped far less by political campaigns than by longer-term causal factors that are generally beyond the control of political parties and candidates (Niemi & Weisberg, 2001, Chap. 1). As a result, research on voting behavior has generally been organized by reference to assumptions about the causal factors that shape the preferences of individual voters *prior* to specific campaigns. However, the literature is also heterogeneous, characterized by competing theories that emphasize the causal relevance of different mechanisms. In this section, we review four major theoretical approaches, discussing their underlying differences as well as relevance to political-sociological research.

Social Psychological Approaches

The classic theories of voting behavior identified factors relating to social groups as the key source of voters' alignments with political parties. Two main approaches to understanding the political effects of social group processes have been proposed. While *social structural* approaches focus on interests group members share by virtue of their (objective) social location, *social psychological* approaches focus on processes through which voters acquire (subjective) identities that derive from socialization and lived experience within specific institutions or contexts.

Social psychological theories emerged in tandem with the first wave of scientific election surveys, and they provided an initial means of making sense of the unexpected results of those surveys. More specifically, the first analyses of National Election Study data from the 1950s suggested a portrait of U.S. voters as ignorant of nearly all aspects of government institutions, policy issues, and even such political concepts as "liberal" (see Converse, 1964). Rejecting idealized views of political behavior in democracies, University of Michigan scholars Campbell, Converse, Miller and Stokes (1960, p. 543) interpreted vote choice as an unreflective and habitual activity, arguing further that American voters were largely incapable of acting on the basis of evaluations of policy issues.

Despite little evidence of political sophistication or factual knowledge, Campbell and his colleagues (1960, Chaps 6–7) found that identification with political parties provided voters with a basis for choosing between candidates, and they hypothesized that once acquired during childhood socialization, party identification became a lasting component of voters' identity throughout the life course. The central assumption of *The American Voter* was thus social psychological: voting behavior is a product of long-standing emotional attachments and identification with a specific political party. Complementing this assumption, Campbell and his colleagues (1960, Chap. 10) reported further evidence that partisan voters were able to articulate general images of their preferred party as endorsing positions expected to benefit their social group.

The *American Voter's* social psychological theory defined a large portion of subsequent research over U.S. voting behavior. However, its emphasis on the stable sources of partisanship and the seeming low capacity of voters to acquire either sophistication or factual information was not without controversy. Indeed, one of the liveliest debates during the 1970s concerned the possibility that such changes in the political environment as high levels of social movement activism and the rise of the electronic media led to a transformation of the American electorate (Verba, Nie & Petrocik, 1979). Although subsequent research yielded little evidence for changes in voters' information level or degree of cognitive consistency (Delli Carpini & Keeter, 1996; Smith, 1989), it did provide firm evidence that voters frequently engage in issue voting, evaluating and choosing between candidates on the basis of their policy preferences (see Niemi & Weisberg, 2001, Chap. 10 for a review). And while the largely static portrait of U.S. voting behavior offered by the Michigan scholars provided little explanation for political change, the influence of this theory remains considerable.

The acquisition and individual-level stability of partisanship is a defining element of the social psychological approach, and party identification has generally been treated as an *exogenous* factor within this tradition, summarizing both parents' and other childhood political influences. One subsequent and particularly heated debate relates to the scenario of partisan dealignment, whereby changes in the affective content or political effects of party identification make partisanship a less relevant guide to voting behavior (e.g. Wattenberg, 1996). Responding to this thesis, Bartels (2000) finds evidence of an *increase* in the association of party identification with both presidential and congressional vote choice since the 1970s, calling into question the validity of the dealignment scenario for contemporary U.S. politics.

An equally lively and ongoing debate concerns the possibility that partisanship should be interpreted as an *endogenous* variable. While the Michigan scholars and two decades of subsequent research assumed that partisanship was exogenous, an accumulating body of evidence has suggested that party identification is instead an outcome shaped by long-term changes in voters' preferences as well as short-term changes linked to economic performance and the context of elections (Erikson, MacKuen & Stimson, 2002, Chap. 4; Franklin, 1992; MacKuen, Erikson & Stimson, 1988; Niemi & Jennings, 1991). Predictably, this revisionist challenge has not gone unmet. Employing different models and analyzing different data, proponents of the endogenous theory have marshaled evidence in support of the position that short-term shifts have limited and only gradual effects on the partisan identities of individuals (Green, Palmquist & Schickler, 1998). While this debate is far from reaching a conclusive resolution, the plausibility of the revisionist interpretation of partisanship raises intriguing questions about the malleability of partisan identity over the life course.[2]

Social Structural Approaches

Social structural approaches to voting behavior also emerged during the early years of election studies, but unlike social psychological theories, social structural approaches identify group-based inequalities as generating conflicting interests that produce divergent alignments with political parties. Moreover, while social psychological approaches are often linked to theories of childhood socialization (where the basis for enduring identities are assumed to originate), social structural approaches generally focus on adult experience, and more specifically, on individuals' memberships in groups stemming from such inequalities as those based on class, race, gender, and religion.

Early political-sociological work by Lazarsfeld and Berelson (Berelson, Lazarsfeld & McPhee, 1954; Lazarsfeld, Berelson & Gaudet, 1948, 1968; Lipset, 1981, 1960; Lipset & Rokkan, 1967) developed influential accounts of the impact of social structural factors on voting behavior. Lazarsfeld and Berelson pioneered an "electoral sociology" in their development of what they called the "Index of Political Predisposition," consisting of socioeconomic status, religion, and place of residence (see e.g. Lazarsfeld, 1948, p. 26). Distinguishing between two types of political institution building, Lipset and Rokkan (1967) theorized that nation-building processes establish social cleavages based upon ethnicity, language, and religion, while industrial revolutions lead to a class cleavage based upon property ownership. But instead of social cleavages leading to revolution, conflicts between groups comprising a particular cleavage are routinized into electoral competition between political parties. So long as the groups comprising a specific cleavage believe that candidates of the party with which they are aligned have a chance of gaining elected office, participation by these groups in elections organizes social conflicts in an orderly fashion, in turn conferring legitimacy on political institutions (Lipset, 1981, 1960, Chap. 1; cf. Przeworski & Sprague, 1986). Because they mediate between social conflicts and political party competition, cleavages thus have a central status in explaining the development and stabilization of democracies.

Social structural research constitutes a large but not exclusive share of political-sociological work on voting behavior. The social cleavage approach introduced by Lipset underlies debates concerning patterns of stability versus change in the partisan influence of social class. Subsequent work by Bartolini and Mair (1990) and Manza and Brooks (1999b) has introduced a modified version of this theory. Building from the insights of Bartolini and Mair, we argued that social cleavages vary across three separate dimensions: social structure; group conflict and identification; and finally through political parties organized by reference to the first two dimensions (Manza & Brooks, 1999b, Chap. 2). Because of the slow pace of social structural change, mature social cleavages may experience significant inertia, perhaps conforming to Lipset and Rokkan's (1967) comment that cleavages tend to become "frozen" in place over time. However, because changes in the level of group conflict or identification and the activities of political organizations cannot be ruled out, social cleavages and their political effects can also experience significant trends. Many of the recent debates around voting have centered precisely on the question of whether there has been a "loosening" of the impact of social cleavages on voting behavior (e.g. Evans, 1999a; Franklin et al., 1992; Nieuwbeerta et al., 2002).

In addition to contributions to the developments of models of the social bases of voting behavior, Lazarsfeld, Berelson, and their colleagues' work on political communication during election campaigns highlighted the importance of social networks in shaping the flow of information and the reinforcement of voters' preferences (see especially Berelson et al., 1954, pp. 88–109). This line of analysis has been recovered in the recent work of Huckfeldt and his colleagues (e.g. Huckfeldt & Sprague, 1995). They hypothesize the importance of network-based information to voters' decision-making and behavior, arguing further that such information is routinely transmitted through both strong ties (e.g. involving friends) and weak ties (e.g. involving individuals acquainted solely through a common contact). By reconceptualizing the political effects of social structure as stemming from individuals' unequal access to information and socially-embedded patterns of communicative influence, Huckfeldt and colleagues' (Huckfeldt, Plutzer & Sprague, 1993; Huckfeldt & Sprague, 1991) approach raises important new questions about the potential for larger than "minimal" effects of campaigns and the media, and also the influence of individuals or organizations with central network positions. The full promise of this work has yet to be realized, and network-based theories may hold considerable appeal for political sociologists (see e.g. Weakliem & Heath, 1994).

Economic Approaches

Like social structural approaches, economic theories of voting specify material interests as the key factor underlying political behavior. However, whereas social structural theories identify individuals' politically-relevant interests as emerging from relationships or social positions involving inequalities of status or assets, economic approaches focus on individual's experiences with, and perceptions of, economic opportunities and risks. Furthermore, while social structural theories typically assume that group interests affect behavior independently of individuals' level of awareness or explicit calculation, economic approaches view interests as subjective, equivalent to consciously-held preferences.

The distinction between individual preferences and economic performance underlies the different logics of micro versus macro economic models of voting behavior. Macro models seek to measure the effects of aggregate economic performance, where economic performance is usually measured at the national rather than sub-national level and the relevant data is *aggregate* in nature (i.e. the observed unit is the country and subsequent measures such as per capita income require assumptions about the unobserved levels and effects of such variables among individuals). The macro approach is frequently applied to political forecasting, where election outcomes are predicted as a function of reduced-form models measuring a key aspect of national economic performance (often combined with aggregate data on presidential popularity or partisanship). The macro approach has yielded powerful insights into the partisan political consequences of economic cycles (e.g. Lewis-Beck, 1988), but as discussed below, the occasional failure of forecasting models coupled with questions about non-economic sources of voters' information raise important questions about the apparent simplicity and transparency of economic voting.

The development of micro-economic approaches has led to important theoretical refinements. A number of these are illustrated in the pioneering work of Fiorina (1981). Responding to persistent findings of low political sophistication and seemingly unreflective behavior on the part of voters, Fiorina develops an economic model of vote choice that distinguishes between the retrospective versus prospective orientations of economic expectations and behavior. Whereas *retrospective* voting involves comparisons between current versus past economic evaluations, *prospective* voting requires comparisons between current evaluations versus expectations about future economic performance. Fiorina argues that voters tend to be more concerned with the outcomes of government policies rather than with the details of policy implementation, and that retrospective voting is the more common orientation found in the U.S. electorate. However, Fiorina further hypothesize that voters may frequently use retrospective evaluations to make economic predictions about the future.

The distinction between retrospective versus prospective evaluations provides analytical leverage for understanding the micro-economic dimensions of political behavior. Indeed, while a key accomplishment of the economic approach is to suggest that "citizens are not fools" (Fiorina, 1981, p. 5), retrospective voting theory fits well with findings about the low levels of information among U.S. voters. More specifically, in the absence of extensive policy information, retrospective voters can be expected to make use of comparisons between past and present economic experiences, thereby explaining why economic conditions leading up to elections can strongly impact their outcomes. Low information levels may thus contribute to retrospective voting, and the evaluations presupposed by the latter can be viewed as a short-cut that simplifies political decision-making (Dalton & Wattenberg, 1993, p. 196).

Political Cultural Approaches

Political cultural theories hypothesize the importance of values or attitudes toward specific policies for understanding voters' alignments. Examples of important values are individualism and egalitarianism; examples of policy attitudes are preferences (or against) anti-discrimination ordinances and the public provision of unemployment insurance.

Past research provides evidence that individuals' adherence to many values thought to be politically-relevant is relatively stable over the life course (Alwin, Cohen & Newcomb, 1991), especially if the latter are the product of childhood socialization, including direct transmission by parents and diffusion from educational and media institutions (Erikson & Tedin, 1995, Chap. 5; Sears et al., 1997). Do differences in the distribution of public support for specific values explain patterns of change and stability in voters' political alignments within specific countries? The application of political cultural theories to explaining cross-national differences are developed in related ways in the influential work of Lipset and Inglehart. For Lipset (1963, 1996), values are diffused and legitimated by social institutions such as schools, churches, and the media, and they subsequently shape voters' national identity as well as their expectations about the policy goals that politicians and government should pursue. According to Lipset, the comparative and historical distinctiveness of U.S. politics (including the absence of a labor party and the existence of the developed world's most successful conservative party), stems from an enduring set of values relating to individualism and an antipathy toward institutional authority (Lipset, 1996; Lipset & Marks, 2000).

Recent work by Inglehart (Inglehart & Baker, 2000) advances a similar claim about the importance of political culture, conceptualizing cross-national differences in values as a function of countries' dominant religious tradition coupled with their level of economic development. In his earlier work, Inglehart (1977, 1990) developed the more limited hypothesis that politically-relevant values stem primarily from individual's past and current experiences of economic scarcity. Nevertheless, both strains of theorizing emphasize the partisan relevance of such values as autonomy and the qualitative dimensions of well-being, and Inglehart (1997, Chap. 8) links growing support for these values to change in voter preferences, including the rise of Green parties and new political cleavages surrounding environmentalism in Western Europe during the 1980s. Although the majority of work on values has focused on the latter as a dependent variable (see Sniderman, 1993 for review), the work of Lipset, Inglehart, and their collaborators illustrates how hypotheses about the behavioral effects of values on behavior can be readily derived.

Moving beyond values, factors relating to public opinion (especially policy preferences for or against specific government policies) have increasingly been applied to voting behavior. Analysts have explored such questions as how changes in public attitudes towards issues of race, gender equality, abortion, and gay and lesbian rights have influenced electoral outcomes (e.g. Abramowitz, 1995a; Alvarez & Nagler, 1998; Brooks, 2000). The macro-level analyses of "public mood" by Erikson and his colleagues (2002, Chap. 7) provides evidence that even relatively small shifts in aggregate opinion (as measured by a unidimensional measurement of mass attitudes across a wide range of issues) will affect electoral outcomes. In *The New American Voter*, Miller and Shanks (1996) develop a hierarchical model of vote choice that asserts that policy-related predispositions have both direct and indirect effects on vote choice (the latter through the impact of such preferences on candidate and party evaluations).

Political cultural influences on voting can be interpreted in similar ways to economic voting, enjoying both retrospective and prospective forms, and requiring a certain level of information on the part of individuals. Accordingly, when political cultural factors exert *no* influence over voting behavior, the explanation may stem from either the absence of the relevant evaluation *or* from the perception that parties do not differ significantly with respect to a specific value or policy. By contrast, evidence of an association between policy attitudes and voting behavior suggest the causal relevance of political culture theory.

Rational Choice as a Meta-Theory

Can causal theories of voting behavior be unified under a larger framework of rational choice? This question has been the focus of a number of recent scholarly controversies, and while too numerous to review in detail (see, e.g. Friedman, 1996; Green & Shapiro, 1994), we suggest an important point of possible scholarly consensus concerning the status of the rational choice paradigm. More specifically, the core assumption of rational choice, that voters act to maximize their utility, can be construed as a useful *meta-theoretical* orientation shared by causal theories of political behavior.

How does rational choice apply to our preceding theories of voting behavior? Each theoretical approach can be construed as specifying a particular source of voters' preferences and thus utility. For instance, the economic approach identifies macro and micro-economic sources of voters' utility, while the political cultural theory focuses on the ways in which voters' preferences stem from their adherence to ideological norms or values. Viewed through the lens of rational choice, theories of voting behavior thus share the common concept of utility-maximizing, or what is sometimes referred to as "goal-oriented" political behavior (Carmines & Huckfeldt, 1996).

However, because rational choice by this definition is compatible with multiple (and potentially limitless) sources of voter utility, it neither rejects nor endorses any *specific* theoretical assumptions about the precise sources of utility that influence the actual behavior of voters and the outcome of elections.[3] It is thus likely, for instance, that specific voters in particular countries and historical eras differ considerably in the extent to which the behavior of some is motivated by perceptions of economic security versus uncertainty, while other members of the electorate are more concerned with supporting parties or candidates they expect to safeguard minority rights or to implement harsher criminal sentencing practices (to name but two examples of specific policy measures).[4]

Taken together, the preceding considerations thus identify a key limitation of rational choice as a meta-theory of voting: only through empirical research can scholars attempt to discover what specific goals and preferences motivate voters in particular national and historical contexts, in turn enabling researchers to adjudicate between competing causal theories of voting behavior. But insofar as scholarly progress in meta-theorizing shares with progress in substantive theorizing the requirement that a new meta-theory represents an improvement over its predecessor, this inclusive specification of rational choice may nevertheless be useful as a guide to formulating and evaluating substantive theories of the mechanisms and conceptions of utility that motivate voters. Indeed, as discussed further below, the well-established finding that voting behavior is not random but instead stems from specific sources of voters' identities, beliefs, or social locations casts doubt on the alternative (and inferior) meta-theory of vote choice as an *irrational* act.[5]

METHODOLOGICAL CONSIDERATIONS IN THE STUDY OF VOTING BEHAVIOR

The study of voting behavior has historically spanned an array of research methods and techniques of analysis. For instance, significant, and in some cases landmark, results have been generated through analysis of archival data on Nazi Party memberships in the 1930s (Brustein, 1996), in-depth interviews with American voters during the early 1960s (Lane, 1962), experiments with the impact on voter reasoning of the emotional tone of campaign advertisements (Ansolabehere & Iyengar, 1995) or the rhetorical strategies of politicians (McGraw, Best & Timpone, 1995), and the increasing application of experimental designs to surveys using computer assisted telephone interviewing (Sniderman & Grob, 1996).

Amidst this plurality of research methods, however, the techniques of survey research have played a central role in the study of voting behavior. Indeed, a significant force in the development of postwar voting behavior research has been innovations in survey research and statistical methods,[6] including systematic efforts of scholars at the University of Michigan to carefully design and disseminate high-quality data that have set a nearly universal standard for electoral research. Of further note is the widespread consensus regarding the utility of quantitative techniques (ranging from early tabular analyses through structural equations, regression models for continuous and categorical dependent variables, time series and cross-sectional panel analyses, and other recent statistical innovations; see Bartels & Brady, 1993 for a review).

Nevertheless, the cumulative character of much of voting behavior research and the scarcity of philosophical warfare concerning methodology should not be construed as indicating an absence of controversies over measurement, the connection of theory to data, or as precluding heated substantive debates (which we discuss following the next section).

Issues in the Connection of Theory to Data

Taken at face value, several core assumptions of *The American Voter*, such as that voters are politically unsophisticated, possess extremely low levels of information, and exhibit randomness in responses to survey questions about policy attitudes implies a simple yet meaningful statistical model: political behavior is predicted as a function of a random error term and perhaps idiosyncratic candidate evaluations, but little else. In this model, covariates measuring more substantive factors such as individuals' policy preferences regarding their desired level of government provision are expected to have little or no significant impact on voting behavior. Evaluating the fit of such a model to data is informative, insofar as a poor fit is potentially indicative of the inability of the assumed theory to capture systematic sources of behavioral differences between individual voters.

In the face of potentially disconfirming evidence, theories of voter randomness can nevertheless be revised to yield an alternative version of the theory. More specifically, in keeping with the social psychological approach discussed earlier in this paper, an important further contribution of *The American Voter* was encapsulated in the assumption that much of the behavioral variation among voters is a product of partisan predispositions that endure over the adult life course. This assumption is readily embedded in a statistical model that predicts vote choice as a function of partisanship. Assuming the exogeneity of partisanship, subsequent models can fruitfully compare the respective effects on voting of partisanship versus covariates measuring factors specified by competing theories.

The preceding example is instructive in demonstrating how the specification of a statistical model compels both supporters and critics of a specific theory to confront its core assumptions. However, researchers who reject causal assumptions about partisanship as truly exogenous will tend to question whether a large coefficient estimate establishes sufficient grounds for this assumption, leading to the utility of time series and cross sectional panel analyses that have furthered research on party identification by suggesting its endogeneity (Franklin, 1992; MacKuen et al., 1988; Niemi & Jennings, 1991).

This simple regression set-up described in reference to partisanship is extremely common in the study of voting behavior. Regardless of whether party identification is included as a covariate, one common practice is to compare the size or significance of coefficients, where the latter represent the estimated effects of theoretically-relevant variables. A further comparison involves path-analytic calculation of total versus direct effects, with the total effects derived from a reduced-form model including a sub-set of covariates assumed to affect (without themselves being affected by) all endogenous variables.

A feature common to many studies that seek to develop historical comparisons is the use of multiple cross-sectional surveys. Such data enable the effects of survey year to be controlled. The latter can be interpreted as period effects common to all voters, and when coefficients for other factors are estimated, the resultant change in period effects can be used in hypothesis-testing, providing information about the extent to which such factors explain aggregate patterns of change in the outcome of elections.[7]

The analysis of repeated cross-sectional surveys further enables the estimation of interaction effects involving survey year and other covariates. A substantial amount of scholarly commentary implies the presence of such interactions, where the partisan political effects of factors such as class are assumed to themselves change over time. When there are grounds for anticipating such interactions, the comparison between a main effects model and an alternative model including interactions between survey year and a specific covariate (or multiple covariates) is informative. Furthermore, because the structure of the interrelationship between time and a specific factor is generally unknown, comparisons between competing interaction models that assume linear versus non-linear interaction effects can provide further relevant information.

The possibility of interactions involving time suggest a final methodological consideration in the analysis of political change. More specifically, the distinction between levels versus effects of a specific covariate anticipates two different scenarios of political change. When the *level* of a causally-relevant factor behind vote choice changes monotonically, we can expect such changes to deliver a consistent advantage to a specific party or party family (as, for example, if a declining trend in the proportion of the electorate employed in manual occupations lowers the probability of a left party victory). However, political change can also occur if the political-behavioral effects of a specific covariate itself changes over time (holding constant the level of the latter). Armed with this distinction, researchers may fruitfully gauge the actual ways in which different factors behind vote choice may influence the outcome of elections over time and across different national contexts.

RECENT DEBATES

The Class Cleavage

Much recent political-sociological interest in voting has been prompted by questions about the interrelationship between class and voting behavior, and about the specific possibility that the political-behavioral effects of class have experienced a universal decline in Western democracies. However, despite widespread assertions of the declining political relevance of class (Clark, Lipset & Rempel, 1993; Franklin, Mackie & Valen, 1992; see Manza, Hout & Brooks, 1995; for a review), subsequent research has provided no consistent support for this hypothesis (Evans, 1999b, 2000), suggesting a more complicated pattern of country-specific trends and cross-national differences.

Reassertions of class decline (e.g. Abramson, Aldrich, & Rohde, 1999, Chap. 5; Inglehart, 1997, Chap. 8) frequently rely upon measures of class and political behavior whose flaws have been known since the mid-1980s (Evans,

1999b; Heath et al., 1991; Heath, Jowell & Curtice, 1985; Manza et al., 1995). Studies reporting global decline often rely on dichotomous measures of either class (manual versus non-manual workers) or voting behavior (left versus right party support).[8] The reliance on out-dated measures of class can be a source of biased inferences, since such measures make it impossible to observe either heterogeneous class alignments or trends *within* "manual" and "non-manual" categories. One illuminating example of this problem stems from findings about the economic and political heterogeneity of the middle classes in capitalist democracies (Brooks & Manza, 1997a, b; Gerteis, 1998; Kriesi, 1998; Wright, 1997).

The clearest evidence to date of substantial decline in the class cleavage is in Scandinavia and the U.S. In a careful analysis of Norwegian Election Studies data, Ringdal and Hines (1999) use a multi-category measure of party support and a version of the Erikson-Goldthorpe class scheme (see e.g. Erikson & Goldthorpe, 1992, Chap. 2) to evaluate hypotheses about change in the political-behavioral effects of class. The class cleavage in Norway has declined in magnitude from the 1950s, leaving contemporary levels of Norwegian class voting to resemble the lower levels found on the European continent.

In the U.S., reports of fluctuation without decline through 1992 (Hout et al., 1995) have been supplanted by subsequent findings of declining class voting. Manza and Brooks (1999b, Chap. 3) use a multi-category class scheme and estimates derived from adjudicating between competing models, reporting that recent reductions in the level of support for Democratic candidates among nonskilled workers contributed to an approximately one-third reduction in the magnitude of the overall class cleavage since the 1970s. Weakliem and Heath (1999) use a slightly different class scheme and analyze Gallup and General Social Survey data to test hypotheses about long-term trends in U.S. class voting since the 1930s. They find evidence of declining magnitude of the class cleavage, including *earlier* declining trends between the 1930s and 1950s.

Scholarly assumptions about the centrality of class to British politics informs a lively debate concerning the class cleavage. Early research by Heath et al. (1991) adjudicated competing models of British Election Studies data from 1964 through 1987, reporting a pattern of aggregate change with no net decline in the class cleavage. More recently, Goldthorpe (1999, pp. 81–82) reports significantly lower levels of class voting in 1997, while Nieuwbeerta, Brooks and Manza (2002) find evidence of a decline in British class voting that was concentrated between 1970 and 1980. Although they analyze a different class scheme than these other researchers, Weakliem and Heath's (1999) analysis of election data from the 1930s suggests that British class voting was at its highest point in 1960 (preceded by lower levels in the 1930s and 1940s), shedding further, if complicating, light on this new generation of research.

A further perspective on the class cleavage in voting behavior is offered by recent studies of new democracies in Russia and Eastern Europe. Analyzing a 5-category class scheme and survey data for 1993, 1995, and 1996, Evans and Whitefield (1999) conclude that class differences in Russian presidential voting are both substantial and reflective of emerging ideological differences in attitudes toward market institutions. These findings fit well with Gerber's (2000) analysis of a 1996 survey which provides evidence that divergent economic ideologies lead to different patterns of Russian voter alignments. Taken together, these studies suggest the relevance of further cross-national investigations that evaluate hypotheses about the linkage between class and changes in economic and political institutions.

Whither research on the class cleavage? Sociologists probably need little prompting to continue debates concerning decline, realignment, and stability in the political-behavioral effects of class. However, while this attention has advanced debates and helped to stimulate renewed sociological interest in voting behavior, there are several reasons why a disproportionate focus by political sociologists on the class cleavage may produce diminishing intellectual returns in the immediate future.

First, there are strong theoretical grounds for taking as seriously other causal factors behind voting behavior. Emerging debates concerning such issues as the political influence of religion or new cleavages based on ideology raise important and unanswered questions that have little bearing on class voting research as it has been conceived up to this point. Indeed, evidence is steadily accumulating that social class is but one (and by no means typically the major) source of voter alignments or election outcomes within capitalist democracies. For example, a recent study of class voting within six democracies (Nieuwbeerta et al., 2002) finds that the religious cleavage was *larger* than the class cleavage in two countries in the 1990s, while being comparable to the class cleavage in three countries and smaller than the class cleavage in only one country. On average, class-based differences in the probability of support for one of a pair of party families during the 1990s was approximately 0.10. While such differences are non-trivial, they tend to be smaller than such alternative sources of voter alignments as race or political ideology in the U.S. (cf. Brooks, 2000).

The Religious Cleavage

The influence of religion on political behavior has been the focus of two important strains of research during the past ten years (Manza & Wright, 2002). The first of these has sought to evaluate the hypothesis that the overall effect of religious group memberships on voting behavior has declined over time (Dalton &

Wattenberg, 1993, pp. 199–200), possibly due to receding denominational tensions or the rising importance of other aspects of voters' identities. With levels of religious participation and identification near the highest among Western democracies, the U.S. has been the focus of this research, and paralleling debates over the class cleavage, dichotomous measures of Protestant versus Catholic voting patterns (e.g. Abramson et al., 1999, p. 103) have given way to more sophisticated typologies that seek to capture the major differences that place American Protestants into distinct denominational families.

Using a 7-category scheme that classifies Protestants into liberal, moderate, and conservative categories (and separately identifying Catholics, seculars, Jews, and members of other religious traditions), Manza and Brooks (1997) analyzed National Election Studies data for presidential elections through 1992, finding evidence that while conservative Protestants showed little change in their Republican alignment since the 1960s, liberal Protestants moved from a strong Republican alignment to a position mid-way between the two parties. While our earlier work suggested a modest decline in the magnitude of the religious cleavage, the overall impact of religion on U.S. political behavior was nevertheless substantial. Indeed, the magnitude of the religion cleavage was nearly twice as large as that of the class cleavage during the 1990s (Manza & Brooks, 1999b, Chap. 8), and larger than estimates derived from dichotomous measures.

A recent study by Layman (2001) disputes a number of these findings, analyzing National Elections Studies data for both voting behavior and partisanship in presidential and mid-term election years, and using a number of multi-category schemes that classify Protestant into evangelical, mainline, and Black Protestant traditions. Layman reports evidence of more extensive changes in religion-based voter alignments, arguing that evangelicals, mainline Protestants, and Catholics have become significantly more Republican in their partisanship and voting behavior since the 1970s. However, Layman presents estimates from an analysis that considers only a single statistical model.

More recently, we have developed an updated analysis of religious group membership and vote choice and partisanship in mid-term and presidential elections from 1972 through 2000 (Brooks & Manza, 2002), applying a new typology of religious group memberships developed by Steensland et al. (2000).[9] This analysis corroborates earlier findings, suggesting far less group-specific change in voting behavior than reported by Layman. But our analyses of partisanship are consistent with Layman's results for Catholics and evangelical Protestants. The existence of more extensive changes in party identification than in actual vote choice raises intriguing questions about the complexity of religion-based political alignments, while suggesting a partisan basis for anticipating further shifts in political behavior.

A second strain of research has investigated the widely-debated influence of the Christian Right on voters during the 1980s and 1990s (Woodberry & Smith, 1998). Initial reports from the 1980s suggested little influence: the Moral Majority and its policy positions were found to be unpopular (Buell & Sigelman, 1985); religion-based beliefs suggested more complexity than consistent polarization (Davis & Robinson, 1996); and claims about growing hostilities between orthodox religionists and modernists were largely without empirical foundation (Williams, 1997). However, the finer-grained analyses reported in several recent studies suggest evidence of important changes.

Focusing on evangelicals, Green and his colleagues (Green, Kellstedt, Smidt & Guth, 1988) and Sears and Valentino (2002) present evidence linking evangelicals to a Republican realignment in the South. Analyzing data from a 1996 survey, Regnerus, Sikkink and Smith (1999) report that 20% of respondents reported using information provided by Christian Right organizations, including not only evangelicals but devout Catholics. Using data from National Election Studies surveys, Brooks (2002) finds that level of concern with family decline had a growing effect on vote choice in the 1980s and early 1990s. The concentration of family decline concern among evangelical Protestants and the particularly large effects of church attendance for this group suggests that Christian Right influence over evangelical ministers has diffused to the laity (Brooks, 2002).

Although still developing, the two preceding strains of research contribute to, and refine, debates concerning the partisan political effects of religion. Of particular note, studies of religion and political behavior usefully identify distinct processes of religious influence, ranging from denominational memberships, commitment to religious doctrine, and exposure to congregation-based networks (Sherkat & Ellison, 1999; Wald, Owen & Hill, 1988). Taken as a whole, this literature suggests the continuing if complicated effects of religion factors on voting behavior in the U.S.

The Complexity of Economic Voting

The substantial effects of economic factors on voting behavior are well-documented and widely acknowledged. Indeed, the magnitude of these effects have led some analysts to deliberately ignore non-economic factors in favor of causal approaches based solely upon measures of economic performance coupled with partisanship or presidential popularity (Lewis-Beck & Rice, 1992). One of the most widely-repeated findings of political behavior research is that incumbent parties' candidates are difficult to unseat in periods of prosperity but suffer disproportionately during recessions (Dalton & Wattenberg, 1993).

Whereas positive economic evaluations provide reasons to support a political incumbent, negative evaluations can lead to support for challengers. While the logic of this type of retrospective voting appears straightforward, an important strain of subsequent research has raised far-reaching questions about the proper interpretation and causal origins of economic voting.

A key source of complexity relates to the specific causal mechanisms that underlie such phenomena as anti-incumbent voting. Kiewiet's research (1983) illustrates the importance of conceptualizing and measuring the variable target of economic evaluations: voters' evaluations are *egocentric* when they involve perceptions of economic conditions experienced by an individual; voters' evaluations are *sociotropic* when they involve perceptions of level of *national* economic prosperity. Not only can the distribution of egocentric and sociotropic evaluations diverge, studies within this tradition find *larger* political-behavioral effects of sociotropic evaluations (Kinder & Kiewiet, 1981). In contrast to pocketbook models of voting, individuals appear to weigh more heavily their satisfaction with national rather than personal economic performance when deciding whether to support a political incumbent versus a challenger.

The importance of sociotropic evaluations further suggests the dependence of economic voting upon individuals' level of information about the national economy. This line of reasoning in turn raises critical questions about causal mechanisms behind voters' level of information and their perceptions of national economic performance. For instance, might non-economic factors and institutions such as the media ultimately be behind much of the direction and partisan effects of sociotropic voting?

A provocative answer to this question is provided by Hetherington (1996), who presents evidence that consistently negative reporting on the performance of the American economy before the 1992 presidential election fueled negative economic perceptions. While the subsequent contribution of economic evaluations to the defeat of Republican incumbent George Bush is well-known (Alvarez & Nagler, 1995), the mediocre performance of macro-economic forecasting models coupled with Hetherington's findings regarding media influence suggest that the partisan consequences of retrospective economic voting can be strongly shaped by the content of media coverage.[10]

Taken in summary, this line of research suggests the complexity and diversity of economic voting. Rather than treating economic factors as a single factor, distinctions between retrospective versus prospective, and sociotropic versus egocentric voting, give rise to a rich typology of economically-motivated behaviors. The literature further suggests that while the predictive power of macro-economic models for election outcomes is considerable, the latter represent incomplete explanations in the absence of measures of specific individual-level mechanisms or analyses of the role of the media in translating the economic environment into actual political behavior.

What type of research on economic voting is likely to stimulate interest and subsequent research on the part of political sociologists? Three recent studies by sociologists illustrate contributions to better understanding the causal mechanisms that link macro-economic conditions to political behavior. In an analysis of aggregate data on partisanship and economic performance, Haynes and Jacobs (1994) find that the effects of unemployment and inflation vary across time periods of Democratic versus Republican control of the presidency. For instance, while increased inflation during Republican presidencies results in a shift toward Democratic identification, rising inflation during a Democratic presidency has *no* effect on party identification. Although Haynes and Jacobs cannot directly measure micro-economic attitudes using their ecological data, their findings of interactions between time periods and macro-economic variables suggest the presence of stable beliefs about which party better addresses specific economic problems.

While one of most popular measures of economic interests is income, little work has attempted to measure the political effects of income over time using individual-level data, and a recent study by Brooks and Brady (1999) investigates the type of preferences that mediate the effects of income. Analyzing National Election Studies data from 1952 through 1996, Brooks and Brady find evidence that income has stable partisan effects, with higher income levels disposing voters to favor Republican over Democratic candidates *regardless* of which party controls the presidency. Further analyses suggest that the partisan effects of income are mediated primarily by policy evaluations, especially individuals' level of support for federal activism and welfare state provision. These findings shed additional light on the reasons why rising affluence between 1952 and 1972 had disproportionate political benefits for the Republican Party (Brooks & Brady, 1999, pp. 1361–1362).

The concept of economic voting can also be applied to test hypotheses about what economic factors explain the political behavior or alignment of specific groups. This type of application is pursued by Weakliem and Heath (1994), who analyze data from the 1987 British Election Study to test hypotheses about the sources of class differences in voting behavior. Contrary to initial expectations, Weakliem and Heath find that a sizable portion of class differences remain after controlling for income and economic policy preferences, suggesting the operation of unmeasured factors such as social networks in generating British class voting during the 1980s. Because even findings about the *non*-effects of economic factors can thus be informative, economic variables are useful for analyzing change in the voting behavior of specific groups or with respect to the electorate as a whole.

The Emergence of New Ideological Cleavages

Since the discovery during the 1980s of more extensive levels of issue voting than anticipated by the classic *American Voter* study (Campbell et al., 1960), scholars have anticipated the likelihood of new sources of voter alignments (e.g. Clark & Hoffman-Martinot, 1998; Inglehart, 1990; Schafer, 1991). Significantly extending the focus of past research on social cleavages, the implicit assumption of a strain of recent work is that conflicts involving values or normative preferences can form the basis for partisan cleavages. To express this point another way, so long as differential levels of support for specific values are enduring and of causal relevance to individual's vote choice or partisanship, the latter qualify as cleavages that provide structure and sometimes also pressure for change within a polity. Theoretically, ideological cleavages are further noteworthy in that they tend to exist separately from social cleavages or stratification factors, being grounded instead in childhood or adult socialization effects involving individuals' level of support for specific doctrines or policy ideas.

Partisan conflicts over abortion in the U.S. exemplify a relatively novel ideological cleavage. Abramowitz (1995a) analyzes data from the (1992) National Election Survey, reporting that abortion attitudes had a larger effect on vote choice than such other policy issues as welfare, the (1991) Gulf War, and the economy. Providing a longer historical perspective, Adams (1997) analyzes roll call votes in the U.S. Congress with General Social Survey data, finding evidence that elite and mass polarization grew from low levels during the early 1970s to much higher levels by the mid-1990s (with Democratic but not Republican identifiers and politicians becoming more pro-choice over time).

Brooks (2000) presents evidence for the emergence of new cleavages surrounding issues relating to the civil rights of women, African Americans, and gays and lesbians. While attitudes toward women's rights had virtually no effect on presidential vote choice in the early 1970s, their corresponding effects in the 1990s were substantial, suggesting the growing partisan relevance of women's rights issues and voters' capacity to perceive differences between the major parties' candidates with respect to this issue. Haeberle (1999) focuses on the politicization of conflicts over gay and lesbian rights in the 1990s, presenting further evidence that attitudes toward homosexuality affect both voting behavior and partisanship.

The role of racial attitudes and ideologies in structuring other kinds of political preferences and behaviors, even in the post-Civil Rights era, has generated a rapidly expanding literature (see Edsall & Edsall, 1991; Mendelberg, 2001; Sears et al., 2000; cf. Manza, 2000). Much of the focus in the race politics literature has been to examine how racial attitudes relate to group conflict and policy attitudes, such as towards affirmative action or welfare (e.g. Gilens, 1999; Sniderman &

Carmines, 1997), with research on voting behavior receiving far less attention (but cf. Kinder & Sanders, 1996, Chap. 8; Lawrence, 1997, Chap. 4; Mendelberg, 2001, Chap. 3). Some of the most interesting work on the impact of racial attitudes examines the interaction between local context, racial attitudes, and behaviors, including voting (e.g. Clark, 1994; Giles & Buckner, 1993; Giles & Hertz, 1994; Oliver & Mendelberg, 2000; Taylor, 2000). Explorations of the electoral impact of racial ideologies is, however, still fairly underdeveloped; as scholarship in this area develops in the future, further work on its political effects needs to be undertaken.

A further strain of research has taken as its point of departure Inglehart's thesis (1990) that the rise of postmaterialism affects political behavior and party conflict in Western democracies. Analyzing repeated cross-sectional surveys for 14 West European countries, Knutsen (1995) reports that while individuals' level of support for postmaterial values have substantial effects on party choice, these effects appear relatively stable since the 1970s. Focusing on the U.S., Carmines and Layman (1997) find that postmaterialist values affect voting behavior indirectly (through their influence on attitudes toward national defense and race), while being uncorrelated with attitudes toward abortion and sexuality, suggesting that the material versus postmaterial cleavage is largely independent of newer partisan conflicts (cf. Brooks & Manza, 1994).

While research on new ideological cleavages is still at a relatively early stage of development, the magnitude of cleavages surrounding issues relating to race or individual rights in the U.S. is likely to provide incentive for additional research. A further question raised by recent studies concerns the causal origins of ideological cleavages. While one explanation is that ideological cleavages are the consequences of elites' strategic action (Adams, 1997; Carmines & Stimson, 1989), a contrasting explanation is that ideological cleavages are the product of cohort-specific socialization, in which new generations' experience with economic scarcity or social change disposes individuals to pursue novel and politically-relevant goals (Dalton, Beck & Flanagan, 1984; Inglehart, 1990). These competing views have not yet evolved into a full-blown debate, but which is ultimately superior (or inferior to a third interpretation) represents a viable issue for further research.

Explaining Aggregate-Level Political Change

Of the five major debates we consider, the explanation of electorate-wide political change is the least developed within political sociology. Most theory and research to date has focused on the *individual-level* of analysis, investigating the causal sources of political alignments among individual voters (or groups of voters).

However, it is the outcome of elections, and especially over-time trends in these outcomes, that affect public policy by sending signals about voters' preferences or altering which party or coalition controls government. For these reasons, the explanation of *aggregate-level* political change represents a critical challenge in the study of voting behavior.

How should recent patterns of aggregate political change be explained? One of the most common interpretations of U.S. political change points to the central role played by economic factors in explaining election outcomes. For instance, results of several studies suggest that discontent with the national economy was the single largest factor behind Democrat Bill Clinton's (1992) election (Alvarez & Nagler, 1995; Weisberg & Kimball, 1995), while subsequently higher levels of economic satisfaction fueled Clinton's re-election in (1996) (Alvarez & Nagler, 1998; Pomper, 1997). These studies suggest that voters in the 1990s were performance-oriented, blaming incumbent presidents during periods of economic downturn and rewarding those presiding over periods of growth *without* extrapolating from these evaluations to ideological assessments of the two parties' approaches to economic policy.

Recalling the complexity of economic voting discussed earlier, other scholars have linked economic forces to longer-term factors whose effects consistently benefit one political party (regardless of which party controls the Presidency or Congress). Brooks and Brady's (1999) analysis of National Election Study data for twelve presidential elections finds that higher income levels consistently dispose voters to favor Republican over Democratic candidates because income directly shapes voters' level of support for welfare state provisions and federal activism.

Changes in policy preferences are another important candidate for explaining aggregate political change, given the likelihood that much of the effects of public opinion trends on national policy making are mediated through the outcome of elections (Erikson, MacKuen & Stimson, 2002, Chap. 7; see also Burstein, 1998). Focusing on the early 1980s, Shanks and Miller (1991) report that a conservative shift in voters' policy preferences contributed to the 1980 election of Ronald Reagan, while having less of an impact on his (1984) re-election. Analyzing presidential elections between (1972) and (1996), Brooks (2000) reports that while liberal trends in rights-based attitudes by themselves benefited Democratic candidates, their aggregate effects on elections were offset by the cumulative advantages that other ideological and economic factors conferred on Republican candidates. Focusing on recent elections, Abramowitz and his colleagues (Abramowitz, 1994, 1995b; Abramowitz & Saunders, 1998) develop a case for an emerging Republican realignment, reporting that declining aggregate support for the welfare state coupled with growing conservative identification explain such outcomes as the (1994) mid-term congressional election.

Applications of a social structural approach posit a different causal factor as contributing to aggregate political change: the changing demographic composition of Democratic versus Republican Party support. For example, Beck (1988) argues that the decline of the New Deal coalition (composed of religious minorities, organized labor, and white Southerners) provided important advantages to the Republican Party during the 1980s (see also Lawrence, 1997). Investigating region and religion, J. Green et al. (1998) argue that an evangelical political realignment has produced a single-party (Republican) South, a development that they interpret as facilitating partisan change in the U.S. as a whole. Other analysts have noted such demographic trends as the rapidly growing proportion of Hispanics in the electorate, a trend which may eventually provide an advantage to the Democrats (Manza & Brooks, 1999a, b, Chap. 10). While the effects of these compositional changes on the actual outcome of elections is not directly estimated, the individual-level effects of social structural variables coupled with the tendency for their marginal distributions to shift monotonically suggest the utility of further tests of these hypotheses.

Taken as a whole, the preceding studies establish an important point of scholarly agreement: aggregate political change in the U.S. is rooted not only in short-term factors relating to campaigns or the economic context of an election, but also in long-term factors such as voters' policy preferences. An unresolved question, however, regards the precise causal weight of such factors as economic evaluations, welfare state preferences, and demographic change. And recalling earlier debates over political change in the 1980s (Shafer, 1991), the re-emergence of claims political realignment in the 1990s represents a new focus of debate. Taken in summary, these controversies are likely to stimulate additional analyses, providing scholars with opportunities for further research.

FUTURE DIRECTIONS IN VOTING BEHAVIOR RESEARCH

Since the early 1990s, the study of voting has enjoyed an intellectual renaissance, re-emerging as an important focus and complement to other fields of research within contemporary political sociology. Three key considerations underlie the sociological significance of voting behavior in national elections. First, related research provides accumulating evidence that elections are a powerful and proximate cause of national-level policy making and the ongoing evolution of welfare states. Second, major social and ideological conflicts involving such established cleavages as race, class, and religious doctrine influence, and in turn frequently become institutionalized, by reference to parallel patterns of political party conflict. Third, elections and party conflict can provide significant opportunities to social movement challengers to make policy-relevant claims that, if successful, can facilitate the emergence of new political or societal cleavages. Sociological research on voting behavior is increasingly cognizant of these considerations, and the implied linkages between voting, states, parties, and social groups suggests a broad relevance to political sociologists, scholars of stratification, and analysts of social movements, media, and culture.

In this section, we provide a further perspective on the accomplishments of political-sociological work on voting by examining what we view as two notable dead-ends suggested by our earlier discussion. Far from representing bad news, however, such unproductive avenues of research and debate provide an instructive example of scholarly progress, while reaffirming the intrinsically pluralistic character of theories and debates concerning voting behavior. Guided by these considerations, we conclude by identifying four lines of further inquiry that have the potential to advance research.

The End of Minimalist Views of Voting Behavior

When viewed from the historical perspective of mid-20th century theory and research, the most dramatic intellectual development of the past two decades has been the substantial revision and even rejection of the minimalist portrait of mass political behavior developed by Campbell and his colleagues' (1960) seminal study, *The American Voter*.[11] To be sure, the causal significance that Campbell et al. unearthed with respect to partisanship remains at the center of a significant portion of research, especially as exemplified in studies guided by the social psychological approach. Likewise, the Michigan scholars' seminal findings of low levels of political information are not themselves directly in doubt (Delli Carpini & Keeter, 1996; Smith, 1989).

However, a critical thrust of the past generation of research is that voters' level of information by itself does not prevent either effective political decision-making or goal-oriented behavior; instead, voters implicitly rely on the cues provided by their social locations, retrospective evaluations, and ideological biases (Ferejohn & Kuklinski, 1990; Lupia, McCubbins & Popkin, 2000; Sniderman, Brody & Tetlock, 1991). Moreover, the *embeddedness* of voters within social structures, communicative networks, and ideological identities appears to be a central feature of electoral politics within actually-existing democracies. The growing acknowledgment by researchers of the numerous and long-term sources of voter alignments and political change beyond party identification has moved the field beyond the minimalist interpretation's inferences about citizens' low capacity for issue voting and its subtle implications of voter randomness.[12] Taken as a whole, then, the last generation of research has provided compelling evidence for more structure and coherence in voting behavior than the minimalist view can readily accommodate.

The rejection of minimalism enables richer and more realistic theories of voting behavior to guide empirical investigations, and contemporary research can be interpreted as attempting to systematically sort out the specific causal factors and institutional conditions that generate voter alignments. The re-emergence of sustained research and interest by political sociologists on voting behavior has coincided with the maturation of these scholarly trends. Political sociologists have contributed to each of the five major debates discussed in this paper, providing notable findings about country-specific and comparative trends in class voting (Evans & Whitefield, 1999; Gerber, 2000; Goldthorpe, 1999; Manza & Brooks, 1999a; Nieuwbeerta et al., 2002; Weakliem & Heath, 1999); the political influence of religion (Brooks, 2002; Manza & Brooks, 1997; Regnerus et al., 1999; Steensland et al., 2000; Woodberry & Smith, 1998); the interrelationship of economic factors and political behavior (Brooks & Brady, 1999; Haynes & Jacobs, 1994; Weakliem & Heath, 1994); and the importance of new partisan cleavages and other sources of aggregate-level political change (Brooks, 2000; Clark, 1994; Evans, Heath & Lalljee, 1996; Heath et al., 1991). Complementing their substantive merits, these studies have contributed further by updating theories of voting behavior to explain the operation of partisan alignments that stem from social group factors, economic evaluations, and ideologically-based preferences.

Sociological Theories of Voting Behavior

A persistent tendency within some contemporary work is to equate sociological research on politics with the social structural approach (Dalton & Wattenberg, 1993). This tendency might initially be explained away by virtue of the traditional centrality of stratification research within U.S. sociology, and also by the focus of much past research on class and other social cleavages. Nevertheless, the equation of the social structural approach with sociological research on political behavior appears to sometimes also be motivated by the goal of casting political sociology as deterministic or monocausal in its assumptions.

Our review suggests that this characterization would ultimately be misleading. In this context, it is particularly useful to highlight the sociological content of both the political cultural and social psychological approaches. As evident in classics such as Lipset's *Political Man* (1981, 1960), a causal focus on nation-specific values and patterns of group identification has always been central to sociological interpretations of politics. And as discussed with respect to recent work on new cleavages, a key thematic finding is the large individual- and aggregate-level effects of ideological cleavages (e.g. Abramowitz & Saunders, 1998; Brooks, 2000). Contemporary political-sociological work is thus best viewed as encompassing the same range of heterogeneous theorizing as adjoining fields within political science.

This discussion further suggests the artificiality of searching for one specifically "sociological" theory of voting behavior. Acknowledging the plurality of sociological approaches has beneficial consequences for political sociologists interested in voting behavior, underscoring the importance of questions and controversies associated with different theoretical perspectives, and opening up potentially fruitful opportunities for subsequent research. Given renewed interest in voting behavior by sociologists during the past 15 years, we caution against defining the heterogeneous field of political behavior in such a way that imposes artificial limits on the type of theoretical approach or questions pursued in subsequent research.

Further Directions

Our emphasis on the cumulative yet *plural* character of theoretical approaches and scholarly debates concerning voting behavior implies that there are multiple strains of research that might be productively developed in future work. Indeed, as should be clear from our earlier discussion, while the five major debates we reviewed suggest important shifts of direction and specific points of emerging consensus, none admits of wholesale resolution, and new findings have raised further questions and controversies. We thus conclude our review by identifying four further avenues of potentially significant research, three of which are closely connected to past debates, while the fourth suggests a more novel extension of voting behavior research.

A first line of research relates to the social structural approach and past debates concerning the historical evolution and possible decline of the class cleavage. From their inception, debates over the interrelationship between social class and political party conflict have involved theories that generalize from specific countries to capitalist democracies as a whole, focusing not only on class but on other cleavages defined by enduring patterns of inequality (Lipset, 1981, 1960). While the cross-national dimensions of the class cleavage are only now starting to emerge (e.g. Evans & Whitefield, 1999; Weakliem, 1999; Weakliem & Heath, 1999), historical and comparative analyses of other social cleavages such as gender remain relatively rare (Nieuwbeerta et al., 2002).

In this context, one hypothesis which merits evaluation is that the partisan alignment of women in Scandinavia has been central to the electoral success of the Swedish Social Democrats (Huber & Stephens, 2001). Given the centrality of gender to the Anglo American democracies (O'Connor, Orloff & Shaver, 1999), the level and effects of gender inequalities within North America, Britain, and Australasia could also be productively pursued in further research. Such research is likely to stimulate productive scholarly debates. Indeed, a potentially fruitful means of theorizing gender cleavages is to contrast state- versus society-centered approaches: whereas a state-centered approach suggests gender-based political alignments are shaped by policy feedback, a societal approach suggests the *prior* relevance of gender cleavages to elections and national policies.

In general, the limited amount of research to date on such cleavages as gender and class suggests the importance of national context and thus the challenge of reformulating cleavage theories to properly account for unmeasured factors associated with country location. Further research may be able to take advantage of the greater availability of high-quality data to develop comparisons over time, across countries, and between specific social cleavages to better understand the partisan political effects of stratification, and also the degree to which the latter complement or interact with institutional factors.

A second line of further research that involves a comparative dimension builds from debates over the religion cleavage. Given the organizational strength and durability of religion in the U.S., it is perhaps not surprising that the growing and increasingly sophisticated literature on religious factors and electoral politics has had a predominantly American focus. Given this orientation, further research might productively develop cross-national comparisons to evaluate the re-emergence of debates concerning U.S. exceptionalism (Lipset, 1996). Coming from a different perspective, new strains of research on Western Europe provide evidence that cross-national trends in religious participation are considerably more complicated than anticipated by secularization or market-based theories (Chaves & Gorski, 2001), raising questions about how country-specific patterns of religious change may relate to aggregate or individual-level political change.

Further, because religion often involves meaning systems that persist beyond individual's current levels of church attendance, the linkages between institutional participation and voters' identities may prove more complicated than initially expected. Indeed, if the ideological legacies of different religious traditions endures despite considerable religious-organizational change or even decline, such processes may underlie contemporary patterns of cultural conflict between as well as within the developed democracies.

Complementing this line of discussion, the political cultural and economic approaches suggest that ideological and economic factors merit further investigation. With respect to between-country comparisons, this third line of research may be facilitated by the increased availability of appropriate data sources for comparative political research. While the development and availability of comparable measures of such factors across countries represents a non-trivial challenge, a useful starting point provided by the economic approach is household or individual income (Hibbs, 1987), and factors suggested by political cultural research (Lipset, 1996; Sears & Valentino, 2002) include welfare state attitudes, and measures of racism or anti-immigrant attitudes. Building from research on new cleavages in U.S. politics discussed earlier (e.g. Abramowitz, 1995a; Abramowitz & Saunders, 1998; Adams, 1997; Brooks, 2000, 2002), the historical dimension of within-country analysis suggests considerable opportunities for theoretically-relevant research.[13] Likewise, the effects of religious traditions as a source of partisan values (Inglehart & Baker, 2000) merit further consideration as a potential means of understanding partisan political conflicts involving nationalism, individualism, and family institutions. Given the small-to-intermediate levels of class voting discovered in most democracies to date, broadening political-sociological research on voting to analyze factors of this sort represents a particularly timely task for future research.

A fourth and final avenue of further research stems from controversies concerning the trajectories and causes of welfare state retrenchment in the contemporary era. It should be emphasized that both the actual extent of, and causal mechanisms behind, welfare state downsizing or the adoption of market-oriented policies are the subject of unresolved debates. While one possibility is that retrenchment is an extension of established cleavages surrounding policy making (Zylan & Soule, 2000), another view is that these conflicts represent a fundamental transformation involving novel issues and constituencies (Pierson, 1996), while a third interpretation emphasizes the interplay between historical contingency and path dependency in explaining specific policy struggles (Skocpol, 1996). Nevertheless, precisely because this literature is in a formative stage and relates to ongoing processes, political sociologists seeking to develop connections between voting behavior and welfare state research may be able to introduce and subsequently answer far-reaching questions about the possible role of elections (and prior processes of economic and ideological change) in generating pressures for or against policy retrenchment. By addressing such issues, further work might accordingly contribute to the growing body of research concerning the linkages between electoral processes and the historical origins and ongoing development of national political institutions.

NOTES

1. For important exceptions, see Hamilton (1972), Knoke (1976), and Form (1985).
2. Another influential, strand of social psychological research on group identities – more often applied to explaining attitudes than voting behavior – that is worth noting here,

although we do not have the space to consider it in detail is research on racial, gender, or other kinds of symbolic group attachments. For further discussion with references to this literature, see Manza and Brooks (1999b, pp. 17–19).

3. Using as an example scholarly controversies concerning the explanation of Republican Party advantage in the 1980s, an economic interpretation might emphasize voters' negative assessments of the incumbent Democratic president during the late 1970s, while a political-cultural interpretation might identify voters' shifting preferences for such normative goals as a smaller federal government as disproportionately benefiting Republican candidates. Because both explanations are consistent with the rational choice approach (e.g. that voters expected to receive greater utility from Republican candidates), this meta-theoretical assumption cannot distinguish the underlying theoretical disagreement about the precise causal sources of U.S. voters' preferences in the 1980s.

4. We emphasize that rational choice applications to understanding political behavior should thus not be conflated with "pocketbook" or egoistic models of vote choice, given the inclusive definition of utility increasingly endorsed by rational choice scholars. See, e.g. Fiorina (1990) for an instructive formulation of rational choice approaches to the (otherwise intractable) problem of explaining voter turnout which assume that voters attach an intrinsic value to their participation in elections.

5. This preceding point is useful in understanding debates concerning rational choice because it suggests the specific empirical grounds for criticizing (and thus, in principle, rejecting) the rational choice meta-theory. More specifically, if persistent evidence was unearthed that voting behavior was truly random, then the latter would lead to the rejection of vote choice as a goal-oriented activity.

6. The centrality of survey research should not be construed as a warrant for underestimating the contributions enabled by the use of other research methods. To return to our earlier examples, the archival research of Brustein (1996) offers evidence for an occupational and economic source of Nazi Party support, while the interviews of Lane (1962) represent an early corrective to the once-dominant view of incohererence and randomness among voters, and the experimental tradition reminds scholars about the subtle but pervasive political effects of media and political communication by politicians (McGraw et al., 1995; for a review, see Kinder, 1998).

7. For instance, if initially large and increasing coefficients for survey year dummy variables shrink to nil when covariates for economic evaluations are measured in a statistical model, this result would provide evidence that changes in the distribution of economic evaluations explain the pattern of change in election outcomes represented by the initial coefficients for survey year. For a discussion of related methodological details, see Firebaugh (1997).

8. A further problem affecting all studies reporting global decline of which we are aware stems from the practice of developing estimates that are derived from a single statistical model without providing evidence that the latter is preferable to theoretically-meaningful alternatives. Nieuwbeerta and De Graaf (1999), for instance, rely upon a single statistical model that they use to derive estimates for 20 separate countries; influential reports of decline by Abramson et al. (1999) and Inglehart (1990, 1997) are based upon a single measure (the Alford index) that they fail to justify by reference to prior analysis of competing models.

9. Like the 7-category scheme used by Layman (2001), Steensland et al.'s (2000) typology distinguishes evangelical, mainline, and black Protestants, and does so using a consistent interpretation of denominational differences.

10. While Hetherington's findings refer to a specific historical context, they are highly consistent with the results of other studies of media influence on voters' reasoning. For instance, reporting on specific policy issues raises the likelihood that voters will evaluate the performance of politicians using the criteria provided by news stories (Iyengar & Kinder, 1987). Accumulating studies of media influence thus suggest more than minimal effects (Kinder, 1998), and in addition to the example of priming discussed above, news reporting routinely influences public opinion through agenda-setting (influencing perceptions of what issues constitute the most important national problems). For further discussion, see Manza and Cook (2002).

11. We borrow the term "minimalism" from Sniderman and Tetlock's (1986) description of Converse's (1964) interpretation of U.S. public opinion as reflecting non-attitudes.

12. See Evans, Heath and Lalljee (1996) for complementary results regarding the coherence of voters' preferences and political alignments in Britain.

13. See Heath, Jowell and Curtice (2001) for an instructive over-time study that investigates the respective roles of social structural change, trends in public policy preferences, and the strategic positioning of political parties in explaining voter alignments and election outcomes in Britain since the 1970s.

ACKNOWLEDGMENTS

We thank Arthur Alderson, Elizabeth Armstrong, Jason Beckfield, David Brady, *RPS* editor Betty Dobratz, and the reviewers for their comments.

REFERENCES

Abramowitz, A. (1994). Issue evolution reconsidered: Racial attitudes and partisanship in the U.S. electorate. *American Journal of Political Science, 38*, 1–24.

Abramowitz, A. (1995a). It's abortion, stupid: Policy voting in the 1992 presidential election. *Journal of Politics, 57*, 176–186.

Abramowitz, A. (1995b). The end of the democratic era? 1994 and the future of congressional election research. *Political Research Quarterly, 48*, 873–889.

Abramowitz, A., & Saunders, K. (1998). Ideological realignment in the U.S. electorate. *Journal of Politics, 60*, 634–652.

Abramson, P., Aldrich, J., & Rohde, D. (1999). *Change and continuity in the 1996 and 1998 elections.* Washington, DC: Congressional Quarterly Press.

Adams, C. (1997). Abortion: Evidence of an issue evolution. *American Journal of Political Science, 3*, 718–737.

Alvarez, M., & Nagler, J. (1995). Economics, issues and the perot candidacy: Voter choice in the 1992 presidential election. *American Journal of Political Science, 39*, 714–744.

Alvarez, M., & Nagler, J. (1998). Economics, entitlements, and social issues: Voter choice in the 1996 presidential election. *American Journal of Political Science, 42*, 1349–1363.

Alwin, D., Cohen, R., & Newcomb, T. (1991). *Political attitudes over the life span: The bennington women after fifty years.* Madison: University of Wisconsin Press.

Ansolabehere, S., & Iyengar, S. (1995). *Going negative: How political advertisements shrink and polarize the electorate*. New York: Free Press.

Bartels, L. (2000). Partisanship and voting behavior, 1952–1996. *American Journal of Political Science*, *44*, 35–50.

Bartels, L., & Brady, H. (1993). The state of quantitative political methodology. In: A. Finifter (Ed.), *Political Science: The State of the Discipline* (pp. 121–158). Washington, DC: American Political Science Association.

Bartolini, S., & Mair, P. (1990). *Identity, competition and electoral availability*. New York: Cambridge University Press.

Beck, P. A. (1988). Incomplete realignment: The Reagan legacy for parties and elections. In: C. Jones (Ed.), *The Reagan Legacy: Promise and Performance* (pp. 145–171). Chatham: Chatham House Publishers, Inc.

Berelson, B. R., Lazarsfeld, P. F., & McPhee, W. (1954). *Voting: A study of opinion formation in a presidential campaign*. Chicago: University of Chicago Press.

Brooks, C. (2000). Civil rights liberalism and the suppression of a republican political realignment in the U.S., 1972–1996. *American Sociological Review*, *65*, 482–505.

Brooks, C. (2002). Religious influence and the politics of family decline concern: Trends, sources, and U.S. political behavior. *American Sociological Review*, *67*, 191–211.

Brooks, C., & Brady, D. (1999). Income, economic voting, and long-term political change in the U.S., 1952–1996. *Social Forces*, *77*, 1339–1374.

Brooks, C., & Manza, J. (1994). Do changing values explain the new politics? A critical assessment of the postmaterialist thesis. *Sociological Quarterly*, *35*, 541–570.

Brooks, C., & Manza, J. (1997a). Class politics and political change in the U.S., 1952–1992. *Social Forces*, *76*, 379–408.

Brooks, C., & Manza, J. (1997b). The social and ideological bases of middle class political realignment in the United States, 1972–1992. *American Sociological Review*, *62*, 191–208.

Brooks, C., & Manza, J. (2002). Evangelicals, mainliners, Catholics: The religious cleavage and partisanship in U.S. national elections, 1972–2000. Unpublished manuscript. Department of Sociology. Indiana University, Bloomington.

Brustein, W. (1996). *The logic of evil: The social origins of the Nazi party, 1925–1933*. New Haven: Yale University Press.

Buell, E., Jr., & Sigelman, L. (1985). An army that meets every Sunday? Popular support for the moral majority in 1980. *Social Science Quarterly*, *66*, 426–434.

Burstein, P. (1998). Bringing the public back in: Should sociologists consider the impact of public opinion on public policy? *Social Forces*, *77*, 27–62.

Campbell, A., Converse, P. E., Miller, W., & Stokes, D. E. (1960). *The American voter*. New York: Wiley.

Carmines, E., & Huckfeldt, R. (1996). Political behavior: An overview. In: R. Goodin & H. Klingemann (Eds), *A New Handbook of Political Science* (pp. 223–254). New York: Oxford University Press.

Carmines, E., & Layman, G. (1997). Value priorities, partisanship, and electoral choice: The neglected case of the United States. *Political Behavior*, *19*, 283–316.

Carmines, E., & Stimson, J. (1989). *Issue evolution: Race and the transformation of American politics*. Princeton: Princeton University Press.

Chaves, M., & Gorski, P. (2001). Religious pluralism and religious participation. *Annual Review of Sociology*, *27*, 261–281.

Clark, T. (1994). Race and class versus the new political culture. In: T. Clark (Ed.), *Urban Innovation: Creative Strategies for Turbulent Times* (pp. 21–78). Thousands Oaks: Sage Publications.

Clark, T., & Hoffman-Martinot, V. (Eds) (1998). *The new political culture.* Boulder: Westview Press.

Clark, T., Lipset, S. M., & Rempel, M. (1993). The declining political significance of social class. *International Sociology, 8,* 293–316.

Converse, P. (1964). The nature of belief systems in mass publics. In: D. Apter (Ed.), *Ideology and Discontent* (pp. 206–261). New York: Free Press.

Dalton, R., Beck, P., & Flanagan, S. (1984). Electoral change in advanced industrial democracies. In: R. Dalton, S. Flanagan & P. Beck (Eds), *Electoral Change in Advanced Industrial Democracies: Realignment or Dealignment?* (pp. 3–22). Princeton: Princeton University Press.

Dalton, R., & Wattenberg, M. (1993). The not so simple act of voting. In: A. Finifter (Ed.), *Political Science: The State of the Discipline* (pp. 193–219). Washington, DC: American Political Science Association.

Davis, N., & Robinson, R. (1996). Are the rumors of war exaggerated? Religious orthodoxy and moral progressivism in America. *American Journal of Sociology, 102,* 756–787.

Delli Carpini, M. X., & Keeter, S. (1996). *What Americans know about politics and why it matters.* New Haven, CT: Yale University Press.

Edsall, T., & Edsall, M. (1991). *Chain reaction: The impact of race, rights, and taxes on American politics.* New York: Norton.

Erikson, R., & Goldthorpe, J. H. (1992). *The constant flux.* Oxford: The Clarendon Press.

Erikson, R. S., MacKuen, M. B., & Stimson, J. A. (2002). *The macro polity.* New York: Cambridge University Press.

Erikson, R. S., & Tedin, K. (1995). *American public opinion: Its origins, content, and impact* (5th ed.). Boston: Allyn and Bacon.

Esping-Andersen, G. (1990). *The three worlds of welfare capitalism.* Princeton: Princeton University Press.

Evans, G. (Ed.) (1999a). *The end of class politics? Class voting in comparative context.* New York: Oxford University Press.

Evans, G. (1999b). Class and vote: Disrupting the orthodoxy. In: G. Evans (Ed.), *The End of Class Politics? Class Voting in Comparative Context* (pp. 323–334). New York: Oxford University Press.

Evans, G. (2000). The continued significance of class voting. *Annual Review of Political Science, 3,* 401–417.

Evans, G., Heath, A., & Lalljee, M. (1996). Measuring left-right and libertarian-authoritarian values in the British electorate. *British Journal of Sociology, 47,* 129–155.

Evans, G., & Whitefield, S. (1999). The emergence of class politics and class voting in post-communist Russia. In: G. Evans (Ed.), *The End of Class Politics? Class Voting in Comparative Context* (pp. 254–277). New York: Oxford University Press.

Ferejohn, J. A., & Kuklinski, J. H. (Eds) (1990). *Information and democratic processes.* Urbana: University of Illinois Press.

Fiorina, M. (1981). *Retrospective voting in American national elections.* New Haven: Yale University Press.

Fiorina, M. (1990). In: J. Ferejohn & J. Kuklinski (Eds), *Information and Democratic Process* (pp. 329–342). Urbana: University of Illinois Press.

Firebaugh, G. (1997). *Analyzing repeated surveys.* Thousand Oaks, CA: Sage Publications.

Form, W. (1985). *Divided we stand: Working class stratification in America.* Urbana: University of Illinois Press.

Franklin, C. (1992). Measurement and the dynamics of party identification. *Political Behavior, 14,* 297–309.

Franklin, M., Mackie, T., & Valen, H. (1992). Introduction. In: M. Franklin, T. Mackie & H. Valen (Eds), *Electoral Change* (pp. 329–342). New York: Cambridge University Press.

Friedman, J. (Ed.) (1996). *The rational choice controversy: Economic models of politics reconsidered.* New Haven: Yale University Press.

Gerber, T. (2000). Market, state, or don't know? Education, economic ideology, and voting in contemporary Russia. *Social Forces, 79,* 477–521.

Gerteis, J. (1998). Political alignment and the American middle class, 1974–1994. *Sociological Forum, 13,* 639–666.

Gilens, M. (1999). *Why Americans hate welfare.* Chicago: University of Chicago Press.

Giles, M. W., & Buckner, M. (1993). David Duke and black threat: An old hypothesis revisited. *Journal of Politics, 55,* 702–713.

Giles, M. W., & Hertz, K. (1994). Racial threat and partisan identification. *American Political Science Review, 88,* 316–326.

Goldthorpe, J. (1999). Modeling the pattern of class voting in British elections, 1964–1992. In: G. Evans (Ed.), *The End of Class Politics? Class Voting in Comparative Context* (pp. 60–82). New York: Oxford University Press.

Green, J., Kellstedt, L., Smidt, C., & Guth, J. (1998). The soul of the south: Religion and the new electoral order. In: C. Bullock & M. Rozell (Eds), *The New Politics of the Old South: An Introduction to Southern Politics* (pp. 261–276). Lanham: Rowman & Littlefield Publishers, Inc.

Green, D., Palmquist, B., & Schickler, E. (1998). Macropartisanship: A replication and critique. *American Political Science Review, 92,* 883–899.

Green, D., & Shapiro, I. (1994). *Pathologies of rational choice theory: A critique of applications in political science.* New Haven: Yale University Press.

Haeberle, S. (1999). Gay and lesbian rights: Emerging trends in public opinion and voting behavior. In: E. Riggle & B. Tadllock (Eds), *Gays and Lesbians in the Democratic Process: Public Policy, Public Opinion, and Political Representation* (pp. 146–169). New York: Columbia University Press.

Hamilton, R. F. (1972). *Class and politics in the United States.* New York: Wiley.

Haynes, S. E., & Jacobs, D. (1994). Macroeconomics, economic stratification, and partisanship: A longitudinal analysis of contingent shifts in political identification. *American Journal of Sociology, 100,* 70–103.

Heath, A., Jowell, R., & Curtice, J. (1985). *How Britain votes.* London: Pergamon.

Heath, A., Jowell, R., & Curtice, J. (2001). *The rise of new labour: Party policies and voter choices.* New York: Oxford University Press.

Heath, A., Jowell, R., Curtice, J., Evans, G., Field, J., & Witherspoon, S. (1991). *Understanding political change: The British voter, 1964–1987.* London: Pergamon.

Hetherington, M. (1996). The media's role in forming voters' national economic evaluations in 1992. *American Journal of Political Science, 40,* 372–395.

Hibbs, D. (1987). *The political economy of industrial democracies.* Cambridge: Harvard University Press.

Hicks, A. (1999). *Social democracy and welfare capitalism: A century of income security politics.* Ithaca, NY: Cornell University Press.

Hout, M., Brooks, C., & Manza, J. (1995). The democratic class struggle in the United States, 1948–1992. *American Sociological Review, 60,* 805–828.

Huber, E., & Stephens, J. (2001). *Development and crisis of the welfare state: Parties and policies in global markets.* Chicago: University of Chicago Press.

Huckfeldt, R., Plutzer, E., & Sprague, J. (1993). Alternative contexts of political behavior: Churches, neighborhoods, and individuals. *Journal of Politics, 55,* 365–381.

Huckfeldt, R., & Sprague, J. (1991). Discussant effects on vote choice: Intimacy, structure, and interdependence. *Journal of Politics, 53,* 122–158.

Huckfeldt, R., & Sprague, J. (1995). *Citizens, politics, and social communication: Information and influence in an election campaign.* New York: Cambridge University Press.

Inglehart, R. (1990). *Culture shift in advanced industrial society.* Princeton: Princeton University Press.

Inglehart, R. (1997). *Modernization and postmodernization: Cultural, economic, and political change in 43 societies.* Princeton: Princeton University Press.

Inglehart, R., & Baker, W. (2000). Modernization, cultural change, and the persistence of traditional values. *American Sociological Review, 65,* 19–51.

Iyengar, S., & Kinder, D. (1987). *News that matters.* Chicago: University of Chicago Press.

Kiewiet, R. (1983). *Macroeconomics and micropolitics: The electoral effects of economic issues.* Chicago: University of Chicago Press.

Kinder, D. (1998). Communication and opinion. *Annual Review of Political Science, 1,* 167–197.

Kinder, D., & Kiewiet, R. (1981). Sociotropic politics: The American case. *British Journal of Political Science, 11,* 129–161.

Kinder, D., & Sanders, L. (1996). *Divided by color.* Chicago: University of Chicago Press.

Knoke, D. (1976). *The social bases of political parties.* Baltimore: Johns Hopkins University Press.

Knutsen, O. (1995). Party choice. In: J. van Deth & E. Scarbrough (Eds), *The Impact of Values* (pp. 460–503). New York: Oxford University Press.

Kriesi, H. (1998). The transformation of cleavage politics. *European Journal of Political Research, 33,* 165–185.

Lane, R. E. (1962). *Political ideology: Why the American common man believes what he does.* New York: Free Press.

Lawrence, D. (1997). *The collapse of the democratic presidential majority.* Boulder, CO: Westview Press.

Lazarsfeld, P. F., Berelson, B. R., & Gaudet, H. (1948, 1968). *The people's choice.* New York: Columbia University Press.

Layman, G. (2001). *The great divide: Religious and cultural conflict in American party politics.* New York: Columbia University Press.

Lewis-Beck, M. (1988). *Economics and elections.* Ann Arbor: University of Michigan Press.

Lewis-Beck, M., & Rice, T. (1992). *Forecasting elections.* Washington, DC: Congressional Quarterly Press.

Lipset, S. M. (1963). *The first new nation: The United States in historical and comparative perspective.* New York: Basic Books, Inc.

Lipset, S. M. (1981, 1960). *Political man.* Expanded edition. Baltimore: Johns Hopkins University Press.

Lipset, S. M. (1996). *American exceptionalism: A double-edged sword.* New York: Norton.

Lipset, S. M., & Marks, G. (2000). *It didn't happen here: Why socialism failed in the United States.* New York: Norton.

Lipset, S. M., & Rokkan, S. (1967). Cleavage structures, party systems, and voter alignments: An introduction. In: S. M. Lipset & S. Rokkan (Eds), *Party Systems and Voter Alignments* (pp. 1–64). New York: Free Press.

Lupia, A., McCubbins, M. D., & Popkin, S. L. (Eds) (2000). *Elements of reason: Cognition, choice, and the bounds of rationality.* New York: Cambridge University Press.

MacKuen, M., Erikson, R., & Stimson, J. (1988). Macropartisanship. *American Political Science Review, 83*, 1125–1142.

Manza, J. (2000). Race and the underdevelopment of the American welfare state. *Theory and Society, 30*, 819–832.

Manza, J., & Brooks, C. (1997). The religious factor in U.S. presidential elections, 1960–1992. *American Journal of Sociology, 103*, 38–81.

Manza, J., & Brooks, C. (1999a). Group size, turnout, and political alignments in the development of U.S. party coalitions, 1960–1992. *European Sociological Review, 15*, 369–390.

Manza, J., & Brooks, C. (1999b). *Social cleavages and political change: Voter alignments and U.S. party coalitions.* New York: Oxford University Press.

Manza, J., & Cook, F. L. (2002). A democratic polity? Three views of policy responsiveness to public opinion in the United States. *American Political Research*, forthcoming.

Manza, J., Hout, M., & Brooks, C. (1995). Class voting in capitalist democracies since World War II: Dealignment, realignment, or trendless fluctuation? *Annual Review of Sociology, 21*, 137–163.

Manza, J., & Wright, N. (2002). Religion and political behavior. In: M. Dillon (Ed.), *Handbook of the Sociology of Religion.* New York: Cambridge University Press.

McGraw, K., Best, S., & Timpone, R. (1995). What they say or what they do? The impact of elite explanation and policy outcomes on public opinion. *American Journal of Political Science, 39*, 53–74.

Mendelberg, T. (2001). *The race card: Campaign strategy, implicit messages, and the norm of equality.* Princeton: Princeton University Press.

Miller, W. E., & Shanks, J. M. (1996). *The new American voter.* Cambridge, MA: Harvard University Press.

Niemi, R., & Jennings, K. (1991). Issues and inheritance in the formation of party identification. *American Journal of Political Science, 35*, 970–988.

Niemi, R., & Weisberg, H. (2001). *Controversies in voting behavior* (4th ed.). Washington DC: Congressional Quarterly Press.

Nieuwbeerta, P., Brooks, C., & Manza, J. (2002). Class vs. religious vs. gender cleavages: Parties and societies in comparative perspective. Unpublished manuscript. Department of Sociology, Indiana University.

Nieuwbeerta, P., & De Graaf, N. D. (1999). Traditional class voting in 20 postwar societies. In: G. Evans (Ed.), *The End of Class Politics? Class Voting in Comparative Context* (pp. 24–56). New York: Oxford University Press.

O'Connor, J., Orloff, A., & Shaver, S. (1999). *States, markets, families: Gender, liberalism and social policy in Australia, Canada, Great Britain and the United States.* New York: Cambridge University Press.

Oliver, J. E., & Mendelberg, T. (2000). Reconsidering the environmental determinants of white racial attitudes. *American Journal of Political Science, 44*, 574–589.

Pierson, P. (1996). The new politics of the welfare state. *World Politics, 48*, 143–179.

Pomper, G. (1997). The presidential election. In: G. Pomper (Ed.), *The Election of 1996: Reports and Interpretation* (pp. 173–204) Chatham, NJ: Chatham House Publishers, Inc.

Powell, G. B. (2000). *Elections as instruments of democracy.* New Haven: Yale University Press.

Przeworski, A., Sprague, J. (1986). *Paper stones: A history of electoral socialism.* Chicago: University of Chicago Press.

Regnerus, M., Sikkink, D., & Smith, C. (1999). Voting with the Christian right: Contextual and individual patterns of electoral influence. *Social Forces, 77*, 1375–1401.

Ringdal, K., & Hines, K. (1999). Changes in class voting in Norway, 1957–1989. In: G. Evans (Ed.), *The End of Class Politics? Class Voting in Comparative Context* (pp. 182–202). New York: Oxford University Press.

Sears, D. O., Sidanius, J., & Bobo, L. (Eds) (2000). *Racialized politics.* Chicago: University of Chicago Press.

Sears, D. O., & Valentino, N. (2002). Race, religion, and sectional conflict in contemporary partisanship. Unpublished manuscript. Department of political science, UCLA.

Sears, D. O., Van Laar, C., Carrillo, M., & Kosterman, R. (1997). Is it really racism? The origins of white Americans' opposition to race-targeted policies. *Public Opinion Quarterly, 61,* 16–53.

Shafer, B. (1991). *The end of realignment? Interpreting American electoral eras.* Madison: University of Wisconsin Press.

Shanks, J. M., & Miller, W. (1991). Policy direction and performance evaluation: Complementary explanations of the Reagan elections. *British Journal of Political Science, 20,* 143–235.

Sherkat, D., & Ellison, C. (1999). Recent developments and current controversies in the sociology of religion. *Annual Review of Sociology, 25,* 363–394.

Skocpol, T. (1996). *Boomerang.* New York: W. W. Norton & Co., Inc.

Smith, E. (1989). *The unchanging American voter.* Berkeley: University of California Press.

Sniderman, P. (1993). The new look in public opinion research. In: A. Finifter (Ed.), *Political Science: The State of the Discipline* (pp. 219–245). DC: American Political Science Association.

Sniderman, P., Brody, H., & Tetlock, P. (1991). *Reasoning and choice: Explorations in political psychology.* New York: Cambridge University Press.

Sniderman, P., & Carmines, E. G. (1997). *Reaching beyond race.* Cambridge: Harvard University Press.

Sniderman, P., & Grob, D. (1996). Innovations in experimental design in attitude surveys. *Annual Review of Sociology, 22,* 377–399.

Sniderman, P., & Tetlock, P. (1986). Interrelationship of political ideology and public opinion. In: M. Herman (Ed.), *Political Psychology: Contemporary Problems and Ideas* (pp. 62–96). San Francisco: Jossey-Bass Publishers, Inc.

Steensland, B., Park, J., Regnerus, M., Robinson, L., Wilcox, B., & Woodberry, R. (2000). The measure of American religion: Toward improving the state of the art. *Social Forces, 79,* 291–318.

Taylor, M. C. (2000). The significance of racial conflict. In: D. Sears, J. Sidanius & L. Bobo (Eds), *Racialized Politics* (pp. 118–136). Chicago: University of Chicago Press.

Verba, S., Nie, N., & Petrocik, J. (1979). *The changing American voter* (Enlarged ed.). Cambridge: Harvard University Press.

Wald, K., Owen, D., & Hill, S., Jr. (1988). Churches as political communities. *American Political Science Review, 82,* 531–548.

Wattenberg, M. (1996). *The decline of American political parties, 1952–1994.* Cambridge: Harvard University Press.

Weakliem, D. (1999). Class voting, social change, and the left in Australia, 1943–1996. *British Journal of Sociology, 50,* 609–630.

Weakliem, D., & Heath, A. (1994). Rational choice and class voting. *Rationality and Society, 6,* 243–270.

Weakliem, D., & Heath, A. (1999). The secret life of class voting: Britain, France, and the United States since the 1930s. In: G. Evans (Ed.), *The End of Class Politics? Class Voting in Comparative Context* (pp. 98–133). New York: Oxford University Press.

Weisberg, H., & Kimball, D. (1995). Attitudinal correlates of the 1992 presidential vote: Party identification and beyond. In: H. Wiseberg (Ed.), *Democracy's Feast: Elections in America* (pp. 72–111). Chatham: Chatham House Publishers.

Williams, R. (Ed.) (1997). *Culture wars in American politics: Critical reviews of a popular myth.* New York: Aldine de Gruyter.

Woodberry, R., & Smith, C. (1998). Fundamentalism et al.: Conservative protestants in America. *Annual Review of Sociology, 24,* 25–56.

Wright, E. (1997). *Class counts: Comparative studies in class analysis.* New York: Cambridge University Press.

Zylan, Y., & Soule, S. (2000). Ending welfare as we know it (Again): Welfare retrenchment, 1989–1995. *Social Forces, 79,* 623–652.

CLASS AND NON-VOTING IN COMPARATIVE PERSPECTIVE: POSSIBLE CAUSES AND CONSEQUENCES IN THE UNITED STATES

Harold R. Kerbo and Juan J. Gonzalez

ABSTRACT

The purpose of this article is to review the recent state of the debate over class and voting behavior since the early 1990s, with a particular focus on the important and neglected issue of class and non-voting in the United States. Recent research suggests that class voting has been in decline in the United States and stands considerably below the level of class voting in most other industrial nations, though there have been swings to higher and lower levels of class voting in all industrial nations since the 1930s, including the United States. Other recent evidence suggests, however, that the United States is most different in the level of non-voting among lower classes. When non-voting by the lower classes is considered we come to understand that class voting is comparatively lower in the United States because the lower classes have largely withdrawn active support from the Democratic Party, rendering Democratic and Republican voters much more similar in class backgrounds in recent decades. In this paper we critically examine the evidence of

Political Sociology for the 21st Century
Research in Political Sociology, Volume 12, 175–195
ISSN: 0895-9935/PII: S0895993503120074

non-voting and class and its effects on the American society, particularly on levels of income inequality and rates of poverty. Finally, we suggest future research that may help us understand differences in class non-voting and political outcomes in the United States.

INTRODUCTION

After the 2000 presidential election in the United States, an election in which region of the country seemed to be one of the determining factors in voting for the Democratic or Republican candidate, it is perhaps fitting that the old debate over class voting has returned to the social science "consciousness." The question of class voting is perhaps particularly puzzling in the United States because the 2000 presidential election came just before the country passed a milestone of its longest economic boom in history. But it was an economic boom which corresponded with sharply divided outcomes for the American people. For the last couple of decades, if not longer, the United States has had the highest level of income inequality among major industrial nations.[1] The 1990s continued a trend of growing income and wealth inequality, longer working hours and fewer benefits for most workers, and lingering high rates of absolute and relative poverty compared to other industrial nations. At the other end of the stratification system, those in the highest wealth categories and executives of the largest 500 corporations were expanding their wealth and income at unprecedented rates (Keister, 2000; Kerbo, 2000, Chap. 2; Mishel, Bernstein & Schmitt, 2001).

In the face of this growing economic inequality, the presidential election of 2000 in the United States showed less evidence of voting along class and income lines than any presidential election in the last 10 or 20 years. Union members and minorities continued to vote heavily for the Democratic candidate, but for other Americans it seemed as if class issues hardly mattered when they went to the polls. Indeed, one of the best predictors of voting for George W. Bush over Al Gore ended up being church attendance (*International Herald Tribune*, March 27, 2001). After church attendance, gun ownership turned out to be the second strongest predictor of voting Republican (Greenberg, 2000). Equally puzzling when comparing the United States to other industrial nations, in the face of growing inequality, just over half of those eligible bothered to vote at all, and those who did so were concentrated in the higher income and educational segments of the population (U.S. Bureau of Census, *Statistical Abstracts of the United States*, 2001, p. 251; Manza & Brooks, 1999, p. 50).

Given these recent trends in voting, it is not surprising that social scientists have increasingly engaged in debates over the issue. Indeed, at stake is a sub-paradigm of class and class-conflict in modern social science theory. New books with titles such as *The Breakdown of Class Politics* (Clark & Lipset, 2001), *The End of Class Politics?* (Evans, 1999), and *Comparing Democracies: Elections and Voting in Global Perspective* (LeDuc, Niemi & Norris, 1996) have brought together some of the most respected American and European social scientists to consider the issue. In one of the more complex analyses of class voting in 20 industrial nations in the second half of the 20th century, Nieuwbeerta (2001) shows there was indeed a steady decline in class voting in the United States between 1945 and 1990.[2] Of the 20 nations in the data set, 18 showed some declines in class voting in the period (Nieuwbeerta, 2001, p. 127).[3] Taking a somewhat longer perspective (1935–1993), Weakliem (2001) found class voting highest in Britain, somewhat lower in France, and much lower in the United States, though all three countries were mostly in a down cycle from the 1980s (Weakliem, 2001, p. 199).[4] Weakliem's suggestion is that the ups and downs are related to periods in which class or non-class issues dominate the historical period. Research by Winders (1999) on voter turnout in the United States from the 1840s suggests temporary class-based social movements are associated with the few times there has been much class voting at all in the United States. But despite this renewed interest in class and voting there is an almost complete neglect of *lower class non-voting in the United States* compared to other industrial nations (Manza & Brooks, 1999, p. 259). Voter turnout, in general, is lower in the United States compared to most other industrial nations, but what is most different in the United States is *non-voting* by the lower classes.

The primary purpose of this paper, therefore, is to examine the relatively neglected issue of class and *non-voting* in comparative perspective. Recent and innovative research on the subject is analyzed which indicates that lower class disenfranchisement in the United States is comparatively more extreme than previously realized. Explanations of this American contrast, however, are inadequate, and research is sketchy. Further, little serious attention has been given to the possible relationship between lower class non-voting and comparatively high rates of poverty and income inequality in the United States. We conclude with a suggested research agenda for both the causes and effects of lower class non-voting in the United States.

CLASS NON-VOTING IN THE UNITED STATES

We can begin with Table 1 which indicates that voter turnout is lower in the United States compared to most other industrial nations. It is true that some countries in Europe have laws requiring people to vote, but such laws are seldom enforced and

Table 1.   Comparative Voter Turnout in National Elections, 1998.

Country	Percent voting
United States	36
Switzerland	43
Japan	59
Canada	69
France	71
UK	72
Netherlands	73
Spain	77
Norway	78
Austria	80
Sweden	81
Germany	82
Italy	83
Denmark	86
Belgium	91
Australia	95

Source: United Nations, Human Development Report, 2000 (2001, Table 25).

research has found this to be only one of several factors influencing voter turnout (Mahler, 2002). It is also important to note that 1998 was an off-year election in the United States with traditionally lower voter participation. Further, a recent study by the U.S. Census Bureau (*Voting and Registration in the Election of November of 1998*, 2000) puts the revised percent voting at 41.9%, still the lowest ever recorded by the Census Bureau. As usual for a presidential election year, the voter turnout in 2000 was higher, but still only 54.7% bothered to vote (U.S. Bureau of Census, *Statistical Abstracts of the United States, 2001*, p. 251; U.S. Census Bureau, *Voting and Registration in the Election of November of 2000*, 2001).[5]

Table 2 suggests that the issue of class *non-voting* should be one of major importance to the examination of class and politics in the United States. Since 1984 only 20 to 40% of the lowest income groups in the United States have bothered to vote compared to 60 to almost 80% of people among upper income groups. In 1998, as noted above, there was a drop in voter participation, but the variance by income remained the same. Further analysis of the 1998 turnout by the Census Bureau (*Voting and Registration in the Election of November of 1998*, 2000, Table D) also indicates the *variance in voter turnout by income remains the same across all race and ethnic categories*. That is, high income blacks and Hispanics turn out to vote in percentages very close to those of high income whites. A breakdown by income for voter participation in the 2000 elections as shown in Table 2 indicates similar results. Considering voter turnout between 1960 and 1992, Manza and

Table 2. Voting Rates by Income, USA: 1984–2000.[a]

Family income	Percent voted					
	1984	1988	1992	1996	1998	2000
Under $5,000	37.5	34.7	32.4	37.9	21.1	28.2
$5,000–9,999	46.2	41.3	39.5	38.3	23.9	34.7
$10,000–14,999	53.5	47.7	46.8	46.7	30.4	37.7
$15,000–19,999	57.1	53.5	55.7	52.8		
					34.6	43.4
$20,000–24,999	61.1	57.8	62.5	52.8		
$25,000–34,999	67.0	64.0	69.5	56.6	40.2	51.0
$35,000–49,999	72.9	70.3	75.7	62.6	44.0	57.5
$50,000 and over	76.0	75.6	79.9	72.8		
$50,000–74,999					49.9	65.2
$75,000 and over					57.3	71.5

Source: U.S. Bureau of the Census, 1989, Current Population Reports, Voting and Registration in the Election of November 1988, series P-20, No. 440, 1989, p. 4; 1993, Voting and Registration in the Election of November 1992, series P-20, No. 466, p. 55. www.census.gov (voting in the 1996 election); U.S. Census Bureau, Voting and Registration in the Election of November of 1998, 2000, Table C; detailed tables, U.S. Census Bureau, www.census.gov/voting, internet release, February 27, 2002, Table 8.
[a] Figures are for U.S. citizens voting, not total population (see Casper & Bass, 1998). The 1998 and 2000 data used slightly different income categories. For example, $15,000 to $24,999 was used instead of dividing the category at $19,999.

Brooks (1999, pp. 194–195) show that low income groups remain the least likely to vote, with the white-non-white voting difference declining.

Data pertaining to the income and class positions of non-voters in European nations are less comprehensive but indicate that non-voters are *not concentrated in the lower class or lower income groups*. Weakliem and Heath (1999) have shown that neither Britain nor France have non-voting by class as does the United States. Also, data from the 1960s and 1970s show there was no significant difference in a larger sample of European nations in voter participation by class and education (Burnham, 1982; Piven & Cloward, 2000, pp. 41–43; Powell, 1986). As would be expected, with little evidence that class and non-voting are related in European countries, there has been almost no research on the subject by European social scientists. For example, only one research article on class and non-voting in Spain in the past decade could be located, which incidentally concluded that it was a non-issue because non-voting was not related to class position (Boix & Riba, 2000).[6]

Class and non-voting would also be less of an issue in the United States if non-voters in the lower income groups were equally likely to vote for Republicans as for Democrats. Recent research, however, suggests this is not the case. For example, Weakliem and Heath (1999, p. 120) have found that "Over the whole period [1936–1992] Democratic voters have become more middle class voters relative to non-voters, while Republicans have remained unchanged. Putting these two facts together, class differences between the two major parties have decreased while class differences between major party voters and non-voters have increased, as Verba, Nie and Kim (1978, p. 309) predict." Manza and Brooks (1999, p. 197) arrive at a similar conclusion with their voting data. From a comparative perspective, the United States again presents a major contrast: Weakliem and Heath (1999, p. 122) also found that in Britain, Labour voters are in fact more working class than non-voters, while in France, Socialist voters and non-voters are similar, and Communist voters are by far more working class than non-voters.

ATTEMPTED EXPLANATIONS OF NON-VOTING AMONG LOWER INCOME GROUPS

With the exception of works by Piven and Cloward (1988, 2000) and Teixeira (1987), very little research has been done on why there are such large differences in voter turnout by income in the United States. Piven and Cloward (1988, p. 96) divide the explanations into two groups; those which "blame" the non-voters themselves and suggest that "non-voting results from one or another of the characteristics of the non-voters..." and those which focus on political institutions. From a long historical perspective, Piven and Cloward's work is among the second group and has focused on how political factors have reduced voting among the lowest income groups, and even how politicians have purposely written off low income groups. In summary, Piven and Cloward (1988, 2000) attempt to show how upper class interests slowly captured the major political parties and moved them away from issues that would attract lower class interests and initiated barriers making it more difficult for lower income groups to vote. With this perspective, Piven and Cloward were among the most active in promoting the "Motor-Voter" legislation which finally passed in 1993 making it easier to get low income people registered to vote. But as the 1996 to 2000 voter turnout suggest, and Piven and Cloward (2000) admit, the "Motor-Voter" bill, while increasing voter registration, had almost no effect on increasing actual voter turnout among lower income groups in the United States.

Other explanations for non-voting among the lower classes in the United States, still from an institutional perspective, cite how the American political system leads the two major parties to lack strong ideological differences in order to attract the middle mass of voters (Franklin, 1996; Jackman & Miller, 1995; Teixeira,

1987; Vanneman & Cannon, 1987; Verba et al., 1978). Moving away from an institutional perspective, still others cite less political knowledge among the lower classes and less educated, and thus less interest in politics. It is also suggested that working class turnout is low because of less organization among the lower classes to motivate voting (Houtman, 2001; Winders, 1999). Others cite the more extreme individualism in the United States leading to detachment from broader institutions (Inglehart, 1990; Rose & McAllister, 1986), while still others suggest more psychological factors related to fatalism and less political efficacy among the lower classes (Wolfinger & Rosenstone, 1980). Teixeira (1987), interestingly, finds that shifts in newspaper readership, especially reading about political events, is related to education and income and leads to non-voting.

At present, the little theoretical interest which does exist on the subject of class and non-voting has not generated much in the way of comprehensive multivariate research able to distinguish the strength of the various explanations for non-voting. One reason is that the usual comparative studies are hampered by a low number of cases when trying to do statistical analysis of advanced industrial nations. This is especially a problem because it is the United States which is most different. As a result, "studies of electoral turnout have invariably struggled with the 'deviant' U.S. case (see e.g. Jackman, 1987; Jackman & Miller, 1995; Powell, 1986)" (Mahler, 2002, p. 11). Using an innovative data set to examine the relationship between levels of inequality and voter turnout, Mahler (2002) has recently overcome some of these problems. Mahler was able to obtain data on income inequality from the Luxemburg Income Study and voter turnout in governments below the national level (e.g. states in the United States, lander in Germany) to create 184 cases for analysis.[7] For the question of class and income differences and voter turnout, however, the research is only suggestive because Mahler had European data on non-voting only, not non-voting by income or class.

Including national level data for 16 nations in North America and Europe on the income ratio between the top 10% and bottom 10% income groups, as well as the Gini Index, Mahler (2002, p. 12) found a significant relation between income inequality and voter turnout: the higher the income inequality in the nation, the lower the voter turnout. Removing the case of the United States from the data, however, renders the correlation non-significant. With data from below the national government level in these 16 nations (thus, 184 cases) over four time periods in the second half of the 20th century (with 1996 the last period), Mahler (2002, p. 13) finds a significant and stronger relationship between income inequality and voter turnout (again, higher inequality in the regions related to lower voter turnout). This finding obviously points to an interesting observation for the United States as well; income inequality by states vary considerably (with some states having income inequality more on par with European nations like Germany and

Sweden), as does voter turnout. Considering the 50 U.S. states alone, there is also a significant correlation between income inequality and voter turnout (Mahler, 2002, p. 15). While Mahler's research *does not show directly that it is the lower income groups who are more likely to be non-voters* when income inequality becomes comparatively high, combined with the American case and research such as that of Weakliem and Heath (1999) described above, it seems reasonable to suggest that certain conditions/factors lead a higher percentage of lower income people to drop out of voter participation when income inequality is comparatively high.

Mahler (2002) was able to examine a few other variables possibly related to non-voting, but few of the suggested explanations noted above could be tested. Using his large data set of sub-national government levels in 16 major industrial nations, Mahler (2002, p. 21), for example, found that attempts to assure higher rates of voter registration (such as laws requiring registration) are related to higher voter turnout. Perhaps more significantly, Mahler was able to show that a measure of political competitiveness is related to higher rates of voter turnout: In countries/local districts with more political competitiveness between parties the voter turnout is higher. This has been one of the major untested arguments of many noted previously who describe how major political parties in the United States have abandoned lower class voters, rather than lower class voters initiating the abandonment. Mahler's (2002, p. 21) measure of "electoral disproportionality" (laws requiring a higher vote count before smaller parties obtain representation), however, was not related to voter turnout.

CLASS VOTING AND NON-VOTING: OUTCOMES

Given the comparatively high and growing levels of economic inequality in the United States, coupled with the rather unique position of low voter turnout for low income groups in the United States, one would think that considerable research attention would be focused on the possible link between the two. Such, however, has not been the case. We finally do have some direct research on the possible link, but it is useful to examine case studies suggesting a link between political activity and inequality before considering multivariate empirical analysis.

The United States is in contrast to most European Union nations with respect to income inequality, voter turnout, and working class political activity, but the contrast between the United States and Germany is in some ways most extreme. Several measures indicate that the United States has the highest income inequality among major industrial nations while Germany ranks fairly low on income inequality (Kerbo, 2000, pp. 26–29; Kerbo & Strasser, 2000; Mishel, Bernstein & Schmitt, 1999; Smeeding & Grodner, 2000; World Bank, 2000). German

Table 3.   Changes in the Middle Class, 1980–1995.[a]

Country	As percent of all households, 1995	Percent change in middle class, 1980–1995
Australia	27.6	−2.6
Canada	35.8	+2.8
France	39.4	+3.7
Germany	43.9	+2.4
Netherlands	38.7	−2.3
Norway	45.3	+3.9
Sweden	52.7	−1.3
Great Britain	32.6	−3.9
United States	27.3	−4.4

Source: Pressman (2001).
[a] Data for some countries are from 1979 to 1994. Middle class is defined as between 75% and 125% of median income in the country.

workers are among the most highly paid in the world, with more benefits, and a shorter working week, compared to workers in almost all other industrial nations. American workers, on the other hand, have below average pay, longer working hours, fewer benefits, and more temporary jobs (see Kerbo, 2000, Chaps 2 and 15; Kerbo & Strasser, 2000). German corporate executives receive less than half the salary and benefits of American top executives (Mishel, Bernstein & Schmitt, 1999, p. 213). Another major trend in the United States has been a shrinking middle class as the income of lower class families stagnate or decline while the upper 20% of Americans have experienced increasing real wages. As can be seen in Table 3, analysis of the Luxembourg Income Study data indicate that the middle income group in the United States (defined as income between 75% and 125% of median income) has been reduced most, while in Germany the middle income group has been steadily growing (Pressman, 2001).

One struggles to explain this contrast between the United States and Germany without recognition of the importance of class political engagement (such as class voting and non-voting). Before World War II, Germany had one of the highest levels of income inequality (Chirot, 1986, p. 163). Since World War II, however, we can trace the political victories of German workers in achieving stronger labor unions that have again and again won significant wage and benefit settlements. Most importantly, during the 1950s (and strengthened in the 1970s) German labor was successful in legitimizing their position through the "Co-determination Laws" or "Works Constitution Act" passed by the national government which gives employees extensive influence in corporations. For example, this "Works Constitution Act" requires approximately half of corporate board members to be elected from employees of the corporation. It also requires the establishment of a "works council" of elected employees (usually among lower ranked employees) in all but the smallest companies. These elected members of the "works councils" have extensive rights in all decisions made within each company (Thelen, 1991; Turner, 1991).[8] Any violation of these employee rights by management will likely end up in the labor court system created by the "Works Constitution Act," with management's disputed actions suspended for years until a final court decision is rendered. In summary, German workers today are said to have a "dual system" of representation; the works council acts in each separate company to protect employee interests, while strong labor unions are politically active in protecting worker interests regionally and nationally, bringing their members out to vote, and working as an effective lobby organization in each German state (lander) and on the national level.

In the United States since World War II we can trace a far different labor history. For American employees it has been a half century of declining influence, to a large extent led by government actions against labor rights (Griffin, Wallace & Rubin, 1986; Tilly & Tilly, 1998). Studies such as that of Useem (1984) are able to show how increased political action by the American corporate elite from the late 1970s set the stage for increased U.S. government actions reducing the influence of labor, especially during the 1980s. The primary point is that this history of class politics in the second half of the 20th century in Germany and the United States may help us understand the different situations for workers in these two countries as we begin the 21st century. Research noted earlier shows less class voting in the United States in the second half of the 20th century, with growing non-voting among the lower classes. In contrast, works such as those by Useem (1984) and Domhoff (2002) indicate increasing political involvement by the U.S. corporate class. In Germany this research has shown class voting has been higher, and political activity by labor unions has become stronger since World War II (Thelen, 1991; Turner, 1991). These contrasting cases alone should stimulate more comparative research to find out the degree to which class voting and non-voting can produce differing outcomes for the lower classes.

We should also note the political activism of the U.S. elderly population and their declining rates of poverty in recent decades. We can begin with voting rates: while every other age group has had a drop in the percentage going to the polls since 1964, the percentage of those 65 and older who vote has held steady in most years, but has generally increased. In the presidential election of 1964, 66.1% of those 65 or old voted. By the 1980 presidential election the voter turnout for the U.S. elderly was 65.1%, and then 76.6% in the 2000 election. For the general population, the voter turnout in 1964 was 69.3%, then 59.2 in 1980 and 54.7 in 2000. For other age groups, especially those under 30 years of age, the drop was even more dramatic. Added to these figures is the increase of those 65 and older as a percent of the overall population. In 1980, for example, those 65 and older accounted for 24.1 million voters compared to 32.8 million by 2000.[9] In short, it can be argued that the numbers voting and the political activism of groups such as the American Association of Retired People have made politicians in the United States recognize the 65 and over population as a major political force to be reckoned with.

Examination of the poverty rates among the 65 and older population provides the second piece to the case analysis. Since poverty figures have been consistently estimated in the United States from 1959, only one group of Americans has had a strong and consistent rate of poverty reduction. In 1959 the poverty rate for those 65 and over was almost 35%, highest for any age group. By 1970 it was down to 24.6%, then 15.3 by 1975, 15.7 in 1980, 12.6 in 1985, 12.4 in 1990, and 10.2 for 2000. Only the working age population, 18–64, had a lower poverty rate in 2000 at 9.4%. All age groups had drops in their rate of poverty during the 1960s, but the rate for those 65 and older was the highest in 1959 and showed the largest and most sustained decline. Those below 18 years old, for example, had a poverty rate in the 28% range in 1959, but then the rate hovered around 20% for most years since 1980. Analysis of transfer payments, taxes, and market income show that it has been transfer payments, primarily in the form of an expanded Social Security System from the mid-1960s, that has brought most of the elderly population out of poverty and kept them out. Especially effective was the political decision in 1972 by Congress to peg annual Social Security check increases to the consumer price index (Tufte, 1978). No other major segment of the U.S. population had a guaranteed inflation hedge, which was especially important during the high inflation years of the 1970s.[10] The Democratic Party is seen as most responsible for promoting the expansion of the Social Security System and the Democratic Party has received the benefits: by 1994 those 65 and older were more strongly in favor of the Democratic Party than any other age group. Some 28% of those 65 and older said they strongly support the Democratic Party, with a majority in support when those weakly favoring the Democratic Party are included, compared to only 15% strongly supporting the Democratic Party in the general population (U.S. Bureau of Census, *Statistical Abstracts of the United States, 1999*, 2000, p. 299).

POLITICAL ENGAGEMENT AND INCOME INEQUALITY: COMPARATIVE EVIDENCE

When we consider the general issue of class political activity and class inequalities more generally, comparative case studies have suggested a relationship somewhat consistent with the contrasting cases of the United States and Germany outlined

Table 4. Class Voting and Comparative Impact of Welfare Benefits on Reducing Poverty.[a]

Country	Poverty (pre-welfare payments)	Poverty (after welfare payments)	Percent reduction	Class voting[b]
Sweden	34.1%	6.7%	−80.4%	4
Denmark	26.9	7.5	−72.1	4
England	29.2	14.6	−50.0	4
Belgium	28.4	5.5	−80.6	3
Germany	22.0	7.6	−65.5	3
Australia	23.2	12.9	−50.0	3
Netherlands	22.8	6.7	−70.6	2
France	21.6	7.5	−65.3	2
Italy	18.4	6.5	−64.7	2
Spain	28.2	10.4	−63.1	2
Canada	23.4	11.7	−50.0	1
United States	26.7	19.1	−28.5	1

Source: Constructed from data presented by Smeeding (1997), Mishel, Bernstein and Schmitt (1999, p. 377), Nieuwbeerta (2001).
[a] Poverty measured by income below 50% of median income in the nation. Data are available from 1989 to 1994.
[b] Ranking of class voting from lowest (1) to highest (4) from Nieuwbeerta (2001). The lowest class voting was found in the United States and Canada (around 0.5 on the Thomsen Index for most years), with relatively low levels in France, Italy, Netherlands, and Spain (Thomsen Index scores of around 1.0); intermediate levels in Australia, Austria and Germany (Thomsen Index of around 1.5); and higher levels (Thomsen Index of around 2.0) in Scandinavian countries and Britain (Nieuwbeerta, 2001, p. 125).

above (Esping-Anderson, 1990; Goodin et al., 1999). Data presented in Table 4, while certainly not conclusive and limited to only 12 countries, also suggests class voting may be related to income inequality and is worth brief discussion. Comparing pre-welfare payment poverty (relative poverty defined as below 50% of median income) with post-welfare payment poverty, Table 4 indicates that the United States lags behind other major industrial nations in government action to reduce poverty. In the far right column is the estimated level of class voting in each country from Nieuwbeerta (2001). One could argue that the 28.5% reduction in poverty through U.S. government action would be greater if there was greater class voting in the United States or if low income Americans voted in percentages equal to upper income groups, the U.S. elderly, or low income groups in other industrial nations. Table 4 does not suggest there is a strong correlation between class voting and poverty reduction, but countries low on class voting have lower poverty reduction or income inequality reductions through government action compared to the countries found to have the highest levels of class voting in Nieuwbeerta's (2001) research. The biggest exception is Great Britain since the Thatcher years which has had growing inequality in the 1990s and, using the new Purchasing Power Parity (PPP) measure of income, may even have a higher rate of absolute poverty than the United States (15.7% compared to 13.6% for the United States in the late 1990s; see Smeeding, Rainwater & Burtless, 2001, p. 51). For the United States, though, the key point is that compared to European nations, the United States is most different in *non-voting* by the lower classes, not just class voting in general. This non-voting, it could be argued, is the most important factor in less poverty reduction in the United States.

A number of other studies have shown similar results on state action and poverty or income inequality reduction using the large data set on income inequality compiled by the Luxembourg Income Study. For example, Behrendt (2000) has used the LIS data to analyze poverty reduction in major industrial nations through time. His analysis suggests a pattern similar to the class voting findings of Nieuwbeerta (2001), that is, a relationship between class voting and poverty reduction. Kim (2000) found that poverty reduction in industrial nations is strongly related to "welfare effort" – that is, simply how many resources are put into the welfare state, rather than the "efficiency" of state agencies. The line up of poverty reduction among the countries in Kim's analysis is again rather close to the class voting findings of Nieuwbeerta (2001), though again with exception of the U.K., which is now low in poverty reduction since the Thatcher years. Ritakallio (2001), using LIS data from 1980 to 1995, finds all major industrial countries have had growing income inequality when considering only market income, but most nations have kept inequality stable with income transfer programs, with the major exceptions of the USA and Canada. The amount of reduction in market income inequality due to state policies again follows rather closely the class voting patterns in Nieuwbeerta's (2001) research. Mahler (2001) has found that increases in income inequality because of economic globalization has been mediated by political variables. Income inequality is increasing with globalization in the United States and a few other countries, but in most nations Mahler's (2001) research suggests that government intervention has lessened the increases in inequality or even prevented the increase. Again we find apparent effects from the class voting differences noted by Nieuwbeerta (2001). Finally, as shown in Table 3, we can again note that Pressman (2001), using LIS data, has found a mix of middle class decline among industrial nations in recent years. The pattern of middle class decline or expansion in Table 3 is somewhat consistent with the pattern of class voting in Nieuwbeerta's (2001) research.

Finally, returning to Mahler's (2002) most recent research on income inequality and voter turnout discussed in some detail above, we have broader evidence of a link between voter turnout and income inequality (but again, no direct measure of voter turnout by income). In addition to the association between income inequality in a nation and subregions to voter turnout, Mahler also examined his data from the other direction – voter turnout to income inequality. In his words, "In sum, a three stage least squares model that includes a number of control variables, incorporates several proposed sources of cross-national variance in turnout, and allows for a non-recursive relationship between inequality and turnout confirms the central conclusion of this paper that electoral turnout is an important factor in explaining cross-regional variance in income inequality" (Mahler, 2002, p. 21). Because Mahler's data measure voter turnout per se and not class differences in voter turnout more specifically, we cannot directly link lower class non-participation in elections and higher inequality. But Mahler's research strongly suggests a likely link.

In one of the few studies to consider the issue of non-voting and poverty rates in the United States, Teixeira (1987) presents data showing non-voters were more likely to be poor in the 1960s. However, with a continuing decline in voter participation through 1980, Teixeira (1987) shows there were many other groups also among non-voters by then. Thus, any impact on poverty reduction by mobilizing non-voters in 1980 would depend upon "which *parts* of that population are mobilized into the electoral arena" (Teixeira, 1987, p. 111). We might add that there is no guarantee that non-voters among the lower classes would vote for liberal Democratic Party candidates who would work to reduce poverty and income inequality when elected. However, we should note again that since 1980, research by Weakliem and Heath (1999) suggests that both the Democratic and Republican Parties are now dominated by middle class voters in contrast to the past in which the Democratic Party had a greater proportion of lower income voters. This suggests that mobilizing low income voters today would bring more gains to the Democratic Party and possibly more elected officials supportive of government action to reduce poverty.

CONCLUSION AND SUGGESTIONS FOR FURTHER RESEARCH

It seems likely that the relationship between class and politics is mainly a function of the inclusive/exclusive character of the lower classes of any given welfare regime: the less inclusive the welfare regime, the less inclusive the politics; the less class politics, the less political participation, and so on. As Piven and Cloward (2000) note, one key reason the poor and lower classes do not vote is that neither political party in the United States has seriously sought out their vote in recent decades. And Winders' (1999) research suggests that since 1840 it has been the relatively rare periods of lower class social movement activity that have made the major political parties incorporate working class issues. Yet this sequence doesn't imply the class character of the political system just disappears: it increasingly becomes an issue of voters and non-voters. Quite often the idea that class politics is over finds support in the evolution of American voting. But this is misleading for several reasons. Among the most important reasons seems to be that the liberal welfare regime in the United States is the least inclusive of all major industrialized nations, which corresponds with the characteristic exclusiveness of American politics (Shier, 2000), in such a way that if it is true that the influence of class over voting is decreasing by comparison with race or gender over time, the pattern of non-voting is increasingly class-biased. Since 1964, Democratic voters have become more middle class voters relative to non-voters, while Republicans have remained unchanged (Weakliem & Heath, 1999, p. 120).

Turning to a possible research agenda, one obvious problem with most research in recent years has been its focus on the question of the existence of class voting patterns in the United States and other countries, but with very little research on class non-voting. Only recently has more research considered class and non-voting in comparative perspective, such as Weakliem and Heath (1999) and Mahler (2002). Also, the research that has been done on class voting in comparative and historical perspective remains primarily descriptive. We find some associations between class and voting vs. non-voting, and we find associations between voter turnout and levels of inequality, but additional research is needed suggesting causal relations more directly.

To most accurately understand differences in class voting and non-voting, it is likely that more qualitative comparative-historical research will be needed to specify some of the possible factors involved. There are quite probably a number of causes for differences in class voting and non-voting in addition to economic conditions in each country. Factors such as class identification, union organization, type of political system, differences in educational systems, and national value orientations most likely influence voter turnout, all of which interact in complex ways. For example, there is more variation among European nations on many of these variables than social scientists seem to recognize. Educational systems, for example, differ considerably, as do values orientations that can effect political behavior (Hampden-Turner & Trompenaars, 1993; Hofstede, 1991). With respect to Germany, it is argued that the high wages and worker protection described earlier are primarily related to laws protecting workers passed in the 1950s and expanded in the 1970s. This is in contrast to Sweden where continuing higher levels of union membership and labor union political activity are said to be more responsible for the high level of poverty reduction we considered in Table 4 (Thelen, 1991; Turner, 1991). Also, very little research on class voting and its outcomes has been done on Japan, the second largest industrial society. Japan was a country with comparatively low income inequality until economic change brought Japan to a medium level of inequality in the 1990s (Kerbo, 2000, Chaps 2 and 14). But Japan is a country described as having a low level of political democracy where unelected government ministry elites have most influence over political policies (Gao, 2001; Johnson, 1982; Kerbo & McKinstry, 1995). As Verba et al. (1987) suggest, Japan is also a country which has low to medium income inequality *without* significant government intervention to reduce inequality compared to the European countries that were included in our Table 4 (Verba et al., 1987). It is likely that class voting would be low in Japan using standard measures like those employed by Weakliem and Heath (1999, p. 120). To the extent all of this is accurate, it is likely that there are factors operating to influence class voting, non-voting, and political outcomes that we would be unaware of with restricting analyses to North America and Europe.

After more qualitative comparative studies among industrial nations have been undertaken to uncover the many factors which are possibly related to class voting, non-voting, and their outcomes, then these factors can be explored using larger data sets and the more typical comparative multivariate analysis as done by Weakliem and Heath (1999) and Mahler (2002). At that point, of course, we will also need more direct measures of non-voting by class and income across European nations than Mahler's (2002) research was unable to uncover. But this research should also give consideration to other measures of class categories when estimating class voting. Recent research has used Goldthorpe's class categories in addition to the simple manual/non-manual class distinction (Goldthorpe, 1999, 2001; Nieuwbeerta, 2001), but Wright's class categories relying on property and authority position in addition to occupational position has been shown to produce different results in social mobility studies (Wright, 1997). Other studies have shown that class measured with more Marxian concepts seems more related to value orientations such as levels of individualism and political perspectives (Burns, 1992). Further, we know there has been some changes in old working class communities and social organization among the poor which could impact voter turnout. For example, Wilson (1987) has found that growing inequality in minority communities has shifted the more affluent out of old neighborhoods, thus reducing community organization in the neighborhoods. Likewise, Eckstein (2001) has found that old style working class communities overlapping with ethnic status have more community organization which might effect such things as voting.

Finally, in addition to these other variables that might effect class voter turnout, future research and theory need to give greater attention to interaction between the two main types of explanations for non-voting – characteristics of voters vs. characteristics of political institutions. It is quite likely that political regimes which begin to ignore working class issues have an impact on the characteristics of lower class individuals (such as greater feelings of alienation), which affect voter turnout, which in turn lead political actors to turn their attention to other voter coalitions, further alienating lower class voters, and so on in a downward cycle. Comparative research should be able to help us understand how such a cycle could start or be prevented when including richer data sets from other industrial nations.

NOTES

1. See Smeeding and Grodner (2000), Mishel, Bernstein and Schmitt (1999), Kerbo (2000, pp. 26–29), and various World Bank Reports.
2. In addition to the typical and simple manual vs. non-manual indicator of class, Nieuwbeerta also used the more complex EGP seven class scheme developed by Goldthorpe and Erikson (Erikson & Goldthorpe, 1992).
3. But there was certainly variation. The lowest class voting was found in the United States and Canada (around 0.5 on the Thomsen Index for most years), with relatively low levels in France, Italy, Netherlands, and Spain (Thomsen Index scores of around 1.0); intermediate levels in Australia, Austria and Germany (Thomsen Index of around 1.5); and higher levels (Thomsen Index of around 2.0) in Scandinavian countries and Britain (Nieuwbeerta, 2001, p. 125).
4. Weakliem and Heath (1999) developed a more complex score for left vs. conservative party voting in the United States, France, and Great Britain than found in the usual "Alford index" to examine class voting (also see Weakliem, 2001).
5. As usual it is Switzerland that is close to the United State in low voter turnout. Switzerland's unique "regional pluralist system," however, makes local politics much more important for most Swiss compared to national elections (Benini, 1999).
6. "Extending the models of a psychological and sociological nature for explaining Spanish abstention, this study demonstrates that the level of participation depend to a large extent on strictly political factors: overall satisfaction of the electorate with the political situation, the introduction of political parties and their power of mobilization, the level of associationism and social capital, the degree of electoral competitivity . . ." (our translation) (Boix & Riba, 2000, p. 128).
7. All of the Luxembourg Income Study research cited in this paper can be found at http://www.lisproject.org/publications/wpapersf.htm
8. A couple of examples spelled out in detail in the "Codetermination Laws" are useful to quote (German Federal Ministry of Labor and Social Affairs, 1991, pp. 18–19):

> [Works councils have] a genuine right of codetermination in a series of matters such as: working hours, e.g. the introduction of short-time work . . . the fixing of job and bonus rates and comparable performance-related remuneration.
>
> In the case of recruitments, gradings, re-gradings and transfers the employer must obtain the consent of the works council. If the works council refuses its consent it can be substituted only by a decision in lieu of consent by a labor court.
>
> Dismissals are effective only if the works council was consulted in advance . . . .

The Codetermination Laws go on to specify that the company must open all its financial books to the works council if it is requested. Finally, it is useful to note that these laws pertain to all companies, German or foreign, that set up operations in Germany and hire

German employees (Kerbo & Strasser, 2000, pp. 46–51; Lincoln, Kerbo & Wittenhagen, 1995).

9. All of these data can be found in U.S. Bureau of Census, *Statistical Abstracts of the United States, 2001* (2002, pp. 250–251); U.S. Census, *Voting in the 2000 Election* (2001, p. 12).

10. These data can be found in the U.S. Bureau of Census, *Measuring 50 years of Economic Change* (1998,Table C-21); U.S. Bureau of Census, *Poverty in the United States, 2000* (2001, p. 4); Danziger, Haveman and Plotnick (1986, p. 54); U.S. Bureau of Census, *Measuring the Effects of Benefits and Taxes on Income and Poverty* (1992, Table 1).

REFERENCES

Behrendt, C. (2000). Holes in the safety net? Social security and the alleviation of poverty in comparative perspective. Luxembourg Income Study Working Paper No. 259.

Benini, A. (1999). *Modern Switzerland: A volume in the comparative societies series*. New York: McGraw-Hill.

Boix, C., & Riba, C. (2000). Las bases sociales y políticas de la abstención en las elecciones generales españolas (The social and political basis of abstention in Spanish general elections: Individual resources, strategic mobilization and electoral institutions). *Revista Española de Investigaciones Sociológicas, 90*, 95–128.

Burnham, W. D. (1982). *The current crisis in American politics*. New York: Oxford University Press.

Burns, T. J. (1992). Class dimensions, individualism, and political orientation. *Sociological Spectrum, 12*, 349–362.

Casper, L., & Bass, L. E. (1998). Voting and registration in the election of November 1996. Washington, DC: Current Population Reports P20–504.

Clark, T. N., & Lipset, S. M. (Eds) (2001). *The breakdown of class politics: A debate on post-industrial stratification*. Washington, DC: Woodrow Wilson Center Press.

Chirot, D. (1986). *Social change in the modern era*. New York: Harcourt Brace Jovanovich.

Danziger, S., Haveman, R. H., & Plotnick, R. D. (1986). Antipoverty policy: Effects on the poor and non-poor. In: S. H. Danziger & D. H. Weinberg (Eds), *Fighting Poverty: What Works and What Doesn't* (pp. 50–77). Cambridge, MA: Harvard University Press.

Domhoff, G. W. (2002). *Who rules America? Power and politics* (4th ed.). New York: McGraw-Hill.

Eckstein, S. (2001). Community as gift-giving: Collectivistic roots of volunteerism. *American Sociological Review, 66*, 829–851.

Erikson, R., & Goldthorpe, J. H. (1992). *The constant flux: A study of class mobility in industrial societies*. Oxford: Clarendon Press.

Esping-Anderson, G. (1990). *The three worlds of welfare capitalism*. Princeton: Princeton University Press.

Evans, G. (Ed.) (1999). *The end of class politics? Class voting in comparative context*. Oxford: Oxford University Press.

Franklin, M. N. (1996). Electoral participation. In: L. LeDuc, R. G. Niemi & P. Norris (Eds), *Comparing Democracies: Elections and Voting in Global Perspective* (pp. 216–235). Thousand Oaks, CA: Sage.

Gao, B. (2001). *Japan's economic dilemma: The institutional origins of prosperity and stagnation*. Cambridge, UK: Cambridge University Press.

German Federal Ministry of Labor and Social Affairs (1991). *Co-determination in the Federal Republic of Germany (legal texts)*. Bonn: Der Bundesminister fnr Arbeit und Sozialordnung Referat Presse.

Goldthorpe, J. H. (2001). Class and politics in advanced industrial societies. In: T. N. Clark & S. M. Lipset (Eds), *The Breakdown of Class Politics: A Debate on Post-Industrial Stratification* (pp. 105–120). Washington, DC: Woodrow Wilson Center Press.

Goldthorpe, J. H. (1999). Modeling the pattern of class voting in British elections, 1964–1992. In: G. Evans (Ed.), *The End of Class Politics?* (pp. 59–82). Oxford: Oxford University Press.

Goodin, R. E., Headey, B., Muffels, R., & Dirven, H. (1999). *The real worlds of welfare capitalism*. Cambridge, England: Cambridge University Press.

Greenberg, S. (2000). The progressive majority and the 2000 elections. A report on post-election national surveys. *The Institute for America's Future* (December 15).

Griffin, L., Wallace, M., & Rubin, B. (1986). Capitalist resistance to the organization of labor before the new deal: Why? How? Success? *American Sociological Review, 51*, 147–167.

Hampden-Turner, C., & Trompenaars, A. (1993). *The seven cultures of capitalism*. New York: Doubleday.

Hofstede, G. (1991). *Cultures and organization: Software of the mind*. New York: McGraw-Hill.

Houtman, D. (2001). Class, culture, and conservatism: Reassessing education as a variable in political sociology. In: T. N. Clark & S. M. Lipset (Eds), *The Breakdown of Class Politics: A Debate on Post-Industrial Stratification* (pp. 161–196). Washington, DC: Woodrow Wilson Center Press.

Inglehart, R. (1990). *Culture shift in advanced industrial society*. Princeton: Princeton University Press.

Jackman, R. W. (1987). Political institutions and voter turnout in the industrial democracies. *American Political Science Review, 81*, 405–424.

Jackman, R. W., & Miller, R. A. (1995). Voter turnout in the industrial democracies during the 1980s. *Comparative Political Studies, 27*, 467–492.

Johnson, C. (1982). *MITI and the Japanese miracle*. Stanford: Stanford University Press.

Keister, L. A. (2000). *Wealth in America: Trends in wealth inequality*. Cambridge, England: Cambridge University Press.

Kerbo, H. R. (2000). *Social stratification and inequality: Class conflict in historical, comparative, and global perspective* (4th ed.). New York: McGraw-Hill.

Kerbo, H. R., & Strasser, H. (2000). *Modern Germany: A volume in the comparative societies series*. New York: McGraw-Hill.

Kerbo, H. R., & McKinstry, J. (1995). *Who rules Japan: The inner circles of economic and political power*. Westport, Conn.: Praeger.

Kim, H. (2000). Anti-poverty effectiveness of taxes and income transfers in welfare states. Luxembourg Income Study Working Paper No. 228.

LeDuc, L., Niemi, R. G., & Norris, P. (Eds) (1996). *Comparing democracies: Elections and voting in global perspective*. Thousand Oaks, CA: Sage.

Lincoln, J. R., Kerbo, H. R., & Wittenhagen, E. (1995). Japanese companies in Germany: A case study in cross-cultural management. *Journal of Industrial Relations, 25*, 123–135.

Mahler, V. A. (2002). Exploring the subnational dimension of income inequality: An analysis of the relationship between inequality and electoral turnout in developed countries. Luxembourg Income Study Working Paper No. 292.

Mahler, V. A. (2001). Economic globalization, domestic politics and income inequality in developed countries: A cross-national analysis. Luxembourg Income Study, Working Paper No. 273.

Manza, J., & Brooks, C. (1999). *Social cleavages and political change: Voter alignments and U.S. party coalitions*. New York: Oxford University Press.

Mishel, L., Bernstein, J., & Schmitt, J. (2001). *The state of working America, 2000/2001*. Ithaca, NY: Cornell University Press.

Mishel, L., Bernstein, J., & Schmitt, J. (1999). *The state of working America, 1999*. Ithaca, NY: Cornell University Press.

Nieuwbeerta, P. (2001). The democratic class struggle in postwar societies: Traditional class voting in twenty countries, 1945–1990. In: T. N. Clark & S. M. Lipset (Eds), *The Breakdown of Class Politics: A Debate on Post-Industrial Stratification* (pp. 121–135). Washington, DC: Woodrow Wilson Center Press.

Piven, F. F., & Cloward, R. A. (2000). *Why Americans still don't vote: And why politicians want it that way*. Boston: Beacon Press.

Piven, F. F., & Cloward, R. A. (1988). *Why Americans don't vote*. New York: Pantheon Books.

Pressman, S. (2001). The decline of the middle class: An international perspective. Luxembourg Income Study Working Paper No. 280.

Powell, G. B., Jr. (1986). American voter turnout in comparative perspective. *American Political Science Review, 80*, 17–43.

Ritakallio, V. (2001). Trends in poverty and income inequality in cross-national comparison. Luxembourg Income Study Working Paper No. 272.

Rose, R., & McAllister, I. (1986). *Voters begin to choose: From closed-class to open elections in Britain*. London: Sage.

Shier, S. E. (2000). *By invitation only: The rise of exclusive politics in the U.S.* Pittsburgh: University of Pittsburgh Press.

Smeeding, T. M. (1997). Financial poverty in developed countries: The evidence from LIS. Luxembourg Income Study Working Paper No. 155.

Smeeding, T., & Grodner, A. (2000). Changing income inequality in OECD countries: Updated results from the Luxembourg Income Study (LIS). Luxembourg Income Study Working Paper No. 252.

Smeeding, T., Rainwater, L., & Burtless, G. (2001). United States poverty in cross national context. *Focus, 21*, 50–54.

Teixeira, R. A. (1987). *Why Americans don't vote: Turnout decline in the United States, 1960–1984*. New York: Greenwood Press.

Thelen, K. A. (1991). *Union of parts: Labor politics in postwar Germany*. Ithaca, NY: Cornell University Press.

Tilly, C., & Tilly, C. (1998). *Work under capitalism*. Boulder, CO: Westview Press.

Tufte, D. (1978). *Political control of the economy*. Princeton, NJ: Princeton University Press.

Turner, L. (1991). *Democracy at work: Changing world markets and the future of labor unions*. Ithaca, NY: Cornell University Press.

United Nations (2001). *Human development report, 2000*. New York: Oxford University Press.

Useem, M. (1984). *The inner circle: Large corporations and the rise of business political activity in the U.S. and U.K.* New York: Oxford University Press.

Vanneman, R., & Cannon, L. W. (1987). *The American perception of class*. Philadelphia: Temple University Press.

Verba, S., Nie, N. H., & Kim, J. (1978). *Participation and political equality: A seven-nation comparison*. Cambridge: Cambridge University Press.

Verba, S. et al. (1987). *Elites and the idea of equality*. Cambridge, MA: Harvard University Press.

Weakliem, D. L. (2001). Social class and voting: The case against decline. In: T. N. Clark & S. M. Lipset (Eds), *The Breakdown of Class Politics: A Debate on Post-Industrial Stratification* (pp. 197–224). Washington, DC: Woodrow Wilson Center Press.

Weakliem, D. L., & Heath, A. (1999). The secret life of class voting: Britain, France and the United States since the 1930s. In: G. Evans (Ed.), *The End of Class Politics?* (pp. 97–136). Oxford: Oxford University Press.

Wilson, W. J. (1987). *The truly disadvantaged: The inner city, the underclass, and public policy.* Chicago: University of Chicago Press.

Winders, B. (1999). The roller coaster of class conflict: Class segments, mass mobilization, and voter turnout in the U.S., 1840–1996. *Social Forces, 77,* 833–860.

Wolfinger, R. E., & Rosenstone, S. J. (1980). *Who votes?* New Haven: Yale University Press.

World Bank (2000). *World development report, 2000/2001.* New York: Oxford University Press.

Wright, E. O. (1997). *Class counts: Comparative studies in class analysis.* Cambridge: Cambridge University Press.

PRACTICING PROGRESSIVE POLITICS IN A CONSERVATIVE STATE: REFLECTIONS OF A NORTH CAROLINA LEGISLATOR

Paul Luebke

ABSTRACT

For twelve years as a legislator in the North Carolina General Assembly, I have observed and participated in widespread political debate. Key subjects have included the state's budget and tax policies, as well as cultural issues such as the death penalty, guns, and the public display of religion. During this same period, with time out for legislative leaves, I have taught sociology, including a seminar in political sociology, at the University of North Carolina at Greensboro.

This article focuses on the roles played by progressive activists (both outsiders and insiders) and progressive Democratic politicians in trying to win legislative battles against more entrenched conservative forces. It finds that the progressive coalition can sometimes persuade moderate Democrats to adopt more progressive public policy. The specific steps taken are discussed in detail. The article also provides examples of the progressive coalition's losses.

Political Sociology for the 21st Century
Research in Political Sociology, Volume 12, 197–210
© 2003 Published by Elsevier Science Ltd.
ISSN: 0895-9935/PII: S0895993503120086

INTRODUCTION

Both before and during my time in office, political sociologists have debated the significance of corporate power and of New Right culture in national and state government. William Domhoff (1996, 1998, 2003), for example, argues that any successful progressive policy making takes place in a political environment dominated by a corporate class.

In a similar vein, Dan Clawson and his co-authors (1998), conclude that the political agenda is dominated by corporate political action committees and wealthy individuals whose campaign contributions "obligate" both Democrat and Republican politicians to support a pro-corporate agenda. Both Domhoff and Clawson et al. believe progressive battles can be won in the U.S. Congress or state legislatures, but such victories are infrequent.

An alternate position, frequently identified with Theda Skocpol, contends that politicians can make policy with minimal influence from corporate leaders (Skocpol, 1980; Skocpol & Amenta, 1985). Anthony Orum (2001) expresses a similar view. He considers corporate interests as "the winds that blow the sails of the ship of state." While they *can* affect the course that is sailed, the sailors steering the course are state officials (Orum, 2001, p. 136).

The New Right ideology that underlies cultural conservatism has been well-articulated in two books by Rebecca Klatch (1987, 1999). Klatch notes that both libertarian ideas and those usually associated with the Christian Right are part of a political movement that seeks to sustain or restore conservative culture nationally and in each of the fifty states. My book, *Tar Heel Politics 2000* (Luebke, 1998), examines in North Carolina the strength of these New Right ideas, which I term traditionalism. *Tar Heel Politics 2000* also examines for North Carolina the issues of corporate power and the state previously raised by Domhoff, Skocpol and others.

This article looks primarily at progressive activists and progressive Democratic politicians. It focuses on how these progressives work with moderate Democrats and oppose political interests representing large corporations and organizations that advocate cultural conservatism. The article provides more understanding of what Sidney Tarrow (1988) calls the "intermediate level of political processes" by examining how politicians make policy when confronted by various pressure groups.

The research is based on observation during my twelve-years as a progressive Democrat in the North Carolina General Assembly. The specific examples emerge both from my early years, beginning in 1991 as a backbencher, and between 1999 and 2002 as a co-chair of the House Finance Committee and a member of the House Democratic leadership group.

THE CASE STUDY: NORTH CAROLINA AS A CONSERVATIVE STATE

Political scientist V. O. Key in his classic volume, *Southern Politics*, labeled North Carolina a "progressive plutocracy" (Key, 1949). While progressive in the sense of having made the greatest shift among the Southern states from agrarianism to industrialism, North Carolina's state government in the first half of the twentieth century was clearly controlled by wealthy industrialists. A key feature both then and now is the hostility of North Carolina corporate interests to organized labor. North Carolina today ranks among the least unionized of the fifty states. Of significance for political policy making is the fact that the AFL-CIO plays only a marginal role in state politics. It is this weakness of the labor movement that most differentiates North Carolina state politics from the politics of similarly industrialized states in the Midwest or Northeast (Luebke, 1998, Chap. 6).

North Carolina is also a culturally conservative state. Like most other Southern states, its predominant Protestant denomination is Baptist. Baptist religious values affirm a traditional social order. Although strongest in the small town and rural areas of North Carolina, this cultural traditionalism has a major impact on political battles in the North Carolina General Assembly (Luebke, 1998, Chap. 2). In sum, North Carolina is conservative in both its political-economic and cultural values.

THE PROGRESSIVE MINORITY: ACTIVISTS AND POLITICIANS

Despite the dominance of economic and cultural conservatism in North Carolina, progressive activist organizations, rooted primarily in the state's cities, play a key role in providing a political alternative to conservatism. These activists are part of what William Julius Wilson has termed the "multiracial progressive coalition in national politics" (Wilson, 1999, p. 12). In this case, however, the activists are focused on changing public policy at the state level. The activists must work in tandem with progressive Democratic legislators – about 20% of the Democrats in the legislature – as well as with the moderate Democrats who currently hold most of the legislative leadership positions.

The Outsider Activist

Outsider activists and outsider organizations view their joint role as promoting a perspective that is largely absent from everyday political debate in government.

Outsiders do not see political victory as imminent. They use demonstrations, teach-ins, magazine and newspaper op-ed articles, and informational picketing at public sites to place their issues into the public's consciousness. They try to influence both the media and politicians themselves.

In the present decade, progressive outside activists can by themselves rarely force politicians to take action. Nevertheless, they do create an overall climate more conducive to progressive political change. At the national level from the 1960s into the 1980s, outsider activists did successfully challenge and influence incumbent politicians. During the mid-1960s, for example, this outsider role was critical to drawing public attention to the negative side of the U.S. war in Vietnam. In the 1970s, California's mostly-Latino United Farm Workers Union relied on non-Latino outsiders across the United States to support publicly the boycott of products of specific California growers who were refusing to bargain collectively with the union. In the 1980s, anti-apartheid activists demanded that U.S. corporations withdraw from economic activity in South Africa.

The critical component of outsider activism is that this political advocacy does not include direct negotiations with politicians. The outsider activist wants the issue to become a public issue. Other political actors are expected to negotiate the specific changes in public policy.

The Insider Activist

Like the outsider, the insider activist has ideological preferences. Insider activists from advocacy organizations seek to pressure the two-party structure directly because they feel that the political options from which politicians normally make choices are too narrow. The outsider activist also shares this preference for more policy options. Insider activists focus on specific policies in a legislative body that they wish to change rather than on the broader public appeals made by the outsider. Insider activist organizations in North Carolina also generally have more resources than do the outsider organizations (McCarthy & Zald, 1977). They are likely to have paid staff who have both the time and the expertise to lobby the legislature on behalf of progressive causes.

At the level of national and state politics, "pro-choice" insider activists seek to preserve or expand women's reproductive rights, while "pro-life" insider ac-tivists simultaneously work to limit or deny these rights altogether. In city politics, neighborhood groups are prime examples of insider activism. Not all groups define "neighborhood protection" in the same way, but insider neighborhood activists are close monitors of their local political scene. They typically work tirelessly to per-suade politicians to cast what the activists consider to be "pro-neighborhood" votes.

Because insider activists are trying to influence politicians' decisions directly, they – unlike the outsiders – must be familiar with a legislative chamber and its personalities. Insiders must also accommodate to some extent to the politicians' definitions of the situation (e.g. what policy choices seem "realistic") and to the political culture. Insiders must, for example, look "respectable" if they appear before a city council or a state legislature, and they risk marginalization if they reject the norms of civility that prevail in those bodies (Luebke, 1981). This need to conform may be peculiar to Southern culture and less important in political debate in, for example, Michigan or Massachusetts.

Letters, phone calls, e-mails, and meetings with politicians are the stock-in-trade of the insider activist. Unlike the op-ed essay of the outsider, which typically focuses on long-term political change, an insider's message would more likely hammer away at a specific policy, such as an upcoming vote in the state legislature on curbing emissions from coal-fired power plants. Insider activists must mobilize volunteer supporters from legislative districts statewide. This hometown activist contact with the politician is crucial because those same hometowners will be the ones voting in the politician's next election.

Insider and outsider activists are linked in that the more strongly the outsider movement has caught the attention of the public, the media, and politicians, the stronger the bargaining power of the insider activists. For example, a successful outsider campaign for healthy air makes it easier for insider activists to convince politicians to vote to institute strict auto emissions testing.

Further, insider activists may persuade outsiders to participate temporarily in the more limited objective of a specific legislative vote. In that sense, outsiders can also play the role of an insider when they send e-mail messages to legislators or attend a press conference along with insider activists and progressive legislators.

Insider activists need to persuade the media that their issue enjoys widespread organized political support. Once persuaded, reporters provide publicity for the issue through their news stories (Gamson, 1992). The activists need the media recognition to build additional support for their issue and also because some politicians doubt that an issue is real if they have not seen it covered in the newspapers.

Another variable affecting the ability of insider activists to win policy battles is the strength and content of their messages to politicians (Klandermans, 1997). Progressive insider activists must learn to differentiate among politicians. Progressive legislators, while a distinct minority, need to be worked with closely, both to develop legislation and to organize a grass-roots strategy. The second key group, the moderate legislators, includes most of the legislative leadership. As moderate party leaders they must be convinced, for example, that specific services should be preserved even if taxes must be raised. To be successful, insider activists must develop a message that can gain support from the more egalitarian progressive legislators as well as from the more moderate party leadership.

The Moderate Politician

Typically, the Democratic Party leaders at national and state levels are moderate politicians. These are not "rock-the-boat" legislators; they see their role as sticking to the middle-of-the road. These politicians rely heavily on corporate PACs and wealthy individuals for the funds to run their own and their party's re-election campaigns (Clawson et al., 1998). While they recognize that their party has a platform and consequently a voting base that prefers certain policies, moderates are also aware of the demands of their corporate funders. Currently, this means a minimum of both taxes and regulations on business. For example, moderate Democratic leaders in Congress or in North Carolina face a difficult challenge in developing an annual budget. How do they satisfy their business and wealthy financial backers who want stable or reduced taxes, while simultaneously satisfying the progressive politicians and insider and outsider activists who demand increased spending for programs that benefit the historic middle- and low-income voting base of the Democratic party? (Domhoff, 1998, Chaps 7 and 8).

The Progressive Politician

Progressive politicians in North Carolina today are exclusively within the Democratic Party. They are both African-American and white. In urban areas such as Durham, Chapel Hill or Charlotte, the white progressive legislators win because a majority of whites and virtually all blacks who reside in their districts vote Democratic. This white support for Democrats in these cities contrasts with the rest of North Carolina, where, depending on the election, 60 to 70% of the whites vote for most or all of the Republican ticket (Luebke, 1998, p. 189).

African-American legislators, most of whom are progressive on both economic and cultural issues, win their seats either because of bi-racial Democratic support in the cities, or because, in small-town and rural eastern North Carolina, their districts are either majority-black or majority-influenced (i.e. 40 to 50% of the voting age population is African-American).

Because they are elected from such Democratic districts, progressive politicians do not rely on corporate PACs to fund their re-election campaigns. Unlike their moderate Democratic colleagues, progressive Democrats are willing to advocate publicly to close corporate tax loopholes and/or increase taxes on corporations and upper-income families in order to adequately fund education and human services programs. As a result, when they run for re-election, these progressive politicians receive both financial and "shoe-leather" campaign support from insider and outsider activists.

WINNING ACCEPTANCE FROM COLLEAGUES

To be able to forge compromises with moderate politicians, progressive politicians must in their first months on the job understand the initiation process whereby they, as rookie politicians, can become accepted onto the politician team. This is an area where a professor turned politician may face particular difficulty, because of the assumption in the dominant culture that academicians are too out of touch with "the real world." For example, in an article in the most influential newspaper that covers the legislature, Raleigh's *News and Observer*, a reporter wondered just before my first term started whether I could successfully make the transition from academic author of a book on North Carolina politics to the give-and-take atmosphere of the General Assembly. In retrospect, I recognize that during my initial 1991–1992 term, I often gave longer speeches than did most members in House floor debate, and my debate had a lecturing tone that in fact violated legislature norms. Adding this style to my substantive challenging of the pro-corporate agenda made me somewhat suspect in the eyes of some of my colleagues.

Aware at least that my political values were to the left of most of my colleagues, I looked for ways to demonstrate that I was otherwise "normal." This included going out to dinner with colleagues, discussing freight and passenger rail service (both past and present), chit-chatting about the men's basketball rivalry between Duke and UNC at Chapel Hill, and joining the legislative basketball team even though I am a very mediocre basketball player.

Perhaps most importantly, I invited a group of legislators who were avid baseball fans to be my guests at a Durham Bulls game. My willingness to host an evening watching minor league baseball and enjoying ballpark fare was an indicator to fellow legislators that I was "OK." As my first year progressed, I felt increasing acceptance. This was indicated formally in a post-session survey of legislators conducted by a state-government watchdog group; I was ranked the second "most effective" legislator among the sixteen freshmen in the 1991 session.

Political sociologists should not be surprised that rookies in a political body, whatever their previous occupations, are tested on whether or not they can take a joke. For example, because I teach nine hours a week at UNC Greensboro, my legislative colleagues loved to insist that I did not work the remaining 31 hours of the 40-hour work week. Finally, the rookie learns to wear the legislative uniform ("business attire" for men and women), and to adapt to the ritual of frequent hand shaking.

ACHIEVING LEGISLATIVE SUCCESS

The progressive politician must first analyze the social forces that underlie political conflict. The conservative orthodoxy on both cultural and corporate issues that prevails in many governmental settings today in the United States, including the North Carolina General Assembly, forces progressive politicians to assess how best to fight an uphill battle. Fundamental to winning this battle is persuading sufficient moderate Democrats that a particular policy should be part of the mainstream package. It includes convincing moderate Democratic leaders that progressive insider activists represent politically-active citizens across the state.

An example of this interplay between progressive politicians and insider activists occurred during the budget battle in the 2001 North Carolina legislature. The goal of the progressive insider activist was to ensure that education and social services programs were not gutted by politicians who wanted to produce a balanced budget solely by cutting programs. Instead, by calling for more revenues, progressive insider activists and their progressive politician allies focused on the importance of closing corporate loopholes and raising taxes on the wealthy. The insider activists entitled their campaign "Save Services/Raise Revenues," shorthand that could be easily remembered by politicians, the media, and the public.

In 2001, the insider activists relied on e-mail networks. By sending a message to interested listservs across the state about the urgency of contacting their legislators on one particular weekend in July 2001, insider activists based in the state capital mobilized a huge constituency of other activists across the state. More than four hundred messages, mostly personally composed letters, on the theme of Save Services/Raise Revenue arrived in legislators' e-mail inboxes over the weekend. As Hill and Hughes (1998, pp. 43–44) noted in their study of cyberpolitics, it is likely that these e-mail messages were simply a new method of communication from citizens who were already insider or outsider activists.

These well-timed messages helped progressive Democrats persuade the rest of the Democratic majority in the State House to support a tax bill that would raise the revenue to reduce cuts in the state's education and human services budget. While the tax bill compromise included a sales tax increase that the progressive politicians and activists disliked, the activist-politician coalition could take credit for ensuring that some progressive tax measures were included in the compromise. Also, the budget cuts were far less severe than they would have been without the work of the progressive coalition.

Another successful legislative campaign, begun in the late 1990s, sought to outlaw the death penalty for the mentally retarded. It is a good example of how progressive legislators worked with outsider and insider activists on a non-economic cultural issue. Outsider activists, in North Carolina, nationally and even internationally, first helped shape the debate by calling outright for state abolition of the death penalty. For more than a decade, whenever there was a scheduled execution, North Carolina outsider activists drew media attention by holding a vigil at one or more sites around North Carolina for six hours before the state's scheduled 2 a.m. execution time. It ensured that the public watching the 11 p.m. news would see an opposition voice to the death penalty.

Taking advantage of increased public awareness of criticism of the death penalty in North Carolina, progressive politicians decided to take action. However, they recognized that support for abolition was minimal among legislators. Instead of introducing bills to abolish the death penalty in North Carolina, the progressive politicians persuaded mainstream Democratic politicians to allow an official study commission to meet during 1999 and 2000 to consider death penalty issues. The study commission collected data on three points: the case for a death penalty moratorium; the case for additional reporting by prosecutors of racial data of both perpetrators and victims to access potential racial discrimination in death penalty cases; and the case for stopping the execution of the mentally retarded. In a "tough on crime" state like North Carolina, all these issues faced varying levels of opposition.

Progressive politicians, with the assistance of insider activists who testified at study commission hearings, recognized that in raising three controversial issues, the least controversial issue had the best chance of success. In this case, this meant that the progressive politician-activist alliance was most able to win support from mainstream politicians for the prohibition of the execution of the mentally retarded. By presenting arguments for three bills that would weaken the death penalty's prominent place in North Carolina's criminal justice system, the progressives gained mainstream Democratic support for one of the three options. The Democratic majority in both the House and Senate succeeded in passing the important bill to protect the mentally retarded from this punishment. North Carolina's bill became law in October 2001, eight months before the 2002 U.S. Supreme Court decision that declared such executions cruel and unusual punishment. The Supreme Court majority opinion acknowledged that the increasing number of states passing such prohibitions – North Carolina was the 18th state of the 38 states that allow capital punishment – affected their decision.

Regarding economic issues, a reality for the progressive Democratic politician in North Carolina today is that political leaders of both major parties allow large corporations to play a dominant role in establishing political agendas. In the

North Carolina General Assembly, the typical member is "pro-business." To be sure, pro-business can be defined in numerous ways. At the present time, business interests define pro-business as meaning maximizing benefits from government while shifting the cost of government to others, especially to lower-income individuals. The business lobby seeks to establish its position as eminently reasonable and beyond debate, the only logical position for, say, a state legislature to take. This argument is frequently reinforced with the claim that if State A raises business taxes or increases government regulation of business, the business will happily relocate in its entirety to State B.

This is a powerful message to most moderate and conservative politicians, who typically accept the corporate definition of the situation as beyond dispute. But a progressive politician necessarily brings two different insights to this analysis. The first is that business minimizing its own taxes represents just one definition of business self-interest. Since the corporations' survival is dependent on trained employees who emerge from a taxpayer-funded education system, it could equally be argued that it is in the self-interest of businesses and their major stockholders to pay higher taxes to fund education. A second argument that progressive politicians bring to the legislative debate is that pro-business is not the only or best world-view. There is no reason why, in a democratic society, the preferences of business lobbies should be able to overwhelm the needs of the developmentally-disabled, the at-risk children, or the low-income elderly who cannot afford prescription medication.

PROGRESSIVE AND CONSERVATIVE FRAMING OF THE ISSUES

Progressive politicians are borrowing from political sociology when they consider how to frame their issues and choose language to combat the conservative orthodoxy. They know that how issues are presented in debate will greatly affect a bill's chances of passage. Their framing efforts indicate that "master frames" to legitimate political action (cf. Snow & Benford, 1992) are constructed not only by movement activists, but also by progressive politicians. For example, in a culturally traditional state like North Carolina, funding for HIV/AIDS prevention programs has succeeded because the illness has been framed as a consequence of drug abuse rather than of homosexual behavior. Similarly, progressive activists and legislators who sought to require safe storage of handguns in the home framed the issue in 2001 as a way to save children's lives, rather than as an attempt to regulate the ownership of guns. However, conservative activists, notably from the National Rifle Association, defeated the safe-storage legislation by countering with their own frame. They successfully argued that safe storage requirements would make gun-owning citizens unable to defend themselves against household intruders. Also in 2001, progressive activists and politicians sought to defeat an effort by New Right Republican legislators and activists to allow the posting of the Ten Commandments in North Carolina's public schools. Progressives framed the issue as a need for the legislature to recognize the increasing diversity of North Carolina. But the conservative frame – that North Carolina is overwhelmingly a Christian state and that the bill did not force non-Christians to read the Ten Commandments – was much more persuasive to the House majority.

Besides the framing of issues, another task for progressive politicians is to speak out publicly on their policy preferences. Without hearing from progressive politicians, it is easy for the news media to presume that only the views of moderate or conservative leaders are valid (cf. Bachrach & Baratz, 1963). To counter such media perception, progressive politicians can give credibility to activists by endorsing their proposals at press conferences. Politicians, precisely because they have been elected to office, have a certain legitimacy in the media's eyes, and this legitimacy can be transferred to the progressive activists by their politician allies.

Finally, the progressive politician has the advantage of being able to introduce and advocate for bills in legislative committees, and thereby expand the parameters of legitimate political debate. Often, business lobbyists and moderate and conservative politicians at national and state levels, will declare, for example, that new taxes, or at least new taxes on business and the wealthy, are "not on this session's agenda." A politician who disagrees with that statement can introduce bills that place the burden on these previously-exempted groups.

Indeed in North Carolina, the mainstream tax debate usually focuses on one question: whether to raise the sales tax, which falls disproportionately on the middle and low income majority, or whether to raise no new taxes at all. A major achievement of progressive legislators during my twelve years in the General Assembly has been to introduce bills that close business loopholes, raise taxes on the wealthy, and provide tax relief for the lower-income majority. While these bills have failed more often than they have succeeded, their introduction has widened the discussion of possible policy alternatives (cf. Luebke & Zipp, 1983).

In 1998, for example, an unusual coalition of progressive Democrats and anti-tax Republicans successfully eliminated the 4% state sales tax on groceries that had been on the books since 1961. And on two occasions, 1991 and 2001, huge budget shortfalls enabled progressive Democratic politicians to convince moderate and conservative Democrats that a higher tax bracket on the highest 2% of incomes was an appropriate policy.

PROGRESSIVE ACTIVISTS AND LEGISLATORS' HOME DISTRICTS

Progressive politicians cannot succeed without the progressive insider activists, who can excel at placing a human face on potential budget cuts in public education or mental health services. The direct constituent contact in legislators' home districts that the insiders arrange makes a difference because politicians often overlook the human dimension of service cuts. Budget language focuses on the millions of dollars in reduced expenditures statewide and not on the specific examples in each legislative district of the low-income elderly who will lose their home health care or the teacher's aides who will lose their jobs. The example that means the most to a legislator is when a voting constituent is providing the specifics, focusing on a situation within the legislator's district. Constituent pressure, arranged by the insider activists, on moderate and conservative Democrats can persuade those same politicians to be more willing to vote for a budget package that avoids deep service cuts.

Likewise, the progressive activist cannot succeed without the progressive politician. The insider must rely on progressive politicians to achieve the activist's policy goals. These progressive politicians provide the crucial link between the activists and the moderate Democratic politicians who typically direct policy.

DISCUSSION

In the North Carolina case, outsider and insider activists along with their politician allies successfully persuaded the General Assembly to ban the execution of the mentally retarded. But on two other cultural issues, gun control and the public school posting of the Ten Commandments, the conservative orthodoxy prevailed. On the issue of corporate power in state politics, the political agenda of corporate interests became the political starting position for the moderate Democrats who controlled the House. Corporations wanted to avoid tax burdens on business and the wealthy. While corporate interests voiced support for public education improvements, they wanted a consumer tax, the general sales tax, to pay for such programs (Luebke, 1998, pp. 43–46). From time to time, a vigorous coalition of progressive activists and politicians not only saved public education and human services programs in the budget, but even shifted some of the tax burden toward big corporations and the wealthy. Such progressive victories were, however, the exception rather than the rule.

Overall, state legislators did not act autonomously but rather adhered mostly to pro-business values that were openly hostile to progressive tax policy. My experiences in North Carolina are generally in accord with the positions of Domhoff and Clawson. Regarding cultural issues, the New Right ideology studied by Klatch has a significant hold on legislative politics in North Carolina.

For other states, I would hypothesize that large corporate interests shape the legislative debate and that progressive activists and legislators face an uphill battle similar to the conflict in North Carolina. The exception would likely be in those states whose labor unions still retain significant clout in the state legislature. I would further hypothesize that the political power of cultural conservatives is in many states far less than in North Carolina. The critical variable, in my analysis, is the extent to which religious diversity and other kinds of diversity are a taken-for-granted reality in that state. I would expect Mississippi and Montana to have a political debate on cultural issues that resembles North Carolina's, but that the Massachusetts legislature would be less receptive to New Right activism.

Finally, to increase our understanding of legislative politics, I would recommend that more political sociologists, if they themselves do not wish to be politicians, conduct open-ended interviews with state legislators about the substance and process of legislative politics. One recent study in North Carolina found that politicians were remarkably forthright in talking about the difficulty of striking a balance between the desires of their home town constituents and the requests of the corporate lobbyists (cf. Fenno, 1978; Shirley, 2002). The study (Shirley, 2002) suggests that much could be learned from legislator interviews that of course promised anonymity to the interviewees. Should I retire from the General Assembly (or "be retired" by the voters of my district), such interviews with North Carolina legislators would be high on my research agenda.

ACKNOWLEDGMENTS

I wish to thank MaryBe McMillan, the anonymous reviewers, and the editors for their constructive comments on earlier drafts.

REFERENCES

Bachrach, P., & Baratz, M. (1963). Decisions and non-decisions: An analytical framework. *American Political Science Review, 57*, 632–642.

Clawson, D., Neustadtl, A., & Weller, M. (1998). *Dollars and votes*. Philadelphia: Temple University Press.

Domhoff, G. W. (1996). *State autonomy or class dominance*. New York: Aldine de Guyer.

Domhoff, G. W. (1998). *Who rules America? Power and politics in the year 2000*. Mountain View, CA: Mayfield Publishing Company.

Domhoff, G. W. (2003). *Changing the powers that be: How the left can stop losing and win.* Lanham, MD: Rowman & Littlefield.

Fenno, R. (1978). *Home style: House members in their district.* Boston: Little Brown.

Gamson, W. (1992). *Talking politics.* Cambridge: Cambridge University Press.

Hill, K., & Hughes, J. (1998). *Cyberpolitics: Citizen activism in the age of the internet.* Lanham, MD: Rowman and Littlefield.

Key, V. O., Jr. (1949). *Southern politics in state and nation.* New York: Knopf.

Klandermans, B. (1997). *The social psychology of protest.* Oxford: Blackwell Publishers.

Klatch, R. E. (1987). *Women of the new right.* Philadelphia: Temple University Press.

Klatch, R. E. (1999). *A generation divided: The new left, the new right and the 1960s.* Berkeley: University of California Press.

Luebke, P. (1981). Activists and asphalt: A successful anti-expressway movement in a 'new south city'. *Human Organization, 40,* 256–263.

Luebke, P. (1998). *Tar Heel politics 2000.* Chapel Hill: University of North Carolina Press.

Luebke, P., & Zipp, J. (1983). Social class and attitudes toward big business in the United States. *Journal of Military and Political Sociology, 11,* 251–264.

McCarthy, J., & Zald, M. (1977). Resource mobilization and social movements: A partial theory. *American Journal of Sociology, 82,* 1212–1241.

Orum, A. (2001). *Introduction to political sociology* (4th ed.). Upper Saddle River, NJ: Prentice Hall.

Shirley, W. B. (2002). Political compromise: How North Carolina legislators reconcile the differences between their constituents and PACs. M. A. Thesis. Department of Sociology, The University of North Carolina at Greensboro.

Skocpol, T. (1980). Political response to capitalist crisis: Neo-Marxist theories of the state and the case of the new deal. *Politics and Society, 10,* 155–202.

Skocpol, T., & Amenta, E. (1985). Did the capitalists shape social security? *American Sociological Review, 50,* 572–575.

Snow, D. A., & Benford, R. D. (1992). Master frames and cycles of protest. In: A. D. Morris & C. McClurg Mueller (Eds), *Frontiers in Social Movement Theory* (pp. 133–155). New Haven: Yale University Press.

Tarrow, S. (1988). National politics and collective action: Recent theory and research in Western Europe and the United States. *Annual Review of Sociology, 14,* 421–440.

Wilson, W. J. (1999). *The bridge over the racial divide.* Berkeley: University of California Press.

PART III:
SOCIAL MOVEMENTS

EMERGING TRENDS IN THE STUDY OF PROTEST AND SOCIAL MOVEMENTS

Pamela E. Oliver, Jorge Cadena-Roa
and Kelley D. Strawn

ABSTRACT

Four important trends in the study of social movements are discussed: expanding the case base beyond the social reform movements of Europe and Anglo-America to encompass other regions and types of movement; a theoretical synthesis that integrates protest with institutional politics and focuses on mechanisms and processes rather than causes and effects; a growing focus on events as units of analysis; and increasing integration of social psychological and cultural theories of social construction with structuralist accounts of movements. Taken together, they promise theory that is both broader in scope and better able to address the diversity of social movements.

INTRODUCTION

Fifty years ago, sociologists considered protest to be an undemocratic intrusion into politics. In the wake of the movements of the 1960s, protest is now seen as an important adjunct to democratic polities and a significant factor in the transition from authoritarian to democratic regimes. The study of protest and social movements has mushroomed from a marginalized and almost-dying sub-specialty of social psychology in the 1960s to a large specialty area of

Political Sociology for the 21st Century
Research in Political Sociology, Volume 12, 213–244
© 2003 Published by Elsevier Science Ltd.
ISSN: 0895-9935/PII: S0895993503120098

sociology in its own right with significant ties to political, organizational, and cultural sociology as well as to social psychology. Social movements theorists see protest as "politics by other means," and it is now well recognized that extra-institutional and institutional politics are intertwined and interdependent.

Since the 1970s, scholars of social movements have developed a productive body of theory and research around the interrelated theoretical orientations generally labeled resource mobilization, political process, and framing theories. There are excellent reviews available of these theoretical traditions (e.g. Benford & Snow, 2000; McAdam, McCarthy & Zald, 1996) and we cannot do justice to them here. Instead, our agenda is forward-looking, seeking to pick up several key trends in the study of social movements that we believe should be important in the coming decades. All involve transcending old categories and boundaries and all combine methodological and theoretical advances. Partisans view some of these trends as coming from theoretically incompatible standpoints, but we do not. Instead, we see them as addressing different important features of a complex reality. The field of social movements is broad, and no article of this length can possibly do justice to every significant trend. Even with our restricted scope, we have had to reduce or eliminate our coverage of some topics to meet the word limits of this piece. Despite these limits, we are confident that the trends we highlight are among the most important.

We treat the first two trends more briefly, and the other two in more detail. The first trend is that the case base underlying mainstream social movements theory is expanding beyond the reform movements of Anglo-America and Western Europe. Regionally, "general" theories are beginning to take account of Eastern Europe, Latin America, Asia, and Africa. Substantively, ethnic conflict, democratization movements, and revolutions have been added to social reform movements as central topics of concern, and concepts of regime-movement relationships and the organization of protest have been broadened to encompass authoritarian regimes and the complex dependency relations of nations in the world economy.

This broader empirical base has fed into the second trend, a broad and unfinished attempt to rework the core theory of the relation between social movements and politics. Older theory focusing on the inputs and outputs of social movements as units of analysis is giving way to new theory which views movements as imperfectly bounded sets of processes and mechanisms capturing complex relations between movements and states.

Changing theory has been linked to the third trend, increased use of event analysis in social movement research. Analyses of the distributions of events have long been part of the repertoire of movement research, but their use is growing and has led to new research on the interrelations of different kinds of acts over time. We give special attention to methodological and theoretical issues that arise because new media are the major source of event data.

The fourth trend that needs to grow involves moving past the old structuralist versus constructionist debates, and an acceleration of the rapprochement between theories grounded in political sociology on the one hand and social psychology and cultural sociology on the other. This involves abandoning false dichotomies such as rational versus emotional, political versus psychological, material versus cultural and growing appreciation of the underlying unities. We offer what we believe are some important clarifications among concepts and levels of analysis in this area.

In selecting these trends, we have omitted many important lines of work. What unifies these is that they are parts of the general project of developing a broader, more dynamic and fluid conception of the terrain of movement processes. Protest event analysis and social constructionist theory may seem to be at opposite ends of a theoretical continuum – certainly specific research projects tend to work on one or the other, and specific researchers in one stream all too often disparage the work in the other – but any valid conception of social movements must be able to encompass both.

EXPANDING THE CASE BASE

All theories, no matter how abstractly stated, are grounded in empirical cases. Mainstream sociological social movement theory developed in the context of the reform movements of the U.S. and Western Europe, and this base shaped the theory. As Tilly (1978) argued long ago, the "social movement" as understood in the U.S. and Western Europe co-evolved with relatively stable popular democracies. Regimes vary greatly in their popular legitimacy, stability, readiness to repress, and responsiveness to popular mobilization as well as in their capacity to contain and channel inter-group conflicts within the nation-state. These matter even in comparing European nations, but the range of variation is severely truncated when only the dominant industrial nations of U.S. and Western Europe are considered. Regimes elsewhere are generally less stable or less democratic, or both. Cases from other regions highlight the limitations of prior theory, and point to new problems to study.

The democratization wave of the 1990s opened a new range of research about the form and role of protest movements and their relations to regimes in authoritarian and post-authoritarian conditions (e.g. Alvarez, Dagnino & Escobar, 1998; Cook, 1996; Escobar, 1992; Escobar & Alvarez, 1992; Foweraker, 1995; Foweraker & Craig, 1990; Hipsher, 1996, 1998a, b; Mainwaring, 1987, 1989; Mainwaring &

Viola, 1984; Oxhorn, 1995; Sandoval, 1998; Schneider, 1995; Stokes, 1995). Linz and Stepan's (1996) detailed comparative investigations of democratizing states have identified the ways in which the specific character of the authoritarian state as well as the timing and sequence of reforms have shaped the trajectory of democratization as well as ethnic conflicts and other social turmoil. Protest and social movements play crucial roles in these processes and are affected by them.

Movements in nations that are not dominant in the world economy have different configurations arising from their economic dependency, including severe material deprivation among large segments of the population and the strictures of austerity programs. A separate literature has focused narrowly on protests directed at austerity programs and neoliberal reforms (Walton, 1989; Walton & Ragin, 1990; Walton & Seddon, 1994; Williams, 1996) and, in a very limited way, on collective protest following austerity (Auvinen, 1996, 1997), but these have done little to integrate regional distinctions and unique national contexts into the broader realm of social movements theory.

A growing literature examines international and transnational movements and issue networks as well, with special emphasis on how these formations relate to and affect national politics and movements. Space does not permit a review of this work, but see Smith, Chatfield and Pagnucco (1997), Keck and Sikkink (1998), or Guidry, Kennedy and Zald (2000) for reviews.

Until recently, there has been little sustained attempt to bring mainstream social movement theory into dialogue with experiences outside Anglo-America and Europe. Scholars of movements in other regions largely ignored or found wanting general social movement theory in addressing the movements of their regions, and "mainstream" theorists of social movements generally ignored other regions in formulating their theories. Even as late as 1996, a major conference volume edited by McAdam, McCarthy and Zald titled *Comparative Perspectives on Social Movements* treated only cases from the U.S. and Europe (although there were a couple of Eastern European cases) and appeared not even to mention Africa, Latin America, or Asia. By contrast, McAdam, Tarrow and Tilly's (2001) most recent theoretical synthesis includes cases from Mexico, Kenya, the Philippines, India, and China in addition to those from Europe.

While the body of work for Asia and Africa has grown of late, the most sustained dialogue so far between "regional" studies and "mainstream" theory has centered on Latin American movements. Latin American universities have a long tradition of scholarship with respect to social movements and collective action in their own countries. Beginning in the late 1980s, several edited volumes critically juxtaposed Latin American traditions and those of U.S./European social movements theory, seeking to develop an understanding of popular protest that started with the Latin American experience (Eckstein, 1989; Escobar & Alvarez, 1992; Jaquette, 1994;

Jelin, Zammit & Thomson, 1990). The articles in these volumes address a broad and eclectic range of collective action topics including peasant and grassroots organizations, violence and revolutionary protest, women's organizations and their role in local community movements and broader identity issues, democratization, the role of the Catholic Church in mobilization, and the utility of the "new social movements" framework in Latin America.

Subsequent Latin American work has engaged many of the major theoretical issues in the study of movements. Following trends elsewhere in the field, women/feminism/gender topics have become quite prominent in Latin American research. A number of these have focused on the conflicts within women's movements internationally and the prospects for bridging these gaps (Ehrick, 1998; Guy, 1998; Safa, 1996). Some have engaged broader contemporary topics like feminism, identity, and democracy (Huiskamp, 2000), gender and citizenship (Schild, 1997), and how gender shapes political protest (Einwohner, Hollander & Olson, 2000), while others address much more localized problematics, like the role of women in the rise of urban movements (Massolo, 1999).

Recent work has also engaged important topics relating to culture, identity, and "new social movements" in the Latin American context. Projects have sought to link identity formation and its relationship to violence and citizenship (Schneider, 2000), democratization and regime change (Huiskamp, 2000), and class relations (Veltmeyer, 1997). The relevance of social movements in the context of civil society is also a recurrent theme. Alvarez, Dagnino and Escobar (1998) draw on contemporary civil society paradigms to argue that the rise in democratization in Latin America has not diminished the significance of social movements. At the same time, Beasley-Murray (1999) argues that the civil society paradigm does not adequately account for the rapid rise of religious fundamentalist movements in Latin America. Still others have argued that culture and civil society are essential dimensions for understanding increased regional integration as a product of neo-liberalism (Jelin, 2001), and that mobilization in the Latin American context must be theorized by integrating "new social movement" concepts with more conventional resource and organizational elements (Mascott, 1997; Zamorano Farías, 1999).

The contemporary work focusing on the unique mobilization experience of Latin America addresses a number of additional topics. The role of the Catholic Church in grassroots mobilization remains a topic of interest (López Jiménez, 1996), while the spread of evangelical and fundamentalist religious organizations throughout Latin America has received considerable attention, particularly with respect to how these relate to indigenous and community movements (Canessa, 2000; Le Bot, 1999) and their relation to social changes brought about by economic crises and neo-liberal policies (Gill, 1999; Misztal & Shupe, 1998). Other areas of focus have been land reform, peasant movements, and the unemployed (Kay, 1998; Larroa Torres, 1997; Petras & Veltmeyer, 2001), the convergence of environmental awareness and social mobilization (Dwivedi, 2001; Stonich & Bailey, 2000), urban movements and community/neighborhood organization (Ellner, 1999; Fernandez Soriano, Dilla Alfonso & Castro Flores, 1999), the transnationalization of mobilization (Mato, 2000; Stonich & Bailey, 2000), and regional integration and liberalization (Brysk & Wise, 1997; Jelin, 2001).

PROTEST AND POLITICS: FROM OUTCOMES TO CONSEQUENCES

The growing case base has fed into a broadening and reworking of theory. The political process synthesis knits together political opportunities, framing and mobilization structures as an integrated account of the sources of social protest (McAdam, McCarthy & Zald, 1996). As useful as this synthesis has been, there is a growing belief that it is too static and categorical, with its focus on inputs and outputs between movements and regimes as distinct actors (Goldstone, 1998). There are growing attempts to theorize the dynamic interplay and interconnection between movements, parties, regimes and other actors as social change unfolds (Goldstone, 2002). McAdam, Tarrow and Tilly (2001) have called for a conceptual shift, away from looking for invariant causes and effects to looking for mechanisms and processes that occur in many different kinds of movements and that lead to different outcomes depending on the specific contexts within which they occur. Metatheoretically, this involves a shift away from physics as a model, with its mechanical inputs and outputs. Oliver and Myers (2003a) and Koopmans (2002) suggest that population biology and evolution provide a different meta-theoretical model: in evolution, the same mechanisms and processes (e.g. mutation, differential fertility and mortality, environmental pressure) generate widely different outcomes. Biologists can study the common features of these mechanisms and processes, the bounds they put on what is possible, and at the same time they recognize how these commonalities act to generate extreme diversity in species.

One aspect of this theoretical shift is to reframe old debates about movement "outcomes" and the relation between movements and regimes. Early resource mobilization/political process research viewed outcomes in relatively simple ways. Tilly's polity model (1978) viewed movements as "challengers" who lack routine access to decision-makers. Once they succeed, they become polity members with routine access to decision making. Gamson (1975, 1990) refined this to a two-dimensional typology: being accepted as a member of the polity (i.e. as having institutional access), and gaining new advantages (i.e. as achieving policy goals). Analytic reviews of studies of movement success may be found in Giugni (1998) and Burstein, Einwohner and Hollander (1995). Recent work has moved beyond the dichotomy of "success" and "failure" or even the idea of "outcomes," with its connotations of intentionality, and is instead considering "consequences." Actions can have wide-ranging and unintended consequences. One line of work picks up on the expansion of the case base, and expands the conception of how movements might affect regimes. Giugni (1998) distinguishes among incorporation, transformation and democratization. *Incorporation* occurs when movements or part of them are absorbed into the polity or into the existing institutional arrangements and procedures of society without altering the basic rules of the game. This path may lead to institutionalization, when movements become part of routine politics, or preemption when movement demands are integrated into governmental policy or legislation without opening the polity. *Transformation* requires fundamental changes in the social and political structures and institutions of society due to transfers of power that alter extant power relations within society. Revolutions are the most radical form of transformation, but movements often produce institutional change that alters power relations in a non-revolutionary way. Some of these transformations relate to transitions from authoritarian rule. *Democratization* develops when a transfer of power modifies the mutual rights and obligations between states and its citizens. Incorporation, transformation and democratization are not mutually exclusive processes but ideal types. Democratization presupposes at least some degree of incorporation and transformation.

New theorizing focuses on the dynamic interactions between regimes and movements. There is a growing recognition that movements and regimes change together or "co-evolve" (Koopmans, 2002; Oliver & Myers, 2003a). One pattern has been shifting tactics of social control of protests. Instead of battling protesters in the streets, police agencies increasingly turned to processes of channeling and negotiation to blunt the disruptive force of protests while allowing protesters to have their say (della Porta, 1996, 1999; della Porta & Reiter, 1998; McCarthy, McPhail, Smith & Crishock, 1998; McPhail, Schweingruber & McCarthy, 1998; Rasler, 1996). Movements, in turn, have evolved in response to shifting police practices. Protests in the U.S. became more routine and less disruptive in the 1980s and 1990s (Oliver & Myers, 1999). As the mutual evolution and adaptation continued, the late 1990s saw the growth of a new generation of disruptive protesters who sought ways to evade police channeling and increase the disruption of their events (Smith, 2001).

In addition to broadening the conception of political outcomes, scholars increasingly recognize the importance of broader patterns of change in culture, opinions, and lifestyles. An early voice in this shift was Gusfield (1981), who talked about "linear" and "nonlinear" conceptions of social movements, and stressed that movements could have many diffuse consequences that go far beyond the question of whether a particular goal has been attained. Oliver (1989) similarly envisioned a way of thinking about social movements as chains of action and reaction. Most scholars working in the field have long since recognized that movements have byproducts and unintended consequences (e.g. Deng, 1997; Giugni, 1999), and that "success" or "failure" hardly describe most of a movement's effects (Tilly, 1999, p. 268). Other kinds of consequences include movement spillover effects (McAdam, 1988; Meyer & Whittier, 1994) in which one social movement inspires, influences, and provides personnel to other movements and effects on the subsequent personal life trajectories of activists; changes in public discussion (della Porta, 1999; Koopmans & Statham, 1999; Melucci & Lyyra, 1998); changes in the public definition of social issues (Gusfield, 1981); collective identity of social groups (Taylor & Whittier, 1992); and changes of meaning in everyday life (Melucci, 1985).

PROTEST EVENT ANALYSIS

As theory has increasingly recognized the importance of ongoing strategic dynamics and mutual adaptation to understanding social movements, new theoretical and methodological tools are required to support this theory. One of the most important has been a growing emphasis on events rather than organizations or movements as units of analysis. Sewell (1996) argues for an emphasis on events in qualitative historical research, and this is likely to be a productive avenue for more qualitative research. However, most event-oriented studies have been quantitative. Quantitative studies of protest event time series have long had a place in the study of social movements, including for example Tilly (1995), McAdam (1982), and Koopmans (1993), and it has long been recognized that focusing only on organizations missed important non-organizational (or hidden organizational) sources of collective action (Oliver, 1989). The growth of the quantitative analysis of protest accelerated with the application of event history analysis by Susan Olzak (1987, 1989, 1992), Sarah Soule (1997, 1999; Soule, McAdam, McCarthy & Su, 1999; Soule & Zylan, 1997), Myers (1997, 2000; Myers & Buoye, 2001) and others. Analysis of quantitative event series has allowed for more specific testing of hypotheses about the workings of the different elements of the political process models.

Event analysis is especially appropriate for the new directions of theorizing, for several reasons. First, events are (at least potentially) *commensurate* across different kinds of movements, thus facilitating unified theory of mobilization.

There do remain important questions about what to count as an "event," and there is no consensus on some single definition of what a protest event is.[1] The majority opinion favors "minimalist" definitions for data collection that includes a very broad range of events, with factors such as size or disruptiveness incorporated as control variables in analyses. Second, event-centered analysis readily incorporates time dynamics and mutual causality. The actions of challengers and regimes can be treated as mutually causative over time, and covariates can also vary over time. Analyses can move beyond a focus on single movement organizations or issues and into the realm of quantitative modeling of protest as a more generalized social phenomenon.

Third, an events approach can handle mobilization failure and decline, as well as its rise. It avoids the problem of sampling on the dependent variable, i.e. of only researching instances in which mobilization succeeded, because it is possible to identify the predictors or consequences of protest not occurring (or of occurring at a low rate). This promises to contribute to a much more sophisticated understanding of broader mobilization dynamics. Finally, an events approach permits study of the ways in which events affect other events (Oliver, 1989) through innovation (McAdam, 1983), diffusion (Myers, 2000; Olzak, 1987, 1989; Soule, 1997), and adaptive learning (Macy, 1990).

These advantages of event-centered analysis have led some to predict that events will lead to a unification of collective action theory and research. In particular, it is a source of optimism for those who contend that the broader field of collective action theory has been long on theory in recent decades but short on empirical evidence (Koopmans & Rucht, 1999).[2] But there are also cautions. While acknowledging the value of event analyses, Tarrow (1998) warns that there is substantial historical variation in the ways that political events, political processes, and political opportunities interrupt the "normal" flow of events over time.

Event-based research provides new data that feed theory development. Fillieule (1998) examines the national "protest rhythmology" of France in the 1980s, while Oliver and Myers (1999) show similar rhythms for a U.S. city in the 1990s. Rucht's (1996) analysis of right-wing radicalism in Germany shows that its decline after the peak in 1991 and 1992 was tied to the emergence of counter-movements and the reaction of key political actors and the state. Gentile (1998) shows that radical right parties and xenophobic organizations and protest rose together in Switzerland (1984–1993), even though neither sought alliance with or entry into the other.

Event data are not limited to Western countries where democracy is already institutionalized. Examining the post-communist countries of the Slovak Republic, Slovenia, and Hungary, Szabo (1996) argues that political protest is central in processes of regime change and the consolidation of new systems, and finds that the majority of protest forms are familiar (marches, rallies, strikes, etc.), but new protest forms are emerging as post-communist regimes consolidate. Ekiert and Kubik (1998) treat collective protest as a measure of democratic consolidation in Poland between 1989 and 1993, concluding that protest was "economy-centered" and came from predominantly mainstream groups, suggesting that Polish democracy had yet to accommodate protest as a "complement" to other institutions of representation. Within a similar context of transition from communist authoritarian rule to republican state structures, Beissinger (1998) examines the four-year protest wave that characterized the state-formation experience of former Soviet countries. Through event analysis, Beissinger is able to demonstrate how, contrary to conventional interpretations, the apparent increase in violent protest over the period was not a general characteristic, but rather one attributable almost exclusively to conflict over the definition of new political boundaries that were slower to emerge. Mueller (1999) uses event data to critique Western-derived models of protest cycles. Drawing on the 1989 protest cycle in the former East Germany, she argues models derived from Tarrow's analysis of Italian protest cycles lack fit in the non-Western, "distintegrating Leninist regime" case.

Events analysis also permits deliberate operationalization and testing of specific premises of mainstream social movements theory. A number of studies test hypotheses about the relation between protest and opportunity structures. Soule et al. (1999) examine the mutual causal effects of Congressional opportunity structures and women's movement protest, finding that political events affect protests but that protests have no effect on outcomes. Kerbo and Shaffer (1992) analyze unemployment protests from 1890 to 1940 and argue that elite statements recognizing unemployment as an issue and supporting welfare programs represented a moment of substantially broader opportunity for the unemployed to act, and that this accounted for the higher level of protest in the early 1930s compared to 1890–1900. McCammon, Campbell, Granberg and Mowery (2001) argue for a broader view of opportunity structures that is not restricted to the state, and show that the successes of state-level women's suffrage movements (1866–1919) were affected by prior changes in "gendered opportunities," i.e. expectations about women's roles in political participation, in addition to more conventional political opportunities and resources.

Event-centered analysis has addressed the claim that "new social movements (NSMs)" in Europe are qualitatively different from those in the United States (Kriesi, Koopmans, Duyvendak & Giugni, 1995). Koopmans (1996) argues against the claim that NSMs have always reoriented what he calls "patterns of extra-parliamentary political participation" in Europe. Analysis of protest events suggest that, contrary to the claim of NSM theorists, only in some countries does protest succeed in shifting claims away from traditional conflicts. Kriesi, Koopmans, Duyvendak and Giugni (1992) identify two dimensions of state structure which affect political opportunities: (1) strength, or ability to impose outputs; and (2) the extent to which states are "exclusive" (repressive, confrontative, polarizing) versus "integrative" (facilitative, cooperative, assimilative). They show that movement outcomes varied across this 2×2 typology and that the new social movements are just as affected by these structures as other movements. Moreover, the typology is consistent with an "opportunity structures" argument.

There has also been event-centered hypothesis testing outside the industrialized regions of the U.S. and Europe. In two studies of Palestinian protest events in the West Bank between 1976 and 1985, Khawaja (1994, 1995) uses parametric event history models to test resource mobilization, modernization, and deprivation theories with respect to mobilization. These studies find that each theoretical perspective, when tested alone, has at least some predictive power. However, when modeled together, only the resource variables retain their explanatory power, supporting resource mobilization theory. Walton and his collaborators (Walton, 1989; Walton & Ragin, 1990; Walton & Seddon, 1994) focus specifically on protest events directed against "liberalization" economic reforms in countries that are forced to renegotiate their foreign debt obligations with the International Monetary Fund, the World Bank, and other international actors (like the U.S. and Europe). With varying emphasis, these works test relative deprivation, resource mobilization, and world-systems/dependency explanations of the occurrence of protest events, finding some support for resource mobilization and world system theories.

Events and News Media Data

Most event data comes from newspapers or other news archives. For this reason, a correct understanding of the news media is a major methodological and theoretical priority for events researchers. The "selection bias" problem involves assessing the extent to which news sources represent some "true" account of the underlying protest events. Prior to the 1970s, analytical understanding of media bias was limited to what Mueller (1997) calls "representational" approaches, which simply held, without evidence, that the most prominent sources in use (the *New York Times* and the *World Handbook of Political and Social Indicators*) were the best available representations of protest. Some still argue for an essentially representational approach on the grounds that selection bias can be assumed to be relatively constant or systematic and will not significantly alter the results of research focused on analytical questions (see Koopmans, 1998). Beginning in the 1970s, however, most discussion has focused on "media model" approaches (Mueller, 1997), beginning with Danzger (1975), who argued that contextual factors conditioned whether conflicts got reported in the *New York Times*, and Snyder and Kelly (1977) who followed this with a "functional model" that held coverage to be a product of event "intensity" and media "sensitivity." Efforts that followed these sought to define which dimensions of bias were most important and to address ways of controlling bias (see Franzosi, 1987; Jackman & Boyd, 1979; Rucht & Ohlemacher, 1992 among others).

McCarthy, McPhail and Smith (1996) refocused selection bias debates by using official police permit records of protests in Washington, DC, in 1982 and 1991 to identify a "population" of protest events against which media reports could be compared. In line with Snyder and Kelly, they found clear evidence of selection bias, and concluded that event size was the most important factor in determining if events got covered. Additionally, they found that some event forms were less likely to be covered (notably vigils) and that the amount of news coverage an issue had been receiving predicted the probability that a protest about it would be covered.

Two subsequent research projects that also assessed news sources against police records deepened the theoretical conception of the problem. Hocke (1998) draws on the much broader ProDat data collection project (Rucht & Neidhardt, 1998) to develop an analysis of how a composite "news value" scale determines which events in Freiburg, Germany, get news coverage and those that do not. Consistent with McCarthy et al. (1996), Hocke finds that events with a higher news value score were more likely to get local news coverage, and more likely to be reflected in national news sources. However, his strategy of summing all "news value" elements into one composite scale prevented analysis of the relative importance of the individual factors. Oliver and her associates compared local event coverage in Madison, Wisconsin to police records of both permitted and unpermitted protests. They first assessed the coverage of protests as compared to other kinds of public collective events (Oliver & Myers, 1999) and then focused more narrowly on what they call message events and their relation to institutional politics (Oliver & Maney, 2000). In their data, the probability that a protest gets news coverage varies significantly from year to year, and is clearly associated with political and electoral cycles. Notably, the variation was large enough to make it appear that protest had declined in a year when it had actually increased. There were also complex interactions protests tied to institutional politics that were substantially more likely to be covered than other protests, but institutional politics competed with protest for space in the "news hole" so that both kinds of protests were less likely to be covered when the legislature was in session. They argue for theorizing the "tripartite" relations among protest, politics, and news media.

McCarthy, Smith and their associates have used their Washington, DC, data to examine media *description* bias (McCarthy et al., 1998; Smith, 2001). They show

how the media covers "hard" and "soft" details about protest events, as well as how electronic and print media represent each of these differently. They find that hard news, when reported, is largely reported accurately by both media. However, on soft news factors, electronic representations tend to be much more "thematic," emphasizing the purpose and significance of an event, while print media tend to be more "episodic," with greater coverage of protestor goals and details of the event.

McPhail, Schweingruber and McCarthy (1998) provide a detailed and rigorous examination of description bias of the 1995 March for Life, held in Washington, DC. While the complexity of the data definition and collection process precludes an elaboration of it here, of note is that the investigators were able to define, create, and test a set of variables to measure description bias, and to implement this schema in a real setting. Examining both television and newspaper reports on the event, they found that only a small portion of event coverage was given to describing the collective action, that those elementary descriptions were indeed details that coders had recorded, and that what was described were the behaviors most prevalent as reflected in the collected data. With this project, the investigators were able to establish an initial framework for examining description bias, and one that will undoubtedly be useful for future refinement of the issue.

These studies are just the beginning of what needs to be done. Maney and Oliver (2001) use newspaper data to assess police records and discuss the factors that affect whether police will record an event. They argue that no source can be treated as an unproblematic record of events, and that all sources must be cross-validated against other sources. There is a growing recognition that multiple sources are preferable to any single source, and that claims for the comprehensiveness of any source cannot be accepted without cross-validation by comparison with other sources. Oliver and Myers (2003b) call for modeling the creation of event records as a necessary underpinning of events research.

INTEGRATING STRUCTURAL AND CONSTRUCTIONIST THEORIES

Simultaneous with the rise of quantitative event studies has been a quite different trend, the rise of social constructionist theories of social movements. Although constructionist theories are usually framed as opposed to structuralist accounts, there is a growing appreciation for the need to integrate structural political theories of movements with constructivist theories rooted in social psychology and cultural sociology. Within sociology, the study of social movements has long stood at the intersection of political sociology and social psychology. The rise of new social movements and new social movements theory coincided and comingled with the rise of cultural sociology. Different intellectual traditions and political sensibilities have led to oppositions formed around false dichotomies: politics versus social psychology, rationality versus emotion, social structure versus social construction, resources versus culture, interests versus frames. At stake in these false dichotomies are images of the fundamental character of people in and around social movements, and the ways in which they interact with the social, political, and economic structures around them.

The "young Turks" of resource mobilization in the 1970s disparaged prior theories which attempted to explain the massive social movements of the 1960s from individual psychologies or hidden Freudian motives, and argued that people's stated reasons for protesting could be taken at face value, that protesters were no less rational than the people they were protesting against.[3] The capacity to mobilize could not be taken for granted, and resources and opportunities were critical. Focusing on structural factors rather than individual psychologies, resource mobilization theorists tended uncritically to assume a rational action model of individual choices. With the inevitability of academic cycles and some poetic justice, they in their turn were criticized by the next generation as imagining that people are nothing more than unthinking unemotional puppets of their material conditions. Although rational action theory is grounded in subjective expected utility theory, which treats interests as subjective, and there were clear recognitions by resource mobilization writers that grievances could be and were constructed, the attention of resource mobilization and then political opportunity theorists was focused on the constraints of structure and the problems of organizing, not on issues of social construction.

But movements not only develop rational and strategic actions, they continuously draw from cultural memories and repertoires, from values and moral principles to redefine situations, events, and relations in ways that would legitimate action, sanction inaction, gain bystanders' sympathy, reduce governments' ability to use social control resources, and attract media attention to reach distant publics. Movement actors try to appeal not only to audiences' reason or self-interest, but also to their values and normative judgment. They attempt to redefine what is going on and why. Social movements are not only mobilizations of protesters, displays of force, and threats of disruption of public order. Movements also have moral and cultural dimensions that involve insurgents' and publics' consciousness, beliefs, and practices.

The social-constructionist perspective can be summarized in terms of what Merton (1948) called a theorem basic to the social sciences: "If men define situations as real, they are real in their consequences" (Thomas & Thomas, 1928, p. 572). There is no single way in which people go about defining situations and attributing meaning to things and relations. Analytically, this process involves psychological, social-psychological and cultural dimensions and processes. These dimensions interact with resources, opportunities and strategies in a relational, conflictual and open-ended way.

Social constructionist theories take as problematic both the way a given structural situation is defined and experienced and the meanings that will be attached to actions. Just as the structuralists tended to ignore construction processes, the constructionists have not generally theorized the ways in which material conditions constrain meaning-making processes. Social-constructionist orientations in social movements are broadly organized around four concepts: framing, identity, culture and emotions. The practitioners within each tradition are working on different central problems with different core insights and methodologies. Social psychological perspectives that examine how individuals make meaning in social contexts work differently from cultural perspectives that examine how meanings are made at a societal level. Social psychological and cultural perspectives are present to varying degrees in work organized around each of these concepts, and a failure to distinguish the social psychological and cultural levels of analysis has contributed to some confusion in all of them.

Framing

In the early 1980s, a number of social movement scholars with social psychology backgrounds called for attention to cognitive and ideational factors such as interpretation, symbolization, and meaning.[4] Particularly influential has been the concept of strategic framing of grievances elaborated by Snow and Benford (Snow & Benford, 1988, 1992; Snow, Rochford, Worden & Benford, 1986) who redirected attention to "subjective" dimensions in the analysis of social movements. They make the point that grievances are a matter of differential interpretation and that variation in their interpretation across individuals, social movement organizations (SMOs), and time can affect whether and how they are acted upon. Thus, the link between intensely felt grievances and susceptibility to movement participation is not immediate or necessary – between grievances and action lies interpretation. They argue that actors "often misunderstand or experience considerable doubt or confusion about what it is that is going on and why" (Snow et al., 1986, p. 466). Framing concepts enable us to examine empirically the process through which a given objective situation *is defined and experienced*. Framing a situation in a new way, adopting an injustice frame, for example, may lead people to consider what was previously seen as an unfortunate but tolerable situation as inexcusable, unjust or immoral. For action to occur, injustice frames should be accompanied by shifts in attributional orientation that shift blame or responsibility from self to system.

Framing denotes "an active, process-derived phenomenon that implies agency and contention at the level of reality construction" (Snow & Benford, 1992, p. 136). Thus, mobilization depends not only on the existence of structural strain, availability and deployment of tangible resources, opening or closing of political opportunities, and a cost-benefit calculus, but also on the way these variables are *framed* and the degree to which they *resonate* with targets of mobilization (Snow & Benford, 1988, p. 213).

Although beginning with the social psychological concern with how individuals interpret events, framing theorists also viewed frames in cultural terms. Social movements are conceived of as *producers of meaning* and functioning as *signifying agents* (Snow & Benford, 1992, p. 151). Movement activists are seen as strategic actors, consciously seeking to draw on old frames or create new ones which will resonate with their targets and enhance movement mobilization or goal-attainment. Their ability to do this is constrained by the cultural meanings their audience brings to the interaction. Accordingly, movements play an active role in cultural change by challenging mainstream meanings. For reviews of framing theory and research, along with some criticisms, see Benford (1997) and Benford and Snow (2000).

Framing theory has become almost fully integrated into the political process synthesis. Standard political process theory explications routinely devote sections to framing processes (e.g. McAdam et al., 1996) and it is well recognized that movement frames affect resources and opportunities. Recent concerns have been raised that framing concepts have been spread too broadly to encompass problems that are better treated with the concept of "ideology" (Oliver & Johnston, 2000) or "discourse" (Ferree & Merrill, 2000). As the serious engagement with the construction of movement ideas proceeds, we expect to see more overt theorizing of ideologies and discourses, in addition to frames, and their relation to political processes.

Culture

What accounts for frame resonance? According to Snow and Benford (1992, p. 140), the degree of frame resonance is attributed to the degree of fit between framings and the "life world of adherents and constituents as well as bystanders." But their analysis does not go any further into the causes of "resonance." A cultural approach is needed to address this question. How does culture matter in accounting for the origins, trajectories and outcomes of social movements? Under what conditions is culture a constraint or facilitator of social movements? Under what circumstances does culture inspire or impede collective action? The answer to these questions depends on how we understand culture.

In the last two decades, we have observed what Sewell (1999, p. 36) considers an "academic culture mania" set in several disciplines and sub-disciplines that have produced numerous definitions and operationalizations of the concept of culture. Following Sewell, there are two fundamentally distinct meanings of the term culture. The first is a theoretical category: culture (in the singular) is contrasted with some other abstract category of social life that is not culture, such as economy, politics or biology. In this sense, culture is a realm of social life defined in contrast to some other non-cultural realm or realms. The second meaning is a concrete, bounded body of beliefs and practices associated to an identifiable society or social group. In this sense, scholars talk of cultures (in plural) as distinct worlds of meaning.

In the first sense culture is used to mean that social processes are not the mere results of political, economic or social structures. This challenges dichotomous conceptions – such as culture versus structure, cultural versus instrumental rationality, cultural versus political goals of social movements – that usually emphasize the second part of the duality at the cost of the analysis of their interaction, or at least a more careful analysis of cultural dimensions (Alvarez et al., 1998). For reviews see Polletta (1997) and McAdam (1994).

In the second sense, culture stands for the symbols and signs whose meaning has a generalized status, provides categories for understanding, relates and sorts elements of social life in hierarchical orders, as well as mediates between and blends with structure and action (Alexander & Smith, 1993; Alexander, Smith & Sherwood, 1993; Sewell, 1999). The meanings attached to signs and symbols are subject to contention and reinterpretation. The bounded sets of differences between the meanings of signs and symbols that stand for things and relations in social life constitute cultures (plural). Thus, cultures in this sense allow us to identify and pin down specific meanings a given society or social group attributes to things and social relations and analyze how they favor or constrain social movements and their practices at different points of its life-course.

Thus, culture is not a set of independent variables that affect certain dependent variables. Most movement dimensions can be reinterpreted from a culturalist point of view. Movements have their origins and are shaped within dominant cultures (Morris, 1984). Movements challenge dominant meanings thus transforming mainstream culture and institutions (Baierle, 1998). Movements create their own culture that may facilitate or impede mobilization, resistance, recruitment and solidarity (Fine, 1985; Scott, 1990). Movements construct ends of action within cultural templates (Rubin, 1998). Movements find means ("tools") for action from host cultures (Swidler, 1986). Movements perform and produce culture through the symbols they create and the public behavior of their members (Fantasia & Hirsh, 1995; Hunt, 1984). Movements produce cultural goods in the form of narratives, texts and myths (Fine, 1995). States may appropriate popular culture to create a mass base for politics (Mosse, 1975).

Identities

Identity is one of the most important and most confounded concepts in the study of social movements. "New social movements" theory argued that creating and maintaining identities had become the central purpose of "new" movements. Johnston, Laraña and Gusfield (1994) seek to bring some order to this confusion by distinguishing among individual identities, collective identities, and public identities. In brief, individual identities concern what people think about themselves, collective identities concern what groups think about themselves, and public identities concern how groups are viewed in a wider public discourse. Social psychology and symbolic interaction traditions treat individual identities, and the way they are formed in social interaction with other people and cultural representations. Cultural sociology treats public identities, and the way they are constructed through discourse. Groups' collective definitions of the meaning and purpose of the group (collective identities, narrowly defined) bring together social psychological and cultural processes. Unfortunately, their clarifications seem to have been ignored and the term "collective identity" is broadly used to refer to all three.

Polletta and Jasper's (2001, p. 285) otherwise excellent and thorough review of research on identities seems not to distinguish these meanings:

> To avoid overextension of the concept, we have defined collective identity as an individual's cognitive, moral, and emotional connection with a broader community, category, practice, or institution. It is a perception of a shared status or relation, which may be imagined rather than experienced directly, and it is distinct from personal identities, although it may form part of a personal identity.

Despite this clear definition equating the term collective identity with the extent of an individual's attachment or relation to a group, their detailed critical review of the ways in which research has used the identity concept to explain movement emergence, recruitment strategy and outcomes gives examples of all three types of identity formation. Similarly, Tilly (1998) uses the term "political identities" in a way that refers largely to individuals and discusses the collective nature of collective identities, but does not clearly demarcate the different levels at which identities are formed.

Individual identities are not necessarily individualist. Social psychologists know that individuals may think of themselves as integrally part of (defined by) some larger group. At the individual level, a movement identity focuses on the extent to which an individual's self-identity includes identification with a movement. Such identities may be referred to as movement identities, activist identities, ethnic or national identities, etc. When actors take on these identities, they merge their sense of self with the larger movement. Their actions cannot be understood in simple cost-benefit terms, but as directed towards preserving and maintaining their identity, their sense of self. Research problems about this kind of identity concern the processes through which individuals come to identify with a broader movement, group, or stance, and the ways such identities influence people's decisions about their movement participation. The term "identity" in this sense is often used indistinguishably from "solidarity," but the two terms cut differently. To feel solidarity with a group is to have strong positive feelings for and commitment to a group. (We discuss the emotional side of identity below.) But identity is about how you see yourself. It would substantially aid clarity if people would not use the term "collective identity" to refer to individuals' views of their relation to a group, but this is probably a vain hope.

Cultural conceptions of identity are found in what Johnston et al. (1994) call collective or public identities. Melucci's (1989) treatment of collective identity refers to the understandings people have about the meaning and purpose of a particular group or movement. For Melucci and others in this tradition, it is important to understand that groups and movements are discursively created in ongoing interaction. Whether a series of events or a set of individuals add up to a movement is discursively created, as is the meaning or purpose of that movement. The idea of the collective identity in this sense is not about the attachment of individuals to the group, but about the nature of the group or movement. Research problems about collective identities in this sense concern the ways they are formed through discursive practices and in ongoing political interaction with other groups and movements. Melucci does not draw the distinction Johnston et al. make between collective and public identities, seeing groups' constructions of themselves as of a piece with their constructions in public, but the distinction seems a useful one. It is useful to think of a group's collective identity construction as impacted by its members' self-constructions on the one hand and the public construction of its identity on the other. Public constructions happen in a discursive space where relatively disembodied ideas interact with other ideas, and are only loosely tied to the self-perceptions of individuals and groups. There is a close, but insufficiently explored, relation between collective identity in this sense and framing (Hunt, Benford & Snow, 1994).

In terms of their relations to structuralist categories, individual identities are especially relevant for understanding why some individuals and not others join and become committed to movements, and why they persist in activism even in the face of movement decline (Friedman & McAdam, 1992; Polletta & Jasper, 2001). Collective identities are relevant for understanding how groups define their boundaries, goals, strategies, and tactics, and why they rule certain kinds of action in or out of bounds regardless of external judgments of efficacy (Jasper, 1997), as well as why they have different definitions of what it means to be a good collectively-oriented member of the group (Lichterman, 1996; Taylor & Whittier, 1992). Public identities are relevant for understanding how and why groups occupy locations in public political space that are often at variance with their self-perceptions. Clearly understanding the distinction between collective identities and public identities will explain why a particular group of individuals may terminate or abandon one organizational formation and create a new one with a different name and public self-presentation. Ethnic or national identities are public identities, in the sense of defining what it means to be a "Negro" or "good American" or "Muslim" in public discourse.

Of course, public contestations over public identities do not ensure individuals' adoption of these identities into themselves, and groups enact rituals and police boundaries to foster individuals' identification with the group (Berezin, 2001; Taylor & Whittier, 1992). Individual, collective, and public identities are in constant interaction with one another, but as theory moves forward, it will be increasingly important to maintain distinctions and clarify the relations among them.

Emotions

Berezin (2001) stresses that identities have an emotional component. Few scholars of social movements defend the binary opposition of emotion and reason, but a full incorporation of emotions into movement theory has lagged the incorporation ideational constructions. As Benford (1997) points out, frame analysts have ignored emotions, thus failing to elaborate on the mediating role that emotions have in the communication and interpretation that goes on among movements and its publics. Older collective behavior theories assumed a discontinuity between rational ordinary behavior and emotional collective behavior, and sought to explain it (see McPhail, 1991, for a review). Social movement theories built in the 1970s reacted against the "myth of the madding crowd" (McPhail, 1991), denied the alleged discontinuity between individual and collective action, and stressed the rationality and political goals of social movements. Resource mobilization theory assumed rational actors weigh costs and benefits of participation vis-à-vis non-participation, and pursued goal-oriented action constrained and enabled by the availability of resources at their disposal (Jenkins, 1983; McCarthy &

Zald, 1973, 1977). Political process models focus upon the relations between movements and the state, and generally lack any explicit social psychological model, but tacitly assume rational action and a direct relationship between material conditions and subjective interests. Rationalists recognized hope or "cognitive liberation" (McAdam, 1982) as the probability of making a difference, a necessary component of rational action.

Subsequent groups of scholars argued that this lacuna led to distorted theory (see e.g. Goodwin, 1997; Goodwin, Jasper & Poletta, 2000; Jasper, 1998). The articles collected by Goodwin, Jasper and Polletta (Goodwin et al., 2001) demonstrate the ways in which analyzing emotions can enrich the understanding of social movements. Emotions are pervasive in social movements and play an important role in different points of a movement's life course (Aminzade & McAdam, 2001). Activists undertaking risky actions have to manage fear (Goodwin & Pfaff, 2001). Kinship ties and sexuality can disrupt a movement (Goodwin, 1997). Sometimes for instrumental reasons emotions are hidden from the public and only displayed backstage. Robnett (1998) argues that Civil Rights Movement leaders displayed a calm rationality in an instrumental way in order to maintain their legitimacy with the state, while emotions clearly prevailed behind the scenes. Activists around sexual abuse both need to manage their own emotions to maintain their own health, but to manage their public displays of emotion for strategic effect (Whittier, 2001). Public displays of anger make actors look and feel more empowered, but sometimes a display of the fear and pain of victimization is strategically necessary.

Even as emotions are incorporated into social movements theory, that theory has to acknowledge the dichotomization of emotion and reason in much of the larger society. Feminists contend that separating passion and reason not only dichotomizes thought and feeling but also elevates "abstract masculinity" over women's standpoint. Feminist scholars have been vocal critics of the rationalist bias in Western thinking that privileges rational, independent, self-interested action over action that is driven by emotion, undertaken collectively, and motivated by altruism or the desire to affirm the group (Taylor, 1995). Feminist groups try to channel emotions tied to women's subordination (fear, shame, resignation) into emotions conducive to protest (anger). The rationalist bias pervades the culture and affects movements' collective identities. Movements perceived as emotional are often not considered respectable. To gain respectability movement activists may develop a "vocabulary of emotions" to rationalize their participation to others and to themselves. The animal rights activists Groves (1995) studied in the southern United States, reproduced organizationally the dominant gender division of emotion: recruiting men was considered a strategic device to bring credibility to the movement because men were believed less emotional and more rational than women. As a consequence, male activists were often chosen for spokesperson and leadership positions while women tended to be overlooked for those positions.

CONCLUSIONS

Our review has highlighted four important and widespread trends in the study of protest and social movements that should continue. First, "mainstream" theory should continue to address a geographically and substantively broader empirical base, breaking out of a preoccupation with Anglo-America and Europe and becoming truly global in its orientation. This broader base will open new empirical problems that will point to weaknesses in current theory and lead to the development of new theory. Second, social movements theory should continue the tendency to treat "social movements" not as a class of objects, but as a pointer to a class of relationships between non-institutional and institutional political actors. This involves a growing focus on mechanisms and processes that occur in many different movements, and decreasing attempts to develop universal propositions about the causes, effects, or trajectories of whole movements. This theoretical project is currently nascent and unformed. We expect that the final two trends we have identified will contribute to this theoretical project. Event-based studies should continue to grow as one of the best empirical and theoretical approaches for testing and expanding theory focusing on mechanisms and processes. Finally, structuralist and constructivist theories should become integrated. Researchers should spend less time criticizing other approaches for what they did not say, and devote attention to understanding how structures constrain social construction, and how social construction gives meaning to structures. Scholars should recognize the differences between the social psychological and cultural traditions and, thus, be able more explicitly to draw on both as they develop their theories.

Knowledge-building requires a division of labor. A Durkheimian organic solidarity through difference and mutual dependence should be our goal, not agreement on one common theoretical agenda and mode of research. Event-based theory and social constructionist theory are different projects, but both are crucial to the larger complex project of developing better theory for social movements processes. So are many of the smaller streams of work that we have not highlighted in this essay. Practitioners of these different strands of work should follow their own logic, and not seek to pursue one single amorphous agenda. In general, constructionists prefer qualitative research methods, and events researchers quantitative methods. Nevertheless, we believe that each can learn from the other and there are likely to be points of at least partial convergence. There are qualitative researchers focused on events and quantitative researchers focused on the construction of ideas. Both events studies and constructionist studies recognize that a "social movement" is a loosely-bounded phenomenon that changes and evolves in dynamic interaction with other elements in a field. Breaking movements down into events is one possible way to get a research handle on unfolding construction processes. The shifting content of speeches, pamphlets, conversations and other communications can be treated as events, and examined over time. Research is already finding that protest actions interrelate with other forms of public discourse (Koopmans & Statham, 1999). This does not mean that the two projects can be folded into each other. But it does mean that there is much to be gained from each gaining insights from the other.

Both constructionist projects and events-oriented projects need fully to engage the insights from the first and second trends we noted. That is, they need to be grounded in empirically a truly international terrain of cases and examples, and they need fully to recognize the ways in which the "social movement" is intertwined with institutional politics and other sectors and processes in society. No movement or movement process operates in isolation. Culture, identities, frames and emotions develop and evolve in ongoing interaction with each other and with the "structural" elements of a social system. The cultural or social psychological processes within a movement are never contained wholly within that movement but always draw on developments in other movements and in the larger society. Social movements and protest waves evolve not from their own internal logics, but from the dynamics of their interactions with regimes and news media and their competition with other movements (Oliver & Myers, 2003a). The challenge of future theorizing is to recognize these complexities without being defeated by them, to find theoretical and methodological strategies for bringing enough order to these complex interactions that we may study them. New theorizing by Oliver and Myers (2003a) and Koopmans (2002) proposes co-evolution as the master paradigm for analyzing these complex interactive relations, but it is too soon to tell whether they have correctly identified the most productive approach.

We end with one comment that arises more from current events than recent scholarship. After the movements of the 1960s, social protest has come to be seen as a vehicle for democracy, as a tool to be used by the less powerful to accomplish equality- and justice-generating political ends. There are always a few researchers studying hostile or anti-democratic movements, but they have been a minority whose work is rarely mentioned in treatments of general movement theory. In these early years of the 21st century, we have been repeatedly reminded that protest is not always peaceful and not always tied to pro-democratic tendencies. In this, we may wish to remember the theorists of the 1950s and 1960s, who tried to make sense of totalitarian movements and genocide, and developed the very theories that were rejected by the next generation as stigmatizing and psychologizing movement activists. It seems to us that one test of any theory of social movements is that we be able to use the same theory to explain processes in movements we celebrate and those we abhor, or at least to provide a genuinely theoretical account of how they differ. This is not to abandon our duty as citizens to apply moral or ethical standards to judge movements as different, even if we believe their underlying causal mechanisms are the same. But there is a broad tendency to give structural accounts of movements we laud, and psychological accounts of those we disparage. A genuinely integrated theory should be able to explain how movements we consider good and those we consider evil can both arise from the same sets of mechanisms and processes.

NOTES

1. For good overviews of events, their advantages, and limitations, see Olzak (1989), Rucht and Ohlemacher (1992), Koopmans (1998), and Tarrow (1998), among others.

2. This is a generalization of much more specific critiques. The "resource mobilization" dimension of contemporary theory has been the focal point for the vast majority of these, but the inability of critics to develop an alternative further underscores the more general problem of a "theory/empirical data gap" as described by Koopmans and Rucht. See Turner (1981), Kerbo (1982), Kitschelt (1991), and Goodwin and Jasper (1999) for specific critiques of mainstream social movement theory.

3. Space does not permit a review of either the older psychological traditions or their resource mobilization critics. See Jenkins (1983) for a review of resource mobilization.

4. For example Cohen (1985), Ferree and Miller (1985), Gamson, Fireman and Rytina (1982), Klandermans (1984), McAdam (1982), Turner (1983). Note that the Ferree and Miller paper circulated unpublished for years and influenced and was explicitly credited by McAdam (1982).

REFERENCES

Alexander, J. C., & Smith, P. (1993). The discourse of American civil society. *Theory and Society, 22*, 151–207.

Alexander, J. C., Smith, P., & Sherwood, S. J. (1993). Risking enchantment. *Culture, 8*, 10–14.

Alvarez, S. E., Dagnino, E., & Escobar, A. (Eds) (1998). *Cultures of politics – politics of cultures*. Boulder: Westview Press.

Aminzade, R., & McAdam, D. (2001). Emotions and contentious politics. In: R. Aminzade, A. J. Goldstone, D. McAdam, E. J. Perry, W. H. Sewell Jr., S. Tarrow & C. Tilly (Eds), *Silence and Voice in the Study of Contentious Politics* (pp. 14–50). New York: Cambridge University Press.

Auvinen, J. (1996). IMF intervention and political protest in the third world. *Third World Quarterly, 17*, 377–400.

Auvinen, J. (1997). Political conflict in less developed countries, 1981–1989. *Journal of Peace Research, 34*, 177–195.

Baierle, S. G. (1998). The explosion of experience. In: S. E. Alvarez, E. Dagnino & A. Escobar (Eds), *Cultures of Politics – Politics of Cultures* (pp. 118–138). Boulder: Westview Press.

Beasley-Murray, J. (1999). Learning from Sendero. *Journal of Latin American Cultural Studies, 8*, 75–88.

Beissinger, M. R. (1998). Event analysis in transitional societies: Protest mobilization in the former Soviet Union. In: D. Rucht, R. Koopmans & F. Neidhardt (Eds), *Acts of Dissent* (pp. 284–316). Berlin: Sigma.

Benford, R. D. (1997). An insider's critique of the social movement framing perspective. *Sociological Inquiry, 67*, 409–430.

Benford, R. D., & Snow, D. A. (2000). Framing processes and social movements. *Annual Review of Sociology, 26*, 611–639.

Berezin, M. (2001). Emotions and political identity. In: J. Goodwin, J. Jasper & F. Polletta (Eds), *Passionate Politics* (pp. 83–98). Chicago and London: The University of Chicago Press.

Brysk, A., & Wise, C. (1997). Liberalization and ethnic conflict in Latin America. *Studies in Comparative International Development, 32*, 76–104.

Burstein, P., Einwohner, R. L., & Hollander, J. A. (1995). The success of political movements. In: J. C. Jenkins & B. Klandermans (Eds), *The Politics of Social Protest* (pp. 275–295). Minneapolis: University of Minnesota Press.

Canessa, A. (2000). Contesting hybridity. *Journal of Latin American Studies, 32*, 115–144.

Cohen, J. L. (1985). Strategy or identity: New theoretical paradigms and contemporary social movements. *Social Research, 52*, 663–716.

Cook, M. L. (1996). *Organizing dissent*. Pennsylvania: The Pennsylvania State University Press.

Danzger, M. H. (1975). Validating conflict data. *American Sociological Review, 40*, 570–584.

della Porta, D. (1996). Social movements and the state. In: D. McAdam, J. D. McCarthy & M. N. Zald (Eds), *Comparative Perspectives on Social Movements* (pp. 62–92). New York: Cambridge University Press.

della Porta, D. (1999). Protest, protesters, and protest policing. In: M. Giugni, D. McAdam & C. Tilly (Eds), *From Contention to Democracy* (pp. 66–96). Boulder: Rowman & Littlefield.

della Porta, D., & Reiter, H. (Eds) (1998). *Policing protest*. Minneapolis: University of Minnesota Press.

Deng, F. (1997). Information gaps and unintended consequences of social movements: The 1989 Chinese student movement. *American Journal of Sociology, 102*, 1085–1112.

Dwivedi, R. (2001). Environmental movements in the global south. *International Sociology, 16*, 11–31.

Eckstein, S. (1989). *Power and popular protest*. Berkeley: University of California Press.

Ehrick, C. (1998). Madrinas and missionaries. *Gender and History, 10*, 406–424.

Einwohner, R. L., Hollander, J. A., & Olson, T. (2000). Engendering social movements. *Gender and Society, 14*, 679–699.

Ekiert, G., & Kubik, J. (1998). Protest event analysis in the study of democratic consolidation in Poland, 1989–1993. In: D. Rucht, R. Koopmans & F. Neidhardt (Eds), *Acts of Dissent* (pp. 317–348). Berlin: Sigma.

Ellner, S. (1999). Obstacles to the consolidation of the Venezuelan neighbourhood movement. *Journal of Latin American Studies, 31*, 75–97.

Escobar, A. (1992). Culture, economics, and politics in Latin American social movements. In: A. Escobar & S. E. Alvarez (Eds), *The Making of Social Movements in Latin America* (pp. 62–85). Boulder: Westview Press.

Escobar, A., & Alvarez, S. E. (Eds) (1992). *The making of social movements in Latin America.* Boulder: Westview Press.

Fantasia, R., & Hirsh, E. L. (1995). Culture in rebellion. In: H. Johnston & B. Klandermans (Eds), *Social Movements and Culture* (pp. 144–159). Minneapolis: University of Minnesota Press.

Fernandez Soriano, A., Dilla Alfonso, H., & Castro Flores, M. (1999). Movimientos comunitarios en Cuba. *Estudios Sociologicos, 17*, 857–884.

Ferree, M. M., & Merrill, D. A. (2000). Hot movements, cold cognition. *Contemporary Sociology, 29*, 454–462.

Ferree, M. M., & Miller, F. D. (1985). Mobilization and meaning: Toward an integration of social psychological and resource perspectives on social movements. *Sociological Inquiry, 55*, 38–61.

Fillieule, O. (1998). 'Plus ça change, moins ça change.' Demonstrations in France during the 1980s. In: D. Rucht, R. Koopmans & F. Neidhardt (Eds), *Acts of Dissent* (pp. 199–226). Berlin: Sigma.

Fine, G. A. (1985). Can the circle be unbroken? Small groups and social movements. In: E. Lawler (Ed.), *Advances in Group Processes* (Vol. 2, pp. 1–28). Greenwich: JAI Press.

Fine, G. A. (1995). Public narration and group culture. In: H. Johnston & B. Klandermans (Eds), *Social Movements and Culture* (pp. 127–143). Minneapolis: University of Minnesota Press.

Foweraker, J. (1995). *Theorizing social movements.* London: Pluto Press.

Foweraker, J., & Craig, A. L. (Eds) (1990). *Popular movements and political change in Mexico.* Boulder: Lynne Rienner.

Franzosi, R. (1987). The press as a source of socio-historical data. *Historical Methods, 20*, 5–16.

Friedman, D., & McAdam, D. (1992). Collective identity and activism. In: A. D. Morris & C. M. Mueller (Eds), *Frontiers in Social Movement Theory* (pp. 156–173). New Haven: Yale University Press.

Gamson, W. A. (1975). *The strategy of social protest.* Homewood: Dorsey.

Gamson, W. A. (1990). *The strategy of social protest* (2nd ed.). Belmont: Wadsworth.

Gamson, W. A., Fireman, B., & Rytina, S. (1982). *Encounters with unjust authorities.* Homewood: Dorsey Press.

Gentile, P. (1998). Radical right protest in Switzerland. In: D. Rucht, R. Koopmans & F. Neidhardt (Eds), *Acts of Dissent* (pp. 227–252). Berlin: Sigma.

Gill, A. (1999). Government regulation, social anomie and Protestant growth in Latin America. *Rationality and Society, 11*, 287–316.

Giugni, M. (1998). Was it worth the effort? *Annual Review of Sociology, 24*, 293–371.

Giugni, M. (1999). How social movements matter. In: M. Giugni, D. McAdam & C. Tilly (Eds), *How Social Movements Matter* (pp. xiii–xxxiii). Minneapolis: University of Minnesota Press.

Goldstone, J. A. (1998). Social movements or revolutions? In: M. Giugni, D. McAdam & C. Tilly (Eds), *How Social Movements Matter* (pp. 125–145). Minneapolis: University of Minnesota Press.

Goldstone, J. A. (Ed.) (2002). *States, parties, and social movements.* New York: Cambridge University Press.

Goodwin, J. (1997). The Libidinal constitution of a high-risk social movement. *American Sociological Review, 62*, 53–69.

Goodwin, J., & Jasper, J. (1999). Caught in a winding, snarling vine: The structural bias of political process theory. *Sociological Forum, 14*, 27–54.

Goodwin, J., Jasper, J., & Polletta, F. (2000). Return of the repressed. *Mobilization, 5*, 65–84.

Goodwin, J., Jasper, J., & Polletta, F. (Eds) (2001). *Passionate politics.* Chicago and London: The University of Chicago Press.

Goodwin, J., & Pfaff, S. (2001). Emotion work in high-risk social movements. In: J. Goodwin, J. Jasper & F. Polletta (Eds), *Passionate Politics* (pp. 282–300). Chicago and London: The University of Chicago Press.

Groves, J. M. (1995). Learning to feel. *The Sociological Review, 43*, 435–461.

Guidry, J. A., Kennedy, M. D., & Zald, M. N. (Eds) (2000). *Globalizations and social movements*. Ann Arbor: University of Michigan Press.

Gusfield, J. (1981). *Drinking-driving and the symbolic order*. Chicago: University of Chicago Press.

Guy, D. J. (1998). The politics of Pan-American cooperation. *Gender and History, 10*, 449–469.

Hipsher, P. L. (1996). Democratization and the decline of urban social movements in Chile and Spain. *Comparative Politics, 28*, 273–297.

Hipsher, P. L. (1998a). Democratic transitions and social movement outcomes. In: M. Giugni, D. McAdam & C. Tilly (Eds), *From Contention to Democracy* (pp. 149–167). Boulder: Rowman & Littlefield.

Hipsher, P. L. (1998b). Democratic transitions as protest cycles. In: D. S. Meyer & S. Tarrow (Eds), *The Social Movement Society* (pp. 153–172). Oxford: Rowman & Littlefield.

Hocke, P. (1998). Determining the selection bias in local and national newspaper reports on protest events. In: D. Rucht, R. Koopmans & F. Neidhardt (Eds), *Acts of Dissent* (pp. 131–163). Berlin: Sigma.

Huiskamp, G. (2000). Identity politics and democratic transitions in Latin America. *Theory and Society, 29*, 385–424.

Hunt, L. (1984). *Politics, culture, and class in the French Revolution*. Berkeley: University of California Press.

Hunt, S. A., Benford, R. D., & Snow, D. A. (1994). Identity fields. In: E. Laraña, H. Johnston & J. R. Gusfield (Eds), *New Social Movements* (pp. 184–208). Minneapolis: University of Minnesota Press.

Jackman, R. W., & Boyd, W. A. (1979). Multiple sources in the collection of data on political conflict. *American Journal of Political Science, 23*, 434–458.

Jaquette, J. S. (Ed.) (1994). *The women's movement in Latin America: Participation and democracy* (2nd ed.). Boulder: Westview Press.

Jasper, J. (1997). *The art of moral protest*. Chicago: The University of Chicago Press.

Jasper, J. (1998). The emotions of protest. *Sociological Forum, 13*, 397–424.

Jelin, E. (2001). Cultural movements and social actors in the new regional scenarios. *International Political Science Review, 22*, 85–98.

Jelin, E., Zammit, J. A., & Thomson, M. (1990). *Women and social change in Latin America*. Geneva: Zed Books.

Jenkins, C. (1983). Resource mobilization theory and the study of social movements. *Annual Review of Sociology, 9*, 527–553.

Johnston, H., Laraña, E., & Gusfield, J. R. (1994). Identities, grievances, and new social movements. In: E. Laraña, H. Johnston & J. R. Gusfield (Eds), *New Social Movements* (pp. 3–36). Minneapolis: University of Minnesota Press.

Kay, C. (1998). El fin de la reforma agraria en America Latina? *Revista Mexicana de Sociologia, 60*, 63–98.

Keck, M. E., & Sikkink, K. (1998). *Activists beyond borders*. Ithaca, NY: Cornell UP.

Kerbo, H. R. (1982). Movements of 'crisis' and movements of 'affluence'. *Journal of Conflict Resolution, 26*, 633–645.

Kerbo, H. R., & Shaffer, R. A. (1992). Lower class insurgency and the political process. *Social Problems, 39*, 139–154.

Khawaja, M. (1994). Resource mobilization, hardship, and popular collective action in the West Bank. *Social Forces, 73*, 191–220.

Khawaja, M. (1995). The dynamics of local collective action in the West Bank. *Economic Development and Cultural Change, 44*, 147–179.

Kitschelt, H. (1991). Resource mobilization theory: A critique. In: D. Rucht (Ed.), *Research on Social Movements*. Boulder: Westview.

Klandermans, B. (1984). Mobilization and participation. *American Sociological Review, 49*, 583–600.

Koopmans, R. (1993). The dynamics of protest waves. *American Sociological Review, 58*, 637–658.

Koopmans, R. (1996). New social movements and changes in political participation in Western Europe. *West European Politics, 19*, 28–50.

Koopmans, R. (1998). The use of protest event data in comparative research. In: D. Rucht, R. Koopmans & F. Neidhardt (Eds), *Acts of Dissent* (pp. 90–110). Berlin: Sigma.

Koopmans, R. (2002). Protest in time and space. In: D. A. Snow et al. (Eds), *The Blackwell Companion to Social Movements*. Oxford: Blackwell.

Koopmans, R., & Rucht, D. (1999). Protest event analysis – Where to now? *Mobilization, 4*, 123–130.

Koopmans, R., & Statham, P. (1999). Ethnic and civic conceptions of nationhood and the differential success of the extreme right in Germany and Italy. In: M. Giugni, D. McAdam & C. Tilly (Eds), *How Social Movements Matter* (pp. 225–251). Minneapolis: University of Minnesota Press.

Kriesi, H., Koopmans, R., Duyvendak, J. W., & Giugni, M. G. (1992). New social movements and political opportunities in Western Europe. *European Journal of Political Research, 22*, 219–244.

Kriesi, H., Koopmans, R., Duyvendak, J. W., & Giugni, M. G. (Eds) (1995). *New social movements in Western Europe*. Minneapolis: University of Minnesota Press.

Larroa Torres, R. M. (1997). El papel del campesinado en la reforma agraria y la definicion de las politicas agrarias de America Latina. *Estudios Latinoamericanos, 4*, 93–107.

Le Bot, Y. (1999). Churches, sects and communities. *Bulletin of Latin American Research, 18*, 165–174.

Lichterman, P. (1996). *The search for political community*. New York: Cambridge University Press.

Linz, J. J., & Stepan, A. (1996). *Problems of democratic transition and consolidation*. Baltimore: The Johns Hopkins University Press.

López Jiménez, A. (1996). Politica y religion en America Latina. *Politica y sociedad, 22*, 91–101.

Macy, M. W. (1990). Learning theory and the logic of critical mass. *American Sociological Review, 55*, 809–826.

Mainwaring, S. (1987). Urban popular movements, identity and democratization in Brazil. *Comparative Politics, 21*, 131–159.

Mainwaring, S. (1989). Grassroots popular movements and the struggle for democracy: Nova Iguacu. In: A. Stepan (Ed.), *Democratizing Brazil* (pp. 168–204). New York: Oxford University Press.

Mainwaring, S., & Viola, E. (1984). New social movements, political culture, and democracy. *Telos, 61*, 17–52.

Maney, G. M., & Oliver, P. E. (2001). Finding event records. *Sociological Methods and Research, 29*, 131–169.

Mascott, M. A. (1997). Cultural politica y nuevos movimientos sociales en America Latina. *Metapolitica, 1*, 227–239.

Massolo, A. (1999). Defender y cambiar la vida. Mujeres en movimientos populares urbanos. *Cuicuilco, 6*, 13–23.

Mato, D. (2000). Transnational networking and the social production of representations of identities by indigenous peoples' organizations of Latin America. *International Sociology, 15*, 343–360.

McAdam, D. (1982). *Political process and the development of black insurgency: 1930–1970*. Chicago: University of Chicago Press.

McAdam, D. (1983). Tactical innovation and the pace of insurgency. *American Sociological Review*, *48*, 735–754.

McAdam, D. (1988). *Freedom Summer*. New York: Oxford University Press.

McAdam, D. (1994). Culture and social movements. In: E. Laraña, H. Johnston & J. R. Gusfield (Eds), *New Social Movements* (pp. 36–57). Philadelphia: Temple University Press.

McAdam, D., McCarthy, J. D., & Zald, M. N. (Eds) (1996). *Comparative perspectives on social movements*. New York: Cambridge University Press.

McAdam, D., Tarrow, S., & Tilly, C. (2001). *Dynamics of contention*. New York: Cambridge University Press.

McCammon, H. J., Campbell, K. E., Granberg, E. M., & Mowery, C. (2001). How movements win. *American Sociological Review*, *66*, 49–70.

McCarthy, J. D., McPhail, C., & Smith, J. (1996). Images of protest. *American Sociological Review*, *61*, 478–499.

McCarthy, J. D., McPhail, C., Smith, J., & Crishock, L. J. (1998). Electronic and print media representations of Washington, DC demonstrations, 1982 and 1991. In: D. Rucht, R. Koopmans & F. Neidhardt (Eds), *Acts of Dissent* (pp. 113–130). Berlin: Sigma.

McCarthy, J. D., & Zald, M. N. (1973). *The trend of social movements in America*. Morristown: General Learning Press.

McCarthy, J. D., & Zald, M. N. (1977). Resource mobilization and social movements. *American Journal of Sociology*, *82*, 1212–1242.

McPhail, C. (1991). *The myth of the madding crowd*. New York: Aldine de Gruyter.

McPhail, C., Schweingruber, D., & McCarthy, J. D. (1998). Policing of protest in the United States, 1960–1995. In: D. della Porta & H. Reiter (Eds), *Policing Protest* (pp. 49–69). Minneapolis: University of Minnesota Press.

Melucci, A. (1985). The symbolic challenge of contemporary movements. *Social Research*, *52*, 789–816.

Melucci, A. (1989). *Nomads of the present*. Philadelphia: Temple University Press.

Melucci, A., & Lyyra, T. (1998). Collective action, change and democracy. In: M. Giugni, D. McAdam & C. Tilly (Eds), *From Contention to Democracy* (pp. 203–227). Boulder: Rowman & Littlefield.

Merton, R. K. (1948). The self-fulfilling prophecy. *Antioch Review*, 193–210.

Meyer, D. S., & Whittier, N. (1994). Social movement spillover. *Social Problems*, *41*, 277–298.

Misztal, B., & Shupe, A. (1998). Fundamentalism and globalization. In: A. Shupe & B. Misztal (Eds), *Religion, Mobilization, and Social Action* (pp. 3–14). Westport, CT: Praeger.

Morris, A. D. (1984). *The origins of the civil rights movement*. New York: Free Press.

Mosse, G. (1975). *The nationalization of the masses*. New York: H. Fertig.

Mueller, C. (1997). Media measurement models of protest event data. *Mobilization*, *2*, 165–184.

Mueller, C. (1999). Claim "radicalization?". *Social Problems*, *46*, 528–547.

Myers, D. J. (1997). Racial rioting in the 1960s. *American Sociological Review*, *62*, 94–112.

Myers, D. J. (2000). The diffusion of collective violence. *American Journal of Sociology*, *106*, 173–208.

Myers, D. J., & Buoye, A. J. (2001). Campus racial disorders and community ties, 1967–1969. *Research in Social Movements, Conflicts and Change*, *23*, 297–327.

Oliver, P. E. (1989). Bringing the crowd back in. In: L. Kriesberg (Ed.), *Research in Social Movements, Conflict and Change* (Vol. 11, pp. 1–30). Greenwich: JAI Press.

Oliver, P. E., & Johnston, H. (2000). What a good idea! Ideologies and frames in social movement research. *Mobilization*, *5*, 37–54.

Oliver, P. E., & Maney, G. M. (2000). Political processes and local newspaper coverage of protest events. *American Journal of Sociology, 106*, 463–505.

Oliver, P. E., & Myers, D. J. (1999). How events enter the public sphere. *American Journal of Sociology, 105*, 38–87.

Oliver, P. E., & Myers, D. J. (2003a). *The co-evolution of social movements*. Mobilization.

Oliver, P. E., & Myers, D. J. (2003b). Networks, diffusion, and cycles of collective action. In: M. Diani & D. McAdam (Eds), *Social Movement Analysis*. New York: Oxford University Press.

Olzak, S. (1987). Causes of ethnic conflict and protest in urban America, 1877–1889. *Social Science Research, 16*, 185–210.

Olzak, S. (1989). Analysis of events in the study of collective action. *Annual Review of Sociology, 15*, 119–141.

Olzak, S. (1992). *The dynamics of ethnic competition and conflict*. Stanford: Stanford University Press.

Oxhorn, P. D. (1995). *Organizing civil society*. Pennsylvania: The University of Pennsylvania Press.

Petras, J., & Veltmeyer, H. (2001). Are Latin American peasant movements still a force for change? *Journal of Peasant Studies, 28*, 83–118.

Polletta, F. (1997). Culture and its discontents. *Social Inquiry, 67*, 431–450.

Polletta, F., & Jasper, J. (2001). Collective identity and social movements. *Annual Review of Sociology, 27*, 283–305.

Rasler, K. (1996). Concessions, repression and political protest in the Iranian revolution. *American Sociological Review, 61*, 132–152.

Robnett, B. (1998). African American women in the civil rights movement. In: K. M. Blee (Ed.), *No Middle Ground. Women and Radical Protest* (pp. 65–95). New York: New York University Press.

Rubin, J. (1998). Ambiguity and contradiction in a radical popular movement. In: S. E. Alvarez, E. Dagnino & A. Escobar (Eds), *Cultures of Politics – Politics of Cultures* (pp. 141–164). Boulder: Westview Press.

Rucht, D. (1996). Recent right-wing radicalism in Germany. *Research on Democracy and Society, 3*, 255–274.

Rucht, D., & Neidhardt, F. (1998). Methodological issues in collecting protest event data. In: D. Rucht, R. Koopmans & F. Neidhardt (Eds), *Acts of Dissent* (pp. 65–89). Berlin: Sigma.

Rucht, D., & Ohlemacher. (1992). Protest event data. In: M. Diani & R. Eyerman (Eds), *Studying Collective Action*. London: Sage.

Safa, H. I. (1996). Beijing, diversity and globalization. *Organization, 3*, 563–570.

Sandoval, S. A. M. (1998). Social movements and democratization. In: M. Giugni, D. McAdam & C. Tilly (Eds), *From Contention to Democracy* (pp. 169–201). Boulder: Rowman & Littlefield.

Schild, V. (1997). New subjects of rights? Gendered citizenship and the contradictory legacies of social movements in Latin America. *Organization, 4*, 604–619.

Schneider, C. L. (1995). *Shantytown protest in Pinochet's Chile*. Philadelphia: Temple University Press.

Schneider, C. L. (2000). Violence, identity and spaces of contention in Chile, Argentina and Colombia. *Social Research, 67*, 773–802.

Scott, J. C. (1990). *Domination and the arts of resistance*. New Haven: Yale University Press.

Sewell, W. H., Jr. (1996). Three temporalities. In: T. J. McDonald (Ed.), *The Historic Turn in the Human Sciences* (pp. 245–280). Ann Arbor: University of Michigan Press.

Sewell, W. H., Jr. (1999). The concept(s) of culture. In: V. Bonnell & L. Hunt (Eds), *Beyond the Cultural Turn* (pp. 35–61). Berkeley: University of California Press.

Smith, J. (2001). Globalizing resistance. *Mobilization, 6*, 1–19.

Smith, J. G., Chatfield, C., & Pagnucco, R. (Eds) (1997). *Transnational social movements and global politics.* Syracuse, NY: Syracuse University Press.

Snow, D. A., & Benford, R. (1988). Ideology, frame resonance, and participant mobilization. In: B. Klandermans, H. Kriesi & S. Tarrow (Eds), *From Structure to Action* (Vol. 1, pp. 197–217). Greenwich: JAI Press.

Snow, D. A., & Benford, R. (1992). Master frames and cycles of protest. In: A. D. Morris & C. M. Mueller (Eds), *Frontiers in Social Movement Theory* (pp. 133–155). New Haven: Yale University Press.

Snow, D. A., Rochford, E. B., Jr., Worden, S. K., & Benford, R. D. (1986). Frame alignment processes, micromobilization, and movement participation. *American Sociological Review, 51,* 464–481.

Snyder, D., & Kelly, W. R. (1977). Conflict intensity, media sensitivity and the validity of newspaper data. *American Sociological Review, 42,* 105–123.

Soule, S. A. (1997). The student divestment movement in the United States and tactical diffusion. *Social Forces, 75,* 855–882.

Soule, S. A. (1999). The diffusion of an unsuccessful innovation. *Annals of the American Academy of Political and Social Science, 566,* 120–131.

Soule, S. A., McAdam, D., McCarthy, J., & Su, Y. (1999). Protest events: Cause or consequence of state action? *Mobilization, 4,* 239–255.

Soule, S. A., & Zylan, Y. Z. (1997). Runaway train? *American Journal of Sociology, 103,* 733–762.

Stokes, S. C. (1995). *Cultures in conflict.* Berkeley: University of California Press.

Stonich, S. C., & Bailey, C. (2000). Resisting the blue revolution. *Human Organization, 59,* 23–36.

Swidler, A. (1986). Culture in action, symbols and strategies. *American Sociological Review, 51,* 273–286.

Szabo, M. (1996). Repertoires of contention in post-communist protest cultures. *Social Research, 63,* 1155–1182.

Tarrow, S. (1998). Studying contentious politics. In: D. Rucht, R. Koopmans & F. Neidhardt (Eds), *Acts of Dissent* (pp. 33–64). Berlin: Sigma.

Taylor, V. (1995). Watching for vibes. In: M. M. Ferree & P. Y. Martin (Eds), *Feminist Organizations: Harvest of the New Women's Movement* (pp. 223–233). Philadelphia: Temple University Press.

Taylor, V., & Whittier, N. E. (1992). Collective identity in social movement communities. In: A. D. Morris & C. M. Mueller (Eds), *Frontiers in Social Movement Theory* (pp. 104–129). New Haven: Yale University Press.

Thomas, W. I., & Thomas, D. S. (1928). *The child in America.* New York: Knopf.

Tilly, C. (1978). *From mobilization to revolution.* Reading: Addison-Wesley.

Tilly, C. (1995). *Popular contention in Great Britain, 1758–1834.* Cambridge, MA: Harvard University Press.

Tilly, C. (1998). Political identities. In: M. P. Hanagan, L. P. Moch & W. T. Brake (Eds), *Challenging Authority* (pp. 3–16). Minneapolis: University of Minnesota Press.

Tilly, C. (1999). From interactions to outcomes in social movements. In: M. Giugni, D. McAdam & C. Tilly (Eds), *How Social Movements Matter* (pp. 253–270). Minneapolis: University of Minnesota Press.

Turner, R. (1981). Collective behavior and resource mobilization as approaches to social movements. *Research in Social Movements, Conflict, and Change, 4,* 1–24.

Turner, R. (1983). Figure and ground in the analysis of social movements. *Symbolic Interaction, 6,* 175–181.

Veltmeyer, H. (1997). New social movements in Latin America. *Journal of Peasant Studies, 25,* 139–169.

Walton, J. (1989). Debt protest and the state in Latin America. In: S. Eckstein (Ed.), *Power and Popular Protest* (pp. 299–328). Berkeley: University of California Press.

Walton, J., & Ragin, C. (1990). Global and national sources of political protest: Third world responses to the debt crisis. *American Sociological Review*, *55*, 876–890.

Walton, J., & Seddon, D. (1994). *Free markets and food riots*. Oxford: Blackwell.

Whittier, N. (2001). Emotional strategies. In: J. Goodwin, J. Jasper & F. Polletta (Eds), *Passionate Politics* (pp. 233–250). Chicago and London: The University of Chicago Press.

Williams, H. L. (1996). *Planting trouble*. San Diego: University of California-San Diego.

Zamorano Farías, R. (1999). Dilemas politicos sobre los movimientos socials. *Revista Mexicana de Sociologia*, *61*, 201–232.

QUALITATIVE RESEARCH ON SOCIAL MOVEMENTS: EXPLORING THE ROLE OF QUALITATIVE DESIGNS IN EXAMINING CONTENTIOUS POLITICAL ACTION

Timothy B. Gongaware and Robert D. Benford

ABSTRACT

The proliferation of social movements and their growing importance has spawned an expansion of scholarship on collective action. Recent social psychological, cultural and narrative shifts in movement research have yielded a resurgence in the use of qualitative methods to study such contentious politics. The bulk of the research questions contemporary movement scholars currently pose warrant qualitative designs. These questions, many of which were first posed by the second Chicago school collective behavior scholars decades before, include questions of interpretive frameworks, culture, identities, narratives, other group processes and structures. We review the various qualitative techniques social movement scholars currently employ, highlight their relevance to the constructivist project and speculate on the future of qualitative methods in addressing questions pertaining to globalization, framing processes, collective identities, narratives and emotions.

Political Sociology for the 21st Century
Research in Political Sociology, Volume 12, 245–281
Copyright © 2003 by Elsevier Science Ltd.
All rights of reproduction in any form reserved
ISSN: 0895-9935/PII: S0895993503120104

INTRODUCTION

The contentious politics of recent decades has made social movements an increasingly important and legitimate area of scholarly inquiry (Meyer et al., 2002). Indeed, Tarrow (1998) suggests that social movements are potentially becoming an institutionalized part of most, if not all, democratic societies (see also Meyer & Tarrow, 1998). Given their growing importance in contemporary political arenas, and their potential to expedite or forestall social change, it is important that we spend time exploring the shifts in the questions scholars have asked about social movements and how researchers have responded to such shifts in their choices of research techniques. This paper responds to that challenge by directing our focus to the use of qualitative methods in the pursuit of knowledge about social movements.

Over the past century and a half, dramatic changes have occurred in the development of theories on collective behavior and social movements as well as in the kinds of questions scholars have asked (McPhail, 1991; Snow & Davis, 1995). Most notably, in recent decades the social psychological, cultural and narrative shifts in movement research have (re)turned scholarly attention to the negotiated and contested meanings, definitions, concepts, characteristics, symbols and other interactional phenomena that are central to social movement emergence, dynamics and outcomes. Such shifts in questions have occurred at a time when new perspectives have (re)emerged to challenge the primacy of positivism in social scientific research (cf. Guba & Lincoln, 1994; Miller & Holstein, 1993; Schwandt, 1994).

Though certainly not new, the ideas expounded upon in the constructivist paradigm, and similarly in naturalist, interpretivist, and constructionist perspectives, pose just such a challenge. At its base, the constructivist controversy calls into question the positivistic notion that an objective world exists which can be gathered and examined from a controlled distance. As Guba and Lincoln (1994) observe, such a position legitimizes the use of research techniques that allow knowledge to be summarized in "time- and context-free generalizations, some of which take the form of cause-effect laws" (p. 109). Indeed, this positivistic position requires the use of methods which ensure a degree of detachment between the researcher and the researched so as to maintain proper control over what is researched.

In place of this objectively independent reality, a position such as that of constructivism substitutes a view that there are multiple realities and that these realities are constructed through the interactions of social elements, particularly the interactions of individuals living in that world. Research methods based in such a tradition, then, must retain a focus on that interactive construction, and requires a means of observing and/or engaging in the process of construction itself so as to explore the what, how and why of such processes (Guba & Lincoln,

1994; Gubrium & Holstein, 1997). Qualitative methods are one such way that an investigator can attend to the dynamics and results of the constructions.

Certainly a radical position on constructivism might seem to preclude the use of any method that does not bring a researcher into direct engagement with the research subjects being studied. However, we do not believe that such a radical position is necessary, nor even prudent. Instead, we would argue, along with Denzin (1978), Fielding and Fielding (1986) and others, that prudent, rigorous investigation is not a matter of using either one or the other, but is a matter of what one type of research technique may provide that adds to the knowledge which the other produces. Nevertheless, we are sympathetic to the project of constructivism, especially as it challenges researchers to avoid sole use of indirect techniques for generating knowledge, techniques that require a researcher to maintain an objective distance from the researched.

In the following review of qualitative research on contentious politics, we high-light the shifts in questions concerning social movements, the use of qualitative research techniques in attempting to find "answers," and their importance given the questions that are emerging as the future of movement research. Our review explores the unique capacity of qualitative methods for capturing the naturalistic context, the interactional dynamics and the meanings of subjective experiences in a setting and/or phenomena under study. In doing so we seek to highlight the importance of these techniques for increasing knowledge and understanding with an eye toward elaborating on the methods' relationships to the constructivist project. Finally, we show that the methods have been and will continue to be important in providing a foundation for the development of grounded conceptual frameworks and theories of collective action.

QUALITATIVE QUESTIONS FOR SOCIAL MOVEMENT RESEARCH

In the pursuit of scientific knowledge, it is the questions we ask which structure the means we use to develop our understandings of the world around us (Lofland, 1996). To understand the use of qualitative methods in social movement research it is important to understand both the questions that they have been used to explore, as well as the kinds of questions that they can be expected to answer. In general, qualitative methods can be used to explore questions regarding, among other things, the characteristics, definitions, meanings, symbols and, especially, *processes* associated with collective action as well as the ways these are constructed, regarded, experienced, disseminated and otherwise deployed by social movement participants.

Qualitative methods can provide researchers access to both the front and back regions of social movements (Goffman, 1959) to facilitate understandings of movement processes and the situated actions of participants. Interestingly, the various swings of the theoretical, and thus methodological, pendulum in collective action research have only recently swung back to questions that are most appropriate for the use of qualitative methods. For several years prior to the resurgent interest in ideational and other cultural foci, research questions regarding collective action drew on assumptions concerning human behavior that pre-empted the need for deep qualitative exploration. However, in the past two decades the study of social movements has yielded a reformulation of those assumptions and the resulting questions. As a result, scholars are now pressed to make use of a method which can answer questions of human behavior as it is influenced by the context, ambience, nature and essence of a setting and the interactions that take place within it.

The Founding Questions

Early collective behavior studies questioned the impact of group context on the behavior of individuals. Researchers asked "what happens when people are in groups?" and "why do people act the way they do in groups?" Their theories posited the notion of a "collective mind" that spread through social contagion (LeBon, 1895). Drawing on these theories, later models continued to ask about the effects of broad group processes, and developed more complex models to explain individual behavior.

Blumer (1946) explained the development of a group mind through "interpretive interaction" in which the actions of individuals reproduced and reinforced the actions of others. Similarly, Smelser's (1962) value-added perspective posited the notion that "generalized beliefs" concerning appropriate norms for action were developed and diffused through a crowd via the processes of milling, suggestion and social contagion. According to McPhail (1991), such theories assumed a certain degree of unanimity among individuals in a group; participants were presumed to act uniformly through either a reliance on a collective mind or, as in other models, through a particular predisposition (Hoffer, 1951).

Given this notion of uniformity, what Turner and Killian (1987) refer to as the "illusion of unanimity," in-depth examinations of individual understandings, interactions and processes within the groups were unnecessary. Instead, data for these studies were of broad group processes – data that could be gathered and analyzed indirectly.[1] Drawing on Smelser's (1962) value-added theory, for instance, a researcher could use indirect measures to capture parameters of structural conduciveness, degrees of structural strain, the prevalence of a generalized belief and its speed of dispersion, types of leadership, and degree of social control. Then, because individuals in the susceptible population could be assumed to act in the same way, one could predict the behavior of the group, or, more likely, use the measures to explain it after the fact. Thus, the questions asked here were not directly about human choices of behavior, but were questions of parameters, degrees, amounts, speeds, and types of things that made up the context in which human behavior took place – questions appropriate for the quantitative and experimental research methods that tended to dominate North American sociology at that time.

But not all of the classical theories developed by the unfortunately named "collective behavior" school suffered from the same conceptual and methodological flaws.[2] Indeed, many of the questions now being pursued by contemporary movement scholars, were first formulated by collective behavior scholars most of whom were members of what has been referred to as the "second Chicago school of sociology" (Fine, 1995a; Snow & Davis, 1995).[3] According to Snow and Davis (1995), the second Chicago school was concerned primarily with the "*processual development and dynamics*" (p. 191) of collective behavior and social movements. They go on to observe that the "themes that make it a distinctive approach include: (1) emergence; (2) symbolization; (3) cognitive and affective transformation; (4) interactive determination; and (5) fluidity" (1995, pp. 191–192). These same themes run through much of the more contemporary questions delineated below, themes which qualitative methods are most well-suited to address. Unfortunately, the lion's share of the second Chicago school's formative work was thrown out with the bath water, the result of a paradigm shift within the field of social movements in the 1960s.

Corresponding with the rise of the New Left in the 1960s (Diggins, 1992; Gitlin, 1980), social movement scholars jettisoned virtually all social psychological models, not only those which framed participation in collective action as irrational, or at the very least not individually rational, but also those which focused on ideational, interactional, and constructivist dynamics. While some early movement research had focused on collective behavior that was not highly regarded by the researchers,[4] scholars of the 1960s were, in many cases, involved in the movements they studied (Benford, 1993b; Jenkins, 1983). The result was a reformulation of the context in which movements form.

The general perspective was that grievances were always present, and thus could not be used to explain movement emergence (Jenkins & Perrow, 1977; McCarthy & Zald, 1977; Oberschall, 1973). Instead, movement actors were highly rational beings who weighed the costs and benefits of movement participation (McCarthy & Zald, 1977; Oliver, 1980; Olson, 1965). Given the proper mobilization of resources such as selective incentives, individuals would rationally choose to participate. Using this as a starting point, the second Chicago school's interpretive questions were dropped, and scholars focused instead on amounts, types and means related to movement resources, organization and resource mobilization.

Mueller (1992) points out that the primary research questions of this perspective asked about the resources available to a movement, how they were organized, how the state facilitated or impeded mobilization and about the outcomes of mobilization. Taking this further, researchers developed a political process model by focusing on the location of movements, the conflicts they brought with them and their impact on larger social settings (Jenkins & Perrow, 1977; Kriesi et al., 1995; McAdam, 1982; Tarrow, 1998). Similar to those earlier theories which assumed irrationality in participation, the basic assumption in these models, that rationality was uniform, seemingly explained individual behavior; again, in-depth examinations of individual behavior and its relationship to ideas, interpretations, and symbolic interaction was rendered unnecessary.

However, beginning in the early 1980s, scholars began to reconsider the individual in social movements – to reproblematize grievance interpretation and thus to rethink movement participation. Armed with a definition of the movement actor as rational, but aware of the impact of context on perception and of perception on rationality (Ferree, 1992), scholars asked questions about the contexts in which meanings are constructed and transformed, about the ways movements arise from and develop their own culture, about the processes by which actors are defined, resist hegemonic labels and redefine themselves, and about the language that aids in all of these. It is in these closely tied, mostly overlapping, areas that questions developed which led to the recent resurgence of qualitative methods in the study of social movements.

Questions of Interpretive Frameworks

Both resource mobilization and political opportunity theories begged the question: what is the impact of people's interpretations of grievances in the emergence and activity of a movement? Attempts to reinsert grievances into the model (Walsh, 1981), and the notion that people may perceive costs and benefits differently (Klandermans, 1984) led to questions that warranted more in-depth study than could be afforded through indirect methods. Here, questions go to the heart of the meanings that people construct and use in regard to the problems addressed by the movement, the solutions posited by the movement and the rationales people use to justify their activity. Drawing upon social constructionist theories (Berger & Luckmann, 1966; Miller & Holstein, 1993; Spector & Kitsuse, 1977), researchers ask questions about the linkages of individual meanings with those of a social movement, about the individual experiences of meaning construction within a movement, and about the processes of interaction between movements and other social groups.

In asking about individual linkages to social movements, scholars look into the specific ways a movement attempts to mobilize participants. Through direct exploration of movements, researchers developed the notion of *collective action frames*: the grammar participants both develop and use to understand what they are doing, why they are doing it, and for explaining it to others (Benford, 1993b; Snow et al., 1986; Steinberg, 1998; Williams & Benford, 2000).[5] In making use of this idea, others have pursued questions of what types of frames exist and how they are developed, used, modified, contested and diffused (Benford, 1993a; Capek, 1993; Coy & Woehrle, 1996; Diani, 1996; Gerhards & Rucht, 1992; Snow & Benford, 1999; Williams & Williams, 1995). These questions are most easily answered when researchers are able to observe directly the actions of individuals and their interactions with movement insiders and outsiders.

Moving further into the examination of individual behavior, questions of meaning construction focus around the actual experiences of individuals within movements. Researchers ask why particular claims about grievances might appeal to some people but not to others (Snow & Benford, 1988). Others seek out specific practices such as how types of movement participants develop their understandings of participation, or how individuals in different social locations are able to make specific contributions to the process of developing collective action frames (Gongaware, 2003; Prindeville & Bretting, 1998). Still others are involved in exploring the experiences of movement participants in the process of cognitive liberation (Nepstad, 1997), the process through which people come to recognize and then act on political opportunities (McAdam, 1982).

Finally, recognizing that interpretation does not occur in a vacuum, researchers focused on the interactions of social movements with other groups. Researchers examined how interpretations of problems, solutions and motivations to act are drawn from interactions with other social movements (Carroll & Ratner, 1996; Mooney & Hunt, 1996; Snow & Benford, 1992). Here, rather than broad patterns of cause and/or effect, the researchers explore specific patterns of interaction. Blum and Vandewater (1993), for example, noted the impact of changes in individual economic conditions on a movement's collective action framing. Additionally, Gotham (1999) analyzed how political opportunities and ideational shifts in political culture affects the motivation to develop frames and their relative potency.

Questions in this area look to the development of meaning through interaction. As the interactions occur on a day-to-day basis and through various channels of communication, not all of which are accessible by those outside the movement, qualitative designs that allow immersion into the setting yield the richest and most varied data (Snow et al., 1986b). The analysis of movement documents, the observations and participation in activities and conversations, and the interviews conducted with movement members allow the researcher a first-hand glimpse at what transpires in the construction of meaning.

Questions in the Cultural Turn

Concurrent with the shift in focus to issues of interpretation and meaning construction, researchers turned to issues of culture. In early movement analysis, culture tended to be viewed simply as a source of values and norms that act as ends (Blumer, 1946; Smelser, 1962). However, with the reformulation of the movement actor as rational, and the insertion of constructionist ideas of movement development, culture came to be seen as a "tool kit" available to individuals in formulating strategic actions, motivations and meanings (Swindler, 1995).

Questions in this area work to assess the impact of a cultural tool kit – comprised of common activities, ideologies, world views, "discrete beliefs, images, feelings, values, and categories, as well as bundles of these components" (Jasper, 1997, p. 12) – on the interactive development of social movements. Johnston and Klandermans (1995) cogently encapsulated the pressing questions regarding movements and culture:

> We should try to answer questions about why and how movements are stimulated or frustrated by cultural characteristics of host societies . . . how framing activities penetrate the black box of mental life to affect behavior, how public discourse generates collective action frames, how socially constructed meanings influences action mobilization . . . [and] how interacting individuals produce movement culture and to what extent movement culture fosters or hinders mobilization (pp. 22–23).

Answering this challenge, scholars have examined the interaction of movements with the larger cultural system, the tool kit elements themselves, and the development of a unique movement culture.

The relation of a social movement with the culture of the host society has been found to provide a number of different opportunities and constraints in the development of meanings. By going in-depth and asking specific questions about the relation of the two, culture has been found to not only influence the meanings people create in a movement, but serves as an important template for the way participants create and present meanings (Kubal, 1998). To get at that interaction of culture and movements, research has delved into processes of media (Goldman & Whalen, 1990) and political ideology (Klatch, 1994), influences on participant understandings and constructions, as well as processes by which general cultural meanings impact the organizational structure of social movements (Robnett, 1996).

While some research asks about the influence of mainstream culture, others ask about local cultures and their impact on movements. Broadbent (1986) investigated the specific effects that different types of local social fabrics had on mobilization processes and goals across Japanese environmental movements. Elsewhere, Gould (1993) asked why local environmental degradation leads some communities to rebel while others remain politically complacent. In these cases, as well as others, the questions require that a researcher enter into a movement in order to directly observe the interactions that draw upon specific contexts.

To understand the cultural context in which, and from which, a movement develops requires understanding the various elements that comprise that context. This has led many researchers to ask about the impact of specific elements and their use or development in a movement. Shanks-Meile and Dobratz (1991) asked about the development and use of images of white women in white supremacist literature. Others have looked at such elements of the tool kit as images of body weight (Maurer, 1999), use of celebrities as sponsors (Meyer & Gamson, 1995), movement names (Jenson, 1995), artwork (Adams, 2001), music (Eyerman & Jamison, 1998), vocabularies of motive (Benford, 1993b; Silver, 1997), conceptions of power (Benford & Hunt, 1992), and ideas concerning the roles specific types of individuals, such as women, play in social movements (Gongaware, 2003; Krauss, 1993; Robnett, 1996).

Detailed examinations of these elements and their use in a movement can certainly help researchers answer questions about the use of those specific cultural resources. However, broader questions concerning how cultural objects are transformed by movement participants in collective action (Fantasia & Hirsch, 1995), and how movements deal with the interaction of conflicting tool kits in movement building (Lichterman, 1995) can also be addressed through direct examinations of specific elements and processes. Researchers have used the notion of a cultural tool kit to address questions about the unique cultures and their impact on participant attraction, organizational development and tactical choices (Staggenborg, 1998), as well as on the continuity of a movement over time and, especially, through periods of abeyance (Taylor, 1989; Taylor & Rupp, 1993). Such studies, as with many in this cultural turn of movement research, have required sociologists to take the micro-processes of interaction that are a part of movement unity and continuity as the empirical units of focus.

Questioning Collective Identities

Beginning in the mid-1980s, several social movement scholars shifted their attention to questions associated with collective identity.[6] This focus on collective identity corresponded to a rising trend in European movement research referred to as New Social Movements (NSM). The NSM approach generally posits that contemporary movements tend to share the following traits: they lack the class base found in earlier movements; they hold a plurality of ideological beliefs; they are based on shared identities; they act through individuals rather than just as a collective; they strike at personal instead of political targets; they use radically new tactics; they set themselves apart from previous movements; and they tend to be segmented, diffuse and decentralized (see also Cohen, 1985; Johnston et al., 1994; Melucci, 1994). To explore the validity of such claims, scholars needed to employ techniques that were conducive to digging beneath the surface, methods that would reveal the detailed characteristics, constructions and processes of the movements being studied.

By putting the very unity of a social movement into analytic play, the question of emerging collective identities became one of the more important focal topics among scholars of contentious politics. Melucci (1985) argued that, as movements are action systems, the unity of the movement must be questioned and we should direct our focus to questions of the "processes through which a collective becomes a collective" (Melucci, 1995, p. 43). Questions of collective identity quickly became questions of processes that occurred at an interactional level.

Drawing on this call for a shift in both theoretical and methodological focus, researchers have examined a myriad of questions including: processes involved in the development and maintenance of collective identities (Gamson, 1995; Hunt et al., 1994; Taylor & Whittier, 1992), the impact of changing membership on a movement's collective identity (Klandermans, 1994), the links that exist between collective identity construction and movement framing processes (Hunt et al., 1994), the role of internal conflict in collective identity development (Mueller, 1994), and the impact of political institutions and their relationship with civil society on collective identity (Thayer, 1997). In each case, the main focus is on the interactions of movement participants and the processes that take place through those interactions.

In addition to studying collective identity processes, researchers have questioned the impacts of those processes, particularly the influence of such processes on movement activity. Laraña (1994), for example, asked about the impact of political context on the continuity of movement identity. Others have looked in-depth at collective identity processes and asked about their impact on the actual challenges made and the forms of mobilization used by a movement (Taylor & Raeburn, 1995; Taylor & Whittier, 1995).

NSM scholars challenged researchers to reconsider the way they addressed the movements they studied. While Cohen (1985) argues that we must learn about movements from the position of observers in order to assess the "newness" of contemporary movements, the shift in focus to collective identity processes made researchers' participation all the more necessary. Indeed, if only observation is used to address questions of what are inherently action systems, as Melucci (1995) suggests, then "what disappears from the scene ... is collective action as a social production, as a purposive, meaningful and relational orientation" (p. 57).

Exploring Narratives

Questions of interpretation, cultural manifestations, influence and processes of collective identity require researchers to infiltrate movement settings and observe interactions at close range. With the growth of narrative analysis in a wide range of other fields, the focus in movement research is slowly turning to the narratives used and developed by social movement participants and organizations. Davis (2002) notes that there are three main questions addressed through an exploration of narratives: how is human agency and efficacy of that agency expressed?; what is the context and embeddedness of human experience?; and, what is the "centrality of language to the negotiation of meaning and the construction of identity in everyday life?" (p. 3).

In addition to helping researchers understand the use of societal rhetoric in movement development (Billig, 1995; Brulle, 1996), or of the use of narratives to tie a movement to the wider social structures (Nolan, 2002; Tatum, 2002; Williams, 1995), researchers can use narrative analysis to identify important claims or counterclaims of movements (Herzog et al., 1997; McCright & Dunlap, 2000). More importantly, however, researchers can use a focus on narratives to glean insights concerning various movement processes.

Recently, researchers have used narrative analysis to explore the connection between narratives and group actions (Brown, 2002; Yang, 2000), and to explore how movements sustain particular points of view (Polletta, 1998). Other research questions in this area involve explorations of how movements use narratives as a means of internal social control (Benford, 2002), and how narratives are used by movements to connect participants with movement goals and activities (Fine, 1995b; Polletta, 2002; Rothenberg, 2002). The overall benefit of examining the narratives used and produced by movement participants is that it attends not just to the lines of communication, but to the very structure of that communication. In so doing, researchers can explore, characterize, evaluate and explain the elements that comprise what is used by individuals to understand and create meaning, how and to what ends the elements are used, and their changes over time.

Questioning Structures, Characteristics and Group Processes

The foregoing discussion should not be taken to imply that only subjective issues that require qualitative methods have been explored in the past three decades. Obviously, this is not the case and a great deal of important research on movement organization, structures, characteristics and, most notably, the globalization of movements (della Porta et al., 1999; Meyer & Tarrow, 1998) has been conducted. However, we should note that qualitative methods have also been important in answering some of the questions developed out of the resource mobilization perspective, the political opportunity perspective, combinations of these and attempts to synthesize them with the perspectives discussed above.

In regards to organization, scholars have looked at the impact of formal organizational styles, economic conditions and political fields on movement goals and tactics (Ayres, 2001; Bates, 2000; Cress, 1997; Ray, 1998; Wharton, 1987). Others have analyzed the impacts of social movements on other movements and on non-activist organizations (Kurzman, 1998; Meyer & Whittier, 1994) as well as the effects of policing on collective action and social movement organizations (della Porta, 1996). Finally, movement scholars have focused on resources. Cress and Snow (1996), for example, employed ethnographic methods in order to identify and analyze the types of resources and combinations of resources needed to sustain a viable homeless social movement organization.

While not as prevalent in this focal area as in the others described above, qualitative methods have proven to be well-suited for analyzing many structural issues associated with the social movement arena. A plethora of questions have emerged concerning the importance of meanings, perceptions, understandings, frames and their construction in movement organization, structure, activity, characteristics and processes such as globalization, questions more aptly addressed via qualitative techniques. For example, Bob (2002) employed in-depth, face-to-face interviews with members of the Movement for the Survival of Ogoni People, in Nigeria, in order to examine the applicability of political process models to the development of international movements. By speaking directly with movement participants, Bob was able to discover not only that the meanings of opportunities were important as domestic and international support was being built, but could examine the dynamics of how those meanings specifically impacted the mobilization.

The key thread that weaves together studies such as those described in the preceding sections is not necessarily a common theoretical stance, nor even a shared set of assumptions concerning social movements. Rather, it is a shared notion that an important part of exploring collective action includes a detailed examination of the interactions and interactants who comprise the movement(s) under study. Analysis along these lines allows researchers to examine meanings, meaning construction, the cultural tool kit and how it is used/developed, shared notions of the movement and the ways these are communicated among movement participants and outsiders. It is a common commitment to providing detailed examinations using various qualitative methods which aid social scientists in developing understandings of movements and the lived experiences of participants.

QUALITATIVE RESEARCH TECHNIQUES FOR EXAMINING SOCIAL MOVEMENTS

Gathering data to answer questions such as those discussed above, requires techniques that involve getting as close to a movement as possible in order to gather information on the lived reality of movement participants. Questions of interpretation, the cultural tool kit, collective identities and communication processes are all questions of the context in which the reality construction of individuals occurs. The important contribution of qualitative studies is attention to the details and context in which that lived reality occurs through the direct and relatively unimpeded contact of the researcher with the research setting.

In general, the contact of researcher with setting allows the researcher to develop studies that provide what Snow (1999) refers to as the "master warrants" for conducting qualitative research: empirical illumination, methodological accessibility and theoretical development.[7] We direct your attention to these three warrants as they nicely draw together various justifications for the continued use of qualitative research in the study of contentious political action. Certainly, many of these qualitative projects do not directly engage constructivist arguments. However, as the warrants serve to indicate, qualitative methods are valuable as they illuminate hidden dynamics, get at elements which are difficult to access or are unknown, and make use of the information in the development of systematic knowledge; important areas of study that have emerged from the constructivist project.

First, *empirical illumination* refers to the ability of in-depth techniques to highlight little or misunderstood aspects of a setting. Second, *methodological accessibility* refers to the way qualitative methods encourage immersion in the setting which allows data to be gathered on dynamics and processes that might not be accessible or even noticeable from a distance. Finally, *theoretical development* refers to the ability of qualitative studies to provide discoveries of new theories about setting and processes, and to extend or refine existing theories.

To these three warrants we would add a fourth that is particularly important for the study of social movements: communicative accessibility. By *communicative accessibility*, we refer to the ability that qualitative research presentations have to be accessible to a wide range of audiences. Following the methods prescribed for qualitative studies, researchers attempt to keep information in as close to its original form as possible when gathering, analyzing *and presenting* the data. Qualitative research is usually presented in a scholarly framework of relevant concepts and ideas, but authors must *"represent* the particular world [s]he has studied (or some slice or quality of it) for readers who lack direct acquaintance with it" (Emerson et al., 1995, p. 169). A qualitative researcher balances the concepts of the discipline with specific examples from the field in the writing. In so doing, the author makes each more readily understandable to a wider range of audiences: scholars can understand the examples in terms of the concepts, and others, such as policy makers or the movement members themselves, may understand the concepts in terms of the examples.

Reviewing movement literature we find a diverse set of qualitative techniques put into practice that give credence to these master warrants. Researchers have used secondary source analysis, document analysis, individual and group interviews, ethnographic fieldwork, and participatory action research. Most importantly, they have used combinations of these to gather appropriate data for answering their questions.

Unobtrusive Techniques

Unobtrusive, or *non-reactive*, qualitative research designs are comprised of those techniques which do not require direct interaction and intervention in the setting, but do draw directly on information produced by, or for, the setting. The use of these techniques is particularly important where the individuals and groups under study are either temporally or spatially unavailable for direct questioning and/or observation. More importantly, the use of non-reactive techniques minimizes the impact that researchers may have on the setting through either their means of entry or their very presence.

Non-reactive techniques in general involve the observation of setting erosion or accretion: the analysis of things that are taken out of or added to the setting under study. Such items may include the physical environment, physical objects, and thoughts and stories recorded by the participants themselves or by others. Zhao (1998) recently noted the importance of physical environment for movement mobilization and activities. Unfortunately, little has been done in the way of analyzing the ecology of a movement's physical environment. However, a great deal of work has utilized historical and document analysis.

Historical Analysis
Historical analysis is broadly construed as examinations of events or combinations of events via primary and secondary sources in order to uncover and describe

accounts of what happened. Certainly most sociologists "do history" (Tuchman, 1994, p. 307) in that they "address the historical processes relevant to their questions." However, for a qualitative researcher examining social movements, the historical period in which the setting is found is of particular importance as it provides the interpretive point of view from which to understand actors' actions and ideas. History provides the assumptions we live by in our everyday lives and, whether we are aware of it or not, "our activities articulate with our times" (Tuchman, 1994, p. 313).

Historical accounts are particularly useful in terms of Snow's (1999) third warrant for qualitative research: theoretical development. Fantasia and Hirsch (1995) drew on historical analyses of women's changing roles in Algeria in the 1950s to further refine the theory of connections between movements and culture. By examining the changing contexts of elite-opposition interactions, the researchers could trace the process through which traditional cultural objects and practices, such as wearing a veil, were transformed into an expression of opposition to existing elite structures.

The key to a historical analysis is the examination of context. This context is what provides the assumptions that impact an individual's or group's interpretations of the world around them and their subsequent actions. Through historical analysis a researcher can link changes in ideas, behaviors, and practices with changes in historical context. For example, della Porta (1996) draws on secondary sources (e.g. newspaper reports, debates in parliament, and movement and police publications) in order to develop a model for examining the causes, consequences and impact of protest policing. As the context of policing practices changed, so too did the framing activities of movements. Further, the policing practices were found to serve as a barometer of political opportunity in which a movement could or could not act. Using historical analysis, della Porta is able to paint a picture of the changing contexts of policing practices and indicate the impact of police practices on movements.

Understanding and being able to recognize contexts is of crucial importance to qualitative research. It is the ability to provide analyses of events within their context that not only comprises the power of qualitative research, but it is the provision of such context that is necessary for qualitative research reports to fit into the societal ken. In providing the historical context of the setting being studied, other researchers have the ability to make comparisons between and across cases. Additionally, exemplifying our fourth warrant for qualitative research, painting the contextual picture is also important to movements as it allows participants to make evaluative comparisons of the contexts described with their own situations.

Document Analysis
Through document analysis, researchers are able to explore what people do, why they do it and their connections to various ideas. As Miller (1997) has

noted, documents are important as they "are one aspect of the sense-making activities through which we reconstruct, sustain, contest and change our senses of social reality" (p. 77). The documents record and/or express these activities. In movement research, documents include official memos and correspondence, photographs participants take, regalia they develop and wear as expressions of their collective identity and ideas, as well as participant journals, letters and forms of artwork. These documents may be found in officially maintained movement "archives," public archives or in private archival records.

While gaining access to some archives and the integrity of certain collections may be formidable obstacles (Hill, 1993; Webb et al., 1981), obtaining documents provides an important means for penetrating the lived experiences of movement participants. Further, with increased use of the Internet by various groups and organizations, some types of documents and records are more immediately available (Schroer, 1998). Herzog, Dinoff and Page (1997), for example, found that the analysis of the written exchanges on an Internet discussion group allowed them access to philosophical, moral and ethical positions of both animal rights activists and animal researchers. While engaged in these discussions, participants on both sides of the issue made statements and formulated arguments that contained indicators of their cosmologies. The researchers were then able to examine how each of the opposing cosmologies was used, especially as they came into contact with each other in the discussions.

One of the important features of documentation is that it "endures physically and thus can be separated across space and time from its author, producer, or user" (Hodder, 2002, p. 393). This makes document analysis an important part of historical analysis. Ellingson (1995), for example, was able to analyze the editorials, letters to the editor, proceedings of public meetings and narratives of rioting that appeared in six of Cincinnati's daily and weekly newspapers to develop a theory of the dialectical relationship between discourse and action. Without the documents, Ellingson would not have been able to identify the early arguments used by abolitionists and antiabolitionists, how they were carried into and influenced two collective action events, a riot and a raid, and then how these events subsequently influenced later arguments by allowing each side to use the discourse of law and order as a carrier for the expression of their positions.

The endurance of documents through time also aids those researching contemporary movements. Shanks-Meile and Dobratz (1991), for instance, analyzed white supremacist newspaper articles of the 1980s to explore their images of women and the construction of ideas on women's issues. Elsewhere, Tatum (2002) was able to draw on official transcripts of the opening and closing defense arguments in the trial of Dr. Jack Kevorkian to explore how the physician assisted suicide movement uses narratives as a means of persuasion. The documents provided a detailed account in which Tatum could identify the ways that the defense used stories that simply "unfolded so as to make any other outcome than the desired one appear to be a violation of the values the jurors, like other Americans, hold dear" (p. 200), instead of attempting to convince a jury using complex movement frames or the movement's ideology.

The recent narrative turn has made documentation all the more valuable. Documents of various forms capture the narratives that express and structure ideas and contentions of social movements. McCright and Dunlap (2000) examined the "publications concerning climate change distributed via the Internet sites of key conservative think tanks" (p. 500) that were used to delegitimate arguments in policy decisions concerning global warming. Through the identification and analysis of the counterclaims contained in these documents, the authors were able to tap a large-scale movement that might otherwise have been a challenge to penetrate via other forms of research.

Face-to-Face

Many of the important questions developed in social movement research require face-to-face contact with movement participants. Unfortunately, data gathered by researchers using non-reactive techniques do not typically allow them direct observation of the processes that lead to their creation; nor does it allow the researcher to question and probe them for needed details. Through face-to-face techniques such as interviewing and participant observation, a researcher can probe those experiences as well as observe and participate in the lived experiences of movement participants. Further, with increasing attention to the participatory action research model, researchers are developing ways to draw movement participants into the very act of gathering and analyzing data in order to provide findings with greater validity and to provide movements with meaningful and usable information.

Interviews

Interviewing has often been described as the favorite method of sociological research (Denzin, 1978) as it nicely encapsulates the very thing sociologists tend to study: human interaction. In fact, in 1956, Benney and Hughes suggested that "sociology has become the science of the interview" (p. 137). They defined the interview as:

> a relationship between two people where both parties behave as though they are of equal status for its duration, whether or not this is actually so; and where, also, both behave as though their encounter had meaning only in relation to a good many other such encounters (p. 142).

Qualitative interviewing for movement research, then, is a process of engaging movement participants, or those related in some way to a movement, directly in a purposive conversation to ask questions, probe responses and explore emergent lines of inquiry.

Through interviews, researchers may attend to the experiences, thoughts, feelings, intentions, meanings and perceptions of movement members, and can work to reconstruct events they did not observe (Berg, 2001; Rubin & Rubin, 1995). According to Darlington and Scott (2002):

> The in-depth interview takes seriously the notion that people are experts on their own experience and so best able to report how they experienced a particular event or phenomenon (p. 48).

In such a situation, whether structured by a series of questions or left unstructured to allow the respondent to direct the flow of conversation, the researcher works to get at those aspects of activity and experience that are not directly observable.

The ability to capitalize on the stories and perspectives that research subjects relate in an interview, has made this technique particularly valuable in the study of activist identities and collective identities, as well as in exploring explanations of movement membership and participation. Robnett (1996), for example, drew on life histories and personal interviews with African American women of the civil rights movement (as well as archival materials and secondary sources) in order to develop an expanded theory of leadership within social movements. Through the interviews, Robnett was able to capture the stories of women's activities and identify themes and patterns in their work with and for the movement. Specifically, in examining their stories she was able to illuminate the role of women as bridge leaders, as connections between communities and their formal leaders as well as between different communities. Most importantly, by attending to the stories of participant experiences, the interviews helped to highlight the problem of conceptualizing a movement as made up of simply leaders and followers: that there is in fact a range of leadership within a movement.

Interviewing, particularly ethnographic interviewing, is not necessarily restricted to asking questions. In an often overlooked article published twenty years ago in *Qualitative Sociology*, Snow, Zurcher and Sjoberg (1982) outlined a method of interviewing that is particularly well-suited for fieldwork on social movements: "interviewing by comment." The authors argue that asking direct, previously constructed questions of individuals, particularly in formal interview settings, can at times "frame answers by establishing the parameters around the field of acceptable responses" (p. 289), and may only elicit party lines, or put the subject on the defensive. Interviewing by comment, however, makes use of a more naturalistic, and hence less threatening, conversational mode.

By engaging individuals in one of the many conversational styles commonly found in that setting, the researcher creates a space that "allows the interviewee to define the response field in accordance with his or her frame of reference" (p. 289). The authors identify and illustrate eight generic types of comments: puzzlement, humorous, replay, descriptive, outrageous, altercasting, motivational and evaluative. Whether employed consciously or not, we suspect that most social movement scholars who conduct research engage in interviewing by comment.

By making an outrageous comment, Zurcher and Kirkpatrick (1976), for example, were able to elicit information from antipornography crusaders regarding whom the crusaders perceived to be the "enemy," information that twelve hours of questionnaire administration had failed to elicit. Kirpatrick attended a late night meeting of the crusaders who

> were discussing possible speakers for an upcoming "decency" rally. In passing, and in conversational context, Kirkpatrick sought to gain greater specificity from the crusaders about whom they perceived to be the "enemy" of their crusade. "Linda Lovelace would be a good speaker," he commented provocatively. For a moment, the crusaders fell silent. It was an outrageous comment – the "star" of Deep Throat as a speaker at an antipornography crusade! Ridiculous! Animated discussion followed, resulting in important data. The crusaders surprisingly concluded that Lovelace would be an appropriate speaker, since in their formulated opinion she had been exploited by avaricious money grubbers and influenced by misguided sexual liberals. The money grubbers and the liberals were the enemy, not the pornographic performers (Snow et al., 1982, p. 299).

The authors concluded that "[d]irect questions did not reveal, and would not have revealed, that attribution" (p. 299). But Kirkpatrick's outrageous comment did.

Benford's (1993a) study of "frame disputes" within the nuclear disarmament movement further illustrates the utility of interviewing by comment techniques. Benford found that activists would respond more candidly and were less "on guard" when he employed conversational style interviewing rather than confronting them with direct questions. To illustrate, an ongoing debate within the movement pertained to the most appropriate targets of mobilization. Moderate factions of the movement argued that middle class citizens held the keys to social change and should thus be mobilized. The more liberal and radical factions of the movement expressed the view that "women, blacks, the poor and others who have been short-changed under present structural conditions are the ones to be mobilized" (p. 691). After listening for several weeks to intramural debates pertaining to this issue and seeking clarification from the activists via traditional interviewing techniques, Benford offered the evaluative comment that "perhaps the movement could devise a strategy that appealed simultaneously to both lower and middle classes" (p. 691). This elicited a barrage of emotion-laden comments from activists suggesting an unwillingness to reach a compromise in the frame dispute. The comments by a leader of the Texas Mobilization for Survival epitomized the responses Benford's comment stimulated:

> I can't stand the middle class! . . . Fuck the middle class! I don't give a shit about them . . . . As far as I'm concerned, they deserve to get nuked. It's the poor people I care about. That's where we should concentrate our efforts (p. 691).

Where direct questions had failed to tap into the intensity of the feelings held by some activists on this issue, one simple comment yielded rich new data.

Interviews, both the traditional or "interviewing by comment" varieties, are typically used in conjunction with other techniques of data gathering. While in some cases it merely supplements other techniques, in many cases interview data are given equal treatment to enlarge the researcher's understanding of the phenomena. Gotham (1999), for example, made use of document analysis (planning reports, court documents, and newspaper articles) to understand the political opportunities that led to the mobilization of a movement against a proposed expressway. However, by including interviews with local residents, he was able to elicit stories directly from the participants concerning the construction of a community identity and how it was used to both gain a voice in the political arena as well as to mobilize participants. Adding this dimension to his document analysis, Gotham could begin to trace the connection of political opportunities not only with mobilization through structural changes but also with ideational shifts that such opportunities set in motion.

In addition to the one-on-one interviews described above, movement researchers have also employed focus group interviews. Group discussions and interviews are useful when one-on-one interviews are not feasible. More importantly, they are effective ways of capturing the interactive development of ideas, perceptions and various social constructions (Berg, 2001; Gamson, 1992). This is particularly important in examining collective identities, as the interactive back and forth of a group discussion may force out in the open commonly held assumptions about a movement, and accelerate the process of getting at higher levels of meaning held and created by social movements (North, 1998; see also Touraine, 1981). The focus groups used by Silverstein, Auerbach and Grieco (1999), for instance, allowed them to examine first hand how men from the Promise Keepers construct understandings of the support that they received from the movement and their struggles with what the researchers identified as the role-strain of becoming more involved fathers while simultaneously maintaining a traditional role of family leader.

Fieldwork

Fieldwork is, at base, an interactive process that is "created by all of the people in the social situation being studied" (Wax, 1971, p. 363) and makes use of a number of different techniques. Researchers enter and immerse themselves in a setting, observe and record what takes place there, and often participate with setting actors (Berg, 2001; Emerson et al., 1995; Shaffir et al., 1980; Van Maanen, 1988; Wax, 1971). In a majority of cases, the research design also includes interviewing, analyzing documents and exploring the historical context.

This convergence of techniques is of great benefit for social movement research. Using observation alone in the field, a researcher can "follow the natural stream of everyday life" (Adler & Adler, 1994, p. 378) and identify important patterns of behavior. However, by also participating in movement activities, a researcher can develop the skill of thinking in terms of the group(s) being studied in order to draw upon their own experiences in the analysis and representation of the setting (Van Maanen, 1988; Wax, 1971). Identifying, describing and developing understandings of these activities requires not only direct observation and experience but a combination of techniques that provide rich descriptions of what occurs and takes into account the many contextual variables that may influence the setting.

Take, for instance, Hunt and Benford's (1994) exploration of the processes through which activists align their own identities with those of the movement. The study makes use of two separate research projects, each of which included not only participant observation with the movements, but also in-depth interviews and document analysis. By drawing upon these various sources of data gathered by the different techniques, the researchers were able to discover "four moments of identity construction: becoming aware, active, committed and weary" (Hunt & Benford, 1994, p. 493) that are expressed in the ways activists construct and communicate their identities.

Another strength of fieldwork has to do with its ability to get at the many 'taken for granted' notions of participants in social settings (Patton, 2002). Lichterman (1998) has noted the value of participant observation for the exploration of implicit meanings: meanings that are taken for granted as participants "are innovating explicit ideologies, identities, and rituals" (p. 402). Drawing on extensive experiences and observations in the setting, Lichterman was able to identify many of the meanings implicit in conversations and behaviors to explore how movement participants practice citizenship, build group ties and define being activists (see also Lichterman, 1996). Elsewhere, Lichterman (1995) drew upon observations to identify the many taken-for-granted cultural patterns of group bonding that created difficulties for multicultural alliance-building among the activists he studied. By immersing oneself in the setting, a researcher can more easily identify patterns and examine how they operate in lived experience regardless of whether or not they were consciously recognized by movement participants.

Immersion in the field tends to force a researcher to remain open to new discoveries, and to temporarily suspend reliance on pre-existing sets of scientific concepts. This presents an opportunity for the discovery of new concepts and ideas. Klandermans (1994), for example, drew upon extensive experiences with Dutch peace movement activists, and through them was able to recognize the impact of changes in membership composition over time on the transformation of collective identity. More recently, Gongaware's (2003) time in the field led to a discovery of how Native American women can use the marginalized positions into which they tend to be socialized as sources of power in the construction of movement frames and the direction that a movement takes.

Finally, the deeper a researcher penetrates a movement setting the greater the potential for discovery and thus empirical illumination as the researcher observes and experiences what might have been hidden in earlier forays or left out of interview responses. Over time there are changes in who may talk to researchers, in the stories they are told and in their access to different types of information (Snow et al., 1986). Immersion allowed Groves (1997), for instance, to discover numerous differences within the animal rights movement, differences that tend to be down-played in favor of a unified front. The animal rights group he studied tended to maintain a "rational" approach to dealing with animal cruelty. However, by navigating his way deeper into the setting, Groves was able to discover that the movement was composed of individuals with a range of "emotional approaches" that movement members termed as "radical," "welfarists" or "feminine." More importantly, his continued work in and with the movement allowed him to identify many of the important influences that emotions have on the work and ideas of movement participants from both sides of the issue, areas that had previously been hidden.

Participatory Action Research
Advocates for participatory action research (PAR) take seriously Wax's (1971) notion that fieldwork is interactively created by everyone in the research setting. Emphasizing the political aspects of doing research, PAR models encourage the production of knowledge that is both useful to the group studied as well as empowering (Stoecker, 1996). The starting points for PAR include a focus on power and powerlessness, using the lived experiences of research subjects as a way to gain understandings and developing authentic commitment to those being studied through a process of genuine collaboration (Reason, 1994).

The action component stresses a convergence of evaluation and direct participation in the actions of the groups being studied. While qualitative researchers in general are encouraged to give something back to the research subjects from whom they are gathering data, the PAR model encourages a researcher to do this explicitly and directly as a justification for the study (Beckwith, 1996). Taylor (1998), for instance, emphasizes that her study on a postpartum self-help movement led her to disseminate information from the study in order to help women experiencing postpartum depression. Indeed, movement researchers may themselves become ardent activists for the causes they are studying. Gedicks' (1996) research, for instance, provided him the opportunity to actively fight mining operations in Wisconsin alongside Native Americans and environmentalists.

The participatory element of PAR refers to a commitment to including the research subjects in the decision making associated with study designs, implementations and analyses (Reinharz, 1992). Taylor (1998) notes that one of the method's powers is that it draws participants into the research process and increases the use of first hand knowledge for gathering and analyzing data. In her case it allowed her to avoid becoming "another 'expert' involved in creating knowledge that might misinterpret [the experiences of the women she studied]" (Taylor, 1998, p. 373).

Finally, we would argue that PAR can potentially be an important source of information for the movements themselves. Here, the power of qualitative research to be communicatively accessible is of particular importance. For research projects to be useful to groups unfamiliar with scientific language, a project must have clarity in the writing and the use of concrete examples in defining concepts.

Qualitative research, particularly ethnographic work, encourages this clarity (Emerson et al., 1995). Unfortunately, instances where movements draw on a researcher's published work have not been explicitly studied, and tales of such use are often anecdotal. However, Burdick (1995) argues, in examining anthropological PAR, that if and when they are drawn upon, PAR studies have the potential to help "refine debates and self-critiques *within* social movements" (p. 363).

THE PLACE OF QUALITATIVE METHODS IN FUTURE MOVEMENT RESEARCH

Each of the techniques discussed in the preceding section provides a means for gaining direct, in-depth knowledge of movement dynamics, processes, meanings, perceptions, and interpretations. The techniques, especially when used in combination, can help answer a wide range of questions by gathering information from numerous points and providing a rich picture of the social phenomena being explored. While so doing may not directly address the constructivist question of the nature of reality, what comes through in the review of these techniques is that they do answer the constructivist challenge to reduce the distance maintained between researcher and subject so as to be able to directly engage those points where reality is being constructed. Even in doing so, however, the techniques have been developed with an eye towards ensuring a degree of objectivity as they are used in the pursuit of identifying sociological patterns.

We take objectivity here as referring to a basic assumption that reality is, at the very least, empirically knowable. Further, it refers to the notion that a human ken may be developed through the use of a variety of methods working incrementally to overcome deficiencies in existing scientific work (Kirk & Miller, 1986; Sjoberg et al., 1991). To maintain a commitment to objectivity, each technique a researcher uses must remain open to criticism, and a researcher must not only acknowledge the possibility that their conclusions can be disconfirmed through subsequent research but must actively work to do so. Qualitative methods are no exception as there are limitations in generalizability, reliability and validity that must be addressed.

One of the most apparent limitations of conducting qualitative research, is that, by their very nature, they tend to be case-study oriented. In terms of social movements, this typically means examining one social movement organization, or a small group of related SMOs. While increasing the ability to look in-depth, this limits a researcher's ability to generalize from that case to social movements in general and to develop formulas for prediction and/or control. However, it is possible for the knowledge gained in a qualitative case study to be generalized to theoretical positions (Snow & Anderson, 1991; see also Yin, 1984). Further, qualitative techniques allow researchers to develop generalizations about specific kinds of settings that are "intuitive, empirically grounded, and context-specific" (Snow & Anderson, 1991, p. 165; see also Stake, 1978), and which are comprehensible for non-scholarly audiences. Generating this knowledge depends on overcoming a number of threats to the reliability and validity of findings.

Reliability in its basic sense, refers to the reproducibility of a research project by others for the testing of conclusions. However, the reproduction of qualitative case studies is rare. First, finding movement settings with conditions that exactly match those of the original case study can be very difficult, if not impossible.[8] Further, many decisions on where to focus attention are made in the field, and require personal judgments that also make reproduction difficult.

This difficulty must be attended to in the research process to ensure that a researcher's findings are reliable. Through careful research design, it is possible to build in checks concerning the consistency of findings. The persistent review of field notes, for example, serves as a key check (Kirk & Miller, 1986). By comparing findings in and over time, a researcher can attend to variations and lack of variations: do the field notes indicate that a situation or question produced similar results each time it arose? A lack of any variation at all may indicate that the researcher has only tapped a controlled presentation, that is a "party line," constructed collective action frame, movement narrative or vocabulary of motive (Benford, 2002). The key is not to identify unvarying patterns, but ones that are "consistent with respect to the particular features of interest to the observer" (Kirk & Miller, 1986, p. 42).

Consistency may also be checked through the use of multiple researchers in the data gathering, analysis or both. The additional researchers may be other professionals, or, following advocates of participatory methods, individuals from the movement (Reinharz, 1992). Including these individuals allows a researcher to draw on their lived experience with the movement to ensure that the data reliably represents what occurs.

Ensuring the reliability of a research project, however, does not necessarily equate to ensuring its validity. Nevertheless, by virtue of its design and the way in which it is presented, qualitative research tends to have a high degree of apparent validity. Many qualitative researchers, for instance, make use of inductive means for developing and exploring concepts, and nearly all provide evidence of validity by explicitly linking the concepts to concrete examples from the field when presenting findings. However, there are two points in the research process that can threaten validity. The first involves the possibility of asking the wrong questions in the field based on false assumptions of the setting or misinterpretations and misuse of meanings (Kirk & Miller, 1986). The second arises when a researcher interprets information in the course of analyzing and presenting data, again based on personal biases (Altheide & Johnson, 1994).

Each of these can be addressed in and through the research process itself. For those who include movement participants in the data collection and analysis, they have a natural check on the reliability of findings. For those who do not, movement participants can still be used as checks through engaging the participants in casual conversations designed to elicit specific information. Further, research designs that use multiple techniques provide a researcher with opportunities to compare findings from different sources and evaluate emerging ideas (Kirk & Miller, 1986). Additionally, it allows a researcher to remain flexible and sensitive to missteps and misinterpretations during the collection of data before it negatively impacts the study, and allows them to employ alternate strategies if necessary (Kirk & Miller, 1986; Orum et al., 1991; Wax, 1971). By maintaining a commitment, an ethnographic ethic (Altheide & Johnson, 1994), to understanding the movement setting, its contexts and its participants, researchers can bolster the validity of their findings beyond their initial apparent validity.

As with any research design, there are limitations and problems that must be acknowledged and addressed. However, the benefit of developing knowledge with a method that can search a topic area in-depth, that includes variations based on specific contexts, that can add to emerging theories on the topic area and which, by its very nature, tends towards communicative accessibility makes the use of qualitative methods an invaluable tool. In reviewing many recent suggestions for future research, we have noted that qualitative techniques will be indispensable for aiding researchers in answering the questions that are posed.

Oliver, Cadena-Roa and Strawn (2003, this volume) have already noted a number of important trends in the future of social movement research. We agree with their assertion that such trends will direct the attention of scholars towards a more global orientation, to movements as a class of relationships between various actors, to a focus on event-based studies, and to the integration of structuralist and constructivist theories including attention to frames, identities, culture and emotion. Such focal points, although again not directly addressing the question of the nature of reality, acknowledge, in one form or another, the constructivist challenge to examine the construction of meaning, symbols and other elements of our social world. Scholars would appear to need, then, continued focus on the details and context-specific dynamics of movement mechanisms and processes.

Many of these dynamics are those that have emerged from the topic areas noted above and their research is best aided by qualitative research techniques. In terms of interpretation, Benford and Snow (2000) note that future questions should revolve around the processes of movement framing as well as the relationship of frames with movement types, specific collective actions, discursive processes and cultural elements. Additionally, Oliver and Johnston (2000) call for a more detailed exploration of linkages between ideology and movements framing processes. Similarly, in focusing on the cultural tool kit, researchers will continue to focus on how cultural elements are used to construct meaning, especially as they come to be seen as "a set of practices that occurs between power holders and challengers, sympathizers, authorities and other groups" (Steinberg, 2002, p. 224). In each area, the focus is on specific elements, the process of their construction and the contexts in which they are found.

As relative newcomers in social movement studies, the areas of collective identity and narrative pose even greater challenges as researchers illuminate the many theoretical connections among identities, narratives and structure. A fundamental question that is begged by such studies involves whether identity or interest is at the base of individual choice, or if each become more or less salient in different contexts (Polletta & Jasper, 2001). To address this issue, Polletta and Jasper (2001) highlight a number of crucial research areas: how individuals sort out and combine different sources of identity; how people juggle and choose among a range of groups, roles and positions; and, how different elements of the cultural tool kit (e.g. collective memories, emotions, body, place, metaphors and images) are used to construct collective identities (pp. 299–301). The exploration of narratives furthers such inquiries by asking about the connection of events with group lore, the relationship of collective identity with a group's metanarratives and ideology, the links between personal narratives and movement narratives (Benford,

2002), and variances in the importance of stories to different movements (Fine, 2002). Again, the focus of research in this area is in illuminating processes and dynamics within particular contexts for the purpose of further developing extant movement theories.

Overall, the work of movement scholars has been, and will continue to be, the integration of theories regarding structures such as political process and various elements of culture including identities, interpretations, and narratives (Whittier, 2002). In addition to the areas noted above, we believe that continued development of social movement theory can benefit from the assistance of qualitative research. For example, qualitative research will be particularly helpful in answering Buechler's (2002) call for a more macro-oriented focus in theory development. His call notes the ahistorical approach of past theories and challenges scholars to develop theories that attend to current understandings of the state and focuses on examining the impact of movements on the state and of the state on movements within specific historical contexts. The findings of qualitative research projects that are context-specific in nature and address the construction and use of meaning, we believe, can potentially be generalized to these theoretical positions and provide them with the rich details of historical context they need.

One area in which qualitative work will be the most useful, is what scholars have identified as a growing interest in exploring relationships between emotions, social movements and contentious politics (cf. Aminzade & McAdam, 2002; Goodwin et al., 2001). While emotions have certainly not been completely ignored in past research on social movements, the research has tended to be "scattered and ad hoc" (Goodwin et al., 2000, p. 80; see also Blee, 1998; Groves, 1995). However, in recent years there has been a growing interest in the subject, and qualitative research has provided some important benefits for their study.

Goodwin, Jasper and Polletta (2000) note that emotions are both constructed situationally in numerous and varying movement contexts, and they are often repressed at both the individual and group levels. The situational construction and repression of emotions preclude the development and use of quantitative models of emotionality in collective action research. Rather, researchers require techniques that allow processes to be captured as they occur and permit penetration beneath the surface into areas purposively or unwittingly hidden from view. For example, Gould (2002) was able to get at the process used by ACT UP for transforming grief over the AIDS crisis into anger by first examining the emotions at play in leaflets and then interviewing participants to get stories of the emotion work which was used to encourage action. Through systematic examination of movement-produced literature and narratives contained in speeches and newspaper columns, Gould was able to not only identify the connection of a movement's rise and fall to an emotional context, but examine the processes by which that occurred as well.

Elsewhere, Groves (1997) uncovered levels of beliefs concerning positions on animal research and the relations of humans to animals in both an animal rights movement and a pro-animal research movement through the use of ethnographic field research. Although each movement attempted to present a unified front to audiences, Groves' immersion in the setting allowed him to see and explore these hidden levels. Specifically, he explored how individual responses to shame impacted both their position on the issue as a whole, and how they personally understood their relations to animals. Through direct, prolonged contact he was able to identify and observe the dynamics of these patterns.

In essence, qualitative research provides a means for directly attending to the details of context, the lived experience of that context and its continued construction through time. Through its various techniques, researchers can examine the expressions of movement participants and other physical traces they leave behind. They can directly question and probe participant responses concerning experiences in or with movements. Finally, they can directly observe and even experience the very processes and dynamics that must be addressed. Using these qualitative methods, especially in combination, allows scholars to develop rich, communicatively accessible, context-specific findings that direct focus at the processes and results of a construction of reality and which can be generalized to emerging theories of collective action, the participants in these actions and the relations of social movements with other aspects of the cultural and political spheres.

NOTES

1. McPhail (1991) also points out that many of these theories were developed by scholars who either "cited or quoted earlier writers who had done their fieldwork in the same armchair manner" (p. 43).

2. Some critics of classical collective behavior theory created "grotesque, polemical, caricatures" of this school, thereby disregarding its many distinctive contributions to the field (Snow & Davis, 1995, p. 188).

3. According to Snow and Davis (1995), collective behavior and social movement scholars from the second Chicago school of sociology included Joseph Gusfield, Morris Janowitz, Lewis Killian, Orin Klapp, William Kornhauser, Gladys and Kurt Lang, E. L. Quarantelli, Tamotsu Shibutanti and Ralph Turner.

4. LeBon, for instance, made no secret of the fact that he was very disturbed by the violent strikes in the Paris Commune between 1869 and 1871 (McPhail, 1991).

5. For recent reviews and debates regarding the social movement framing perspective, see the following: Benford (1997), Benford and Snow (2000), Fisher (1997), Goodwin and Jasper (1999), Hart (1996), Jasper (1997), Oliver and Johnston (2000), Scheufele (1999), Sherkat (1998), Snow and Benford (2000), Steinberg (1998), Williams and Benford (2000).

6. For a recent review and critique of the collective identity literature, see Polletta and Jasper (2001).

7. For a focused discussion specifically on the warrants of ethnography, see Katz (1997).

8. Indeed, Strauss and Corbin (1990) note that the exact reproduction of the conditions for the study of any social phenomena would be near impossible.

ACKNOWLEDGMENTS

We would like to acknowledge our gratitude for the assistance of Jackie Groce whose skills were invaluable in getting this project underway. Further, we would like to thank the reviewers and editors of *Research in Political Sociology* for their comments and suggestions on earlier drafts of this paper.

REFERENCES

Adams, J. (2001). The makings of political art. *Qualitative Sociology, 24*(3), 311–348.

Adler, P., & Adler, P. (1994). Observational techniques. In: N. Denzin & Y. Lincoln (Eds), *Handbook of Qualitative Research* (pp. 377–392). Thousand Oaks, CA: Sage Publications.

Altheide, D., & Johnson, J. (1994). Criteria for assessing interpretive validity in qualitative research. In: N. Denzin & Y. Lincoln (Eds), *Handbook of Qualitative Research* (pp. 485–499). Thousand Oaks, CA: Sage Publications.

Aminzade, R., & McAdam, D. (2002). Emotions and contentious politics [Special Issue]. *Mobilzation, 7*(2).

Ayres, J. (2001). Transnational political processes and contention against the global economy. *Mobilization, 6*(1), 55–68.

Bates, V. (2000). The decline of a new Christian right social movement organization: Opportunities and constraints. *Review of Religious Research, 42*(1), 19–40.

Beckwith, D. (1996). Ten ways to work together: An organizer's view. *Sociological Imagination, 33*(2), 164–172.

Benford, R. D. (1993a). Frame disputes within the nuclear disarmament movement. *Social Forces, 71*, 677–701.

Benford, R. D. (1993b). You could be the hundredth monkey: Collective action frames and vocabularies of motive within the nuclear disarmament movement. *The Sociological Quarterly, 34*, 195–216.

Benford, R. D. (1997). An insider's critique of the social movement framing perspective. *Sociological Inquiry, 67*, 409–430.

Benford, R. D. (2002). Controlling narratives and narratives as control within social movements. In: J. Davis (Ed.), *Stories of Change: Narrative and Social Movements* (pp. 53–75). Albany, NY: State University of New York.

Benford, R. D., & Hunt, S. A. (1992). Dramaturgy and social movements: The social construction and communication of power. *Sociological Inquiry, 62*, 36–55.

Benford, R. D., & Snow, D. A. (2000). Framing processes and social movements: An overview and assessment. *Annual Review of Sociology, 26*, 611–639.

Benney, M., & Hughes, E. C. (1956). Sociology and the interview: Editorial preface. *American Journal of Sociology, 62*(2), 137–142.

Berg, B. L. (2001). *Qualitative research methods for the social sciences* (4th ed.). Boston, MA: Allyn and Bacon.

Berger, P., & Luckmann, T. (1966). *The social construction of reality: A treatise in the sociology of knowledge*. NY: Doubleday.

Billig, M. (1995). Rhetorical psychology, ideological thinking, and imagining nationhood. In: H. Johnston & B. Klandermans (Eds), *Social Movements and Culture* (pp. 64–84). Minneapolis, MN: University of Minnesota Press.

Blee, K. (1998). White-Knuckle research: Emotional dynamics in fieldwork with racist activists. *Qualitative Sociology, 21*(4), 381–399.

Blum, L., & Vandewater, E. (1993). "Mother to mother": A maternalist organization in late capitalist America. *Social Problems, 40*(3), 285–300.

Blumer, H. (1946). Collective behavior. In: A. M. Lee (Ed.), *Principles of Sociology: A New Outline of the Principles of Sociology* (2nd ed., pp. 167–219). NY: Barnes & Noble.

Bob, C. (2002). Political process theory and transnational movements: Dialectics of protest among Nigeria's Ogoni minority. *Social Problems, 49*(3), 395–415.

Broadbent, J. (1986). The ties that bind: Social fabric and the mobilization of environmental movements in Japan. *International Journal of Mass Emergencies and Disasters, 4*(2), 227–253.

Brown, M. (2002). Moving toward the light: Self, other, and the politics of experience in new age narratives. In: J. Davis (Ed.), *Stories of Change: Narrative and Social Movements* (pp. 101–122). Albany, NY: State University of New York.

Brulle, R. (1996). Environmental discourse and social movement organizations: A historical and theoretical perspective on the development of U.S. environmental organizations. *Sociological Inquiry, 66*(1), 58–83.

Buechler, S. (2002). Toward a structural approach to social movements. *Research in Political Sociology, 10*, 1–45.

Burdick, J. (1995). Uniting theory and practice in the ethnography of social movements: Notes toward a hopeful realism. *Dialectical Anthropology, 20*, 361–385.

Capek, S. M. (1993). The "Environmental Justice" Frame: A conceptual discussion and application. *Social Problems, 40*, 5–24.

Carroll, W., & Ratner, R. S. (1996). Master framing and cross-movement networking in contemporary social movements. *The Sociological Quarterly, 37*, 601–625.

Cohen, J. (1985). Strategy and identity: New theoretical paradigms and contemporary social movements. *Social Research, 52*, 663–716.

Coy, P., & Woehrle, L. (1996). Constructing identity and oppositional knowledge: The framing practices of peace movement organizations during the Persian Gulf War. *Sociological Spectrum, 16*(3), 287–327.

Cress, D. (1997). Non-profit incorporation among movements of the poor: Pathways and consequences for homeless social movement organizations. *The Sociological Quarterly, 38*(2), 343–360.

Cress, D., & Snow, D. (1996). Mobilization at the margins: Resources, benefactors, and the viability of homeless social movement organizations. *American Sociological Review, 61*(6), 1089–1109.

Darlington, Y., & Scott, D. (2002). *Qualitative research in practice: Stories from the field*. Buckingham, England: Open University Press.

Davis, J. (2002). Narrative and social movements: The power of stories. In: J. Davis (Ed.), *Stories of Change: Narrative and Social Movements* (pp. 3–30). Albany, NY: State University of New York.

della Porta, D. (1996). Social movements and the state: Thoughts on the policing of protest. In: D. McAdam, J. McCarthy & M. Zald (Eds), *Comparative Perspectives on Social Movements: Political Opportunities, Mobilizing Structures and Cultural Framings* (pp. 62–92). Cambridge, MA: Cambridge University Press.

della Porta, D., Kriesi, H., & Rucht, D. (Eds) (1999). *Social movements in a globalizing world.* NY: St. Martins Press Inc.

Denzin, N. (1978). *The research act: A theoretical introduction to sociological methods* (2nd ed.). NY: McGraw-Hill Book Co.

Diani, M. (1996). Linking mobilization frames and political opportunities: Insights from regional populism in Italy. *American Sociological Review, 61,* 1053–1069.

Diggins, J. (1992). *The rise and fall of the American left.* NY: W. W. Norton and Company.

Ellingson, S. (1995). Understanding the dialectic of discourse and collective action: Public debate and rioting in Antebellum Cincinnati. *American Journal of Sociology, 101,* 100–144.

Emerson, R. M., Fretz, R., & Shaw, L. (1995). *Writing ethnographic fieldnotes.* Chicago: University of Chicago Press.

Eyerman, R., & Jamison, A. (1998). *Music and social movements: Mobilizing traditions in the twentieth century (Cambridge cultural social studies).* NY: Cambridge University Press.

Fantasia, R., & Hirsch, E. L. (1995). Culture in rebellion: The appropriation and transformation of the veil in Algerian revolution. In: H. Johnston & B. Klandermans (Eds), *Social Movements and Culture* (pp. 144–162). Minneapolis, MN: University of Minnesota Press.

Ferree, M. M. (1992). The political context of rationality: Rational choice theory and resource mobilization. In: A. D. Morris & C. M. Mueller (Eds), *Frontiers in Social Movement Theory* (pp. 29–52). New Haven, CT: Yale University Press.

Fielding, N. G., & Fielding, J. L. (1986). *Linking data.* Beverly Hills, CA: Sage Publications.

Fine, G. A. (Ed.) (1995a). *A second Chicago school? The development of a postwar American sociology.* Chicago: University of Chicago Press.

Fine, G. A. (1995b). Public narration and group culture: Discerning discourse in social movements. In: H. Johnston & B. Klandermans (Eds), *Social Movements and Culture* (pp. 127–143). Minneapolis, MN: University of Minnesota Press.

Fine, G. A. (2002). The storied group: Social movements as "bundles of narratives." In: J. Davis (Ed.), *Stories of Change: Narrative and Social Movements* (pp. 229–245). Albany, NY: State University of New York.

Fisher, K. (1997). Locating frames in the discursive Universe. *Sociological research Online, 2*(3), <http://www.socresonline.org.uk/socresonline/2/3/4.html>

Gamson, J. (1995). Must identity movements self destruct? A queer dilemma. *Social Problems, 42,* 390–407.

Gamson, W. A. (1992). *Talking politics.* New York: Cambridge University Press.

Gedicks, A. (1996). Activist sociology: Personal reflections. *Sociological Imagination, 33*(1), 55–72.

Gerhards, J., & Rucht, D. (1992). Mesomobilization: Organizing and framing in two protest campaigns in West Germany. *American Journal of Sociology, 98*(3), 555–595.

Gitlin, T. (1980). *The whole world is watching: Mass media in the making and unmaking of the new left.* Berkeley, CA: University of California Press.

Goffman, E. (1959). *The presentation of self in everyday life.* Garden City, NY: Anchor Books.

Goldman, M., & Whalen, J. (1990). From the new left to the new enlightenment: The methodological implication of public attention on private lives. *Qualitative Sociology, 13*(1), 85–107.

Gongaware, T. B. (2003). Nurturers and keepers of culture: The influence of native American women on the development of collective action frames. *Research in Social Movements, Conflict and Change, 24.*

Goodwin, J., & Jasper, J. M. (1999). Caught in a winding, snarling vine: The structural bias of political process theory. *Sociological Forum, 14,* 27–54.

Goodwin, J., Jasper, J. M., & Polletta, F. (2000). Return of the repressed: The fall and rise of emotions in social movement theory. *Mobilization, 5*(1), 65–84.

Goodwin, J., Jasper, J. M., & Polletta, F. (Eds) (2001). *Passionate politics: Emotions and social movements.* Chicago: University of Chicago Press.

Gotham, K. (1999). Political opportunity, community identity, and the emergence of a local anti-expressway movement. *Social Problems, 46*(3), 332–354.

Gould, D. (2002). Life during wartime: Emotions and the development of ACT UP. *Mobilization, 7,* 177–200.

Gould, K. (1993). Pollution and perception: Social visibility and local environmental mobilization. *Qualitative Sociology, 16*(2), 157–178.

Groves, J. M. (1995). Learning to feel: The neglected sociology of social movements. *The Sociological Review, 43*(3), 435–461.

Groves, J. M. (1997). *Hearts and minds: The controversy over laboratory animals.* Philadelphia, PA: Temple University Press.

Guba, E. G., & Lincoln, Y. S. (1994). Competing paradigms in qualitative research. In: N. Denzin & Y. S. Lincoln (Eds), *Handbook of Qualitative Research* (pp. 105–117). Thousand Oaks, CA: Sage Publications, Inc.

Gubrium, J. F., & Holstein, J. A. (1997). *The new language of qualitative methods.* New York: Oxford University Press.

Hart, S. (1996). The cultural dimension of social movements: A theoretical reassessment and literature review. *Sociological of Religion, 57,* 87–100.

Herzog, H., Jr., Dinoff, B., & Page, J. (1997). Animal rights talk: Moral debate over the Internet. *Qualitative Sociology, 20*(3), 399–418.

Hill, M. (1993). *Archival strategies and techniques: Analytical field research* (Vol. 31). Newbury Park, CA: Sage Publications.

Hodder, I. (2002). The interpretation of documents and material culture. In: N. Denzin & Y. Lincoln (Eds), *Handbook of Qualitative Research* (pp. 393–402). Thousand Oaks, CA: Sage Publications.

Hoffer, E. (1951). *The true believer.* NY: The new American library.

Hunt, S., & Benford, R. D. (1994). Identity talk in the peace and justice movement. *Journal of Contemporary Ethnography, 22,* 488–517.

Hunt, S. A., Benford, R. D., & Snow, D. A. (1994). Identity fields: Framing processes and the social construction of movement identities. In: E. Laraña, H. Johnson & J. Gusfield (Eds), *New Social Movements: From Ideology to Identity* (pp. 185–208). Philadelphia, PA: Temple University Press.

Jasper, J. M. (1997). *The art of moral protest: Culture, biography and creativity in social movements.* Chicago, IL: University of Chicago Press.

Jenkins, J. C. (1983). Resource mobilization theory and the study of social movements. *Annual Review of Sociology, 9,* 527–553.

Jenkins, J. C., & Perrow, C. (1977). Insurgency of the powerless: Farm worker movements (1946–1972). *American Sociological Review, 42*(2), 249–268.

Jenson, J. (1995). What's in a name? Nationalist movements and public discourse. In: H. Johnston & B. Klandermans (Eds), *Social Movements and Culture* (pp. 107–126). Minneapolis, MN: University of Minnesota Press.

Johnston, H., & Klandermans, B. (1995). The cultural analysis of social movements. In: H. Johnston & B. Klandermans (Eds), *Social Movements and Culture* (pp. 3–24). Minneapolis, MN: University of Minnesota Press.

Johnston, H., Laraña, E., & Gusfield, J. (1994). Identities, grievances, new social movements. In: E. Laraña, H. Johnson & J. Gusfield (Eds), *New Social Movements: From Ideology to Identity* (pp. 3–36). Philadelphia, PA: Temple University Press.

Katz, J. (1997). Ethnography's warrants. *Sociological Methods and Research, 25*(4), 391–423.

Kirk, J., & Miller, M. (1986). *Reliability and validity in qualitative research.* Newbury Park, CA: Sage Publications.

Klandermans, B. (1984). Mobilization and participation: Social-psychological expansions of resource mobilization theory. *American Sociological Review, 49*, 583–600.

Klandermans, B. (1994). Transient identities? Membership patterns in the Dutch peace movement. In: E. Laraña & H. Johnston & J. Gusfield (Eds), *New Social Movements: From Ideology to Identity* (pp. 168–184). Philadelphia, PA: Temple University Press.

Klatch, R. (1994). The counterculture, the new left and the new right. *Qualitative Sociology, 17*(3), 199–214.

Krauss, C. (1993). Women and toxic waste protests: Race, class and gender as resources of resistance. *Qualitative Sociology, 16*(3), 247–262.

Kriesi, H., Koopmans, R., Duyvendak, J. W., & Giugi, M. (1995). *New social movements in western Europe: A comparative analysis.* Minneapolis, MN: University of Minnesota Press.

Kubal, T. (1998). The presentation of political self: Cultural resonance and the construction of collective action frames. *The Sociological Quarterly, 39*(4), 539–554.

Kurzman, C. (1998). Organizational opportunity and social movement mobilization: A comparative analysis of four religious movements. *Mobilization, 3*(1), 23–49.

Laraña, E. (1994). Continuity and unity in new forms of collective action: A comparative analysis of student movements. In: H. Johnston & B. Klandermans (Eds), *Social Movements and Culture* (pp. 209–233). Minneapolis, MN: University of Minnesota Press.

LeBon, G. (1895). *The crowd* (1960 ed.). NY: Viking Press.

Lichterman, P. (1995). Piecing together multicultural community: Cultural differences in community building among grass-roots environmentalists. *Social Problems, 42*(4), 513–534.

Lichterman, P. (1996). *The search for political community: American activists reinventing commitment.* NY: Cambridge University Press.

Lichterman, P. (1998). What do movements mean? The value of participant-observation. *Qualitative Sociology, 21*(4), 401–418.

Lofland, J. (1996). *Social movement organizations: Guide to research on insurgent realities.* New York: Aldine de Gruyter.

Maurer, D. (1999). Too skinny or vibrant and healthy? Weight management in the vegetarian movement. In: J. Sobal & D. Maurer (Eds), *Weighty Issues: Fatness and Thinness as Social Problems* (pp. 209–229). NY: Aldine de Gruyter.

McAdam, D. (1982). *Political process and the development of black insurgency, 1930–1970.* Chicago: University of Chicago Press.

McCarthy, J. D., & Zald, M. (1977). Resource mobilization and social movements: A partial theory. *American Journal of Sociology, 82*(6), 1212–1241.

McCright, A., & Dunlap, R. (2000). Challenging global warming as a social problem: An analysis of the conservative movement's counter-claims. *Social Problems, 47*(4), 499–522.

McPhail, C. (1991). *The myth of the madding crowd.* NY: Aldine de Gruyter.

Melucci, A. (1985). The symbolic challenge of contemporary movements. *Social Research, 52*(4), 789–816.

Melucci, A. (1994). A strange kind of newness: What's new in social movements? In: E. Laraña, H. Johnston & J. Gusfield (Eds), *New Social Movements: From Ideology to Identity* (pp. 101–130). Philadelphia, PA: Temple University Press.

Melucci, A. (1995). The process of collective identity. In: H. Johnston & B. Klandermans (Eds), *Social Movements and Culture* (pp. 41–63). Minneapolis, MN: University of Minnesota Press.

Meyer, D. S., & Gamson, J. (1995). The challenge of cultural elites: Celebrities and social movements. *Sociological Inquiry, 65*(2), 181–206.

Meyer, D. S., & Tarrow, S. (Eds) (1998). *The social movement society: Contentious politics for a new century*. NY: Rowman and Littlefield Publishers Inc.

Meyer, D. S., & Whittier, N. (1994). Social movement spillover. *Social Problems, 41*, 277–298.

Meyer, D. S., Whittier, N. & Robnett, B. (Eds) (2002). *Social Movements: Identity, Culture and the State*. NY: Oxford University Press.

Miller, G. (1997). Contextualizing texts: Studying organizational texts. In: G. Miller & R. Dingwall (Eds), *Context and Method in Qualitative Research* (pp. 77–91). Thousand Oaks, CA: Sage Publications.

Miller, G., & Holstein, J. (Eds) (1993). *Constructionist controversies: Issues in social problems theory*. NY: Aldine De Gruyter.

Mooney, P., & Hunt, S. (1996). A repertoire of interpretations: Master frames and ideological continuity in U.S. agrarian mobilization. *The Sociological Quarterly, 37*(1), 177–197.

Mueller, C. M. (1992). Building social movement theory. In: A. D. Morris & C. M. Mueller (Eds), *Frontiers in Social Movement Theory* (pp. 3–26). New Haven, CT: Yale University Press.

Mueller, C. M. (1994). Conflict networks and the origins of women's liberation. In: E. Laraña, H. Johnston & J. Gusfield (Eds), *New Social Movements: From Ideology to Identity* (pp. 234–263). Philadelphia, PA: Temple University Press.

Nepstad, S. (1997). The process of cognitive liberation: Cultural synapses, links and frame contradictions in the U.S.-central America peace movement. *Sociological Inquiry, 67*(4), 470–487.

Nolan, J., Jr. (2002). Drug court stories: Transforming American jurisprudence. In: J. Davis (Ed.), *Stories of Change: Narrative and Social Movements* (pp. 149–178). Albany, NY: State University of New York.

North, P. (1998). Exploring the politics of social movements through 'sociological intervention': A case study of local exchange trading schemes. *Sociological Review, 46*(3), 564–582.

Oberschall, A. (1973). *Social conflict and social movements*. Englewood Cliffs, NJ: Prentice-Hall.

Oliver, P. (1980). Rewards and punishments as selective incentives for collective action: Theoretical investigations. *American Journal of Sociology, 85*, 1356–1375.

Oliver, P., & Johnston, H. (2000). What a good idea! Ideology and frames in social movement research. *Mobilization, 5*, 37–54.

Olson, M. (1965). *The logic of collective action: Public goods and the theory of groups*. Cambridge, MA: Harvard University Press.

Orum, A., Feagin, J., & Sjoberg, G. (1991). Introduction: The nature of the case study. In: J. Feagin, A. Orum & G. Sjoberg (Eds), *A Case for the Case Study* (pp. 1–26). Chapel Hill, NC: University of North Carolina Press.

Patton, M. (2002). *Qualitative research and evaluation methods* (3rd ed.). Thousand Oaks, CA: Sage Publications.

Polletta, F. (1998). 'It was like a fever': Narrative and identity in social protest. *Social Problems, 45*, 137–159.

Polletta, F. (2002). Plotting protest: Mobilizing stories in the 1960 student sit-Ins. In: J. Davis (Ed.), *Stories of Change: Narrative and Social Movements* (pp. 31–52). Albany, NY: State University of New York.

Polletta, F., & Jasper, J. M. (2001). Collective identity and social movements. *Annual Review of Sociology, 27,* 283–305.

Prindeville, D. M., & Bretting, J. (1998). Indigenous women activists and political participation: The case of environmental justice. *Women and Politics, 19*(1), 39–58.

Ray, R. (1998). Women's movements and political fields: A comparison of two Indian cities. *Social Problems, 45*(1), 21–36.

Reason, P. (1994). Three approaches to participative inquiry. In: N. Denzin & Y. Lincoln (Eds), *Handbook of Qualitative Research* (pp. 324–352). Thousand Oaks, CA: Sage Publications.

Reinharz, S. (1992). *Feminist methods in social research.* NY: Oxford University Press.

Robnett, B. (1996). African-American women in the civil rights movement, 1954–1965: Gender, leadership, and micromobilization. *American Journal of Sociology, 101*(6), 1661–1693.

Rothenberg, B. (2002). Movement advocates as battered women's storytellers: From varied experiences, One message. In: J. Davis (Ed.), *Stories of Change: Narrative and Social Movements* (pp. 203–225). Albany, NY: State University of New York.

Rubin, H., & Rubin, I. (1995). *Qualitative interviewing: The art of hearing data.* Thousand Oaks, CA: Sage Publications.

Scheufele, D. A. (1999). Framing as a theory of media effects. *Journal of Communication, 49,* 103–122.

Schroer, T. J. (1998). White racialists, computers, and the internet: A macro, meso, and microlevel analysis. Unpublished doctoral dissertation, University of Nebraska-Lincoln.

Shaffir, W., Stebbins, R., & Turowetz, A. (Eds) (1980). *Fieldwork experience: Qualitative approaches to social research.* NY: St. Martin's Press.

Shanks-Meile, S., & Dobratz, B. (1991). Sick feminists or helpless victims: Images of women in Ku Klux Klan and American Nazi party literature. *Humanity and Society, 15*(1), 72–93.

Sherkat, D. E. (1998). What's in a frame? Toward an integrated social psychology of social movements. Paper presented at the annual meeting of the international sociological association conference, Montreal, Quebec.

Silver, I. (1997). Constructing social change through philanthropy: Boundary framing and the articulation of vocabularies of motives for social movement participation. *Sociological Inquiry, 67*(4), 488–503.

Silverstein, L., Auerbach, C., & Grieco, L. (1999). Do promise keepers dream of feminist sheep? *Sex Roles, 40*(9–10), 665–688.

Sjoberg, G., Williams, N., Vaughan, T. R., & Sjoberg, A. F. (1991). The case study approach in social research: Basic methodological issues. In: J. R. Feagin, A. Orum & G. Sjoberg (Eds), *A Case for the Case Study* (pp. 27–79). Chapel Hill, NC: The University of North Carolina Press.

Smelser, N. J. (1962). *Theory of collective behavior.* NY: Free Press.

Snow, D. A. (1999). Assessing the ways in which qualitative/ethnographic research contributes to social psychology: Introduction to the special issue. *Social Psychology Quarterly, 62*(2), 97–100.

Snow, D. A., & Anderson, L. (1991). Researching the homeless: The characteristic features and virtues of the case study. In: J. Feagin, A. Orum & G. Sjoberg (Eds), *A Case for the Case Study* (pp. 148–173). Chapel Hill, NC: University of North Carolina Press.

Snow, D. A., & Benford, R. D. (1988). Ideology, frame resonance and participant mobilization. *International Social Movement Research, 1,* 197–217.

Snow, D. A., & Benford, R. D. (1992). Master frames and cycles of protest. In: A. D. Morris & C. M. Mueller (Eds), *Frontiers in Social Movement Theory* (pp. 133–155). New Haven, CT: Yale University Press.

Snow, D. A., & Benford, R. D. (1999). Alternative types of crossnational diffusion in the social movement arena. In: D. della Porta, H. Kriesi & D. Rucht (Eds), *Social Movements in a Globalizing World* (pp. 23–39). NY: St. Martins Press Inc.

Snow, D. A., & Benford, R. D. (2000). Clarifying the relationship between framing and ideology: A comment on Oliver and Johnston. *Mobilization, 5*, 55–60.

Snow, D. A., Benford, R. D., & Anderson, L. (1986b). Fieldwork roles and informational yield: A comparison of alternative settings and roles. *Urban Life, 14*, 377–408.

Snow, D. A., & Davis, P. W. (1995). The Chicago approach to collective behavior. In: G. A. Fine (Ed.), *A Second Chicago School? The Development of a Postwar American Sociology* (pp. 188–230). Chicago: University of Chicago Press.

Snow, D. A., Rochford, E. B., Jr., Worden, S. K., & Benford, R. D. (1986). Frame alignment processes, micromobilization and movement participation. *American Sociological Review, 51*, 464–481.

Snow, D. A., Zurcher, L. A., & Sjoberg, G. (1982). Interviewing by comment: An adjunct to the direct question. *Qualitative Sociology, 5*, 283–311.

Spector, M., & Kitsuse, J. (1977). *Constructing social problems*. Menlo Park, CA: Cummings publishing company.

Staggenborg, S. (1998). Social movement communities and cycles of protest: The emergence and maintenance of a local women's movement. *Social Problems, 45*, 180–204.

Stake, R. (1978). The case-study method of social inquiry. *Educational Researcher, 7*, 5–8.

Steinberg, M. (1998). Tilting the frame: Considerations on collective action framing from a discursive turn. *Theory and Society, 27*, 845–872.

Steinberg, M. (2002). Toward a more dialogic analysis of social movement culture. In: D. Meyer, N. Whittier & B. Robnett (Eds), *Social Movements: Identity, Culture and the State* (pp. 208–225). NY: Oxford University Press.

Stoecker, R. (1996). Sociology and social action: Introduction. *Sociological Imagination, 33*(1), 3–17.

Strauss, A., & Corbin, J. (1990). *Basics of qualitative research: Grounded theory procedures and techniques*. Newbury Park, CA: Sage Publications.

Schwandt, T. A. (1994). Constructivist, interpretivist approaches to human inquiry. In: N. Denzin & Y. S. Lincoln (Eds), *Handbook of Qualitative Research* (pp. 118–137). Thousand Oaks, CA: Sage Publications, Inc.

Swindler, A. (1995). Cultural power and social movements. In: H. Johnston & B. Klandermans (Eds), *Social Movements and Culture* (pp. 25–40). Minneapolis, MN: University of Minnesota Press.

Tarrow, S. (1998). *Power in movement: Social movements and contentious politics* (2nd ed.). NY: Cambridge University Press.

Tatum, J. (2002). Compassion on trial: Movement narrative in a court conflict over physician-assisted suicide. In: J. Davis (Ed.), *Stories of Change: Narrative and Social Movements* (pp. 179–202). Albany, NY: State University of New York.

Taylor, V. (1989). Social movement continuity: The women's movement in abeyance. *American Sociological Review, 54*, 761–775.

Taylor, V. (1998). Feminist methodology in social movement research. *Qualitative Sociology, 21*(4), 357–379.

Taylor, V., & Raeburn, N. (1995). Identity politics as high-risk activism: Career consequences for lesbian, gay and bisexual sociologists. *Social Problems, 42*(2), 252–273.

Taylor, V., & Rupp, L. (1993). Women's culture and lesbian feminist activism: A reconsideration of cultural feminism. In: K. A. Myers, C. Anderson & B. Risman (Eds), *Feminist Foundations: Towards Transforming Sociology* (pp. 328–365). Thousand Oaks, CA: Sage Publications Inc.

Taylor, V., & Whittier, N. (1992). Collective identity in social movement communities: Lesbian feminist mobilization. In: A. D. Morris & C. M. Mueller (Eds), *Frontiers in Social Movement Theory* (pp. 104–129). New Haven, CT: Yale University Press.

Taylor, V., & Whittier, N. (1995). Analytical approaches to social movement culture: The culture of the women's movement. In: H. Johnston & B. Klandermans (Eds), *Social Movements and Culture* (pp. 163–187). Minneapolis, MN: University of Minnesota Press.

Thayer, M. (1997). Identity, revolution, and democracy: Lesbian movements in central America. *Social Problems, 44,* 386–407.

Touraine, A. (1981). *The voice and the eye: An analysis of social movements* (1985 ed.). A. Duff (Trans.). Cambridge, MA: Cambridge University Press.

Tuchman, G. (1994). Historical social science: Methodologies, methods, and meanings. In: N. Denzin & Y. Lincoln (Eds), *Handbook of Qualitative Research* (pp. 306–323). Thousand Oaks, CA: Sage Publications.

Turner, R. H., & Killian, L. M. (1987). *Collective behavior* (3rd ed.). Englewood Cliffs, NJ: Prentice-Hall.

Van Maanen, J. (1988). *Tales of the field: On writing ethnography*. Chicago: University of Chicago Press.

Walsh, E. J. (1981). Resource mobilization and citizen protest in communities around Three Mile Island. *Social Problems, 29,* 1–21.

Wax, R. (1971). *Doing fieldwork: Warnings and advice*. Chicago: University of Chicago Press.

Webb, E., Campbell, D., Schwartz, R., Sechrest, L., & Grove, J. B. (1981). *Non-reactive measures in the social sciences* (2nd ed.). Boston, MA: Houghton Mifflin Co.

Wharton, C. (1987). Establishing shelters for battered women: Local manifestations of a social movement. *Qualitative Sociology, 10*(2), 146–163.

Whittier, N. (2002). Meaning and structure in social movements. In: D. Meyer, N. Whittier & B. Robnett (Eds), *Social Movements: Identity, Culture, and the State* (pp. 289–307). NY: Oxford University Press.

Williams, G., & Williams, R. (1995). All we want is equality: Rhetorical framing in the fathers' rights movement. In: J. Best (Ed.), *Images of Issues: Typifying Contemporary Social Problems* (pp. 191–212). NY: Aldine de Gruyter.

Williams, R. (1995). Constructing the public good: Social movements and cultural resources. *Social Problems, 42,* 124–144.

Williams, R., & Benford, R. D. (2000). Two faces of collective action frames: A theoretical consideration. *Current Perspectives in Social Theory, 20,* 127–151.

Yang, G. (2000). Achieving emotions in collective action: Emotional processes and movement mobilization in the 1989 Chinese student movement. *The Sociological Quarterly, 41*(4), 593–614.

Yin, R. (1984). *Case study research: Design and methods*. Beverly Hills, CA: Sage Publications.

Zhao, D. (1998). Ecologies of social movements: Student mobilization during the 1989 prodemocracy movement in Beijing. *American Journal of Sociology, 103*(6), 1493–1529.

Zurcher, L. A., & Kirkpatrick, R. G. (1976). *Citizens for decency*. Austin, TX: University of Texas Press.

PART IV:
HISTORICAL COMPARATIVE
ANALYSIS OF THE STATE

THEORY, HISTORY AND COMPARATIVE POLITICAL SOCIOLOGY: ASSESSING RECENT ANALYSES OF THE MAKING, UNMAKING AND REMAKING OF STATES

Steven Pfaff and Edgar Kiser

ABSTRACT

Comparative-historical political sociology stands at a crossroads. One direction leads toward history, with a stress on the uniqueness and complexity of particular times, places and events, contingency and chance in determining outcomes, and the dismissal of general theory and systematic testing of propositions. The other direction leads toward social science, with an emphasis on general causal models, theoretical progress through the resolution of anomalies, and transportable propositions with abstractly defined scope conditions. Many contemporary historical sociologists chose to reject general theory in favor of more descriptive analyses of particular times and places, contributing much more to substantive knowledge than to theory. We argue that this is now beginning to change. In spite of sharp theoretical polemics from historicist and positivist camps, comparative-historical

Political Sociology for the 21st Century
Research in Political Sociology, Volume 12, 285–310
ISSN: 0895-9935/PII: S0895993503120116

research in political sociology is moving toward an increasingly productive middle ground. Much new historical work in political sociology is becoming less inductive and descriptive and more theoretical by paying attention to causal mechanisms, the theoretical resolution of anomalies, and the transportability of theoretical arguments across spatially and temporally defined contexts. Evaluating contemporary research on the making, unmaking and remaking of states, we contend that this new historical work is providing political sociology with enhanced substantive/empirical knowledge and new methods, and advancing theory.

INTRODUCTION

The discipline of sociology is marked by a strong presentist bias. Most issues of our major journals contain more articles about contemporary societies than about all other historical societies combined. In addition to favoring the present, most sociological research in the United States examines only the United States. Despite the analytic advantages of historical comparison, comparative-historical research still remains something of a specialty. From a scientific point of view, such a huge sampling bias will distort the questions we ask, the theories we develop, and attempts to test our theories. One of the most basic contributions of historical and comparative sociology is to increase the number of "cases" sociologists can use to test their theories. The population of states is much larger than the sum total of current states. Perhaps more importantly, contemporary states are a biased sample of the population of states, and the United States (or even OECD countries) is not representative of even contemporary states. Adding historical and comparative cases therefore not only allows us to increase our sample size, it also forces us to rethink (and often to revise) our typologies, and raises important questions about the scope of our theories. More generally, historical sociology can provide three main types of things to political sociology: substantive/empirical knowledge (additional data, also useful for putting the present in historical context), new methods, and theory. Of course, we know we are to some extent preaching to the converted – like the social sciences as a whole, political sociology has become more historical and more comparative over the past couple of decades.[1] However, as political sociology has become more historical it has had to face a number of methodological problems. The perils of research designs based upon intensive case studies and comparisons using small samples are well recognized in historical social sciences (see Goldthorpe, 2000; King, Keohane & Verba, 1994; Kiser & Hechter, 1991, 1998; Lieberson, 1991; Lijphart, 1975). Not only does the analyst risk being left with too few cases and too many independent variables to permit analysis,[2] but case studies risk being overly inductive and historical, losing sight of broader theoretical concerns. Because some contemporary historical sociologists have chosen to reject general theory[3] in favor of more descriptive analyses of particular times and places, it has contributed much more to substantive and methodological knowledge than to theory (for a critique of this practice, see Kiser & Hechter, 1991).

Comparative-historical political sociology is at a crossroads. One direction leads toward history, with a stress on the uniqueness and complexity of particular times, places and events, the dominance of contingency and chance in determining outcomes, and the dismissal of general theory and systematic testing of propositions (McDonald, 1996; Somers, 1998). The other direction leads toward social science, with an emphasis on general causal mechanisms, theoretical progress through the resolution of anomalies, and the development of an interconnected body of transportable arguments with abstractly defined scope conditions (Goldthorpe, 2000; King, Keohane & Verba, 1994; Kiser & Hechter, 1991, 1998). Although the issues at stake are important and far from resolved, we do not intend to revisit that debate here. Instead, we will demonstrate that in spite of the sharp theoretical polemics from both camps, comparative-historical research in political sociology is moving toward and beginning to define an increasingly productive middle ground. More specifically, much new historical work in political sociology is becoming less inductive and descriptive and more theoretical – it is paying more attention to causal mechanisms (especially at the micro level), the theoretical resolution of anomalies, and the transportability of theoretical arguments across spatially and temporally defined contexts (by defining scope conditions abstractly).

In large measure, the challenge for historical political sociology has become analyzing historical cases in order to identify general causal mechanisms that are independent of particular events (Abel, 2000; Hedström & Swedberg, 1998; Kiser & Hechter, 1998; Tilly, 2000). As Charles Tilly notes in his survey of five centuries of European revolution, "History's regularities appear not in repeated sequences, replicated structures and recurrent trends on a large scale but in causal mechanisms that link contingent sets of circumstances" (1993, p. 18). Properly understood, causal mechanisms in sociological theory are general and abstract, that is, independent of context. They are the specific processes that operate behind apparent correlations, providing the traction between hypothesized causes and effects (Mahoney, 2001). They are not general theories per se, but elements of general theorizing about social processes that are intermediate to structure and action. Some examples of social mechanisms that have been influential in theorizing state-society relations include threshold and signaling models of collective action (Granovetter, 1978; Lohmann, 1994; Macy, 1991;

Oliver & Marwell, 1993), network diffusion of revolution and radical ideologies (Braun, 1995; Kim & Bearman, 1997), exit-voice dynamics (Dowding et al., 2000; Hirschman, 1993) and competitive selection in religious economies (Stark & Iannaccone, 1994). One misleading suggestion in discussing social mechanisms in historical research is to employ them as an alternative to research agendas driven by general causal models. This line of reasoning in the study of contentious politics tends to treat mechanisms as historically specific, contingent combinations of factors that translate structure into action. Yet bargaining, political mobilization, bureaucratic reorganization, administrative standard-ization, etc. are not so much mechanisms of contention as they are processes operating above general causal mechanisms (Giugni, McAdam & Tilly, 1999; Tilly, 2000).

Properly understood, causal mechanisms are general and abstract, that is, independent of context. This need not render specific case studies unimportant. Case studies in comparative and historical sociology can become opportunities to explore, revise and amend our theories about causal processes. The detail they provide is often essential to identifying causal mechanisms. Moreover, well chosen case studies can test the scope conditions of different mechanisms. For example, studies of places like Ming China, the Ottoman Empire, and Tokugawa, Japan can help us find out whether instrumental rationality is only dominant in advanced western societies. The transportability of insights from historical sociology is necessary to avoid its marginalization. Most sociologists do not find the politics of Capetian France or Song China intrinsically interesting – they care about that work only if it produces insights applicable to other times and places. To put it more positively, the use of transportable causal mechanisms facilitates *cumulative* knowledge by uniting work about different times and places. Perhaps most important, it shows the relevance of studies of the past for understanding the present and future.

One of the most important contributions of historical case studies in the social sciences may be to isolate meaningful anomalies.[4] When informed by general theory, historical and comparative scholarship "reveals anomalies that lead to new questions, and creates conditions under which existing theories can be supplanted by superior ones" (Kiser & Hechter, 1998, p. 785). Extraordinary cases are not only objects of specific description or interpretation, but are analyzed to reveal unusual causal patterns or anomalous outcomes that might be explained by auxiliary propositions consistent with the core postulates of general theory (Bradshaw & Wallace, 1991; Emigh, 1997; Froese & Pfaff, 2001; Kohn, 1987; Lakatos, 1978). Thus, the aim of intensive case-based methods is not so much theoretical generalization, but rather more effective analysis of general processes.

We are not arguing that the increased focus of mechanisms, anomalies, and transportability are the main or even quantitatively the most important trends in contemporary historical political sociology – a compelling test of that claim would require an exhaustive analysis of historical political sociology across its many sub-areas over the past few decades – in other words, a book, not a short paper. Rather, we simply want to demonstrate that the outlines of one possible future direction for political sociology are now becoming visible. Our focus is thus narrow and selective, concentrating on one area in which theory-driven work has been prominent – historical and comparative work that addresses the institution of the state – its making, unmaking, and remaking. Throughout this discussion we will show how a focus on general mechanisms, the identification of meaningful anomalies, and a concern for the spatial and temporal transportability of theory have advanced analysis of the state.

MAKING STATES: STATE FORMATION

One of the most important contributions that historical work can make to political sociology is describing and explaining the processes by which our contemporary political institutions came to be as they are. Knowing their history will greatly enhance our understanding of their current structure and likely developmental trajectory. We thus begin with a short discussion of the literature on initial state formation. We focus on the development of the modern state in the early modern era, but we begin with a few comments about the initial formation of states.

There are ongoing debates about the initial formation of states.[5] Militarist theories suggest that the state originated in warfare (Oppenheimer, 1975). States are forced on the losers by the winners of wars, and used primarily to repress the vanquished. As Nisbet (1976, p. 101) puts it, "the state is indeed hardly more than the institutionalizaton of the war-making apparatus." Engels (1942) also sees the state as oriented toward repression, but for a very different reason. Increasing stratification (instead of war) produces economic winners (a ruling class) and losers, and the winners use the state as an instrument to protect their economic position and property.[6] Evolutionary and ecological theories share Marxist theory's materialism but use it in a very different way. The evolutionary approach contends that material conflict accounts for the origins of the state, but this development precedes the emergence of a formal class structure. In a given environment, if demographic pressures increase the size of societies at the same time that mobility is constrained, this will heighten inter-group competition and create incentives to make war. Chiefdoms and elementary state structures arise to organize collective violence and distribute booty, conquered territories, and slaves (Keeley, 1996; Lenski, 1966). If the evolutionary account is right, then war is not the consequence of class-divided society, but rather war-making creates the conditions for social classes to emerge in primitive societies. Michael Mann (1986, pp. 34–129) has developed a new argument about initial state formation that combines ecological and economic factors. He argues that states form when groups are very dependent on particular areas, such as rich river valleys, because of the high costs of exit. This "caging" allows states to form and extract resources from subjects.

The formation of the early-modern state is basically a story about the centralization of state functions and institutions, as states take over military, judicial, and revenue collection duties. As with initial state formation, there are several different theoretical arguments. Perry Anderson's (1974) innovative argument about the formation of early modern (absolutist) states illustrates the Marxist tendency to explain politics in terms of economics. For Anderson, absolute monarchies were feudal states, and must be understood in the context of the crisis of the feudal mode of production. As a result of the 14th century plague, the land to labor ratio increased substantially. This gave serfs much more power relative to nobles. The nobles found it more costly to extract labor and rents from peasants, and their incomes dropped. Anderson suggests that the state arose to prop up the feudal mode of production and its dominant class. In addition to aiding in the repression of the peasantry, states taxed peasants (but generally not nobles) and used the money to hire nobles to fill high positions in their expanding military and administrative organizations. In effect, the state was acting as a middleman in the exploitation process, taking money (taxes) from non-nobles and giving it (in the form of salaries) to nobles. The absolutist state was an instrument used by the nobility to facilitate neo-feudal exploitation. This argument is problematic in several respects. Most importantly, absolutist states were much more autonomous from dominant classes than Anderson's theory suggests, and many of their policies served interests other than those of the nobility (Skocpol, 1979).

Like theories of initial state formation, many arguments about the formation of early modern states also focus on the role of war. How, and to what extent, does inter-state military competition affect the formation and the structure of early modern states? Poggi (1978) argues that state formation is primarily a product of geopolitical pressures. As the technologies of warfare developed in the medieval era, increased state centralization (thus the ability to extract revenue and field large armies) became a necessary condition for survival. A more recent and more developed version of this argument is made by Tilly (1975, 1990), who argues that "war made states" in the early modern era (see also Mann, 1986). Warfare (along with the repayment of debts from past wars) cost far more than any other state policies in early modern Europe.

Ertman (1997) also argues that war was the main cause of the development and expansion of the state. He develops the argument further by suggesting that the timing of the onset of sustained geopolitical competition determined the form of state administration. States that faced frequent warfare prior to about 1450 tended to construct patrimonial administrations, whereas those that experienced war only after 1450 developed more effective bureaucratic systems. States that were forced by war to develop early had to use older and less effective institutional arrangements, had a limited supply of trained personnel, and had only two cultural models of organization available to them (ecclesiastical and feudal). This explains why they initially used patrimonial administrations characterized by proprietary offices (venal offices and tax farmers), but not why those systems persisted for centuries in spite of the existence of what Ertman claims were more effective alternatives. Here Ertman relies on a very strong version of path dependence – once patrimonial officials became entrenched, they were generally powerful enough to block any reforms, so the choices made by medieval rulers determined the administrative forms of their states for the next five or six centuries.

From this perspective Britain is anomalous, and Ertman addresses and resolves this anomaly. Although it initially developed patrimonial administration due to early warfare, it was fairly bureaucratic by the eighteenth century (at least in the administration of indirect taxes; see Brewer, 1989). Why was Britain able to reform its patrimonial administration when other states could not? Ertman (1997, p. 187) explains this case by arguing that strong legislative institutions like the British parliament after 1688 "allowed reformers operating from within central government to overcome resistance from vested interests." From his perspective, parliament was the only mediating factor that could break the power of proprietary patrimonialism.

The neo-Weberian, state-centered argument that war made states has now clearly supplanted the Marxist argument focusing on economic structure and class power. This perspective has advanced primarily because of its ability to identify general, transportable causal mechanisms and to resolve anomalies. Centeno (1997) shows that war did not impact state making in Latin America the way it did in early modern Europe – a compelling direct test of the transportability of the argument. Kiser and Linton (2001) show that offensive wars had a greater impact on the growth of early modern states than defensive wars in early modern Europe, and that the process was intensified when administrative centralization increased the extractive capacity of states, more precisely defining the causal mechanism linking war and state-making. Finally, Ertman (1997) demonstrates that his model can explain the anomaly of early British administrative reform.

MAKING MODERN STATES: BUREAUCRATIZATION

In spite of the legacy of Weber (and unlike political science, which has a special area of public administration), sociologists do not pay much attention to the implementation of state policy. In part this follows from a presentist bias – since contemporary developed countries generally have few problems with policy implementation, it has not been a major issue in political sociology. Historical work can help fill in this important gap in our understanding of politics. It has done so primarily by elaborating on Weber's ([1922] 1968) arguments about the different types of causal mechanisms (values, instrumental motivations) affecting the relationship between rulers and their administrative staffs.

Gorski (1993) applies Weber's main thesis in *The Protestant Ethic and the Spirit of Capitalism* ([1930] 1998) to the state. He argues that instrumental motivations cannot fully explain the efficiency of state administration in Holland and Prussia. Instead, internalized religious values and religious monitoring mechanisms motivated compliance by tax officials. He contends that one of the main causes of the efficiency of administration in Prussia and Holland was that rulers selected agents on the basis of religious affiliation, and that these agents had religious values that inhibited corruption – the same general mechanism used by Weber to explain the development of capitalism.

Gorski (1993) also suggests an additional causal mechanism linking religious affiliation with low corruption, third party monitoring and sanctioning by churches. If corruption is contrary to religious as well as state rules, and churches enforce those rules, they are indirectly acting as a control mechanism for the state. This part of Gorski's argument provides additional evidence for a general causal argument developed in political science on third party monitoring (Kiewiet & McCubbins, 1991; Weingast & Moran, 1983).

Other historical work on state administration has challenged some of Weber's substantive conclusions. For example, Kiser and Tong (1992) explore the causes of corruption in late imperial China, in part to discover whether instrumental motivations were dominant in this pre-modern, nonwestern setting. They demonstrate that officials in pre-modern Asia reacted to variations in monitoring and sanctioning (the certainty and severity of punishments for corruption) just as their western counterparts did. Moreover, in contrast to cultural socialization arguments, they show that the Confucian education and examination system did not reduce corruption by giving officials pro-state values, but in fact increased it by creating strong long-term network ties that facilitated collusion among officials.

Kiser and Schneider (1994) address Weber's claim that the efficiency of Prussian tax administration was due to its early bureaucratization. Using historical data not available in Weber's time, they show that the Prussian state was much less bureaucratic than Weber thought. Moreover, they demonstrate that particular variations from the bureaucratic ideal type that increased the dependence of officials or strengthened their incentives were the primary causes of efficiency in this case. For example, Prussian rulers used a unique system of caring for injured military veterans. Instead of giving them welfare payments, they gave them positions as collectors of indirect taxes (what we would now call a "workfare" program). Since these officials had poor alternative employment opportunities, they were very dependent on rulers, and thus less corrupt. By creating a high level of dependence, this way of selecting officials was more effective than bureaucratic selection on the basis of merit.

One of the most interesting ongoing debates in this literature concerns whether war facilitates or hinders bureaucratization. Weber ([1922] 1968) argues that states involved in military competition with other states (e.g. Western Europe) would be more likely to bureaucratize than those that were more isolated (e.g. China, Japan). He argues that states not facing the threat of war would retain existing administrative arrangements, whereas those competing militarily would be forced to adopt more efficient bureaucratic forms. In contrast to this, Levi (1988) views war as a consistent impediment to bureaucratization. She argues that war raises the discount rates of rulers, causing them to pursue policies that provide immediate gains even if they are costly in the long term. Thus, rulers facing war would be unlikely to pay the high start-up costs of bureaucratization, but would instead do things like selling offices, which would make bureaucracy much more difficult to implement. The resolution of this debate hinges on making the theory more precise by differentiating types of wars, since only some types will facilitate bureaucratization. Most importantly, wars that result in severe losses may facilitate bureaucratic reforms. One of the main barriers to bureaucratization is the entrenched officials in the state administration who have both the incentives and the power to block reform (Ertman, 1997). These officials will not be dislodged by most wars, but their power will be broken by a severe loss at war, especially one that results in foreign occupation (see Kiser & Schneider, 1994 on Prussia after the Napoleonic conquest).

Another interesting historical question concerns the relationship between revolution and bureaucratization. Several scholars posit a strong positive relationship between revolution and bureaucratization (Ertman, 1997; Skocpol, 1979; Tilly, 1990). For example, Skocpol (1979, pp. 161, 204) argues that the three revolutions she studied brought about the transition from protobureaucracy to bureaucracy, since the "new state organizations forged during the revolutions were more centralized and rationalized than those of the Old Regime." The main counter-argument, developed by Alexis de Tocqueville ([1856] 1955), is that the French state bureaucratized prior to the revolution of 1789. Mann (1993, pp. 462–463) also expresses doubts about the strength of the effects of revolution, noting that the French revolution "promised more bureaucracy than it delivered." Goldstone (1991, pp. 437–444) takes an intermediate position, arguing that revolutions will have some effect on administration (especially elite recruitment), but less than revolutionary ideologies of total transformation suggest. Revolution was clearly neither a necessary nor a sufficient condition for bureaucratization, but it did have some important effects. The most important effect seems to be the one stressed by Skocpol (1979) and Goldstone (1991, p. 437) – revolutions can sweep away entrenched officials opposed to reform. Perhaps the most important impact of both revolutions was to end both tax farming and the sale of offices, two of the most significant patrimonial elements in the pre-revolutionary states (Kiser & Kane, 2001).

In addition to identifying clear causal mechanisms and resolving important anomalies (such as the efficiency of the Prussian state), this historical work on bureaucratization can also help us understand contemporary states – these general arguments are transportable. Although most administrative problems have been solved in the developed world, this is not the case in less developed countries. Many less developed countries have attempted to model their administrative systems on the bureaucracies of the developed West, and almost all of them have found that this type of reform significantly increases the costs of administration without decreasing either tax evasion or official corruption (Gillis, 1989; Shaw, 1981, p. 149). It is easy to see why this would be the case – the technologies of control (transportation, communications, record-keeping) in most contemporary less developed countries are more like those in early modern states than those in contemporary developed states. These countries might be right to imitate Europe, but they would do better imitating the administrative systems of early modern rather than modern Europe (Kiser & Baker, 1994). Since the general arguments are transportable and some of the conditions are similar, historical work on these forms of administration might be directly relevant to contemporary state-making efforts. As it is, much of their inefficiency is due to over-bureaucratization. One of the most interesting questions this raises is why do they over-bureaucratize? Arguments from Meyer et al. (1997) and Dimaggio and Powell (1983) about imitation and institutional isomorphism may provide the best answer.

UNMAKING STATES: REVOLUTION AND REVOLT

Historical and comparative research on the state shows that revolution may be an important factor in state formation, yet the chief relevance of revolutions remains the *unmaking* of states. As much as they are of extraordinary interest for students of politics, the study of revolutions poses considerable obstacles. The scarcity of full-fledged social and political revolutions makes systematic analysis difficult and means scholars typically select on the outcome of revolution, or at least revolt and civil unrest. Many classical studies of revolution provided not so much analysis of causes as they provided descriptive typologies (see e.g. Brinton, 1965; Moore, 1966). Marxist theories of revolution had the advantage of general theory, but in spite of Marx's own sophisticated analysis of revolutionary struggles, often suffered from a teleological bias and from a general failure of predictive accuracy. Indeed, the recurrent failure of any theoretical school to predict major revolutionary upheavals has haunted the historical and comparative study of revolution and provides a real impetus to improve our theoretical arsenal (Collins, 1993; Goldstone, 1994; Kuran, 1995; Tilly, 1995).

The most influential contemporary approach in historical and comparative analysis of revolutions is the "state-centered" theory of revolution (Collins, 1993; Goldstone, 1991, 2000; Goodwin, 2001; Skocpol, 1979). Theda Skocpol's neo-Weberian approach built upon sophisticated class-based analysis of revolution like those of Barrington Moore, Jr. (1966) and Jeffery Paige (1975) to analyze how state-society relations and interstate competition generated revolutionary upheavals.

Rather than focus one-sidedly on class conflict, the state-centered approach concentrates on the state for the simple reason that all successful revolutions involve the incapacitation and capitulation of states. Contemporary state-centered accounts concur that unless a state is controlled by a very weak, exclusive regime with a declining capacity for repression, full-fledged social revolutions are highly unlikely no matter how great the magnitude of popular mobilization (Goldstone, Moishe & Gurr, 1991; Goodwin, 2001; Wickham-Crowley, 1992). Moreover, revolutions only occur because (and if) states matter; that is, when states have unavoidable consequences for the lives of citizens and subjects but obstruct peaceful change, thus worth the risk of challenging them. Popular movements only target states for revolutionary upheavals when it appears, as Trotsky observed, as if there is "no other way out" (Goodwin, 2001).

Goldstone (2001) has done the most to specify a general state-centered model of revolution, regarding revolutions as rare, large-scale events caused by a *conjuncture* of independent causal factors involving the seizure or reconstitution of state power. Goldstone and his colleagues have specified endogenous and exogenous factors that may trigger revolutionary situations of this kind. These may be demographic, as when a swelling population places demands on states they are unable to satisfy, or arise through geopolitical strain and inter-state conflicts that undermine regime performance and legitimacy. He contends that revolutions only occur when a state simultaneously experiences the inability to meet its fiscal needs and obligations;

increasing intra-elite conflicts brought on by insecurity of tenure, competition for elite positions, the spread of heterodox ideologies; and finally where it has a high potential for popular mobilization, especially an aggrieved population with local resources of collective action. Under these conditions states may be unable to prevent the spread of radicalism that challenge the social order. As the state's authority begins to break down, overt conflict (including popular uprisings, military revolts and mutinies) and intra-elite power struggles become more common setting the stage for revolution. Although a change of regime is a likely consequence of state breakdown, it can only be regarded as a revolution if there are substantial changes in political and social organization and the ideology legitimating political institutions.

Skocpol and other state-centered theorists first developed the model to explain "classical" revolutions in modernizing agrarian states in which demographic pressures and economic stagnation helped to initiate state crisis. Yet the full-fledged, highly transformative revolutions of 1789, 1917 and 1949 – as the resonance of these dates suggests – are rare occurrences. State-centered theories have begun to address the problem by looking at a wider array of revolutionary movements across historical contexts. Scholarship on revolution in the "Third World" and in Eastern Europe has confirmed the importance of state crisis, economic instability and the international political climate in making revolutionary upheavals possible (Banac, 1992; Boswell, 1989; Eckstein, 1989; Goodwin, 2001). In these cases old regimes were exclusive and repressive, dependent on the support of foreign governments, and widely opposed by broad categories of citizens sharing common grievances (Ekiert, 1996; Goodwin, 2001; Goldstone, Gurr & Moshiri, 1991). So the constellation of causal factors in a wide range of cases – regimes facing internal and external challenges, elites internally divided and a profound shift in popular loyalty away from the government – is essentially the same. The same basic general argument concerning agrarian revolutions that "regimes fell because they used their nation's resources poorly" (Goldstone, 1991, p. 486) extends to Third World revolutions and the collapse of socialism – these insights are transportable. Indeed, state-centered theory is moving beyond revolutions to understand rebellious collective action more generally, as in pioneering work on prison riots as microrevolutions (Goldstone & Useem, 1999). This movement away from historically specific objects of analysis to general classes of events holds considerable promise to uncover mechanisms of political contention.

One limit of the state-centered approach is that if every revolutionary political transformation undergoes something that can be described as state crisis or breakdown, then the analytical contribution of a state-centered theory is blunted. State crisis may end up being part of both the independent and dependent variables. In his historical survey of five centuries of European history, Tilly

(1993) applies models from the study of social movements. Tilly's approach opens up broader comparative possibilities. He argues that the same factors that account for more conventional forms of contention also explain revolutionary movements. These are mobilization by contending forces and shifting political opportunity structures that signal vulnerability of the state, provide openings to challengers and enrich their resources. Revolutionaries, like all political entrepreneurs seeking public support, require organizations and other social resources to coordinate a movement and communicate with potential supporters.

This approach permits Tilly to more clearly differentiate between rebellion and revolution. For Tilly, revolutionary *situations* occur when contenders advance a competing claim to control of a state, when these contenders have significant sources of popular support, and when the state proves incapable or unwilling to suppress the challenge. But revolutionary *outcomes* are produced only if state elites fail, that is, if polity members defect to the side of the contenders, when they face persistent armed challenges, and when the armed forces are neutralized by defection or demoralization. Tilly argues that revolutionary situations are most likely to appear where there is a discrepancy between state demands and what organized groups of citizens are willing to provide, when state demands threaten collective identities and customary rights attached to them, and when state power is "visibly diminished" (1993, p. 237). In short, revolutionary movements only take shape when the interests of solidaristic and resourceful actors are threatened by the state. A similar argument is evident in Michael Hechter's (2000) research on nationalist revolt which demonstrates how centralizing state administration can spur defensive counter-mobilization by local elites. When centralizing states shift their strategies from indirect to direct rule, the potential for conflict is heightened and national identities likely activated. Civil war, revolution and secession may be the result.

Few would suggest that macro-structural variables should be omitted in explanations of revolution but as we move toward a "fourth generation" (Goldstone, 2001) of theories of revolution, greater efforts are being made to provide more detailed analysis of the micro-level foundations of macro-level events. Recent studies of revolts and revolutions have focused on micro-mobilization processes that account for recruitment and participation. Rational choice approaches have explored the micro-dynamics of mobilization and the rationality of participation (Goldstone & Opp, 1994; Oberschall, 1994; Opp, Voss & Gern, 1995). Studies of ideational diffusion turn to the importance of heterodox ideas in revolutionary mobilization (Kim, 1998; Kim & Bearman, 1997). Other studies explore the network structure of recruitment to high-risk collective action (Gould, 1991, 1995; Opp & Gern, 1993). Finally, evidence of the effect of social identities on mobilization into collective action suggests that leadership by a revolutionary cadre may not be an essential factor if such "soft" incentives as community, reputation, and moral preferences can be activated in mobilization (Calhoun, 1994; Chong, 1991; Pfaff, 1996).

Recent work on revolutions has been especially good at specifying clear, testable causal mechanisms. This began with the work of Goldstone (1991) and Tilly (1993), which was a big improvement in this respect over the earlier work of Moore (1966) and Skocpol (1979). More recently, the focus on micro-level causal mechanisms (Goldstone & Opp, 1994; Oberschall, 1994) has made these theories even more detailed and precise. There has also been important work on non-European and more contemporary revolutions, which has demonstrated that many of the basic causal mechanisms are transportable beyond the European and early modern contexts, and identified some that are not transportable (Goodwin, 2001; Wickham-Crowley, 1992). Finally, the basic analytical framework of the state-centered approach is migrating towards the study of a broader class of rebellions (Goldstone & Useem, 1999).

REMAKING STATES: TRANSITION AND DEMOCRATIZATION

In the wake of recent waves of democratization in the developing world and the collapse of Soviet socialism in Eastern Europe comparative political sociology has been particularly concerned with the *remaking* of formerly authoritarian states. This gave birth to 'transitology,' a general framework for the analysis of political transformation in authoritarian regimes and the consolidation of democratic government (see among others Anderson, 1999; Bunce, 1999; Linz & Stepan, 1996; O'Donnell & Schmitter, 1986; O'Donnell, Schmitter & Whitehead, 1991; Offe, 1997; Przeworski, 1991; Stark & Bruszt, 1998).

The basic comparative transition model identifies stages by which democratic transitions can be understood (Linz & Stepan, 1996; O'Donnell & Schmitter, 1986). Given a set of facilitating conditions such as economic or financial crisis, military defeat and expanding networks of civil society, the first stage in a democratic transition is one of *liberalization*, as counter-elites challenge an existing regime and test the limits of political action and democratic discourse. Counter-elites accelerate declining popular confidence in the state resulting in a mounting crisis of legitimacy. Given the expanding power of counter-elites, liberalization gives way to a *democratization* phase in which the old elites are replaced. In the place of the old rulers, a new constellation typically drawn from progressive elements of the old regime and opposition forces takes power. Finally, there is *consolidation*, in which the new democratic regime and its elites are institutionalized in at least two successive, democratically selected governments.

Juan Linz and Alfred Stepan (1996) concede that transition theory, as the above model suggests, describes cases of gradual, negotiated or "pacted" political transition, rather than revolution (with some justification, of course, as few revolutions lead directly to democracy). The transition model has generally assumed the presence of two necessary factors for peaceful democratic transition. The first is an organized set of collective actors capable of pressing for democracy but moderate enough to compromise with the old elite. The second is the presence of moderate or reformist elements within a regime that have the autonomy and desire to negotiate a transition (Linz & Stepan, 1996, p. 356). Expressed in terms of the contention model, this means that both organization and opportunity are present to make possible negotiation between pragmatic regime elites and moderate opposition groups.

Some studies of transition elude these questions by discounting variation across cases in favor of an analytical focus on geopolitics. In the case of Eastern Europe, the undeniable importance of exogenous factors, particularly Gorbachev and the crisis of the international socialist system, led some to explain the fall of Communist regimes in terms of a general system-level structural collapse (Chirot, 1991; Przeworski, 1991). Przeworski (1991, p. 3) offers a particularly clear repudiation of the utility of historical and comparative political sociology in the analysis of transition: ". . . hundreds of macrohistorical comparative sociologists will write thousands of books and articles correlating background conditions with outcomes in each "Eastern European" country, but . . . they will be wasting their time, for the entire event was one single snowball."

A causal factor identified at such a high level of generality is unlikely to provide a satisfactory explanation of the East European transitions. As Valerie Bunce concludes in her analysis of the institutional decline of socialism, "Although international factors were important, they influenced, rather than caused, what happened" (Bunce, 1999, p. 156). In addition to the persistence of 'really existing' socialist states after 1991, in view of mounting anomalies and historical complications, prominent analysts have increasingly acknowledged varieties of path-dependent transition (Anderson, 1999; Offe, 1997), a multiplicity of "postsocialist pathways" (Stark & Bruszt, 1998) and called for more specified analysis of socialist crisis and transition (Bunce, 1999). Researchers are uncovering multiple transitions in the wake of socialism's decline, including regime collapse in which gradual liberalization and democratization never occur. In these instances, intransigent regimes are brought down by an intense protest wave without negotiation or brokering (Friedheim, 1993; Kitschelt et al., 1999; Linz & Stepan, 1996). There has also been greater attention paid to the sequence of actions that made political breakthroughs, as in research on the role of mid-level officials and loosely organized political contestants in the "velvet" revolutions of Eastern Europe and South Africa (Charney, 1999; Friedheim, 1993; Glenn, 1999).

Transition theory's contribution to political sociology has been largely typological and descriptive, rather than analytic. Although strides have been made in categorizing regime types and pathways to transition, scholars have been reluctant to isolate causal mechanisms (for a more thorough critique, see Tilly, 2000). As a result, the contribution of potentially significant causal processes in transition remains unclear. Popular protest, for example, is sometimes portrayed as a byproduct or symptom of regime crisis, rather than as a potential causal variable. For many theorists of transition, mobilization is treated, inadequately, as a part of the regime's "implosion" or as a secondary factor in bringing actors to the table in negotiating transition pacts. In the transition literature mobilization is generally treated as a causal factor of secondary or even negligible importance. The crucial actors in the democratization process are taken to be elements of the established elite, a rival counter-elite, or a coalition representing both elements (Munck & Skalnick Leff, 1999). These forces include resourceful, well-coordinated groups that make democratic transition possible through negotiation and compromise. Indeed, strategic players with stable political preferences are essential for the underlying game-theoretic logic of transition studies. However, there has been little attention to the difficulties of such players emerging under authoritarian conditions and the problems of collective action that even established sets of actors would surely confront.

As with state-centered studies of revolution, the challenge for students of political transition must be to explain how micro-level processes of mobilization generate identifiable macro-level patterns across cases. One important effort to provide a theory aimed at bridging micro and macro accounts of political change in states is the contention model, based on the political process theory (PPT) of social movements (Gamson, 1990; McAdam, 1982, 1996; McAdam, McCarthy & Zald, 1996; Tarrow, 1991, 1998; Tilly, 1978). As operationalized in the polity model, a broad set of constraints and opportunities usually considered under the rubric of "political opportunity structure" is taken as the key causal mechanism in movement emergence, success and failure. Doug McAdam's (1996) concise definition of political opportunity includes the relative openness or closure of political institutions; the relative stability of elite alignments that support a polity; the presence of elite allies to support challengers; and the state's capacity and propensity to engage in repression. Movement success would seem to depend on both the perception of new opportunities being present and the favorable political environment that enables movement breakthrough and consolidation (McAdam, McCarthy & Zald, 1996, p. 8).

The polity model is the fruit of considerable historical research on the democratization of Western states. It evidences a concern with the historical evolution of political environments and with changing forms of political mobilization and organization (Giugni, McAdam & Tilly, 1998; McAdam, Tarrow & Tilly, 2001; Tarrow, 1998; Tilly, 1986; Tilly, Tilly & Tilly, 1975). Studies demonstrate that as the locus of political power in industrial societies shifted from local settings to national centers, the repertoire of protest and the organization of challengers shifted with it, becoming increasingly pacified along the way. Riotous assemblies, land invasions and the sacking of tax offices – all part of the traditional repertoire of collective action that drew on local sources of solidarity and leadership – were replaced over the course of the 19th century with strikes, protest marches, and petition drives organized by national campaigns as democratic polities took shape (Tilly, 1978; Traugott, 1995).

The clear aspiration of PPT has been to develop a synthetic model of social movements and collective action that would include structural, organizational and cultural explanatory variables (see McAdam, McCarthy & Zald, 1996). PPT is particularly convincing in arguing that analysts cannot afford to ignore the political context in which collective action takes place, yet an over-reliance on political opportunity structure as a dynamic causal mechanism seems to unbalance it. Critics have noted that if opportunities of some kind are understood as a necessary, but not sufficient, causes of protest or as background conditions to mobilizing processes and other movement activity, then their analytical precision is limited (Goodwin & Jasper, 1999).

The political process model of contentious politics was developed primarily to explain conventional, organized social movements in liberal polities – the kind of states that experience few revolutionary movements of any consequence. Many social movements flow from organized groups using new opportunities to seek greater political power. But some are loosely organized reactions to moral indignation, collective animosities, and social insecurity (Horowitz, 2001; Pfaff, 1996; Useem, 1998). And research on collective action has revealed how threshold effects, signaling processes and social diffusion may explain rapid shifts in collective action without political opportunity, organization and ideological framing (Braun, 1994; Kim & Bearman, 1998; Lohmann, 1994; Opp, 1994; Opp, Voss & Gern, 1995). All this suggests that, in its aspiration to apply to a range of phenomena from petitions to strikes to revolutions, the contention model may be at once overly ambitious and not ambitious enough. Petition-drives and revolutionary movements do not differ simply in the scale of their aims, they are forms of collective action conditioned by very different institutional settings. In including such a broad range of causal variables, including everything from state crisis, to external allies, to indigenous social resources, to injustice frames, the contention model becomes a blunt instrument.

The adoption of the concept of social mechanisms in the theory of contentious politics has not yet gone far enough as many of the mechanisms identified in the literature – mobilization, repression, bargaining cycles, coalition formation, extraction and resistance, administrative centralization – are either too broad to be general mechanisms or likely involve multiple, unspecified micro-mechanisms (McAdam, Tarrow & Tilly, 2001; Tilly, 2000). The political process model, however, may have much to say about how movements respond to new opportunities in the process of democratization. Yet, because the political process theory of contentious politics is based on the comparative history of Western European state formation, it does not travel with ease to other institutional contexts where the shape of polities may be very different. And, even in Western democracies, in spite of the clear historical contribution of the approach to understanding the process by which contentious practices were transformed, gaps remain in linking mobilization in social movements to policy change at the state level (Burstein, 1999). In short, outside of specific historical cases studies, it still remains unclear why, when, and how social movements matter to democratization (Giugni, McAdam & Tilly, 1999). While it certainly improves upon the study of transition in comparative politics in analyzing the process of contention, PPT fails to develop a convincing general theory of democratic mobilization. Perhaps because it reflects recent efforts at synthesizing diverse strands in research on collective action and social movements, its primary contribution to date has been more descriptive and substantive than theoretical.

CONCLUSION

Many factors will no doubt determine whether the more inductive/historicist or the more theoretical/scientific form of historical sociology will become dominant in political sociology (we do not expect either to disappear completely), but we hope that their relative success in providing useful explanations of the empirical world will be the deciding factor. This paper has documented the recent increase in work that follows the more social scientific path in one broad area in political sociology – the making, unmaking, and remaking of states. We have not attempted a systematic comparison with work in this area that follows the historicist path (in part because many critical analyses of that work have already been done (see Burawoy, 1991; Kiser & Hechter, 1991; Lieberson, 1991), and in part because we wanted to stress positive developments), nor have we looked at any of the many other areas in political sociology (an analysis work on political culture, for example, would no doubt show a much different distribution). This paper is clearly just a first small step toward moving the debate from abstract theoretical and methodological issues to analyzing the substantive products of these competing positions.

In examining such diverse fields as state emergence, bureaucratization, revolution and democratic transition, we see clear evidence of an emerging middle ground between general theory and specific historical investigation. Much of the strongest work employs comparative and historical inquiry in an effort to identify and analyze causal mechanisms, to make productive use of seemingly anomalous cases, and to develop transportable mechanisms and propositions. This remains, however, a reorientation of research that remains at a fairly infant stage. We anticipate that these new ways around the impasse of exaggerated historicist and positivist positions promise much in their maturity.

One of the most promising signs of the emergence of a more theoretical comparative-historical political sociology is the development and refinement of more formal methods of historical analysis. Many historical sociologists are attempting to reconstruct narrative methods for historical sociology (Abbott, 1992; Aminzade, 1992; Griffin, 1992; Kiser, 1996). Unlike historicists, most sociological narrativists are willing to generalize, and their formal methods have been oriented toward discovering general features of events. Abbott (1992, pp. 428–429) wants to find "typical sequences," and Griffin (1993, p. 1096) tries to understand lynching as "both a historically singular event and as an instance of a class of historically repeated events." Stovel (2001) moves beyond the sequential analysis of a single lynching event to evaluate sequential patterns across cases. Bates et al. (1998) argue that game theory can be used to make the plot structures and actor's choices more explicit. Although this program is still in its infancy, the five case studies they provide show great promise for uniting narrative and general theory using rational choice models (see also Kiser, 1996). Research on state formation and democratic transition seem particularly well placed to profit from new approaches to analytical narratives.

Another way to formalize narrative analysis is by using "process-tracing" and the comparison of historical sequences, the aim of which is the deductive unraveling of complex causal narratives (Goldstone, 1997; King, Keohane & Verba, 1994; Rueschemeyer & Stephens, 1997). This entails the "decomposition of complex narrative into stages, episodes, or events which can be connected by causal sequences that are simpler and easier to explain than the narrative as a whole" (Goldstone, 1997, p. 112). Process tracing is thus a combination of narrative investigation and deductive reasoning based on explicit general theoretical foundations. Clearly, process tracing is well-suited to the analysis of macro level events such as revolutions and the collapse of states in which contingency, multi-causal conjunctures and temporality frustrate cross-sectional analysis.

Many historical sociologists, political scientists, and economists have also begun to stress the path-dependent nature of social and political processes (Aminzade, 1992; Arthur, 1994; David, 1985; Mahoney, 2000; Pierson, 2000). One of the main problems with the concept of path dependence has been its vagueness – it has often been used to refer to any process in which temporality and sequence are important. Recently, that has begun to change. Drawing on the more precise definition of path dependence in economics (Arthur, 1994; David, 1985), historically oriented political scientists (Pierson, 2000) and sociologists (Mahoney, 2000) have both clarified the concept and applied it to the study of politics. The remaining debate mainly concerns whether path dependence is produced by only one causal mechanism, increasing returns (Pierson, 2000) or by power and legitimation mechanisms, as well (Mahoney, 2000). We have seen how the concept of path dependence has been particularly influential in comparative research on the transformation and consolidation of post-Communist societies (Kitschelt et al., 1999; Offe, 1997; Stark & Bruszt, 1998).

Models of narratives, process tracing, and formalizing the notion of path dependence are just three ways to formalize historical analysis. Since these are all fairly new, their track records are too short to support a systematic evaluation of their substantive payoffs at this point, but all are potentially very promising. This short summary of recent methodological developments suggests that, if adopted widely, they could push historical political sociology further down the path of a more productive dialogue between history and social science.

NOTES

1. Political sociology is especially well placed to profit from history, since political elites leave behind more historical traces than other groups. Not only does political sociology benefit from what the elite has left behind, but because rulers must monitor subordinates and have an interest in accurate information upon which to reach decisions the state records a diversity of data through such activities as taxation, conscription and war making, census-taking and policing that can reveal much about ordinary citizens and subjects.

2. One way to address data limitations is through the construction of larger, comparative data sets to test and potentially falsify theories (Goldthorpe, 2000). Another strategy is to use historical records to construct systematic data sets that permit standard statistical evaluation (see e.g. Gould, 1995; Stovel, 2001; Tolnay & Beck, 1995). Where data limitations or the infrequency of occurrences (such as revolutions) obstruct standard statistical approaches, these problems can be confronted through careful case selection and comparisons that help to isolate hypothesized causal relationships. In some instances, historical sociologists have made inventive use of very limited data by assembling plausible evidence for broader inference (see e.g. Stark, 1996).

3. By general theory, we mean an interrelated set of explicit assumptions, abstract models, causal mechanisms, and testable propositions with abstract scope conditions (Kiser & Hechter, 1991, 1998).

4. Historical and comparative analysis also allows researchers to posit plausible counterfactuals to offset the small sample problem. Counterfactuals allow the researcher the opportunity to determine which causal factors or what circumstances in a series of events played a crucial role in determining the actual outcome. Counter-factual analysis is one way to contend with the limits imposed by rare large-scale events in which we hypothetically modify the course of events by altering one or more conditions or variables (King, Keohane & Verba, 1994). Theoretical-historical reflection of this kind allows us to disentangle the complex, multi-causal conjuncture behind the familiar description of events. It also provides us with prospective insights for what might occur in similar settings given a comparable series of events.

5. These debates have been very difficult to resolve due to the scarcity of systematic data. In the case of archaic societies, significant archaeological evidence has been uncovered to support the conflict hypothesis.

6. Another view also sees the state in primarily economic terms, but more benignly. This theory argues that the main function of early states was redistribution – chiefs would facilitate the process of storage and distribution of food (Malinowski, 1926). This theory turns Engels on his head – states take from the rich in order to give to the poor (or, inter-temporally, they take in good times and redistribute in bad).

ACKNOWLEDGMENTS

The authors would like to thank the editors of *Research in Political Sociology* and two anonymous reviewers for their comments on the manuscript.

REFERENCES

Abel, P. (2000). Putting social theory right? *Sociological Theory, 18*(3), 518–523.

Abbott, A. (1992). From causes to events: Notes on narrative positivism. *Sociological Methods and Research, 20*(4), 428–455.

Aminzade, R. (1992). Historical sociology and time. *Sociological Methods and Research, 20*(4), 456–480.

Anderson, L. (1999). *Transitions to democracy*. New York: Columbia University Press.

Anderson, P. (1974). *Lineages of the absolutist state*. London: New Left Books.

Arthur, B. (1994). *Increasing returns and path dependence in the economy*. Ann Arbor: University of Michigan.

Banac, I. (1992). *Eastern Europe in revolution*. Ithaca: Cornell University Press.

Bates, R., Greif, A., Levi, M., Rosenthal, J.-L., & Weingast, B. (1998). *Analytic narratives*. Princeton: Princeton University.

Boswell, T. (1989). *Revolution in the world-system*. New York: Greenwood Press.

Bradshaw, Y., & Wallace, M. (1991). Informing generality and explaining uniqueness: The place of case studies in comparative research. *International Journal of Comparative Sociology, 32*(1–2), 154–171.

Braun, N. (1994). Das schwellenmodell und die leipziger montagsdemonstrationen. *Kölner Zeitschrift für Soziologie und Sozialpsychologie, 46*(3), 482–500.

Braun, N. (1995). Individual thresholds and social diffusion. *Rationality and Society, 7*(2), 167–182.

Brinton, C. (1965). *The anatomy of revolution* (2nd rev. ed.). New York: Vintage.

Bunce, V. (1999). *Subversive institutions: The design and the destruction of socialism and the state.* Cambridge, UK: Cambridge University Press.

Brewer, J. (1989). *The sinews of power.* London: Unwin Hyman.

Burawoy, M. (Ed.) (1991). *Ethnography unbound.* Berkeley, CA: University of California Press.

Burstein, P. (1999). Social movements and public policy. In: M. Giugni, D. McAdam & C. Tilly (Eds), *How Social Movements Matter.* Minneapolis: University of Minnesota Press.

Calhoun, C. (1994). *Neither Gods nor Emperors: Students and the struggle for democracy in China.* Berkeley: University of California Press.

Centeno, M. A. (1997). Blood and debt: War and taxation in nineteenth-century Latin America. *American Journal of Sociology, 102*(6), 1565–1605.

Charney, C. (1999). Civil society, political violence and democratic transitions: Business and the peace process in South Africa, 1990 to 1994. *Comparative Studies in Society and History, 41*(1), 182–206.

Chirot, D. (1991). *The crisis of Leninism and the decline of the left: The revolutions of 1989.* Seattle: University of Washington Press.

Chong, D. (1991). *Collective action and the civil rights movement.* Chicago: University of Chicago Press.

Collins, R. (1993). Maturation of the state-centered Theory of revolutions and ideology. *Sociological Theory, 11*(1), 117–128.

David, P. (1985). Clio and the economics of QWERTY. *American Economic Review, 75*(May), 332–337.

Dimaggio, P., & Powell, W. (1983). The iron cage revisited: Institutional isomorphism and collective rationality in organizational fields. *American Sociological Review, 48*(2), 147–160.

Dowding, K., John, P., Mergoupis, T., & Van Vugt, M. (2000). Exit, voice and loyalty: Analytic and empirical developments. *European Journal of Political Research, 37,* 469–495.

Eckstein, S. (1989). *Power and popular protest: Latin American social movements.* Berkeley: University of California.

Ekiert, G. (1996). *The state against society: Political crises and their aftermath in East Central Europe.* Princeton: Princeton University Press.

Emigh, R. (1997). The power of negative thinking: The use of negative case methodology in the development of sociological theory. *Theory and Society, 26*(5), 649–684.

Engels, F. (1942). *The origins of the family, private property and the state.* New York: International Publishers.

Ertman, T. (1997). *Birth of the leviathan.* Cambridge: Cambridge University Press.

Friedheim, D. (1993). Bringing society back into democratic transition theory after 1989: Pact making and regime collapse. *East European Politics and Societies, 7*(3), 482–512.

Froese, P., & Pfaff, S. (2001). Replete and desolate markets: Poland, East Germany and the new religious paradigm. *Social Forces, 80*(2), 481–507.

Gamson, W. (1990). *The strategy of social protest.* NY: Wadsworth.

Gillis, M. (1989). *Tax reform in developing countries.* Durham: Duke University Press.

Giugni, M., McAdam, D., & Tilly, C. (1998). *From contention to democracy*. Lanham, MD: Rowan and Littlefield.

Giugni, M., McAdam D., & Tilly, C. (1999). *How social movements matter*. Minneapolis: University of Minnesota Press.

Glenn, J. (1999). Competing challengers and contested outcomes to state breakdown: The velvet revolution in Czechoslovakia. *Social Forces, 78*(1), 187–212.

Goldstone, J. A. (1991). *Revolution and rebellion in the early modern world*. Berkeley: University of California Press.

Goldstone, J. A. (1994). Why we could (and should) have foreseen the revolutions of 1989–1991 in the U.S.S.R. and Eastern Europe. *Contention, 2*(2), 127–152.

Goldstone, J. A. (1997). Methodological issues in comparative macrosociology. *Comparative Social Research, 16*, 107–120.

Goldstone, J. A. (2001). Toward a fourth generation of revolutionary theory. *American Review of Political Science, 4*, 139–187.

Goldstone, J. A., & Opp, K.-D. (1994). Rationality, revolution and 1989 in Eastern Europe. *Rationality and Society, 6*, 5–7.

Goldstone, J. A., & Useem, B. (1999). Prison riots as microrevolutions: An extension of state-centered theories of revolution. *American Journal of Sociology, 104*(4), 985–1029.

Goldstone, J. A., Gurr, T. R., & Moshie, F. (1991). *Revolutions of the late twentieth century*. Boulder: Westview Press.

Goldthorpe, J. H. (2000). *On sociology*. Oxford: Oxford University Press.

Goodwin, J. (2001). *No other way out: States and revolutionary movements 1945–1991*. Cambridge, UK: Cambridge University Press.

Goodwin, J., & Jasper, J. M. (1999). Caught in a winding, snarling vine: The structural bias of political process theory. *Sociological Forum, 14*, 27–54.

Gould, R. (1991). Multiple networks and mobilization in the Paris commune. *American Sociological Review, 56*, 716–729.

Gould, R. (1995). *Insurgent identities: Class, community and protest in Paris from 1848 to the commune*. Chicago: University of Chicago Press.

Gorski, P. (1993). The Protestant ethic revisited: Disciplinary revolution and state formation in Holland and Prussia. *American Journal of Sociology, 99*(2), 265–316.

Granovetter, M. (1978). Threshhold models of collective behavior. *American Journal of Sociology, 83*(6), 1420–1443.

Griffin, L. (1992). Temporality, events, and explanation in historical sociology. *Sociological Methods and Research, 20*(4), 403–427.

Griffin, L. (1993). Narrative, event-structure analysis, and causal interpretation in historical sociology. *American Journal of Sociology, 98*(5), 1094–1133.

Hechter, M. (2000). *Containing nationalism*. London and New York: Oxford.

Hedström, P., & Swedberg, R. (1998). *Social mechanisms*. Cambridge: Cambridge University Press.

Hirschman, A. O. (1993). Exit, voice, and the fate of the German Democratic Republic. *World Politics, 45*(2), 173–202.

Horowitz, D. (2001). *The deadly ethnic riot*. Berkeley and Los Angeles: University of California Press.

Keeley, L. (1996). *War before civilization*. Oxford and New York: Oxford University Press.

Kiewiet, D. R., & McCubbins, M. (1991). *The logic of delegation*. Chicago: University of Chicago.

King, G., Keohane, R. O., & Verba, S. (1994). *Designing social inquiry*. Princeton: Princeton University Press.

Kim, H. (1998). The diffusion of ideas: Modeling ideational diffusion in historical context. Unpublished doctoral dissertation, University of North Carolina, Chapel Hill.

Kim, H., & Bearman, P. (1997). The structure and dynamics of movement participation. *American Sociological Review, 62*(1), 70–93.

Kiser, E. (1996). The revival of narrative in historical sociology: What rational choice theory can contribute. *Politics and Society, 24*(3), 249–271.

Kiser, E., & Hechter, M. (1991). The role of general theory in comparative-historical sociology. *American Journal of Sociology, 97*(1), 1–30.

Kiser, E., & Hechter, M. (1998). The debate on historical sociology: Rational choice theory and its critics. *American Journal of Sociology, 104*, 785–791.

Kiser, E., & Tong, X. (1992). Determinants of the amount and type of corruption in state fiscal bureaucracies: An analysis of late imperial China. *Comparative Political Studies, 25*(3), 300–331.

Kiser, E., & Baker, K. (1994). Could privatization increase the efficiency of tax collection in less developed countries? *Policy Studies Journal, 22*(3), 489–500.

Kiser, E., & Schneider, J. (1994). Bureaucracy and efficiency: An analysis of taxation in early modern Prussia. *American Sociological Review, 59*(2), 187–204.

Kiser, E., & Linton, A. (2001). Determinants of the growth of the state: War, revolt, and taxation in early modern France. *Social Forces, 80*(2), 411–448.

Kiser, E., & Kane, J. (2001). Revolution and state structure: The bureaucratization of tax administration in early modern England and France. *American Journal of Sociology, 107*(1), 183–223.

Kitschelt, H., Mansfeldova, Z., Markowski, R., & Toka, G. (1999). *Post-communist party systems.* NY: Cambridge University Press.

Kohn, M. (1987). Cross-national research as an analytic strategy. *American Sociological Review, 52*(6), 713–731.

Kuran, T. (1995). The inevitability of future revolutionary surprises. *American Journal of Sociology, 100*(6), 1528–1551.

Lakatos, I. (1978). *The methodology of scientific research programmes.* Cambridge and New York: Cambridge University Press.

Lieberson, S. (1991). Small N's and big conclusions: An examination of the reasoning in comparative studies based on a small number of cases. *Social Forces, 70*(2), 307–320.

Lijphart, A. (1975). The comparable cases strategy in comparative research. *Comparative Political Studies, 8*(2), 158–177.

Linz, J., & Stepan, A. (1996). *Problems of democratic transition and consolidation.* Baltimore, MD: Johns Hopkins University Press.

Lohmann, S. (1994). The dynamics of informational cascades: The Monday demonstrations in Leipzig, East Germany, 1989–1991. *World Politics, 47*, 42–101.

Lenski, G. (1966). *Power and privilege.* Chapel Hill: University of North Carolina.

Levi, M. (1988). *Of rule and revenue.* Berkeley: University of California.

Macy, M. (1991). Chains of cooperation: Threshold effects in collective action. *American Sociological Review, 56*, 730–747.

Mahoney, J. (2000). Path dependence in historical sociology. *Theory and Society, 29*(4), 507–548.

Mahoney, J. (2001). Beyond correlational analysis. *Sociological Forum, 16*(3), 575–593.

Malinowski, B. (1926). *Crime and custom in savage society.* London: Kegan Paul.

Mann, M. (1986). *Sources of social power* (Vol. 1). Cambridge: Cambridge University Press.

Mann, M. (1993). *Sources of social power* (Vol. 2). Cambridge: Cambridge University Press.

McDonald, T. (Ed.) (1996). *The historic turn in the human sciences.* Ann Arbor, MI: University of Michigan Press.

Meyer, J., Boli, J., Thomas, G., & Ramirez, F. (1997). World society and the nation state. *American Journal of Sociology, 103*(1), 144–181.

McAdam, D. (1982). *Political process and the development of black insurgency, 1930–1970*. Chicago: Chicago University Press.

McAdam, D. (1996). Conceptual origins, current problems, future directions. In: D. McAdam, J. McCarthy & M. Zald (Eds), *Comparative Perspectives on Social Movements*. New York: Cambridge University Press.

McAdam, D., Tarrow, S., & Tilly, C. (2001). *Dynamics of contention*. New York: Cambridge University Press.

McAdam, D., McCarthy, J., & Zald, M. (1996). *Comparative perspectives on social movements*. New York: Cambridge University Press.

Moore, B. (1966). *Social origins of dictatorship and democracy*. Boston: Beacon.

Munck, G., & Skalnick Leff, C. (1999). Modes of transition and democratization. In: L. Anderson (Ed.), *Transitions to Democracy*. New York: Columbia University Press.

Nisbet, R. (1976). *The social philosophers*. St. Albans: Granada.

Oppenheimer, R. (1975). *The state*. New York: Free Life Editions.

Oberschall, A. (1994). Rational choice in collective protests. *Rationality and society, 6*, 79–100.

O'Donnell, G., & Schmitter, P. (1986). *Transitions from authoritarian rule: Tentative conclusions about uncertain democracies*. Baltimore, MD: Johns Hopkins University Press.

O'Donnell, G., Schmitter, P., & Whitehead, L. (1991). *Transitions from authoritarian rule*. Baltimore: Johns Hopkins University Press.

Offe, C. (1997). *Varieties of transition: The East European and the East German experience*. Cambridge: MIT Press.

Oliver, P., & Marwell, G. (1993). *The critical mass in collective action*. New York: Cambridge University Press.

Opp, K.-D. (1994). Repression and revolutionary action: East Germany in 1989. *Rationality and Society, 6*, 101–138.

Opp, K.-D., & Gern, C. (1993). Dissident groups, personal networks and spontaneous cooperation: The East German revolution of 1989. *American Sociological Review, 58*(5), 659–680.

Opp, K.-D., Voss, P., & Gern, C.(1995). *Origins of a spontaneous revolution*. Ann Arbor, MI: University of Michigan Press.

Paige, J. (1975). *Agrarian revolution*. New York: Free Press.

Pfaff, S. (1996). Collective identity and informal groups in revolutionary mobilization: East Germany in 1989. *Social Forces, 75*(1), 91–118.

Pierson, P. (2000). Increasing returns, path dependence, and the study of politics. *American Political Science Review, 94*(2), 251–267.

Poggi, G. (1978). *The development of the modern state*. Stanford: Stanford University.

Przeworski, A. (1991). *Democracy and the market: Political and economic reform in Eastern Europe and Latin America*. NY: Cambridge University Press.

Rueschemeyer, D., & Stephens, J. D. (1997). Comparing historical sequences. *Comparative Social Research, 16*, 55–72.

Shaw, G. (1981). Leading issues of tax policy in developing countries: The economic problems. In: A. Peacock & F. Forte (Eds), *The Political Economy of Taxation*. Oxford: Blackwell.

Skocpol, T. (1979). *States and social revolutions*. Cambridge, UK: Cambridge University Press.

Somers, M. (1998). 'We're no angels': Realism, rational choice and rationality in social science. *American Journal of Sociology, 104*(3), 722–784.

Stark, D., & Bruszt, L. (1998). *Postsocialist pathways*. Cambridge and New York: Cambridge University Press.

Stark, R. (1996). *The rise of Christianity*. Princeton: Princeton University Press.

Stark, R., & Iannaccone, L. (1994). A supply-side reinterpretation of the 'secularization' of Europe. *Journal for the Scientific Study of Religion, 33*(3), 230–252.

Stovel, K. (2001). Local sequential patterns: The structure of lynching in the Deep South. *Social Forces, 79*(3), 843–880.

Tarrow, S. (1998). *Power in movement: Social movements and contentious politics* (2nd ed.). Cambridge, UK: Cambridge University Press.

Tilly, C. (1975). *The formation of national states in Western Europe*. Princeton, NJ: Princeton University Press.

Tilly, C. (1978). *From mobilization to revolution*. Wesley, MA: Addison-Wesley.

Tilly, C. (1986). *The contentious French*. Cambridge, MA: Belknap.

Tilly, C. (1990). *Coercion, capital, and European states, AD 990–1990*. Cambridge, MA: Blackwell.

Tilly, C. (1993). *European revolutions 1492–1992*. Oxford: Blackwell.

Tilly, C. (2000). Processes and mechanisms of democratization. *Sociological Theory, 18*(1), 1–16.

Tilly, C., Tilly, L., & Tilly, R. (1975). *The rebellious century, 1830–1930*. Cambridge, MA: Harvard University Press.

Tocqueville, A. ([1856] 1955). *The old regime and the French revolution*. Garden City: Doubleday.

Tolnay, S., & Beck, E. M. (1995). *A festival of violence: An analysis of southern lynchings, 1882–1930*. Urbana: University of Illinois Press.

Traugott, M. (1995). *Repertoires and cycles of collective action*. Durham, NC and London: Duke University.

Useem, B. (1998). Breakdown theories of collective action. *Annual Review of Sociology, 24*, 215–238.

Weingast, B., & Moran, M. (1983). Bureaucratic discretion or congressional control? Regulatory policy making by the Federal Trade Commission. *Journal of Political Economy, 91*, 765–800.

Weber, M. ([1922] 1968). *Economy and society*. Berkeley: University of California Press.

Weber, M. ([1930] 1998). *The protestant ethic and the spirit of capitalism*. T. Parsons (Trans.), R. Collins (Ed.). Los Angeles: Roxbury.

Wickham-Crowley, T. (1992). *Guerrillas and revolution in Latin America*. Princeton: Princeton University Press.

HISTORICAL CONTINGENCY THEORY, POLICY PARADIGM SHIFTS, AND CORPORATE MALFEASANCE AT THE TURN OF THE 21st CENTURY

Harland Prechel

ABSTRACT

This paper suggests that understanding the policy formation process requires an explicitly historical theory. Historical contingency theory of business political behavior maintains that key variables that affect public policy such as class unity and state autonomy vary historically, class interests are embedded in state structures, and capitalists mobilize politically in response to capital dependence. Capitalist class fractions mobilized in response to capital dependence during three historical periods, but their responses were affected by other causes that vary historically. Like in the late 19th century, big business developed a laissez-faire ideology in the late 20th century. The big business coalition pressured state managers to set up public policies based on the neoliberal assumption that markets create incentives and controls over economic behavior. Subsequent public policies allowed corporations to restructure as the multilayered subsidiary form (MLSF). In the absence of regulation, the embeddedness of the MLSF in these institutional arrangements provided opportunities and incentives for social actors to pursue their self-interest with guile.

Political Sociology for the 21st Century
Research in Political Sociology, Volume 12, 311–340
Copyright © 2003 by Elsevier Science Ltd.
ISSN: 0895-9935/PII: S0895993503120128

INTRODUCTION

The relationship between class power and state power has been the subject of much debate. Marx (1867) maintained that economic relationships are inherently political and state mediation of class conflict reinforces the class structure. Engels (1892) and Lenin (1939) argued that the capitalist class holds instrumental control over the state. Weber (1921) suggested that power is manifested in classes, status groups, and political parties and other organizations such as states and corporations. During the second half of the 20th century, political sociologists began to examine the interrelationships between class power and state power at the local, subnational, and national levels. C. Wright Mills (1956) maintained that business executives, military leaders, and politicians constituted the three domains of power in American society. Mills' analysis initiated criticism, debate, and research on several dimensions of class and state power.

Central to this debate is the pluralist argument that power is relatively equally distributed and multiple groups have access to the political process. Pluralism maintains that the American power structure is made up of many competing groups, most groups have some power resources, the political system is open to multiple interest groups, and if groups feel strongly enough about an issue to mobilize, they have adequate power to change or veto it (Dahl, 1958; Reisman, 1950). Implicit in the pluralist framework is the assumption that states are sufficiently autonomous to remain impartial and protect the rights of all individuals. By the 1980s, some political sociologists elaborated the pluralist state autonomy assumption and argued that: (1) states are power holders in their own right; (2) states' organizational structures and agendas are bases of state autonomy; and (3) state managers act autonomously when exercising power over the policy formation process (Skocpol, 1980).

Although research in the second half of the 20th century has advanced our understanding of the political process, current theories do not account for historical variation in political behavior. For example, pluralism does not specify the historical conditions when veto groups exercise power or when state autonomy exists. The failure to specify the conditions when key variables are expected to have the greatest effect assumes that their effects do not vary historically or that variation in them is of little consequence. Thus, even when they examine historical data, many political sociologists tend to do so from an ahistorical perspective.

In this paper, I address three issues. First, I elaborate historical contingency theory of business political behavior, which incorporates theoretical developments from state theory and economic, historical, and organizational sociology. I suggest that political sociology would benefit by developing a theoretically explicit conception of the relationship between the exercise of power, state structures, and historical conditions. Second, I analyze three historical transitions and show that similar causes affected the policy paradigm shifts that occurred during each transition. Third, I show how the policy paradigm shift that occurred in the late 20th century created opportunities and incentives for capitalists and corporate managers to pursue their self-interests with guile.

HISTORICAL CONTINGENCY OF CLASS POWER AND STATE POWER IN STRUCTURAL NEO-MARXISM

In the 1970s, *structural neo-Marxists* began to develop a conceptual framework to explain historical variation in dimensions of state power and class power. They maintained that the capitalist class consists of *class fractions*, which conform to the relationship each branch of capital has with the economy. These divisions exist among major economic sectors because differential rates of capital accumulation occur within them. Thus, class fractions have specific political economic interests that may be contradictory to those of other classes and capitalist class fractions (Aglietta, 1979; Offe, 1975; Poulantzas, 1978a; Zeitlin, Neuman & Ratcliff, 1976). Because the economy is not dominated by a unified logic of capital accumulation, the political realm is not occupied by a single class or class fraction. Instead, state policy is affected by a "power bloc" of class fractions who control resources vital to the state's economic agenda (Poulantzas, 1978a). The state mediates intraclass conflict because capitalists are unable to resolve the contradictions that emerge in the economic sphere (Poulantzas, 1978b). Conflict resolution among class fractions takes the form of revising public policy in ways that advance capital accumulation. Ruling class control over the state *only* requires that fractions of the capitalist class are capable of establishing sufficient class consciousness to form a "power bloc" that agrees on a general strategy for economic development.

Historical variation in class and state power is explained, in part, by the two dimensions of *relative autonomy*: variation in class consciousness and state structure (Poulantzas, 1978b). First, state autonomy varies historically because capitalist class consciousness changes over time, which affects the capacity of the capitalist class to unify politically and influence public policy. Second, after state structures are created to advance the agendas of big business capitalist-class interests are embedded in the state, which subordinates the state to the capital accumulation process. Thus, even when capitalist class consciousness wanes, the state can only be relatively autonomous because state structures represent capitalist class interests. State structures provide the basis of future policy by establishing the parameters that require state managers to act in ways that advance capitalist class interests. In summary, this conceptual framework suggests that variation in state autonomy is time dependent. It is affected by the historically specific structure of the state and time-based variation in capitalist class consciousness and unity.

HISTORICAL CONTINGENCY THEORY OF POLITICAL BEHAVIOR

Historical contingency theory of political behavior incorporates central ideas from structural neo-Marxism and economic sociology: economic action is embedded in social relations. Whereas Marx (1965) maintained the class relations are central to understanding economic action, Weber (1921) emphasized multiple causes of economic action that vary over time. These causes include the cultural and political-legal arrangements in which markets are embedded. Others have shown that tribal affiliation, political rule, kinship systems, and religion obligations affect market behavior (Dalton, 1968; Granovetter, 1993; Polanyi, 1944; Sahlins, 1972). The conceptual framework herein elaborates two core ideas from these perspectives: (1) the organization of social relations creates the conditions, incentives, and obligations in which market behavior occurs; and (2) the form of embeddedness varies over time.

By the late 1980s, economic and political sociologists began to use the structural neo-Marxist framework to examine public policy. They pointed out that previous research had not demonstrated whether the capitalist class is unified or fragmented (Mizruchi, 1989) or the extent to which capitalist class unity and state autonomy vary historically (Prechel, 1990). This line of theorizing pointed out that much political sociology interprets concepts as empirical absolutes, rather than as theoretical constructs to explain and interpret empirical events. Subsequent research showed that central concepts in political sociology such as class unity and state autonomy vary historically, which provided corrections to previous conceptions of state autonomy.

In contrast to the argument that state autonomy is high and the capitalist class is weak during war and economic downturns (e.g. Block, 1977), historical contingency theory showed that capitalist class fractions are capable of advancing their class-based interests during these historical conditions. During World War II, despite pressure from the state to expand its production capability, the steel industry refused. In response, the state enacted a policy to finance the construction of steelmaking capability, which facilitated this class fraction's capacity to accumulate capital (Prechel, 1990). The state acquiesced because the steel industry refused to provide it with resources that the state was dependent on to achieve its war-making agenda. The steel industry also exercised control over the state in the 1980s when it was less central to capital accumulation in the economy as a whole and the economy was in recession. During this historical period, the steel industry used the state structure of trade-dispute settlement to pressure the pro-free trade Reagan Administration to pass laws that increased protectionism. Specifically, the steel industry used the political-legal structure of the state to file antidumping complaints against several European corporations, which conflicted with the state's agenda to ensure stable trade relations. The steel industry was able to advance its class interests during a period: (1) when the economy was in recession; (2) steel was less central to economic stability and growth; and (3) the Executive Branch advanced a free-trade agenda. This shows that state structures are important not because they ensure state autonomy, but because they provide a basis for capitalist class fractions to pressure state managers to enact public policy that facilitates their narrow capital accumulation agenda, even when it opposes the state's agenda (Prechel, 1991b). Class-based power during these historical conditions was based on capitalists' capacity to mobilize politically and the embeddedness of class interests in state structures. Moreover, the expansion of state structures that advanced capitalist-class interests (e.g. protectionism, subsidies) further strengthened class-based power inside the state.[1]

These counterintuitive causal processes were identified because the theory directed the researcher's attention toward the relational complexities between the bases of class power and state power. Historical contingency theory suggests that political sociologists would benefit from theorizing key concepts such as state autonomy, class unity, and state structure as variables that change over time and allow for the possibility of state structures providing means for classes and class fractions to exercise control over the state (Prechel, 1990, p. 664).

In addition to analyzing the effects of historical variation in state structures, historical contingency theory posits that social actors who enter public service do not leave their class-based interests behind, and the state is not capable of containing state managers' class-based interests. The issue of whether state managers' class-based interests affect public policy is particularly important during the historical transition at the turn of the 21st century. Although presidents have appointed business elites to government positions for decades (Mills, 1956), beginning in the 1980s, Democrat and Republican presidents (i.e. Ronald Reagan, George H. W. Bush, Bill Clinton, George W. Bush) appointed an unprecedented number of corporate executives to head key government agencies. During the same historical transition, the federal government enacted policies based on neo-liberal economic principles that benefitted big business. Instead of assuming that state managers leave their class-based interest behind or that the state is capable of constraining their class-based interests, historical contingency theory posits the following working hypotheses.

A positive relationship exists between state managers with a background in (or ties to) big business and the shift to conservative social policy.

A positive relationship exists between state managers with a background in (or ties to) big business and the shift to business policy based on neo-liberal economics.[2]

Findings from this research can make important contributions to our understanding of political and economic networks by identifying ties among state managers to elites outside the state and the effects of those networks on public policy. This research can also provide information to evaluate the pluralist assumptions that the state is autonomous and that the political system is open to multiple interest groups.

THEORETICAL AND METHODOLOGICAL PRESUPPOSITIONS OF HISTORICAL CONTINGENCY THEORY

An important benefit of theory is to simplify empirical complexities. However, theories with narrow scope conditions preclude the possibility of examining events that are outside its scope. If the scope conditions narrowly focus on events that occur inside the state, then findings are limited to statements about those relationships. Similarly, if theories do not direct researchers' attention to sources of power that exist outside the state, they cannot explain the effects of those sources of power. Moreover, findings from theories with narrow scope conditions that examine few variables run the risk of treating "the outcome as inevitable" (Roy, 1990, p. 25). In the following, I discuss several theoretical and methodological presuppositions that aid in ensuring adequate scope to examine the causal sequences that affect the policy formation process.

First, examining *atypical* cases is important. Atypical cases suggest that a social change has occurred or that existing theory failed to direct researchers' attention toward the phenomena. Although resemblance and generalizability are important, the emphasis on these methodological issues tend to ignore a crucial aspect of the case-oriented method. The primary value of a case study is not in its generalizability, but in determining whether a phenomenon resembles, or differs from, prevailing conceptions of the empirical world and why those resemblances or differences are theoretically important (Prechel, 1994, p. 728). After the key variables that explain the atypical cases are identified, researchers can employ research designs that test those relationships on a sample or population with a large number of cases.

Second, *structure matters*. Social structures provide a memory of the past through a pattern of relations that are "continuously enacted by actors doing things with others" (Abbott, 1997, p. 99; Weick, 1969). As such, social structures provide knowledge of what is required to re-enact the future in such a way that it gives form to social action. After state structure's governing markets are created, these rules and procedures establish the parameters within which economic activity occurs. State structures also create constituents inside and outside the state with an interest in preserving or modifying those structures.

Third, the rationalization of capitalism is characterized by *irrationalities* in the social structure that lead to periodic crises. Rationalization does not conform to the assumption of linearity in much social theory and method. Instead, rationalization is marked by irrationalities that emerge in unpredictable ways (Antonio, 1979; Benson, 1977; Heydebrand, 1977; McNeil, 1978; Prechel, 1991a). Weber was among the first sociologists to show that rationalization is not equivalent to efficiency or rationality. Weber's distinction between formally rational means and substantively rational ends provides a useful analytic tool to convey the irrationality in the rationalization processes. Weber considered bureaucracy the organizational prototype of legal-rational authority and the inevitable accompaniment to the rationalization of capitalist society. The state sets up monetary systems, international trade agreements, and other political-legal structures integral to capitalist development. On the one hand, these state structures create the stability necessary for capitalist production. On the other, economic processes undergo changes that create disjunctures between state structures and capitalist economies. When the political and economic spheres of society move out of equilibrium, capitalists mobilize politically to restore equilibrium between state structures and the economy in order to restore conditions favorable to capital accumulation.

Fourth, *multiple causes* affect an outcome and the effects of causes vary across time. Drawing on Weber's conception of multicausality, historical sociologists maintain that economic, political-legal, and cultural forces constitute the broad categories that influence social action (Kalberg, 1994). These patterned action-orientations may vary in intensity, which suggests that causal forces are historically contingent. The historical comparative method entails an examination of the constellations of factors that constitute the sequence of events that affect the outcome. It is sensitive to multiple conjunctural causes, which do not "anticipate causal uniformity across . . . cases," but expect that "different combinations of causes may produce the same outcome" (Ragin, 1997, p. 36). That is, "different causes combine in different and sometimes contradictory ways to produce roughly similar outcomes in different settings" (Ragin, 1997, p. 36). Identifying multiple conjunctural causes requires an examination of complex interaction affects because "the magnitude of any single cause's impact depends on the presence or absence of other causal conditions" (Ragin, 1997, p. 37).

Fifth, *temporality* is central to understanding change because the capacity of theories to explain the effects of events depends on the degree to which they can account for the temporal dimension of events. The effects of variables are time dependent because complex interdependencies shape the particular pathway a process follows and "the determining force of a property or variable is not constant, but contingent on the entire situation at a given time" (Abbott, 1991, p. 22; also see Isaac & Griffin, 1989). The emphasis on temporality directs researchers' attention toward causes that are historically unique and causes that are constant in one or more cases at different points in time. Both contribute to *turning points*: consequential shifts that redirect a process (Abbott, 1997). In order to identify the causal forces that produce turning points, researchers must first identify *trajectories*: interlocked and interdependent sequences of events (Abbott, 1997). While trajectories represent stability, turning points represent change. Identifying trajectories and turning points are essential to understand historical sequences that cause *transitions*: radical shifts in historical trajectories. Transitions are frequently manifested as organizational *transformations*, which take the form of changes in the social structure of corporations, states, and other organizations. Although transformations are manifested as structures that provide the basis of stability, social change is a historical question because the social actors who enact change are embedded in routines, rules, and structures that are time dependent. Examining historical sequences avoids over and underestimating the effects of events and provides insights into the causal sequence of events (Rueschemeyer & Stephens, 1997). Although historical sequencing does not establish causation, it facilitates the identification of potential causal processes by connecting the outcome (e.g. change in public policy and state structure) to the social actors exercising power.

TIME-DEPENDENT VARIATION

Historical contingency theory suggests that historical variation in the interdependencies of capital-state relations are crucial to understanding the policy formation process. Whereas capitalists are dependent on states to provide the political-legal arrangements within which capital accumulations occurs, the legitimacy of the state is dependent on growth and stability in the economy that operates relatively autonomously from the state (O'Connor, 1973). Understanding the effects of these interdependencies requires that public policy research must "operate within a sufficiently long time frame to determine the variations" in them (Prechel, 1990, p. 648). These interdependencies are affected by historical variation in: (1) state structures; (2) class unity among capitalist class fractions; and (3) class interests represented in the dominant power block. Generalizations are derived through examining historical variation in capital-state relationships and by showing how this variation affects public policy.

In order to narrow the potential causal processes, historical contingency theory focuses on the conditions within which groups that share an interest act or fail to act on that interest (Prechel, 1990; Tilly, 1981). *Conditions* encompass "the structure of available alternatives as well as incentives and constraints" that result "in aggregates of individual actions or of collective decisions" (Hernes, 1976, pp. 515, 534). Specifying the conditions within which social action occurs avoids the problem of over generalization from a specific case. As formal theorists point out, the utility of a theory exists in its application to all cases identified by its scope conditions (Willer, 1996). Identifying scope conditions establishes parameters to formulate hypotheses about when the capitalist class is unified or divided and when the state is more or less autonomous. This framework also aids in avoiding the mistakes of the positivistic search for abstract laws that are incapable of "providing explanations of specific cases" in which the causes are multiple and where the value-relevance of events vary over time (Kalberg, 1994, p. 82).

Historical conditions affect logics of action that emerge to enact policy paradigm shifts and transform state structures. *Logics of action* entail a particular "rationality underlying, and infusing a set of programs and initiatives" that transform abstract principles into policy (Benson & Paretsky, 1998, p. 174). Logics of action vary historically because policy implementation occurs under historical conditions where resolution is dependent on the options and opportunities available. Variations in capital accumulation, ideology, state structure, and class unity affect the opportunities for forming the power block required to set in motion the logic of action necessary for a policy paradigm shift. *Policy paradigms* entail "the overarching set of ideas that specify how the problems facing decision-makers are to be perceived, what goals might be pursued by policy and what sorts of techniques can be used to reach these goals" (Hall, 1992, p. 91).

Focusing on the competing logics of action directs the researcher toward the bases of power and the extent to which the power of one social actor is affected by their structural location in the network of power relations with other social actors engaged in related activities. This relational dimension of power affects decision-makers' motives and actions as well as their opportunities to enact new behaviors. Historical contingencies structure these "motives and actions" as well as the "interests and opportunities for satisfying them" (Prechel, 1990, p. 665). Two important dimensions of relational power are relevant to historical research. First, the power of one social actor resides in the dependence of other social actors; the dependence of A upon B is the basis for B's power (Galaskiewicz, 1985). Second, understanding how power relationships affect behavior entails identifying social actors (e.g. individuals, corporations, classes) and the conditions within which they are willing or unwilling to "risk exclusion from valued resources" (Markovsky, Willer & Patton, 1988, p. 232). Decisions to engage in risk-taking behaviors are affected by historical conditions, which include the opportunities to engage in social acts and the potential sanctions and rewards for engaging in them.

HISTORICAL TRANSITIONS: CAPITAL DEPENDENCE AS A CONDITION

The following illustrates how capital dependence affected three historical transitions. The decision to focus on capital dependence draws from a long line of theorizing, which maintains that the availability of capital is important to the success and survival of the capitalist enterprise and capitalist class privilege. Karl Marx (1867) argued that the need to generate capital internally was a driving force behind capitalists' efforts to extract labor from the labor power they purchased. Max Weber (1921) maintained that decisions concerning capital are defining features of the business enterprise and that the "autonomous action" of the corporation is dependent on availability of capital, which affects its capacity to pursue opportunities in the market. By the 1960s, Galbraith (1967) argued that few changes have had more effect on the 'character of capitalism' than those related to the 'shift in power' associated with external versus internal sources of capital. More recently, researchers suggest that the most important decisions made by managers are those involving the firm's capital structure and who controls their financing (Mintz & Schwartz, 1985; Mizruchi & Stearns, 1994), and that capitalists mobilize politically in order to overcome capital dependence (Prechel, 1990, 2000).

The analysis here uses the historical periodization articulated in the *social structure of accumulation* framework, which maintains that capitalism goes through a cycle that is repeated over time. Social structure of accumulation theory suggests that corporations' profitability depends on institutional arrangements external to the firm, which include the ideological, political, and economic spheres. These institutional arrangements are designed to ensure conditions favorable to capital accumulation and the reproduction of class relations (Gordon, Edwards & Reich, 1982). However, a breakdown in one part of these institutional arrangements undermines capital accumulation (Gordon, 1980). There are three distinct stages in each social structure of accumulation. The initial *exploration* phase follows periods of economic decline and profitability crisis. During this stage, state managers and capitalists experiment with restructuring institutional arrangements. After new institutional arrangements are enacted, *consolidation* occurs. This constitutes a new social structure of accumulation, which provides the foundation for higher profits. The last stage is *decay*, which is characterized by incompatibility within the institutional arrangements. Markets weaken during periods of economic decline and instability. Decay and the subsequent capital accumulation crisis results in a new exploration phase and the cycle is repeated.

The focus here is on *decay-exploration* transitions where new institutional arrangements are politically constructed in response to long-term constraints on capital accumulation. It examines a central proposition of historical contingency theory: when capital dependence increases, the capitalist class unifies because realigning the institutional arrangements is dependent on their collective political power (Prechel, 1990, 2000). The theory also suggests that capital dependence is most extreme during the decay-exploration stage, which creates incentives for capitalists to unify and pursue political solutions to economic problems. The analysis evaluates a second proposition of historical contingency theory: public policies and state structures are politically constructed to institutionalize stability by changing economic conditions (e.g. competition, instability) that threaten capital accumulation in the dominant power block.[3]

1870–1890s DECAY-EXPLORATION TRANSITION

The historical transition at the end of the 19th century transformed the business enterprise from a public organization with few rights into an entity that held many of the same rights as individuals. Prior to the Civil War, the term corporation referred to a broad range of organizations that carried out activities for the public (Roy, 1991, 1997). Corporations had responsibilities to the public, but few rights. Business enterprises existed at the behest of the government and rights were granted by state legislatures through corporate charters. If a corporation located in New Jersey wanted to purchase raw materials that were located in Pennsylvania, it had to obtain permission from the state legislature. Activities that were not granted in the corporation's state charter were not permitted.

However, organizations that developed a public good (e.g. transportation, utilities) were permitted to use the holding company form, which provided them with certain rights. The development and expansion of these economic sectors were facilitated by the financial sector, which arranged financing and underwrote stocks and bonds. However, the flexibility of this corporate form permitted chicanery that ultimately led to financial crises. In some cases, parent holding companies used subsidiaries to siphon off capital that was transferred to top executives and politicians. The 1873 investigation of Credit Mobilier Corporation, a holding company, showed that capital from Union Pacific Railroad was transferred to a member of Congress and other elected state managers (Kindleberger, 1978). In other cases, railroad stocks were overcapitalized. After several financial disasters in the railroad industry in the 1870s and 1880s, capitalists began to look for other investments (Roy, 1991). During that same period, the demand for industrial goods increased but this economic sector was unable to internally generate the capital necessary for expansion. Dependent on external capital markets for financing, industrial capitalists attempted to obtain the assistance of financial capitalists who had extensive expertise in underwriting stocks and bonds in the holding-company subsidiary form. However, the requirement to obtain permission from state legislatures in order to own stock in industrial corporations was an impediment to using the holding company. Capitalists did not want to ask state legislatures for permission to form holding companies thereby making their capital accumulation strategies dependent on state managers' approval and open to public scrutiny. This combination of historical conditions created an incentive for financial and industrial capitalist class fractions to unify and mobilize politically in order to transform the political-legal arrangements in which industrial corporations were embedded.

The subsequent policy paradigm shift created a historical transition that transformed the balance between capitalist-class power and state power. It transferred power to corporate owners by allocating corporations with property rights that were previously reserved for individuals. At the national level, in 1886, the *Santa Clara County v. Southern Pacific Railroad Company* Supreme Court case granted corporations with legal status similar to that of individuals (Derber, 1998). At the subnational level, industrial and financial capitalists lobbied for legislation to permit unrestricted use of the holding-company subsidiary form. In fact, drafts of the New Jersey Holding Company Acts that created the political-legal structure for the industrial holding company were written by James B. Dill, an attorney, whose clients included Standard Oil, J. P. Morgan, and other financial and industrial corporations. In the 1880s, the New Jersey Holding Company Acts provided industrial corporations with a wide range of rights, which included the right to own stock in other corporations. The New Jersey legislation also created the conditions for a 'race to the bottom' where other subnational states (e.g. Delaware) enacted more lenient laws of incorporation in order to obtain revenues from industrial corporations that wanted to restructure as a holding company (for more detail see Prechel, 2000). Holding companies held ownership control over *subsidiary corporations* in which they owned more than 50% of the stock. This policy paradigm shift transformed business enterprises in the industrial sector from entities that had responsibilities and obligations to the public into quasi-private entities with extensive property rights and limited responsibilities to the public.

The holding-company subsidiary form provided the means for rapid consolidation, which facilitated the creation of giant corporations such as AT&T, Ford, General Electric, General Motors, Standard Oil, and United States Steel. In 1901, the holding company was used to merge scores of independent companies into United States Steel Corporation and create the first corporation in the U.S. with a market capitalization of more than $1 billion. Estimates suggest that U.S. Steel was overcapitalized by several $100 million. By the turn of the 20th century, industrial and financial capitalists had used this corporate form to accumulate massive amounts of private wealth.

1920s–1930s DECAY-EXPLORATION TRANSITION

The second historical transition and policy paradigm shift occurred in response to the abuses of the holding company form (e.g. stock overvaluation) and other forms of corporate chicanery. Many of the corporations formed in the late 19th and early 20th centuries had complex financial structures consisting of pyramids of holding companies, subsidiaries, and *affiliate corporations*: business units in which the parent company owns less than 50% of the stock. Much of the capital used to finance this corporate consolidation was obtained from issuing stock and debt. When the economy began to slow in the 1920s, many corporations were unable to generate sufficient cash flows to meet their debt payments. Although some members of the middle and working classes invested in corporate securities, most did not. However, unknown to the public, banks had invested capital from saving accounts in corporate stock. When these corporations filed for bankruptcy, many members of the working and middle classes lost their savings.

In response, the working classes, small businesses, and middle-class professionals challenged the power of big business and pressured state managers to enact public policy that held big business accountable. Although anticapitalist sentiment was widespread, the capitalist class had sufficient power to pressure state managers to pass several favorable business policies (Levine, 1988). However, President Franklin D. Roosevelt and other New Deal liberals were committed to reinvigorating and sustaining capitalism by limiting corporations' capacity to engage in behaviors that undermined capitalist growth and development. These state managers were supported by scholars who were concerned with managerial control in this corporate form. Adolf A. Berle and Gardiner C. Means argued that the holding-company subsidiary form allowed managers to engage in "personal monetary gain" by creating misleading financial statements and shifting capital from parent companies to subsidiary corporations (1932, p. 115).[4] Together with the liberals inside and outside the state, the anti-big business coalition held adequate power to pass a tax on capital transfers from subsidiary corporations to parent holding companies. This legislation was crucial to the public policy paradigm shift that deinstitutionalized the holding-company subsidiary form (Prechel, 2000). Soon after this legislation was passed, corporations began to restructure as the multidivisional form where capital transfers between divisions and the central office were not taxed. Some corporations retained their subsidiaries, but most of those subsidiary corporations operated independent of the parent company.

To stabilize the economy and restore stockholder confidence, in 1933, state managers passed the "truth in securities" law that required corporations to provide investors with financial information prior to issuing stock. In the same year, they passed the *Banking Act of 1933*, sections of which are known as the *Glass-Steagall Act*, which eliminated conflicts of interest by separating ownership of commercial banks from investment banks. In 1934, the government created the *Securities and Exchange Commission* to monitor public corporations. In the following year, the federal government made public-utility holding companies dediversify by requiring that they invest revenues in utilities (e.g. electricity, natural gas, water). The federal government took additional measures to eliminate conflicts of interest when Congress passed the *1956 Holding Company Act*, which established barriers to bank and insurance company mergers.

1970s–1990s DECAY-EXPLORATION TRANSITION

A third historical transition and policy paradigm shift occurred at the end of the 20th century. In the mid-1970s, economic globalization penetrated the U.S. economy, profits declined, and corporations' dependence on external sources of capital increased. At the same time, conservatives became openly critical of government intervention in the economy, embraced free-market economic principles, and began to lobby the Carter administration to eliminate regulations on business. Conservatives argued that government regulation and the Keynesian-welfare state had created a capital shortage, which undermined economic growth and capital investment. This coalition persuasively integrated free-market principles with religious tenants and asserted that public policy based on these ideas would promote moral behavior. This ideology elaborated a *politics of choice*, which asserted that the government unnecessarily intruded into private affairs, infringed on individual choices, and created incentives that produced dysfunctional economic and social behavior, especially among the poor. By the 1980s, the politics of choice became a crucial component of the logic of action and was supported by a political coalition consisting of capitalists and religious groups who mobilized politically to reduce the 'intrusion' of government into 'private' affairs. Despite the fact that corporations are public entities that have access to the public's capital, this ideology opposed public scrutiny of corporate behavior. This is in sharp contrast to 19th century ideology when corporate interests were subordinate to public interests.

NEO-LIBERAL REFORMS, 1980s

A neoliberal logic of action emerged during this historical transition. *Neoliberal logic of action* is based on the ideology that regulatory structures limit corporate flexibility and growth, and that markets provide the proper incentives for economic decisions. Advocates of this logic of action asserted that big business should be afforded the right to pursue its interests, and markets were capable of monitoring and controlling corporate behavior.[5] Despite the pervasiveness of this ideology, protectionist state structures and Keynesian spending policies remained intact. In the 1980s, protectionism increased and government spending escalated in defense and weapon development and in energy exploration and development (Boies, 1989). By the 1990s, government spending increased in pharmaceutical, semiconductor, and software research.

Capitalists and state managers experimented with a range of public policies during this historical transition. This experiment included the transformation of policies governing business, consumer protection, employment, environmental pollution, social welfare, taxes, and workplace safety. By the mid-1980s, conflict emerged between financial and industrial capitalist class fractions, in part, because the *Revenue Tax Act of 1981* was biased toward industrial capital. Policy makers proposed to eliminate the accelerated depreciation system and to extend the investment tax credit, which benefitted a wider range of corporations. This conflict was mediated when state managers passed the *Tax Reform Act of 1986* (*TRA86*), which was presented as a free-market-oriented tax policy to replace a tax system that had been used to create and manipulate industrial policy. Advocates of the *TRA86* maintained that a free-market-oriented tax policy would eliminate economic distortions and inefficient decision making by consumers and managers. A key component of the new business policy was a little known clause that eliminated the New Deal tax on capital transfers from subsidiary corporations to parent companies. Now, industrial corporations could make tax-free capital transfers from subsidiaries to parent companies.

When it became apparent that state managers would pass the *TRA86*, capital dependent corporations rapidly changed to the holding-company subsidiary form by transforming their domestic divisions into subsidiaries (Prechel, 1991a, pp. 438–439). Large parent companies also acquired other corporations that they incorporated as subsidiaries (Prechel, 1997; Prechel, Boies & Woods, 1999). This transformation in the state structure was followed by a rapid change to the *multilayered subsidiary form* (MLSF) in which a parent company at the top of the corporate hierarchy operates as a financial management company, with two or more levels of subsidiary corporations embedded in it (Prechel, 1997, p. 407). In contrast to the late-19th century holding company, the MLSF has extensive market-based accounting controls (Prechel, 1994, 2000). By 1993, the majority of the largest 100 industrial corporations changed to the MLSF where parent companies own stock in legally separate subsidiary corporations. These parent companies more than doubled their number of subsidiary corporations between 1981 and 1993. In 1993, they held ownership control over more than 4,700 subsidiaries. The majority of that change occurred after the *TRA86* was passed (Prechel, 2000, pp. 241–244).

In addition, the antitrust laws and enforcement structures were transformed in a way that allowed corporations to expand their product-line concentration in specific markets. The embeddedness of this corporate form in these political-legal structures simultaneously increased corporations' flexibility and opportunities to engage in business practices that were previously not viable. In addition to using subsidiaries and affiliates, corporations created *partnerships* with third parties to finance their operations. As one CEO put it, the corporation initiated plans to restructure because:

> The new structure would facilitate the entry into new businesses and the formation of joint ventures or other business combinations with third parties. It would also permit greater flexibility in the management and financing of new and existing business operations (Corporate Document, 1986;[6] see Prechel, 1991a, p. 439).

In 1991, regulatory agencies enacted rules that required parent companies to obtain at least 3% of the capital for these partnerships from third parties. Partnerships often included financial corporations who assisted industrial corporations with raising capital. In addition, financial corporations underwrote initial public stock offerings (IPOs) in industrial parent companies and their subsidiaries. Affiliates also became increasingly widespread in the 1990s in order to expand parent companies' network of corporate entities. This expansion was often in related product lines. For example, ChevronTexaco, a supplier of natural gas, owns 26.5% of Dynergy, which is a gas-marketing and trading corporation. In the early 2000s, Dynergy bought and distributed most of the natural gas that ChevronTexaco produced in the continental United States.

The flexibility of the MLSF is not solely due to its organizational characteristics. Flexibility of the MLSF also exists because there are few political-legal structures to monitor and control it. After the late-19th century decisions by the courts and state managers to grant corporations a status previously reserved for individuals, if a corporate activity was not forbidden by law, it was legal. Whereas the holding-company subsidiary form was deinstitutionalized in the 1930s, in the 1980s state managers passed legislation that created incentives to use this corporate form without setting up mechanisms to monitor and control it. Government oversight of corporate governance was designed to monitor and control managerial behavior in the multidivisional form. In the absence of regulations governing the disclosure of financial transactions in affiliates, partnerships and subsidiaries, managers were permitted to engage in a wide range of speculative behaviors.

MORE NEO-LIBERAL REFORMS, 1990s

In the 1990s, big business lobbied to transform public policies and state structures that regulated financial corporations. Employing neo-liberal ideology, big business argued that the federal government should dismantle New Deal Era regulatory structures and replace them with policies that created market incentives. In response to intensive lobbying by big business, in 1995, state managers passed the *Private Securities Litigation Reform Act*, which created legal obstacles to bringing lawsuits against accountants, executives and related occupations for financial fraud. In 1997, state managers began to weaken the *Banking Act of 1933*, which separated financial activities among commercial and investment banks. This New Deal legislation and the *1956 Holding Company Act*, which established regulatory barriers to banks and insurance company mergers, were dismantled in 1999 when Congress passed the *Gramm-Leach-Bliley Financial Services Modernization Act*.

This dimension of the policy paradigm shift allowed big business to create financial conglomerates that provide a range of financial services and products to the same client. These services and products include stock analyses, underwriting stocks and bonds, lending, advising on mergers and acquisitions, and investment advice. Whereas the *Gramm-Leach-Bliley Financial Services Modernization Act* created the potential for multiple conflicts of interests that might result in advising clients to make bad investment decisions, the *Private Securities Litigation Reform Act* reduced the disincentives for giving bad advice.[7] The big business coalition maintained that financial conglomerates could create effective 'Chinese Walls' among corporate entities to ensure that decision-making information was not transferred among entities that provided different financial products and services to the same customer.

By the early 1990s, the *Financial Accounting Standards Board (FASB)* and the *Securities and Exchange Commission (SEC)* became increasingly concerned over several aspects of corporate governance. In 1993, the *FASB* proposed safeguards to ensure that accounting firms more closely monitored corporations' use of stock options. This policy initiative proposed that violations of the rule would be investigated by the *SEC*. In response, big business mobilized politically and pressured appointed and elected state managers to block this legislation. Several elected state managers openly opposed the stricter accounting rules and Joseph Lieberman (D-Conn), whose state is home to several giant accounting firms, sponsored a Senate resolution opposing the change. The resolution passed by an 88–9 vote. The *FASB* and the *SEC* were also concerned over the increase in accounting firms' consulting activities and executive stock ownership in the firms that they audited. These conflicts of interest became increasingly widespread in the 1990s when consulting revenues exceeded audit revenues in accounting firms. When Arthur Levitt, Chairman of the *SEC*, attempted to curtail this activity, the accounting industry launched an intensive lobby effort and made substantial political contributions to members of Congress.[8] Again, big business used the 'Chinese Wall' argument and effectively blocked this public policy initiative.

The historical transitions at the end of the 19th and 20th centuries share three characteristics: capital dependence, the formation of a capitalist class power block, and transformation of state structures. The political-legal structures that were enacted in the late 20th century, which permitted corporations to organize as the MLSF, represent a transformation in corporate property rights. Now, parent companies could exercise managerial control over other corporations in which they held partial ownership. In addition, embedding the MLSF in these new institutional arrangements provided big business with the 'flexibility' to conceal their financial transactions in multiple levels of affiliates, partnerships, and subsidiaries. Neo-liberal ideology was a crucial social force behind the policy paradigm shift that permitted corporations to shroud their financial transactions from the public. Although the advocates of neo-liberal ideology argued that public policy based on market incentives would provide the basis for stability and growth, it had the opposite effect. The new institutional arrangements created incentives for corporations and their managers to engage in business activities that undermined capitalist stability and initiated one of the most volatile periods in stock market history.

CORPORATE MALFEASANCE, CHICANERY, AND SCANDAL

After the political-legal arrangements governing the banking industry were changed, commercial and investment banks merged and created conglomerates including Citigroup, J. P. Morgan Chase, and Merrill Lynch & Company (Morris,

2000). These financial conglomerates created opportunities and incentives for managers to engage in conflicts of interest. For example, stock analysts who issue optimistic reports for a client firm may facilitate closing an investment-banking deal with the same client in another part of the financial conglomerate. Also, overly optimistic stock reports inflate stock values and exaggerate financial strength, which increase the probability of negotiating a lower interest loan. Further, optimistic stock reports contribute to high IPO prices, which aid the financial conglomerate in obtaining investment banking business. In 2000, the lucrative IPO business raised $58.89 billion. The investment-bank fee for IPOs varies, but is typically between 5 and 7%. Assuming that the investment-banking fee of Tyco Corporation's $4.6 billion IPO in its financial subsidiary was 5%, this transaction resulted in $250 million in revenues for the investment bank. Annual IPO bonuses for individual financial managers can exceed $1 million. Thus, in addition to creating corporate structures that provided opportunities for its managers to engage in conflicts of interest, top management created incentives for them to do so. A decision to not engage in this risk-taking behavior excluded these middle-managers from valued financial benefits and career advancement.

These institutional arrangements permitted Merrill Lynch and its affiliate, Merrill Lynch Capital, to provide several financial products and services to Enron Corporation. These services included stock analyses, underwriting Enron stock and bond issues, raising capital from third parties for Enron's LJM2 partnership, investing capital in the LJM2 partnership, and making loans to the LJM2 partnership. The stocks and bonds underwriting fees alone produced $38 million in revenues for Merrill Lynch. Other financial conglomerates such as J. P. Morgan Chase made low-profit loans to corporations in the telecommunications and cable industry and obtained its high-profit investment-banking business (e.g. IPO issues). There is a substantively irrational dimension to behaviors permitted by these new formally rational political-legal arrangements. The distortion of corporations' financial strength and their subsequent bankruptcies eliminated the possibility that J. P. Morgan Chase would receive their investment-banking business. Moreover, Morgan Chase is confronted with absorbing $1.4 billion in bad loans, which places downward pressure on the value of its own stock.

The embeddedness of the MLSF in neoliberal institutional arrangements resulted in a rapid increase in the lucrative IPO market (Prechel, 2000, pp. 264–265) where the financial incentives to participate in conflicts of interest are high. For example, the average first-day increase in IPO shares in 1999 and 2000 was 65% (McNamee, 2002). IPOs were frequently given to preferred customers. Between 1996 and 2000, Salomon Smith Barney, a subsidiary of Citigroup, allocated almost 900,000 IPO shares to Bernard Ebbers, the CEO of

WorldCom, at a time when WorldCom was using Citigroup as a lender on several mergers. In one case, 10,000 shares of an IPO increased from $21.00 on the offering day to $69.13 on the first-day close. If the stock were sold on that day, Ebbers would have realized a profit of $481,300. Whereas preferred customers benefitted from their arrangements with investment banks, overly-optimistic stock reports misled the general public by encouraging them to buy stock in companies that frequently could not meet their own earnings projections.

By the late-1990s, parent companies were using the MLSF to engage in a range of business activities to disguise debt, inflate earnings, and pump-up stock values. Between 1999 and 2002, Merck, a parent company, reported more than $14 billion in non-existent revenue transfers from a subsidiary (i.e. Medco). Using a non-traditional accounting method known as *mark-to-market*, which counts anticipated revenues immediately after closing a deal, it is estimated that Enron reported more than $100 million in anticipated revenues from a single subsidiary. Enron's managers also transferred more than $100 million in debt from a partnership and reported it as revenue in the parent company. These practices give the appearance of a strong cash flow, which inflates stock values and misleads investors. Preliminary evidence also suggests that Enron's managers used partner-ships to transfer more than $37 million to their personal accounts and the accounts of their family members, friends, and other executives. Corporate managers were able to carry out these transactions because public policy was based on the false assumption that markets are capable of regulating financial transactions. Moreover, because these new institutional arrangements treat the corporation like a private entity, there are no reasonably accessible public records of these financial transactions.

The bankruptcy at Enron Corporation revealed that it had concealed $27 billion in off-book debt through an elaborate network of partnerships and subsidiaries that inflated profits and deceived investors (U.S. Congress, 2002). At the same time, Enron compensated its board of directors at approximately $350,000 per year, which was more than double the national average. In addition, Congress passed legislation introduced by Senator Phil Gramm (D-TX) that deregulated the energy industry, one of Enron's main product lines. The embeddedness of the MLSF in these political-legal arrangements made it possible for management to transform Enron into one of the largest corporations in the United States. In 1985, Enron Corporation was created from Houston Natural Gas Corporation, which held *ownership control* (i.e. more than 50% of the stock) in five subsidiaries. By 1999, Enron operated in many different markets and held ownership control in more than 200 domestic subsidiary corporations. When Enron filed bankruptcy on December 2001, it had a market capitalization of approximately $49.5 billion (for more detail see Boies & Prechel, 2002, pp. 309–311). In October 2002, a federal indictment of an Enron manager included 72 counts of wire fraud and money laundering all of which went undetected or unreported in its complex hierarchy of affiliates, partnerships, and subsidiaries.

Despite the efforts of some state managers to more closely monitor corporations, they had little success. For example, SEC Chair, Arthur Levitt, unsuccessfully attempted to control the use of stock options because this form of executive compensation creates incentives for executives to pump up corporate balance sheets in order to inflate stock values. The failure of state managers to enact structures to control the use of stock options permitted executives and directors to take billions of dollars of stockholders equity from companies. Although the $102 million that Kenneth Lay, Enron's CEO, obtained in stock options is high publicized, it is far less than the amount taken by many directors and executives. Of the 25 companies whose stock had "fallen by at least 75% from the highs they reached during the bubble years," 466 managers and directors took $23 billion in risk-free stock options between January 1999 and May 2002 (Fortune, 2002). This same study placed Phil Anschultz, who took $1.57 billion in stock options from QWest Communications, at the top of the list of takers. The same study showed that, during this 29-month period, approximately $66 billion was taken in stock options from the 1,035 corporations included in the study. Because most stock options were not reported on corporations' financial reports, shareholders were unaware of the degree to which this form of compensation lowered the value of their stock and contributed to stock overvaluation. Like in the 1920s, when the stock bubble burst and the stock market 'corrected,' overvalued stocks lost much of their value and a large portion of the working and middle classes' savings (e.g. 401(k) retirement plans) disappeared.

THE ABSENCE OF REGULATION

Although the late 20th century is frequently characterized as an era of deregulation, this is misleading because the 1980s-1990s policy paradigm shift allowed big business to use a corporate form in which many financial transactions were never regulated. As discussed above, after the abuses of the holding-company subsidiary form were exposed in the 1920s and 1930s, the state imposed a tax on capital transfers from legally separate corporate entities (e.g. affiliates, subsidiaries) to parent companies, which deinstitutionalized this corporate form. To avoid paying this capital-transfer tax, corporations restructured many of their subsidiaries as division and changed to the multidivisional form. Although some parent companies retained their subsidiaries, most subsidiary operated as financially independent corporations.

There are two important features of the tax on capital transfers in the holding-company subsidiary form. First, the tax represents a cost, which creates a disincentive to transfer capital from subsidiaries to the parent company, especially if that capital transfer does not result in an authentic financial benefit. Second, payment of the tax creates a public record of the financial transaction. After this capital-transfer tax was eliminated in 1986, there were no easily obtainable records to know when these financial transactions occurred or how they affected corporations' financial stability and stock values. These transactions are even less transparent when they occur from partnerships to parent companies because parent companies are allowed to keep financial transactions in partnerships off their financial statements. This privatization of corporations' financial transactions in the complex MLSF is a primary reason why it required scores of SEC accountants, attorneys, and other investigators months to determine the legality of Enron's capital transfers.

Like the late 19th century when the "robber barons flooded politics with big money" (Derber, 1998), big business spent massive amounts of capital on politics in the late 20th century. For example, in 1999–2000, Enron Corporation donated $114,000 in PAC contributions to President George W. Bush (Weiss, 2002). Enron, its chairman, and its CEO donated an additional $300,000 to Bush's inaugural fund. Between 1989 and 2001, Enron made PAC contributions to 71 of the 100 U.S. Senators and 188 of the 431 members of the House. The largest recipient of Enron's PAC contributions was Senator Kay Bailey Hutchison (Tx-R) who received $101,500. The second largest recipient, Senator Phil Gramm (Tx-R) who received $101,350, was a cosponsor of the *Gramm-Leach-Bliley Financial Services Modernization Act*. Gramm also sponsored legislation that eliminated regulations on energy corporations. Between 1989 and 2001, the total contribution to federal candidates and political parties from Enron was more than $5.9 billion. Between 1997 and 2001, Enron spent an additional $8.7 billion on lobbying. During this same time period, state managers dismantled some regulations and relaxed enforcement of other regulations in the energy industry, which was Enron's largest product line. In addition, state managers assisted Enron in strengthening its position in the global economy by guaranteeing more than $7.2 billion in public financing for its foreign investments.

The above suggests that there is a causal relationship between corporate lobby and PAC expenditures and changes in public policy. The following posits hypotheses to test these relationships.

A positive relationship exists between corporate lobby expenditures and business policy based on neo-liberal economic principles.

A positive relationship exists between corporate lobby expenditures and conservative social policy.

A positive relationship exists between corporate PAC contributions and business policy based on neo-liberal economic principles.

A positive relationship exists between corporate PAC contributions and conservative social policy.

SUMMARY

The historical narrative here identified three policy paradigm shifts in the last 120 years. Beginning in the 1880s, state structures were enacted that defined corporations' legal rights in a way that treated corporations similar to individuals. After these state structures were enacted, if the law did not prohibit an act, it was legal. In the 1920s and 1930s, the widespread corporate scandals in the holding-company subsidiary form compelled state managers to limit its use. However, in the late 20th century, big business argued that it required the increased flexibility of the holding-company subsidiary form to compete in the global economy. Subsequent changes in public policy, most notably, the *Tax Reform Act of 1986* and the *Gramm-Leach-Bliley Financial Services Modernization Act*, permitted increased 'flexibility' for corporations that used the multilayered subsidiary form.

In the absence of political-legal structures that prohibited corporate chicanery at the turn of the 21st century, capitalists and corporate managers were permitted to engage in financial transactions that were previously infeasible or illegal. Many of these transactions occurred in affiliates, partnerships and subsidiaries. These behaviors were permitted because state managers enacted a policy paradigm shift that transformed the institutional arrangements in which corporations are embedded. Like at the end of the 19th century, the embeddedness of the MLSF in contemporary political-legal arrangements provides opportunities for capitalists and their managers to expand their wealth at rates that far exceeded wealth accumulation in most other historical periods. The embeddedness of the MLSF in these political-legal arrangements also permitted big business to construct some of the largest corporations in the world. Whereas the largest 50 *Fortune* 500 industrial firms held less than 30 times as many assets as the smallest 50 firms between 1958 and 1977, this ratio increased to more than 60 times by 1993 (Prechel & Boies, 1998, p. 323). This policy paradigm shift also permitted industrial consolidation through mergers and acquisitions (e.g. Chevron-Texaco, ConocoPhillips, Hewlett-Packard-Compaq Computer), the recombination of corporations that were previously broken up (e.g. parts of Standard Oil were reunited as Exxon-Mobil), and the creation of new giant corporations (e.g. Enron, WorldCom).

Corporate chicanery contributed to one of the most volatile periods in stock market history. The accounting and financial devises used at Enron, Dynegy,

Global Crossing, Merck, QWest, Tyco, WorldCom and other corporations discredit the neoliberal claim that markets are capable of regulating corporations. Also, the temporal relationship between corporate scandals and these political-legal arrangements raise serious questions about the motives of politicians and members of the media who attribute corporate chicanery to individual characteristics (e.g. 'greed,' 'bad apples'). Corporate scandals were not caused solely by the unrestrained pursuit of self-interests. Rather, public policy based on neoliberal ideology created incentives for social actors to engage in risk-taking behavior that advanced their self-interest *and* the interests of the capitalist class. The analysis here shows that market-based neoliberal reforms are fatally flawed because markets do not create moral behavior as advocates imply or assert. In order to advance public welfare, market economies must be embedded in institutional arrangements that constrain, not encourage, the pursuit of economic self-interests.

Discourse that focuses on the decline in ethical standards is ideological because it obscures the reality that big business legitimated the policy paradigm shift at the end of the 20th century as a means to create market incentives. The 'greed' discourse also conceals the reality that after these political-legal arrangements were enacted big business created incentives that rewarded chicanery. The embeddedness of the MLSF in these new institutional arrangements permitted boards of directors and inside managers to increase their personal wealth by engaging in (or ignoring) financial manipulations and transactions that were previously not legal or viable. These institutional arrangements also allowed capitalists and top management to take the vast majority of the wealth that was created during the economic boom at the end of the 20th century.

By examining the 1980s–1990s policy paradigm shift in more detail, political sociologists can make valuable contributions to public policy debates in the 21st century. If state managers enact laws and enforcement structures that effectively limit corporate chicanery and malfeasance, they will be the outcome of several years of political debate. A full year after the chicanery at Enron was exposed to the public, state managers have only enacted the vague and imprecise *Sarbanes-Oxley Act*. Like other vague and imprecise legislation, *Sarbanes-Oxley* will be difficult to enforce. In addition, the *SEC*, which is responsible for enforcing this legislation, is underfunded. Although President Bush signed the *Sarbanes-Oxley Act*, he later denied the budget increase requested by *SEC* Chair, Harvey Pitts, and approved less than 40% of the increase recommended by Congress. Currently, the *SEC* has about 75 employees in its trial unit, and 20 of its attorneys and accountants are working on the Enron case. In the absence of adequate resources and staff, the *SEC* is unable to pursue many cases of corporate corruption.

There are several potential explanations for why state managers have not responded with adequate legislation, enforcement structures and resources to investigate corporate corruption. However, preliminary data suggests that there is a correlation between the business background of state managers and this probusiness policy paradigm shift. Studies indicate that in the 1980s the number of state managers who have business backgrounds and connections to elite social movement organizations increased (Boies & Pichardo, 1992; Jenkins & Ekert, 2000). This trend continued into the 21st century. President George W. Bush and Vice President Dick Cheney are former corporate executives. In addition, George W. Bush appointed several former corporate directors, executives, and lobbyists to key administrative positions. These appointments include the Secretaries of Agriculture, Commerce, Interior and Treasury, and the Deputy Secretaries of Energy and Interior, the EPA Deputy Administrator, the Army Secretary, the National Security Advisor, and the White House Chief of Staff. Also, all five of the current *SEC* commissioners were nominated by President Bush. Further, the accounting oversight board designated by the *Sarbanes-Oxley Act*, which is responsible to set auditing standards and monitor accounting firms, did not have a permanent chairperson as of early December 2002. This inaction hampers enforcement of *Sarbanes Oxley*. However, little research has been done on the extent to which causal relationships exit between state managers background and the enforcement of public policy. By examining this relationship, political sociologists can provide valuable information on this crucial dimension of public policy and state theory.

CONCLUSION

This paper described central aspects of historical contingent theory of business political behavior, showed that historical conditions affect policy paradigm shifts, and examined the relationship between policy paradigm shifts and corporate malfeasance. In response to capital dependence, in the late 19th and late 20th centuries, financial and industrial capitalist class fractions unified and mobilized politically to enact public policies that provided corporations with increased flexibility. During both historical periods, the ideology of self-regulating markets was employed to legitimate public policy permitting the used of the multilayered subsidiary form without establishing controls over it. Although corporations' capital dependence also affected the policy paradigm shift after the Great Depression, corporate chicanery and the failure to ensure economic stability undermined the legitimacy of the capitalist class. This condition limited the power of the capitalist class and reduced its capacity to control public policy, which created opportunities for the working and middle classes to affect this policy paradigm shift.

Although historical transitions represent breaks from the past, policy paradigm shifts and transformations in state structures are not disconnected from the past. State structures provide continuity because they are the product of past policies and are supported by a network of interests inside and outside the state that constrain present choices (Beetham, 1987; Prechel, 1990). Although historical transitions create new opportunities and constraints for decision making, existing state structures provide a memory of the past and a source of class-based power that affect the enactment of the political struggles that transform public policy.

The analysis shows that policy paradigm shifts are explained by multiple causes some of which are constant and others that are time dependent. Whereas capital accumulation crisis is *a* cause of policy paradigm shifts, multiple causes exist, some causes are time dependent, and the "magnitude of any single cause's impact depends on the presence or absence of other causal conditions" (Kalberg, 1994; Ragin, 1997, p. 37). Political outcomes are affected by contradictions that emerge from the historically specific character of the economy, the state structure, the network of interest inside and outside the state, and the irrationality in the rationalization of capitalism. This irrationality became apparent at the turn of the 21st century when neoliberal policies failed to achieve their stated goal of improving the economic well being of the public as a whole. Although the institutional arrangements were substantively rational for the capitalist and managerial classes, they were substantively irrational for the middle and working classes who invested their savings and retirements in overvalued stock in the 1990s.[9] The contradiction between formally rational means and substantive goals is a cause of social change because the resolution of contradiction transforms structures.

This paper suggests that political sociology can benefit by incorporating theoretical developments from other subfields. Organizational sociologists have demonstrated that corporations do not passively respond to changes in their environment. Instead, corporations are social actors that actively structure dimensions of their environment, especially those upon which they are dependent. This dimension of organizational theory is particularly relevant to political sociologists given the interdependencies of states and corporations. Also, studies that examine the extent to which state managers' professional and class backgrounds cause policy paradigm shifts can aid in resolving the long-term debate between pluralist and neo-Marxist theories. Political sociology can also benefit from historical sociology and formal theory by placing greater emphasis on the conditions in which social action occurs. Together with existing theoretical knowledge in political sociology and other subfields in sociology, analyses that examine historical contingencies can advance our understanding of the multiple causes that affect the enactment of public policy and the extent to which causes are constant or vary historically.

NOTES

1. Much of the research that is sensitive to historical variation tends to focus on class power that is located outside the state. These scholars have shown that capitalists mobilized politically to weaken consumer, environmental, and labor protections in the 1970s and 1980s (Akard, 1992) and blocked social policy reforms in the 1980s and 1990s (Akard, 1998; Mintz, 1998) when elite policy councils became more politically active (Benson & Paretsky, 1998; Jenkins & Ekert, 2000).

2. Research in organizational sociology suggests that a relationship exists between the background of top managers and organizational behavior (Fligstein, 1985; but see Prechel & Boies, 1998).

3. The primary focus of SSA theorists is on how long-wave economic cycles contribute to the homogenization and segmentation of workers. Although these theorists do not ignore politics, they give limited attention to policy paradigm shifts.

4. Many scholars narrowly interpret Berle's and Means' to maintain that managers replaced capitalists. This is correct, but it is also an incomplete reading of their work.

5. Despite retaining many Keynesian safeguards in the United States, big business and the U.S. government lobbied for the broad application of neo-liberal reforms in Latin America.

6. Access to this corporation included an agreement to not reveal the identity of the managers or the corporation.

7. Transformation of public policy in the banking industry also resulted in change to the holding company form and the acquisition of branch banks (Morris, 2000).

8. During the 2000 election cycle, the accounting industry contributed $14.5 million to political candidates and parties.

9. For example, the Arkansas Teachers Retirement System invested $30 million in Enron's, now bankrupt, LJM2 partnership.

ACKNOWLEDGMENTS

The author thanks Robert Antonio and anonymous reviewers at Research in Political Sociology for their comments on previous drafts of this paper.

REFERENCES

Abbott, A. (1991). Causality and contingency. Paper presented at the annual meeting of the American Sociological Association, Cincinnati.
Abbott, A. (1997). On the concept of turning point. *Comparative Social Research, 16*, 85–106.
Aglietta, M. (1979). *A theory of capitalist regulation*. London: New Left Books.

Akard, P. (1992). Corporate mobilization and political power. *American Sociological Review*, *57*, 597–615.

Akard, P. (1998). Where are all the democrats?: The limits of economic policy reform. In: C. Lo & M. Schwartz (Eds), *Social Policy and the Conservative Agenda* (pp. 187–209). Malden, MA: Blackwell Publishers.

Antonio, R. (1979). The contradiction of domination and production in bureaucracy. *American Sociological Review*, *44*, 895–912.

Beetham, D. (1987). *Bureaucracy*. Minneapolis, MI: University of Minnesota Press.

Benson, K. (1977). Organizations: A dialectical view. *Administrative Science Quarterly*, *20*, 229–249.

Benson, K., & Paretsky, N. (1998). Active-competitive industrial policy: From elite project to logic of action. In: C. Lo & M. Schwartz (Eds), *Social Policy and the Conservative Agenda* (pp. 169–186). Malden, MA: Blackwell Publishers.

Berle, A., & Means, G. (1932 [1991]). *The modern corporation and private property*. NJ: New Brunswick.

Block, F. (1977). The ruling class does not rule. *Socialist Review*, *7*, 6–28.

Boies, J. (1989). Money, business, and the state. *American Sociological Review*, *54*, 821–833.

Boies, J., & Pichardo, N. (1992). The committee on the present danger: A case for the importance of elite social movement organizations to theories of social movements and the state. *Berkeley Journal of Sociology*, *20*, 57–87.

Boies, J., & Prechel, H. (2002). Capital dependence, business political behavior, and change to the multilayered subsidiary form. *Social Problems*, *49*, 301–326.

Dahl, R. (1958). A critique of the ruling elite model. *American Political Science Review*, *52*, 463–469.

Dalton, G. (Ed.) (1968). *Primitive, archaic and modern economies: Essays of Karl Polanyi*. Boston: Beacon Press.

Derber, C. (1998). *Corporation nation*. New York: St. Martin's Press.

Engels, F. (1892). Socialism: Utopian and scientific. In: H. Tucker (Ed.), *The Marx-Engels Reader* (2nd ed., pp. 683–717). New York: W. W. Norton & Company, Inc.

Fligstein, N. (1985). The spread of the multidivisional form among large firms, 1919–1979. *American Sociological Review*, *50*, 377–391.

Fortune (2002). You bought. They sold (September 2), 64–74.

Galaskiewicz, J. (1985). Interorganizational relations. *Annual Review of Sociology*, *11*, 281–304. Palo Alto, CA: Annual Reviews.

Galbraith, J. K. (1967). *The new industrial state*. New York: New American Library.

Gordon, D. (1980). Stages of accumulation and long economic cycles. In: T. Hopkins & I. Wallerstein (Eds), *Processes of the World System* (pp. 19–45). Beverly Hills, CA: Sage Publications.

Gordon, D., Edwards, R., & Reich, M. (1982). *Segmented work, divided workers*. Cambridge: Cambridge University Press.

Granovetter, M. (1993). The nature of economic relationships. In: R. Swedberg (Ed.), *Explorations in Economic Sociology* (pp. 2–41). New York: Russell Sage Foundation.

Hall, P. (1992). The movement from Keynesianism to Monetarism: Institutional analysis and British economic policy in the 1970s. In: K. Thelen & F. Longstreth (Eds), *Structuring Politics: Historical Institutionalism in Comparative Analysis*. Princeton, NJ: Princeton University Press.

Hernes, G. (1976). Structural change in social progress. *American Journal of Sociology*, *82*, 513–547.

Heydebrand, W. (1977). Organizational contradictions in public bureaucracies. *The Sociological Quarterly*, *18*, 85–109.

Isaac, L., & Griffin, L. (1989). Ahistoricism in time-series analysis of historical processes. *American Sociological Review*, *54*, 873–890.

Jenkins, C., & Ekert, C. (2000). The right turn in economic policy: Business elites and the new conservative economics. *Sociological Forum*, *15*, 307–338.

Kalberg, S. (1994). *Max Weber's comparative-historical sociology*. Chicago IL: University of Chicago Press.

Kindleberger, C. (1978). *Manias, panics, and crashes: A history of financial crises*. New York: John Wiley & Sons, Inc.

Lenin, V. I. (1939). *Imperialism the highest stage of capitalism*. New York: International Publishers.

Levine, R. (1988). *Class struggle and the new deal*. Lawrence, KS: University of Kansas Press.

Markovsky, B., Willer, D., & Patton, T. (1988). Power relations in exchange networks. *American Sociological Review*, *53*, 220–236.

Marx, K. (1867 [1977]). *Capital* (Vol. 1). New York: Vintage Books.

Marx, K. (1965). *Pre-capitalists economic formations*. With an Introduction by: E. Hobsbawn. New York: International Publishers.

McNamee, M. (2002). IPOs: Getting the price right. *Business Week* (September 9), 126.

McNeil, K. (1978). Understanding organizational power: Building on the Weberian legacy. *Administrative Science Quarterly*, *23*, 65–90.

Mills, C. W. (1956). *The power elite*. New York: Oxford University Press.

Mintz, B. (1998). The failure of health-care reform: The role of big business in policy formation. In: C. Lo & M. Schwartz (Eds), *Social Policy and the Conservative Agenda* (pp. 210–224). Malden, MA: Blackwell Publishers.

Mintz, B., & Schwartz, N. (1985). *The structure of power in American business*. Chicago: University of Chicago Press.

Mizruchi, M. (1989). Similarity of political behavior among large American corporations. *American Journal of Sociology*, *95*, 401–424.

Mizruchi, M., & Stearns, L. (1994). A longitudinal study of borrowing by large corporations. *Administrative Science Quarterly*, *39*, 118–140.

Morris, T. (2000). Transformation in the organization of banking: The effects of government policy, 1977–1998. Unpublished doctoral dissertation, Texas A&M University, College Station, Texas.

O'Connor, J. (1973). *The fiscal crisis of the state*. New York: St. Martin's Press.

Offe, C. (1975). The theory of the capitalist state and the problem of policy formation. In: L. Lindberg, R. Alford, C. Crouch & C. Offe (Eds), *Stress and Contradiction in Modern Capitalism* (pp. 124–144). Lexington, DC: Heath and Company.

Polanyi, K. (1944 [2001]). *The great transformation: The political and economic origins of our time*. Boston: Beacon Press.

Poulantzas, N. (1978a). *Classes in contemporary capitalism*. London: Verso.

Poulantzas, N. (1978b). *State, power, socialism*. London: New Left Books.

Prechel, H. (1990). Steel and the state: Industry politics and business policy formation. *American Sociological Review*, *55*, 648–668.

Prechel, H. (1991a). Irrationality and contradiction in organizational change: Transformations in the corporate form of a U.S. steel corporation. *The Sociological Quarterly*, *32*, 423–445.

Prechel, H. (1991b). Conflict and historical variation in steel capital-state relations. *American Sociological Review*, *56*, 693–698.

Prechel, H. (1994). Economic crisis and the centralization of control over the managerial process: Corporate restructuring and neo-Fordist decision making. *American Sociological Review*, *59*, 723–745.

Prechel, H. (1997). Corporate transformation to the multilayered subsidiary form: Changing economic conditions and state business policy. *Sociological Forum*, *12*, 405–439.

Prechel, H. (2000). *Big business and the state: Historical transitions and corporate transformation, 1880s-1990s*. Albany, New York: State University of New York Press.

Prechel, H., & Boies, J. (1998). Capital dependence, financial risk, and change from the multidivisional to the multilayered subsidiary form. *Sociological Forum, 13*, 321–362.

Prechel, H., Boies, J., & Woods, T. (1999). Debt, mergers and acquisitions, changing institutional arrangements and transformation to the multilayered subsidiary form. *Social Science Quarterly, 80*, 115–135.

Ragin, C. (1997). Turning the tables: How case-oriented research challenges variable-oriented research. *Comparative Social Research, 16*, 27–42.

Reisman, D. in collaboration with Denny, R., & Glazer, N. (1950). *The lonely crowd*. New Haven, NJ: Yale University Press.

Roy, W. (1990). Functional and historical logics in explaining the rise of the American industrial corporation. *Comparative Social Research, 12*, 19–44.

Roy, W. (1991). The organization of the corporate class segment of the U.S. capitalist class at the turn of this century. In: S. McNall (Ed.), *Bringing Class Back In* (pp. 139–164). Boulder, CO: Westview Press.

Roy, W. (1997). *Socializing capital: The rise of the large industrial corporation in America*. Princeton, NJ: Princeton University Press.

Rueschemeyer, D., & Stephens, J. (1997). Comparing historical sequences – A powerful tool for causal analysis. *Comparative Social Research, 16*, 55–72.

Sahlins, M. (1972). *Stone age economics*. Chicago, IL: Aldine Publishing Company.

Skocpol, T. (1980). Political response to capitalist crisis: Neo-Marxist theories of the state and the case of the new deal. *Politics and Society, 10*, 155–201.

Tilly, C. (1981). *As sociology meets history*. New York: Academic.

United States Congress (2002). Permanent subcommittee on investigations of the committee on governmental affairs. "The role of the board of directors in Enron's collapse. 107th Congress, Report 107–70.

Weber, M. (1921 [1978]). *Economy and society*. Berkeley CA: University of California Press.

Weick, K. (1969). *The social psychology of organizing*. Reading, MA: Addison-Wesley.

Weiss, S. (2002). *The fall of a giant*. Washington, DC: Center for Responsive Politics.

Willer, D. (1996). The prominence of formal theory in sociology. *Sociological Forum, 11*, 319–332.

Zeitlin, M., Neuman, W., & Ratcliff, R. (1976). Class segments: Agrarian property and political leadership in the capitalist class of Chile. *American Sociological Review, 41*, 1006–1030.

ABOUT THE AUTHORS

Robert D. Benford is Professor and Chair of sociology at Southern Illinois University Carbondale. His published works on framing processes, narratives, collective identity and other social constructionist issues associated with social movements, nuclear politics, war museums, and environmental controversies have appeared in journals such as the *Annual Review of Sociology, American Sociological Review, Social Forces, Journal of Contemporary Ethnography, The Sociological Quarterly, Sociological Inquiry, Peace Review, Current Perspectives in Social Theory, International Social Movement Research*, and *Mobilization*. He currently serves as editor of the *Journal of Contemporary Ethnography*. E-mail: rbenford@siu.edu

Catherine Bolzendahl is a Ph.D. candidate at Indiana University in the Department of Sociology. Her research interests include gender, public opinion, welfare states, religion and political identities. She has recently completed several studies of trends and sources of conflict in U.S. attitudes on issues of gender roles, family, and abortion. Her dissertation will examine gender ideologies and attitudes toward family institutions in the U.S. and Western Europe. E-mail: cbolzend@indiana.edu

Eduardo Bonilla-Silva is an Associate Professor of Sociology at Texas A&M University. He is best known for his 1997 article in the *American Sociological Review* entitled, "Rethinking Racism: Toward a Structural Interpretation," where he argued that Sociology needed to analyze racism not as "prejudice" but as a structural part of the post-1500 world-system. His book *White Supremacy and Racism in the Post-Civil Rights Era* (Lynne Rienner Publishers, 2001) was the co-winner of the 2002 Oliver Cromwell Cox Award. Professor Bonilla-Silva is currently working on two book projects: one (with Ashley Doane) entitled *Whiteout: The Continuing Significance of Racism* (Routledge) and another entitled *Racism without Racists: Color Blind Racism and the Persistence of Racial Inequality in the USA* (Rowman and Littlefield). E-mail: bonilla@tamu.edu

Clem Brooks is Professor of Sociology at Indiana University, Bloomington. His research interests are elections and voting behavior, welfare states and public opinion, social change, and quantitative methods. With Jeff Manza, he is the author of *Social Cleavages and Political Change* (Oxford University Press, 1999). Brooks and Manza are working on several new studies of political change, including a manuscript entitled The Ideological American Voter. E-mail: cbrooks@indiana.edu

Jorge Cadena-Roa is Professor of Sociology at Universidad Nacional Autónoma de México (Torre 2 de Humanidades, 6o. piso, Ciudad Universitaria DF 04510, Mexico). His recent publications include "Strategic Framing, Emotions, and Superbarrio – Mexico City's Masked Crusader" in *Mobilization* 7 (2002) and "State Pacts, Elites, and Social Movements in Mexico's Transition to Democracy" in *Movements, Parties, and States*, edited by J. Goldstone. His current research focuses on the ways movements affected democratization processes in Latin America and the ways laughter may challenge the symbolic order. E-mail: cadena@servidor.unam.mx

David G. Embrick is a doctoral student in the Sociology Department at Texas A&M University. He is interested in the areas of race and ethnicity, gender and sexuality, and social stratification. He has published an article in *Race and Society* (with Eduardo Bonilla-Silva) entitled, "Are Blacks Color Blind Too? An Interview-Based Analysis of Blacks' Views." His current work is an examination of race, gender, and class practices in the workplace (a bread company). He is working on his thesis entitled, "The Making of Whitebread: Race, Gender, and Class in a Bread Company."

Tyrone A. Forman is an Assistant Professor of Sociology and African American Studies, faculty fellow at the Institute for Research on Race and Public Policy, and faculty affiliate at the Institute of Government and Public Affairs at the University of Illinois at Chicago. His primary research interests are in intergroup prejudice and discrimination, American youth and public opinion, and survey research methods. He is currently conducting research in three areas: (1) studies of intergroup relations among people of color; (2) studies of the patterns, trends, and social determinants of young whites' racial attitudes; and (3) studies of the social psychological consequences of racial stratification for African American well-being. His work on these topics has appeared in *Social Problems, Discourse and Society, Perspectives on Social Problems, Youth and Society, Sociological Studies of Children and Youth, Health Education and Behavior*, and *Journal of Studies on Alcohol*. E-mail: tyforman@uic.edu

Timothy B. Gongaware is an Assistant Professor in the Department of Sociology and Archaeology at the University of Wisconsin – La Crosse. His research interests revolve around issues of collective memory creation and maintenance, collective identity, collective action framing and the role of the self in social movement processes. Most recently he published an article in *Research in Social Movements, Conflict and Change* concerning the impact of Native American women on the development of collective action frames in Native American social movements challenging educational issues. E-mail: gongawar.timo@uwlax.edu

Juan J. Gonzalez is a Tenured Professor of Sociology at the Universidad Nacional de Educacion a Distancia in Madrid. He has been an Honorary Fellow in the Department of Sociology, University of Wisconsin-Madison, and a visiting research professor at California Polytechnic State University, San Luis Obispo. He is currently general coordinator of the Spanish research project on "Class Structure, Biography, and Class Consciousness." One of his recent publications is "Class, Citizens, and Classes of Citizens: The Electoral Cycle of Postsocialism" (Spain, 1986–1994), *Revista Espanola de Investigaciones Sociologicas*, 1997.

Herbert H. Haines is Professor of Sociology at the State University of New York at Cortland. His research focuses on social movements that seek to influence crime policy. Haines is the author of *Against Capital Punishment: The Anti-Death Penalty Movement in America, 1972–1994* (Oxford University Press, 1996). His first book, *Black Radicals and the Civil Rights Mainstream: 1954–1970* (University of Tennessee Press, 1988) was selected as an Outstanding Book by the Gustavus Myers Center for the Study of Human Rights in the United States. Haines is currently studying drug policy reform activism. E-mail: haines@cortland.edu

Ronald N. Jacobs is Assistant Professor of Sociology at the University at Albany, State University of New York. His most recent book is *Race, Media, and the Crisis of Civil Society: From Watts to Rodney King* (Cambridge University Press, 2000). E-mail: Rjacobs@csc.albany.edu

Harold Kerbo is a Professor of Sociology at California Polytechnic State University, San Luis Obispo, and currently a Visiting Professor at the University of Oklahoma. He has held Fulbright positions or visiting professor positions in several European countries, Japan, and Southeast Asia. He is the author of *Social Stratification and Inequality: Class Conflict in Historical, Comparative, and Global Perspective* now in its 5th edition. His research interests focus upon comparative social structures in North America, Europe, and Asia.

Edgar Kiser is Professor of Sociology at the University of Washington. He has published several articles in sociology, political science, and economics journals on topics including the determinants of war and revolt, the development and decline of voting institutions, and the centralization and bureaucratization of state administration.

Amanda E. Lewis (Ph.D., University of Michigan, 2000) is an Assistant Professor in the Departments of Sociology and African American Studies at the University of Illinois at Chicago. Her primary areas of research and teaching include race and ethnic relations, sociology of education, and qualitative and ethnographic research methods. She has recently completed an in-depth ethnographic study of the reproduction of racial meaning and racial inequality in schools; the manuscript based on this work is entitled *Race in the Schoolyard: Negotiating the Color Line in Classrooms and Communities* (Rutgers University Press).

Paul Luebke is Associate Professor of Sociology at the University of North Carolina at Greensboro. He has published extensively on politics and society in North Carolina, including *Tar Heel Politics 2000* (UNC Press, 1998). He has also represented Durham since 1991 in the North Carolina State House. E-mail: paull@ncleg.net

Jeff Manza is an Associate Professor of Sociology and Faculty Fellow at the Institute for Policy Research at Northwestern University. In addition to his collaborative work with Clem Brooks on public opinion and voting behavior, he is the co-author (with Christopher Uggen) of a forthcoming book on the political consequences of felon disfranchisement, entitled *Locking Up the Vote* (Oxford University Press). E-mail: manza@northwestern.edu

Pamela E. Oliver is Professor of Sociology at the University of Wisconsin – Madison (1180 Observatory Drive, Madison WI 53705) and past chair of the Political Sociology and Collective Behavior and Social Movements sections of the American Sociological Association. She has published widely in the areas of social movements and collective action theory. Her current work focuses on co-evolution models of social movements, interactions between politics, protests and news media, and racial disparities in imprisonment. E-mail: oliver@ssc.wisc.edu

Steven Pfaff is Assistant Professor of Sociology at the University of Washington. His research interests include comparative and historical sociology, collective action and social movements, political sociology and Central European history. His recent work has appeared in *Social Forces* and *Theory and Society*.

Harland Prechel is Professor of Sociology at Texas A&M University. His research interests include business political behavior, class, and corporate transformation. He has published several articles that examine these issues in journals including the *American Sociological Review*, *Social Problems*, and *Sociological Forum*. His book, *Big Business and the State: Historical Transitions and Corporate Transformation, 1880s–1990s*, analyzes the political construction of the institutional arrangements in which corporations are embedded. The book shows how the institutional arrangements at the end of the 20th century established the conditions for the emergence of the multilayered subsidiary form, which is a variation of the holding company-subsidiary form that was prevalent at the beginning of the 20th century and deinstitutionalized after the Great Depression. E-mail: hprechel@neo.tamu.edu

Kelley D. Strawn is writing his Ph.D. dissertation in the Department of Sociology at the University of Wisconsin-Madison (1180 Observatory Drive, Madison WI 53705). His research examines how economic and political changes since the early 1980s impact the occurrence of protest events in Mexico. E-mail: kstrawn@ssc.wisc.edu

David L. Weakliem is Professor of Sociology at the University of Connecticut. He has published many articles on political sociology, stratification, and quantitative methods, including recent pieces in the *International Journal of Public Opinion Research*, *Electoral Studies*, and the *British Journal of Sociology*.